BUSINESS FLUCTUATIONS AND CYCLES

BUSINESS FLUCTUATIONS AND CYCLES

T. NAGAKAWA
EDITOR

Nova Science Publishers, Inc.
New York

For permission to use material from this book please contact us:
Telephone 631-231-7269; Fax 631-231-8175
Web Site: http://www.novapublishers.com

LIBRARY OF CONGRESS CATALOGING-IN-PUBLICATION DATA

Business fluctuations and cycles / T. Nagakawa (editor).
p. cm.
Includes index.
ISBN-13: 978-1-60021-503-2
ISBN-10: 1-60021-503-3
1. Business cycles. I. Nagakawa, T.
HB3711.B947 2006
338.5'42--dc22

2006102253

Published by Nova Science Publishers, Inc. ✦ New York

CONTENTS

PREFACE

The business cycle or economic cycle refers to the periodic fluctuations of economic activity about its long term growth trend. The cycle involves shifts over time between periods of relatively rapid growth of output (recovery and prosperity), alternating with periods of relative stagnation or decline (contraction or recession). These fluctuations are often measured using the real gross domestic product. One of the government's main roles is to smooth out the business cycle and reduce its fluctuations. To call those alternances "cycles" is rather misleading as they don't tend to repeat at fairly regular time intervals. Most observers find that their lengths (from peak to peak, or from trough to trough) vary, so that cycles are not mechanical in their regularity. Since no two cycles are alike in their details, some economists dispute the existence of cycles and use the word "fluctuations" (or the like) instead. Others see enough similarities between cycles that the cycle is a valid basis of studying the state of the economy. A key question is whether or not there are similar mechanisms that generate recessions and/or booms that exist in capitalist economies so that the dynamics that appear as a cycle will be seen again and again. This new book presents leading-edge research in this field.

Chapter 1 - Economies across time and regions are characterized by large and pervasive job flows. This reallocation process gives the economy great flexibility and potentially allows economic resources to be used where they will be most productive. This chapter reviews the existing job-flow evidence over the business cycle and motivates a theory that combines two driving forces for job flows: learning and creative destruction. I build a framework where the creative destruction force reallocates labor into technologically more advanced firms while the learning force leads labor to firms with better idiosyncratic productivity. The model well replicates the declining firm failure rate with firm age and the skewed firm size distribution. Additionally, it gives rise to interesting hypothesis. First, recessions not only feature a conventional leansing effect as Schumpeter argued in 1934, but also a "scarring effect" by clearing out firms with unrealized potential. Second, the time-consuming learning process suggests slow adjustment of industrial structure. A recession can be followed by a "jobless" recovery as observed recently.

Chapter 2 - In this paper, the authors study the effect of macroeconomic stabilization policy by utilizing the analytical framework of the high-dimensional dynamic Keynesian model of the business cycle, which consists of a set of nonlinear differential equations with many endogenous variables. Endogenous variables in the model include both of private and public real debts, real national income, rate of employment, real capital stock, and real money supply. In the model, money supply, public debt, taxes and government expenditure are intimately related each other through the budget constraint of the 'consolidated government' including the central bank. The authors investigate the macroeconomic impact of fiscal stabilization policy with and without time lags in policy response analytically. It is shown that stability, instability, and cyclical fluctuations emerge according to the choice of the values of policy parameters, among others, the strength of the fiscal stabilization policy and the length of the policy lag.

Chapter 3 - Duration dependent Markov-switching VAR (DDMS-VAR) models are time series models with data generating process consisting in a mixture of two VAR processes. The switching between the two VAR processes is governed by a two state Markov chain with transition probabilities that depend on how long the chain has been in a state. In the present paper the authors analyze the second order properties of such models and propose a Markov chain Monte Carlo algorithm to carry out Bayesian inference on the model's unknowns.

The methodology is then applied to the analysis of the U.S. business cycle. The model replicates rather well the NBER dating, and the authors find strong evidence against duration dependence in expansion phases. As for contractions, there is a very weak evidence in favor of duration dependence. This uncertainty is, however, coherent with the low number of recessions (seven) present in the dataset.

Chapter 4 - Linear relationships between inflation, unemployment, and labor force are obtained for two European countries - Austria and France. The best fit models of inflation as a linear and lagged function of labor force change rate and unemployment explain more than 90% of observed variation ($R^2>0.9$). Labor force projections for Austria provide a forecast of decreasing inflation for the next ten years. In France, inflation lags by four years behind labor force change and unemployment allowing for an exact prediction at a four-year horizon. Standard error of such a prediction is lower than 1%. The results confirm those obtained for the USA and Japan and provide strong evidences in favor of the concept of labor force growth as the only driving force behind unemployment and inflation.

Chapter 5 - This paper suggests that the "home production" and the "underground" sectors are two crucial phenomena for properly understanding the European and the United States business cycles. These sectors spell out the labor reallocation mechanism between market and non-market sectors, and rely upon two important and distinguishing aspects: a different degree of family institutionalization and the incentive for individuals and firms to seek tax-free income. The analysis is fruitfully carried out by reviewing two broad classes of multi-sector dynamic general equilibrium model incorporating different informal sectors. It is surprising, but the literature on the role of informal sectors in macromodels is not large, although their implications are extremely relevant.

Chapter 6 - The authors estimate a system of equations to analyze whether trade and financial linkages influence business cycle synchronization directly or indirectly. The authors use a small, open economy (Spain) as benchmark for the results, instead of the US as generally done in the literature. Neither trade nor financial linkages are found significant in directly influencing business cycle synchronization. Only the similarity in productive structure appears to foster economic integration, after controlling for common policies. Trade linkages are found to increase output synchronization indirectly, by contributing to the similarity of productive structures, which might point to the prevalence of intra-industry trade. The positive influence of financial linkages on output synchronization is even more indirect, by fostering trade integration and, thereby, a more similar productive structure. The net effects of both trade and financial linkages on business cycle synchronization are found statistically significant, but economically very small.

Chapter 7 - The authors propose in this article the use of a procedure for testing unit root cycles in macroeconomic time series. Unlike most classic unit-root methods, which are embedded in autoregressive alternatives, the tests employed in this paper are nested in a fractional model and have standard null and local limit distributions. The tests are first applied to the real US GDP series, the results substantially varying depending on how the authors specify the I(0) disturbances and the inclusion or not of deterministic components in the model. A model selection criterion based on diagnostic tests on the residuals is used in order to determine which may be the best specification of this series. In the second application the authors analyse the monthly structure of the US interest rate (Federal Funds). The results here indicate that there is some kind of intra-year cyclical component in the data, with the number of periods per cycle oscillating between 6 and 12 periods. However, separating the series in two subsamples (1955m1-1981m2, and 1981m3-2001m3), the results show that the length of the cycles is longer during the second part of the sample.

Chapter 8 - This paper empirically analyzes the relationship between international stock prices and international business cycles, specifically focusing on the number of cointegration vectors of each variable. The empirical data were taken from statistics on Germany, Japan, the UK, and the USA tabulated from January 1980 to May 2001. No cointegrating vectors were identified in indices of international stock prices, whereas several were identified in indices of international industrial production. These empirical results suggest that international stock prices do not necessarily reflect international business cycles.

Chapter 9 - In this paper the authors investigate, from the numerical perspective, the 18D core dynamics of a theoretical 39D representation of an applied Keynesian disequilibrium model of monetary growth of a small open economy. After considering the model from the viewpoint of national accounting, the authors provide a compact description of the intensive form of the model, its laws of motion and accompanying algebraic expressions and its unique interior steady state solution. The authors then give a survey of various types of subsystems that can be isolated from the integrated 18D dynamics by means of suitable assumptions. These subsystems and the full 18D dynamics are investigated and compared in the remainder of the paper from the perspective of bifurcation diagrams that separate situations of asymptotic stability from stable cyclical behavior as well as pure explosiveness. In this way the authors lay the foundations for an analysis of business cycle fluctuations in applicable high order macrosystems, which will show, in contrast to what is generally believed to characterize such structural macroeconometric models, that applied integrated macrodynamical systems can have a variety of interesting more or less complex attractors which are surrounded by more or less long-phase transient behavior. Such attractors are obtained in particular when locally explosive situations are turned into bounded dynamics by the addition of specifically tailored extrinsic behavioral nonlinearities. In this way the authors establish a Keynesian theory of endogenously generated business cycles where turning points are caused by globally nonlinear behavior, rather than by complex eigenvalues, around the steady state position of the economy.

Chapter 10 - This paper models the G7 business cycle using a common factor model, which is used to investigate increased stabilization and its impact on business cycle phases. The authors find strong evidence of a decline in volatility in each of the G7 countries. The authors also find a break towards stability in their common business cycle. This reduction in volatility implies that recessions will be significantly less frequent in the future compared to the historical track.

In: Business Fluctuations and Cycles
Editor: T. Nagakawa, pp. 1-23
ISBN 978-1-60021-503-3

Chapter 1

THE DRIVING FORCES OF JOB FLOWS OVER THE BUSINESS CYCLE: THEORY AND EVIDENCE

Min Ouyang
University of California at Irvine

Abstract

Economies across time and regions are characterized by large and pervasive job flows. This reallocation process gives the economy great flexibility and potentially allows economic resources to be used where they will be most productive. This chapter reviews the existing job-flow evidence over the business cycle and motivates a theory that combines two driving forces for job flows: learning and creative destruction. I build a framework where the creative destruction force reallocates labor into technologically more advanced firms while the learning force leads labor to firms with better idiosyncratic productivity. The model well replicates the declining firm failure rate with firm age and the skewed firm size distribution. Additionally, it gives rise to interesting hypothesis. First, recessions not only feature a conventional leansing effect as Schumpeter argued in 1934, but also a "scarring effect" by clearing out firms with unrealized potential. Second, the time-consuming learning process suggests slow adjustment of industrial structure. A recession can be followed by a "jobless" recovery as observed recently.

1. Introduction

Ever since the foundation of real business cycle theory in Kydland and Prescott (1982), the empirical regularities seen in productivity dynamics over business cycles have attracted a great amount of research attention. In recent years with longitudinal micro business data bases becoming more available, our understanding of aggregate productivity as well as its measurements have much improved.[1] We now know that the representative firm paradigm does not hold in the real world. As a matter of fact, economies across time and regions are

[1]The most heavily examined one is the Longitudinal Research Data (LRD) provided by U.S. Census of Bureau.

characterized by a large and pervasive restructuring process due to entry, exit, expansion and contraction of businesses. This restructuring process gives the economy great flexibility and potentially allows economic resources to be used where they will be most productive. Businesses that use outdated technologies, or produce products flagging in popularity, experience employment decreases. And the displaced workers can then be re-employed by entrants or businesses that are expanding. According to Davis and Haltiwanger (1999), in the U.S., roughly thirty percent of productivity growth over a ten-year horizon is accounted for by more productive entering businesses displacing less productive exiting ones.

A body of literature has arisen attempting to empirically synthesize the microeconomic and macroeconomic patterns of reallocation.[2] Much of them have centered on the creation and destruction of jobs, defined by Davis, Haltiwanger and Schuh (1996), as Gross Job Flows. A key stylized fact in this literature is that job reallocation exceeds that necessary to implement observed net job growth. This implies that jobs are continually being reallocated across businesses within the same industry. Davis, Haltiwanger and Schuh (1996) document that this is true even when looking at very narrowly defined industries within specific geographic regions. Hence, the large and pervasive job flows seem to reflect businesses' idiosyncratic characteristics and the resulting heterogeneity in their individual labor demand.

This paper attempts to provide a theoretical framework with heterogeneous businesses that matches the observed job flow patterns. I combine two driving forces for job flows – learning and creative destruction. In the profession, there has been a long tradition of examining each force separately. The idea of creative destruction traces back to Schumpeter (1942), and has been formalized into a class of vintage models by Caballero and Hammour (1994 and 1996) and Aghion and Howitt (1992, 1994). Firm learning, originated by Jovanovic (1982), can be seen in Ericson and Pakes (1995) and more recently in Pries (2004) and Moscarini (2003).

Both theories on their own can match some of empirical evidence, but not all. The vintage models of creative destruction assume that new technology can only be adopted by constructing new businesses, so that technologically sophisticated businesses enter to displace older, outmoded ones. This is supported by the fact, as documented by Davis, Haltiwanger and Schuh (1996), that entry and exit of businesses account for a large fraction of job reallocation. However, while holding some appeal, this prediction runs counter to the prevalent findings that failure rates decrease sharply with business age (Dunne, Roberts, and Samuelson 1989), and that productivity rises with business age (Baily, Hulten and Campbell (1992), Bahk and Gort (1993), Aw, Chen and Roberts (1997), Jensen, McGuckin and Stiroh (2000)). The learning models formalize the idea that businesses learn over time about initial conditions relevant to success and business survival. As learning diminishes with age, its contribution to job flows among businesses in the same birth cohort decreases. While providing an appealing interpretation of the strong and pervasive negative relationship between employer age and the magnitude of gross job flows, the learning models fail to explain the large gross job flows among mature businesses. Moreover, neither learning nor creative destruction alone can explain the fact that creation is more volatile than destruction for young businesses, while old businesses features more volatile destruction.

[2]Due to data limitations, most of the evidence comes from the manufacturing sectors.

In this paper, I propose a model that *combines* learning with creative destruction. I focus on two salient facts of gross job flows: the first is that young plants display greater turnover rates than old plants; the second is that, although job destruction is more volatile than job creation in general, this asymmetry weakens with plant age. In my theoretical framework, two forces interact together to drive job flows: creative destruction reallocates labor into technologically more advanced production units; while learning leads labor to production units with good idiosyncratic productivity. With demand fluctuations, the learning force generates symmetric responses of the creation and destruction, while the creative destruction force makes job destruction more responsive. Since old businesses are surer about their true idiosyncratic productivity of idiosyncratic productivity, the learning force weakens with age. Hence, my model interprets the observed cyclical pattern of job flows as the dominance of learning for young businesses and the dominance of creative destruction for old ones.

With such a framework, additional interesting results arise. First, recessions not only feature the conventional cleansing effect as Schumpeter has argued, but also a "scarring effect" under which potentially good firms are lost. Second, because of the time-consuming learning, demand fluctuations are companied by slow adjustment of industrial structure, even if firms adjust instantaneously. Since the industrial structure adjusts slowly, recessions can be followed by "jobless" recoveries as we have observed recently.

My model stresses two frictions that stifle instantaneous labor reallocation. Entry is costly, which allows different vintages to coexist; learning takes time, so that good and bad firms both survive. Vintage and idiosyncratic productivity together can explain the observed heterogeneous firm-level productivity. The vintage component suggests that entering cohorts are more productive than incumbents.[3] The idiosyncratic productivity component implies that each vintage cohort is itself a heterogeneous group. Vintage and idiosyncratic productivity together also lead to the following productivity dynamics. Creative destruction perpetually drives in entrants with higher productivity. Learning selects out bad firms over time so that as a cohort ages, its average productivity rises but productivity dispersion declines. Data from the U.S. manufacturing sector provides large and pervasive empirical evidence to support these predictions.[4]

The existing empirical literature has advanced learning and creative destruction as powerful tools to understand the patterns of firm turnover and industrial dynamics.[5] The significance of their interaction has also been suggested. Davis and Haltiwanger (1999) note that "vintage effects may be obscured by selection effects; vintage and selection effects may also interact in important ways..." In my model, the interaction of these two forces generates

[3]Although this is often true in the data, some authors such as Aw, Chen and Roberts (1997) find evidence that entrants are no more productive than incumbents. Foster, Haltiwanger and Syverson (2003) propose an explanation by separating two measures for plant-level productivity: a revenue-based measure and a quantity-based measure. They find that entrants are more productive than incumbents in terms of the quantity-based measure, but not in the revenue-based measure because entrants charge a lower price on average. Hence, more productive entrants can appear less profitable when prices are not observed.

[4]For evidence on the cross-cohort and within-cohort productivity distribution, see Baldwin (1995), Balk and Gort (1993), Foster, Haltiwanger and Syverson (2003). For evidence on cohort productivity dynamics, see Balk and Gort (1993) and Jensen, McGuckin and Stiroh (2000).

[5]See Hall (1987), Evans (1987), Montgomery and Wascher (1988), Dunne, Roberts and Samuelson (1989), Bresnahan and Raff (1991), Bahk and Gort (1993), Caves (1998), Davis and Haltiwanger (1999), and Jensen, McGuckin and Stiroh (2000).

the scarring effect of recessions.

The rest of the paper is organized as follows. The next section reviews stylized facts on gross job flows. Section 3 presents the model. Section 4 explores the model's response to demand fluctuations. Section 5 concludes.

2. Evidence on Gross Job Flows

I begin by reviewing findings on the large and pervasive magnitudes of gross job flows. Table 1 presents the statistics on annual job flows in the manufacturing sectors for 10 countries. Most of the studies in Table 1 use plant-level employment changes to calculate gross job flows, where a plant (or an establishment) is a specific physical location at which production of goods or services takes place.[6] Gross job flows are separated into two components: the number of jobs created at expanding and newly born units (job creation) and the number of jobs lost at declining and closing units (job destruction). Job reallocation equals the sum of job creation and job destruction.

Apparently, the job-flow magnitudes are large. According to Table 1, in the western world, roughly 1 in 10 jobs are created and another 1 in 10 jobs are destroyed each year. The large magnitudes of gross job flows are also pervasive. Table 1 suggests that the constant churning of job opportunities observed in the U.S. labor market is also true for many developed and developing economies. Although evidence presented in Table 1 is on the manufacturing sector only, many studies have pointed out that, within countries, gross-job flow rates for nonmanufacturing sectors tend to be even higher than those for manufacturing.
7

Do the observed large job flows reflect the within-industry reallocation of between-industry employment shifts? Defining excess job reallocation as job reallocation minus the absolute value of net employment change, Table 2 presents the faction of excess job reallocation accounted for by employment shifts between industries. In Table 2, employment shifts among the 448 four-digit industries in the U.S. manufacturing sector account for a mere 13% of excess job reallocation. Davis and Haltiwanger (1992) report that, even when sectors are defined by simultaneously crossing 2-digit industry, region, size class, plant age class and ownership type, employment shifts among those 14,400 sectors account for only 39% of excess job reallocation. The same finding holds up in studies for other countries such as Norway and France. The dominance of within-industry reallocation shown in Table 2 suggests that, the large job flows should not arise primarily because of sectoral disturbances or economy-wide disturbances; rather, they are largely driven by plant-level or firm-level heterogeneity in labor demand changes.

Consistent with the above hypothesis, job-flow patterns have been found to differ significantly by employer characteristics, among which employer age is one of the most heavily studied. Next, I present evidence on the relationship between employer age and job-flow patterns. My data source is Davis, Haltiwanger and Shuh's observations of job creation and destruction rates for the US manufacturing sector. The sample covers the statistics

[6]Carreira and Teixeira (2006) use firm-level data.

[7]See Foote (1997) and Nocke (1994), for example.

Table 1. Annual Gross Job Flows in the Manufacturing Sectors. C represents job creation, D job destruction, and R job reallocation.

Country	Coverage	C	D	R	Source
Canada	1974-1992	10.9%	11.1%	21.9%	Baldwin et al (1998)
Chile	1976-1986	13.0%	13.9%	26.8%	Roberts (1996)
Colombia	1977-1991	12.5%	12.2%	24.6%	Roberts (1996)
Denmark	1981-1991	12.0%	11.5%	23.5%	Albaek and Sorensen (1996)
France	1985-1991	10.2%	11.0%	21.2%	Nocke (1994)
Germany	1979-1993	4.5%	5.2%	9.7%	Wagner (1995)
Israel	1971-1972	9.7%	8.2%	17.9%	Gronau and Regev (1997)
Norway	1976-1986	7.1%	8.4%	15.5%	Klette and Mathisssen (1996)
Portugal	1991-1995	9.5%	13.9%	23.4%	Blanchard and Portugal (2001)
Portugal	1992-2000	8.4%	8.0%	16.4%	Carreira and Teixeira (2006)
U.S.A.	1973- 1993	8.8%	10.2%	19.0%	Baldwin et al (1998)

from the second quarter of 1972 to the fourth quarter of 1988. I use their quarterly job creation and destruction series for plants in three different age categories. Recommended by Davis, Haltiwanger and Schuh (1996, p.225), I aggregate the two categories that include the youngest plants. Table 3 and Figure 1 display job-flow patterns with respect to plant age.

In Table 3A, young plants' average job creation rate and destruction rate are both higher than those of old plants. In Table 3B, the variance ratio of job destruction and creation is 4.18 for old plants, suggesting a more volatile job destruction; but it is only 1.32 for young plants, implying approximately equally volatile job destruction and creation. As Table 1 shows, the age differences in magnitude and the relative volatility of destruction and creation *persist* even after separating job-flow rates into those by plant birth, plant death, and continuing operating plants.[8] The related time series are presented in Figure 1, reinforcing those impressions.

Table 3 and Figure 1 reflect the fact that the magnitudes and cyclical responses of job creation and destruction differ significantly by plant age. More specifically, both job creation and destruction rates are larger in magnitude for younger plants. At the same time, job destruction varies more over time than job creation at older plants, while the variation of job creation and that of job destruction at younger plants are much more symmetric. These patterns are also evident with more detailed age categories.

The sharp relationship between plant age and gross job flows, as revealed in Table 3 and

[8]Notice that in Table 1, job creation from plant birth is not zero among old plants, although old plants are those older than 40 quarters. This comes from the definition of plant age and plant birth. Plant age is calculated from the first time a plant is observed with positive employment. Plant birth is recorded when a plant's employment level going from zero to above zero. Some old plants' employment may temporarily drop to zero and rise again, which generates job creation from plant birth at old plants.

Table 2. The Faction of Excess Job Reallocation Accounted for by Employment Shifts Between Industries. N represents the number of industries; F fraction from employment shifts between industries.

Country	Coverage	Classification	N	F	Source
U.S.A.	1972-1988	4-digit SIC Manufacturing	448	0.13	Davis and Haltiwanger (1992)
U.S.A.	1972-1988	2-digit SIC Manufacturing by state	980	0.14	Davis and Haltiwanger (1992)
Norway	1976-1986	5-digit ISIC Manufacturing	142	0.06	Klette and Mathiassen (1996)
France	1985-1991	Detailed industry	600	0.17	Nocke (1994)

Figure 1, suggests the link between plant life cycle and aggregate employment dynamics. This link has been theoretically explored in Campbell and Fisher (2004), who models the adjustment costs that are proportional to the number of jobs created or destroyed. In their environment, a plant currently adjusting employment is more likely to do so again in the immediate future. Since by definition entrants must adjustment employment, the frequency of employment adjustment naturally declines with plant age. Their model well matches the larger job flow rates and heightened employment volatility at young plants, but leaves much of the relative volatility of job destruction and creation unexplained.

The model presented in the next section takes a different approach. My focus is the heterogeneity in plant productivity. I develop a model in which plant-level productivity are decomposed to match the cross-section productivity variation as well as dynamics of productivity distribution observed in the U.S. manufacturing sector. My purpose is to show that such a model developed according to observed productivity dynamics, can also generate aggregate employment dynamics at young and old plants as illustrated in Table 3 and Figure 1.

3. The Model

Consider an industry of plants that combine labor and capital in fixed proportions to produce a single good. Plants hire labor in a competitive labor market. Each plant consists of:

1. machines embodying a technology of some vintage;

2. a group of employees; and

3. an unobservable idiosyncratic productivity component.

There is an exogenous technological progress that drives the most advanced technology, denoted by A, growing over time at rate, $\gamma > 0$. When entering the market, a plant adopts the most advanced technology at the time, which remains constant afterward and becomes

Table 3. Quarterly gross job flows from plant birth, plant death, and continuing operating plants in the US manufacturing sector: 1973 II to 1988 IV. Young plants are defined as those younger than 40 quarters. Cb denotes job creation from plant birth, Dd job destruction from plant death, Cc and Dc job creation and destruction from continuing operating plants.ong old plants, although old plants are those older than 40 quarters. C and D represent gross job creation and destruction. C=Cc+Cb, D=Dd+Dc. All numbers are in percentage points.

A. Means						
Plant type	$E(Cb)$	$E(Cc)$	$\mathbf{E(C)}$	$E(Dd)$	$E(Dc)$	$\mathbf{E(D)}$
all	0.42	4.77	**5.20**	0.64	4.89	**5.53**
young	1.52	6.00	**7.52**	1.24	5.33	**6.56**
old	0.12	4.42	**4.54**	0.47	4.77	**5.24**
B. Variance ratio of job destruction to creation						
plant type	$\boldsymbol{\sigma(\mathbf{D})^2/\sigma(\mathbf{C})^2}$			$\sigma(Dc)^2/\sigma(Cc)^2$		
all	**3.49**			3.64		
young	**1.32**			2.80		
old	**4.18**			3.69		

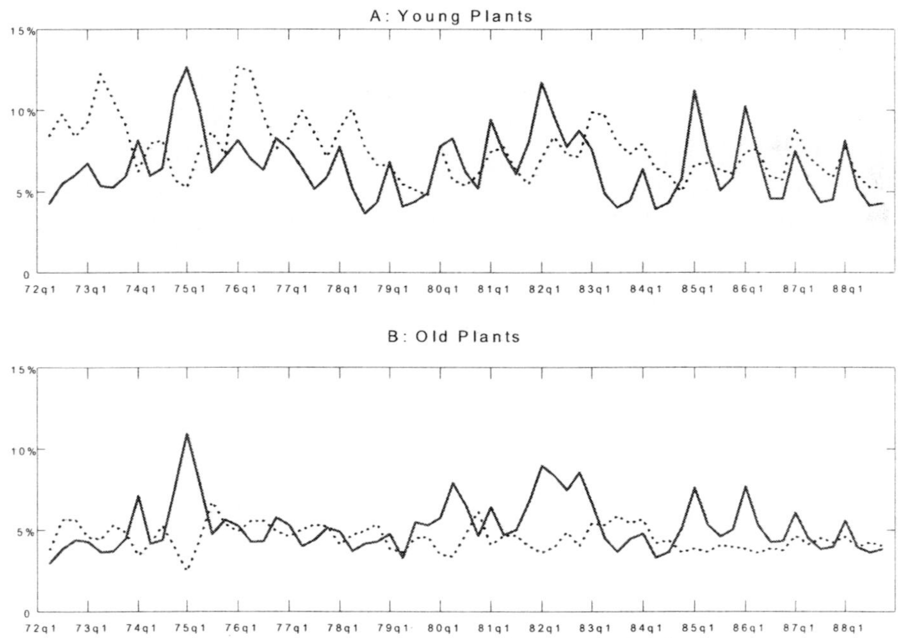

Figure 1. Job flows at young and old plants, 1972:2 – 1988:4. Dashed lines represent the job creation series; solid lines represent job destruction.

this plant's vintage. Let $A(a)$ represent the vintage of a plant of age a, or, in another word, the most advanced technology a periods ago.

$$A(a) = A \cdot (1+\gamma)^{-a}.$$

When entering the market, a plant is also endowed with idiosyncratic productivity, denoted by θ. It can represent the talent of the manager as in Lucas (1978), or alternatively, the location of the store, the organizational structure of the production process, or its fitness to the embodied technology. The key assumption regarding θ is that its value, although fixed at the time of entry, is not directly observable.

Production takes place through a group of workers. n represents the plant's employment level. The output of this plant is given by

$$A(a) \cdot x \cdot n^{\alpha}, \qquad 0 < \alpha < 1$$

where

$$x = \theta + \varepsilon.$$

The shock ε is an i.i.d. random draw from a fixed distribution that masks the influence of θ on output. Output is directly observable. Since the plant knows its vintage, it can infer the value of x. The plant uses its observations of x to learn about θ.

3.1. "All-or-Nothing" Learning

Plants are price takers and profit maximizers. While deciding whether to continue or terminate production and to choose the optimal level of employment, plants attempt to resolve the uncertainty about θ. The random component ε represents transitory factors that are independent of the idiosyncratic productivity θ. By assuming that ε has mean zero, we have $E(x) = E(\theta) + E(\varepsilon) = E(\theta)$.

Given knowledge of the distribution of ε, a sequence of observations of x allows the plant to learn about its θ. Although a continuum of potential values for θ is more realistic, for simplicity it is assumed here that there are only two values: θ_g for a good plant and θ_b for a bad plant. Furthermore, ε is assumed to be distributed uniformly on $[-\omega, \omega]$. Therefore, a good plant will have x each period as a random draw from a uniform distribution over $[\theta_g - \omega, \theta_g + \omega]$, while the x of a bad plant is drawn from an uniform distribution over $[\theta_b - \omega, \theta_b + w]$. Finally, θ_g, θ_b and ω satisfy $0 < \theta_b - \omega < \theta_g - \omega < \theta_b + \omega < \theta_g + \omega$.

Pries (2004) shows that the above assumptions give rise to an "all-or-nothing" learning process. With an observation of x within $(\theta_b + \omega, \theta_g + \omega]$, the plant learns with certainty that it is a good plant; conversely, an observation of x within $[\theta_b - \omega, \theta_g - \omega)$ indicates that it is a bad plant. However, an x within $[\theta_g - \omega, \theta_b + \omega]$ does not reveal anything, since the probabilities of falling in this range as a good plant and as a bad plant are the same (both equal to $\frac{2\omega+\theta_b-\theta_g}{2\omega}$).

This all-or-nothing learning simplifies my model considerably. Since it is θ^e instead of θ that affects plants' decisions, there are three types of plants corresponding to the three values of θ^e: plants with $\theta^e = \theta_g$, plants with $\theta^e = \theta_b$, and plants with $\theta^e = \theta_u$, the prior mean of θ. We define "unsure plants" as those with $\theta^e = \theta_u$. We further assume that the unconditional probability of $\theta = \theta_g$ is φ, and let $p \equiv \frac{\theta_g - \theta_b}{2\omega}$ denote the probability of the

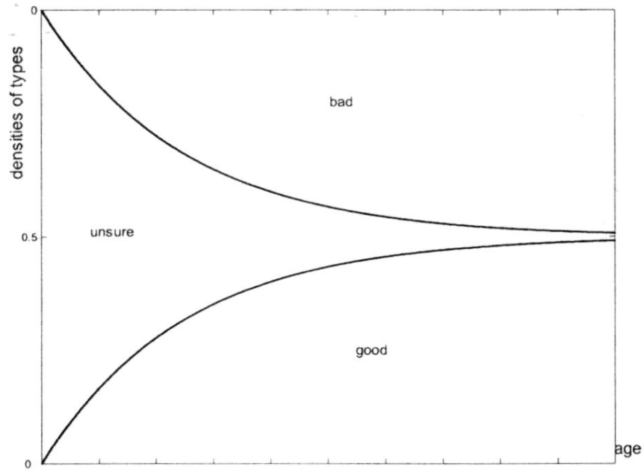

Figure 2. Dynamics of a Birth Cohort with Learning: the distance between the concave curve and the bottom axis measures the density of plants with $\theta^e = \theta_g$; the distance between the convex curve and the top axis measures the density of plants with $\theta^e = \theta_b$; and the distance between the two curves measures the density of unsure plants (plants with $\theta^e = \theta_u$).

true idiosyncratic productivity being revealed every period. Hence a plant's life-cycle is incorporated into the model as follows. A flow of new plants enter the market as unsure; thereafter, every period they stay unsure with probability $1 - p$, learn they are good with probability $p \cdot \varphi$ and learn they are bad with probability $p \cdot (1 - \varphi)$. The evolution of θ^e from the time of entry is a Markov process with values $(\theta_g, \theta_u, \theta_b)$, an initial probability distribution $(\ 0,\quad 1,\quad 0\ )$,and a transition matrix

$$\begin{pmatrix} 1 & 0 & 0 \\ p \cdot \varphi\ , & 1 - p\ , & p \cdot (1 - \varphi) \\ 0 & 0 & 1 \end{pmatrix}.$$

If plants were to live forever, eventually all uncertainty would be resolved because the market would provide enough information to reveal each plant's idiosyncratic productivity. The limiting probability distribution as a goes to ∞ is $\left(\ \varphi,\quad 0,\quad (1 - \varphi)\ \right)$.

Because there is a continuum of plants, it is assumed that the law of large numbers applies, so that both φ and p are not only the probabilities but also the fractions of unsure plants with $\theta = \theta_g$, and of plants who learn θ each period, respectively. Hence, *ignoring plant exit for now*, the densities of the three groups of plants in a cohort of age a as

$$\left(\ \varphi \cdot [1 - (1 - p)^a],\quad (1 - p)^a,\quad (1 - \varphi) \cdot [1 - (1 - p)^a]\ \right),$$

which implies an evolution of the idiosyncratic-productivity plant distribution within a birth cohort as shown in Figure 2, with the horizontal axis depicting the age of a cohort over *time*. The densities of plants that are certain about their idiosyncratic productivity, whether good or bad, grow as a cohort ages. Moreover, the two "learning curves" (depicting the evolution of densities of good plants and bad plants) are concave. This feature is defined as the decreasing property of marginal learning in Jovanovic (1982): the marginal learning effect decreases with plant age, which, in my model, is reflected by the fact that the marginal number of learners decreases with cohort age. The convenient feature of all-or-nothing learning is that, on the one hand, it implies that any single plant learns "suddenly", which allows us to easily keep track of the cross-section distribution of beliefs while, on the other hand, it still implies "gradual learning" at the cohort level.

3.2. Plant Decisions and Industry Equilibrium

We now turn to the supply and demand conditions in this model, and to the economics of creative destruction. This sub-section considers a *recursive competitive (partial) equilibrium* definition which includes as a key component the law of motion of the aggregate state of the industry. The aggregate state is (F, D). F denotes the distribution (measure) of plants across vintages and expected idiosyncratic productivity. D is an exogenous demand parameter; it captures aggregate conditions and is fully observable. The law of motion for D, denoted H_D, is exogenous. The law of motion for F, denoted H_F, is such that $F' = H_F(F, D)$. The part of F that measures the number of plants with belief θ^e and age a is denoted $f(\theta^e, a)$. The following sequence of events implies that H_F captures the influence of entry, exit and learning:

First, entry and exit occur by observing the aggregate state. Second, each surviving plant adjusts its employment and produces. Third, the industry equilibrium price is realized. Fourth, plants observe revenue and update beliefs. Then, another period begins.

3.2.1. Plant Employment Decision

We assume *costless* employment adjustment each period. Accordingly, a plant adjusts its employment to solve a *static* profit maximization problem. With wage rate normalized as 1, θ^e as a plant's current belief of its idiosyncratic productivity, and P as the equilibrium price, a plant's employment is,

$$\begin{aligned} n(\theta^e, a) &= \underset{n_t \geq 0}{\arg\max} E\left[P \cdot A(a) \cdot x \cdot n^{\alpha} - n\right] \\ &= [\alpha \frac{PA\theta^e}{(1+\gamma)^a}]^{\frac{1}{1-\alpha}} \end{aligned} \tag{1}$$

where θ^e can take on three values θ_g, θ_b or θ_u as suggested by all-or-nothing learning process. And the corresponding expected plant-level output is

$$q(\theta^e, a) = (\alpha P)^{\frac{\alpha}{1-\alpha}} \left(\frac{A\theta^e}{(1+\gamma)^a}\right)^{\frac{1}{1-\alpha}}. \tag{2}$$

The corresponding *expected* value of the single-period profit maximized with respect to n_t is,

$$\pi(\theta^e, a) \equiv (\alpha^{\frac{\alpha}{1-\alpha}} - \alpha^{\frac{1}{1-\alpha}}) \cdot \left[\frac{PA\theta^e}{(1+\gamma)^a}\right]^{\frac{1}{1-\alpha}}. \tag{3}$$

3.2.2. Plant Exit Decision

A plant exits as long as the expected value of staying drops below the outside option value W. The value of W is the same for all plants in the industry regardless of their vintages and idiosyncratic productivity. The exit decision of a plant is forward-looking: plants have to form expectations about both current and future profits, based on its expected idiosyncratic productivity θ^e, age a, and the aggregate state (F, D). Let $V(\theta^e, a; F, D)$ be the value of staying in the market for a plant with age a and belief θ^e. Then V satisfies:

$$\begin{aligned} V(\theta^e, a; F, D) &= \pi(\theta^e, a; F, D) + \beta \cdot E\{\max[W, V(\theta^{e'}, a+1; F', D')] | \theta^e, F, D\} \quad (4) \\ \text{subject to} &: F' = H_F(F, D), D' = H_D(D) \end{aligned}$$

We assume that parameters are such that $V(\theta_b, a; F, D) < 0$ for any a, F and D: the expected value of staying of a bad plant at any age is always negative. Therefore, bad plants always exit.

(2) suggests that $\pi(\theta^e, a; F, D)$ decreases in a: plants with older vintages are less profitable. It follows that, holding other parameters constant, $V(\theta^e, a; F, D)$ also decreases in a. Therefore, each period there exists a maximum plant age for each θ^e, denoted $\overline{a}(\theta^e; F, D)$, so that plants with θ^e exit if they are older than $\overline{a}(\theta^e; F, D)$.

3.2.3. The Entry Size

The industry features continual entry. To fix the size of entry, we further assume that each entrant has to pay an entry cost c to enter the market, and c satisfies

$$c = c_0 + c_1 \cdot f'(\theta_u, 0; F, D), \qquad c > 0, c_1 \geq 0.$$

$f'(\theta_u, 0; F, D)$ denotes the entry size with aggregate state (F, D). We let the entry cost depend positively on the entry size to capture the idea that, for the industry as a whole, *fast* entry is costly and adjustment may not take place instantaneously. This can arise from a limited amount of land available to build production sites or an upward-sloping supply curve for the industry's specific capital.[9] The free entry condition equates a plant's entry cost to its value of entry, and can be written as

$$V(\theta_u, 0; F, D) = c_0 + c_1 \cdot f(\theta_u, 0; F, D). \quad (5)$$

As more new plants enter, the entry cost is driven up until it reaches the value of entry. At this point, entry stops.

3.2.4. Industry Equilibrium

Let $Q(F, D)$ represent the industry-equilibrium output, A recursive competitive equilibrium in this industry is a law of motion H_F, a value function V, and a pricing function P such that:

1. V satisfies (3);

[9]See Goolsbee (1998) for related empirical evidence.

2. $F' = H(F, D)$ is generated by the appropriate summing-up of plants' entry, exit, and learning. Let $f'(\theta_u, 0; F, D)$ denote the part of F' that measures the number of plants with belief θ^e and age a ,

$$
\begin{aligned}
f'(\theta_u, 0; F, D) &= \frac{V(\theta_u, 0; F, D) - c_0}{c_1}; \\
f'(\theta_u, a; F, D) &= (1-p) \cdot f(\theta_u, a-1) \text{ for } 0 < a \leq \overline{a}(\theta_u; F, D); \\
f'(\theta_g, a; F, D) &= f(\theta_g, a-1) + p\varphi \cdot f(\theta_u, a-1) \text{ for } 0 < a \leq \overline{a}(\theta_g; F, D); \\
f'(\theta_u, a; F, D) &= 0 \text{ for } a > \overline{a}(\theta_u; F, D), \text{ and } f'(\theta_g, a; F, D) = 0 \text{ for } a > \overline{a}(\theta_g; F,
\end{aligned}
$$

3. $Q(F, D)$ equals the sum of all staying plants' output: [10]

$$Q(F, D) = \sum_{a=0}^{\overline{a}(\theta_g; F, D)} q(\theta_g, a; F, D) \cdot f'(\theta_g, a; F, D) + \sum_{a=0}^{\overline{a}(\theta_u; F, D)} q(\theta_u, a; F, D) \cdot f'(\theta_u, a; F$$

4. $P(F, D)$ satisfies:

$$P(F, D) = \frac{D}{Q(F, D)}, \tag{6}$$

Three essential parts capture the key component of the equilibrium – the law of motion for plant distribution H_F: the entry size $f(\theta_u, 0; F, D)$, good plants' maximum age $\overline{a}(\theta_g; F, D)$, and unsure plants' maximum age $\overline{a}(\theta_u; F, D)$. These three parts, together with the all-or-nothing learning, update F to F'. F' gives the industry-equilibrium output and price by conditions 3 and 4, and serves as part of the aggregate state for the next period.

4. The Steady State

In the model described above, new plants embodied with the latest technology keep coming in; the sizes of incumbents grow or shrink, depending on what they learn and how fast the technology updates; and those realized as bad plants or with outdated technology are continually being thrown out. Thus, the industry keeps retooling new technology and getting rid of bad plants, resulting in a reallocation process where labor flows into more productive units. This process is driven by two forces – learning and creative destruction.

Before exploring the response of the industry to demand fluctuations in Section 4, this section addresses the firm distribution and job-flow margins at the steady state – when demand remains time-invariant.

4.1. Solving for a Steady State

I define a steady state as a recursive competitive equilibrium with time-invariant aggregate states: D is *and is perceived* as time-invariant: $D = H_D(D)$; F is also time-invariant: $F =$

[10]Although industry-level output should equal the sum of *realized* plant-level output, it can be shown that the expectation error and the random noise cancel out within each age cohort so that the sum of *expected* plant output equals the sum of *realized* output.

$H_F(F, D)$. Since H_F is generated by entry, exit and learning, a steady state must feature time-invariant entry and exit for $F = H_F(F, D)$ to hold. Thus, it can be summarized by $\{f^{ss}(0, D), \overline{a}_u^{ss}(D), \overline{a}_g^{ss}(D)\}$, with $f^{ss}(0, D)$ as the steady-state entry size, $\overline{a}_g^{ss}(D)$ as the maximum age for good plants, and $\overline{a}_u^{ss}(D)$ as the maximum age for unsure plants.

> *Lemma 1: unsure firms exit the market earlier than good firms;* $\overline{a}_u^{ss}(D) < \overline{a}_g^{ss}(D)$.
>
> *Lemma 2: at a steady state, P is declining at the same rate (γ) as A grows, so that the value of $A \cdot P$ stays time-invariant.*

Lemma 2 states that the steady-state price declines at the same rate as the technology grows.[11] Since entrants embodied with better technology keep entering and firms with outdated technology keep exiting, the *mean* level of technology in the industry increases over time. With the mean technology increasing, the industrial output is driven up continuously, so that, holding demand constant, price level declines.

Using Lemma 1 and Lemma 2, the following equation can be derived from good firms' exit condition:

$$PA = \left(\frac{\alpha^{\alpha} - \alpha}{\alpha^{\frac{\alpha}{1-\alpha}}}\right)^{1-\alpha} \cdot \frac{[(1-\beta)W]^{1-\alpha}}{\theta_g} \cdot (1+\gamma)^{\overline{a}_g^{ss}(D)} \tag{1}$$

Substituting equation (1) into unsure firms' exit conditions, I get:

$$(1+\gamma)^{\frac{\overline{a}_g^{ss}(D)-\overline{a}_u^{ss}(D)}{1-\alpha}} \left(\frac{\theta_u}{\theta_g}\right)^{\frac{1}{1-\alpha}} + \beta p p_0 \left\{ \frac{\left[\frac{(1+\gamma)^{\frac{\overline{a}_g^{ss}(D)-\overline{a}_u^{ss}(D)}{1-\alpha}} - \beta^{\overline{a}_g^{ss}(D)-\overline{a}_u^{ss}(D)}}{(1+\gamma)^{\frac{1}{1-\alpha}} - \beta}\right] - }{\left(\frac{1-\beta^{\overline{a}_g^{ss}(D)-\overline{a}_u^{ss}(D)}}{1-\beta}\right)} \right\} = 1 \tag{2}$$

(2) determines the value of $\overline{a}_g^{ss}(D) - \overline{a}_u^{ss}(D)$.

> *Proposition: the steady-state difference between good firms' exit age and unsure firms' exit age is independent of demand.*

Since demand (D) is not in (2), $\overline{a}_g^{ss}(D) - \overline{a}_u^{ss}(D)$ is independent of demand. With $\overline{a}_u^{ss}(D) = \overline{a}_g^{ss}(D) - \left(\overline{a}_g^{ss}(D) - \overline{a}_u^{ss}(D)\right)$, the steady-state entry size $f^{ss}(0, D)$ and the good firms' exit age $\overline{a}_g^{ss}(D)$ are jointly determined by the demand condition and free entry condition. $\{f^{ss}(0, D), \overline{a}_u^{ss}(D), \overline{a}_g^{ss}(D)\}$ is the solution for a steady state corresponding to demand level D.

The model reveals the "insulation" effect in Caballero and Hammour (1994): entry margin and exit margin absorb changes in demand simultaneously. In the extreme case with entry cost independent of entry size (i.e., a constant c), exit ages remain constant and changes in demand are completely accommodated by the entry size. In that case, the whole system in my model becomes recursive: $\overline{a}_g^{ss}(D) - \overline{a}_u^{ss}(D)$ is determined by (2); with entry cost as a constant and $\overline{a}_u^{ss}(D)$ replaced by $\overline{a}_g^{ss}(D) - \left(\overline{a}_g^{ss}(D) - \overline{a}_u^{ss}(D)\right)$, the free entry

[11] The model with only creative destruction in Cabellero and Hammour (1994) implies similar result.

Table 4.

Calibrated Parameters

	Symbol	Value
annual discount rate	β	$\frac{1}{1+0.065}$
annual learning Pace	p	0.20
annual technological pace	γ	0.028
probability of being a good firm	p_0	0.5
idiosyncratic productivity of good firms	θ_g	3
idiosyncratic productivity of bad firms	θ_b	1
entry cost parameters	c_0	0.403
	c_1	0.500
The outside option value	W	5

condition, which equates entry cost to the value of entry, gives the value of $\overline{a}_g^{ss}(D)$; with $\overline{a}_g^{ss}(D)$ and $\overline{a}_u^{ss}(D)$ solved independent of D, $f^{ss}(0, D)$ is determined by the demand condition. Therefore, with entry cost independent of entry size, changes in demand only affects the entry size.

4.2. The Steady-State Firm Distribution

I calibrate the model using parameter values summarized in Table 4. The annual discount rate and the technological pace come from Caballero and Hammour (1994) Entry cost function is assumed linear: $c(f^{ss}(0, D)) = c_0 + c_1 \cdot f^{ss}(0, D)$. Figure 3 presents the steady-state firm distribution across ages and expected idiosyncratic productivity.

There are two ways to interpret Figure 3. First, it displays the steady-state life-cycle dynamics of a representative cohort with the horizontal axis depicting the cohort age *across time*. Firms enter in size $f^{ss}(0, D)$ as unsure. As the cohort ages and learns, bad firms are thrown out so that the cohort size declines; good firms are realized, so that the density of good firms increases. After $\overline{a}_u^{ss}(D)$, all unsure firms exit because their vintage is too old to survive with $\theta^e = \theta_u$. However, firms with $\theta^e = \theta_g$ stay. Afterwards, the cohort contains only good firms and the number of good firms remains constant because learning has stopped. Good firms live until $\overline{a}_g^{ss}(D)$. The vintage after $\overline{a}_g^{ss}(D)$ is too old even for good firms to survive.

Second, Figure 3 also displays the firm distribution across ages and idiosyncratic productivity at any one time, with the horizontal axis depicting the cohort age *cross section*. At the steady state, firms of different ages coexist. Since older cohorts have lived longer and learned more, their size is lower and their density of good firms is higher. Cohorts older than $\overline{a}_u^{ss}(D)$ are of the same size and contain only good firms. No cohort is older than $\overline{a}_g^{ss}(D)$.

4.3. The Steady-State Job Flows

How does the steady-state job flows in my model look like? From a purely accounting point of view, there are two margins for job creation and three for job destruction. As seen in Figure 3. jobs are created either by new entrants at *the entry margin*; or by *new* good

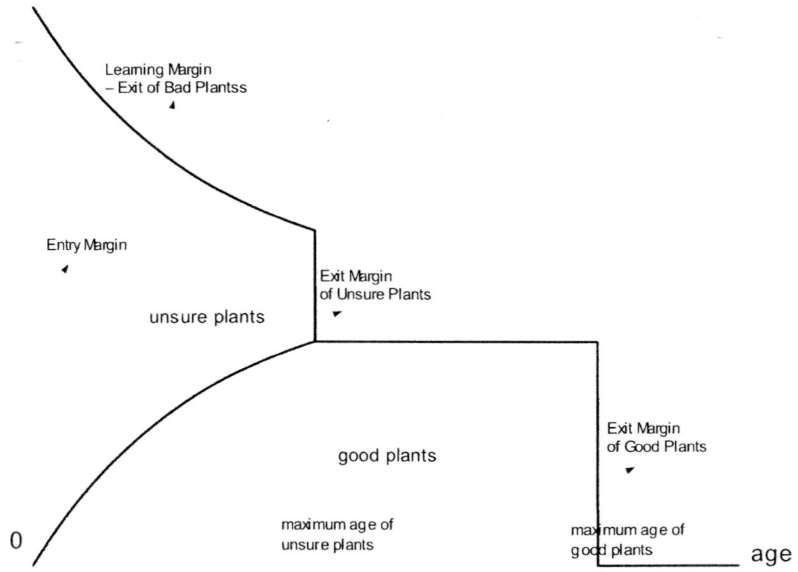

Figure 3. The Steady-state Plant Distribution across Ages and Expected Idiosyncratic Productivity, or Dynamics of a Birth Cohort with both Learning and Creative Destruction. the distance between the lower curve (extended as the horizontal line) and the bottom axis measures the density of good firms; the distance between the two curves measures the density of unsure firms.

firms at the *positive learning margin* (shown in Figure 3 as the lower concave line). Jobs are destroyed either at *the exit margin* as old vintages leave, or at *the negative learning margin* (shown in Figure 3 as the upper convex line) by firms that just learn they are good, or at *the aging margin* by good firms and non-learning unsure firms whose vintages are growing old. The force of creative destruction and the force of learning together drive the steady-state job flows. The force of creative destruction drives the job creation at the entry margin and job destruction at the exit margin and at the aging margin. The learning force drives the job creation at the positive learning margin and the job destruction at the negative learning margin.

Figure 3 displays a strong pattern for job flows with respect to firm age. The force of creative destruction strengthens but the learning force weakens with firm age. As cohort ages, less and less firms learn. Note that for firms aged older than $\overline{a_u}^{ss}$, learning effect disappears and only creative destruction force exists.

Section 2.3 has argued that the employment level of a firm (with vintage $A(t-a)$ and θ^e) equals $[\alpha \cdot \frac{PA}{(1+\gamma)^a} \cdot \theta^e]^{\frac{1}{1-\alpha}}$. Lemma 2 further implies that, at a steady state, the firm-level employment equals

$$[\alpha \cdot \frac{PA}{(1+\gamma)^a} \cdot \theta^e]^{\frac{1}{1-\alpha}}$$

Apparently, firm-level employment is affected by both the force of creative destruction and the force of learning. The force of creative destruction takes effect through $\frac{PA}{(1+\gamma)^a}$: with a higher a, older vintage tends to destroy jobs. The learning force takes effect through the dynamics of θ^e: firms create jobs they learn they are good (the value of θ^e changes from θ_u to θ_g), and destroy jobs when they learn they are bad (the value of θ^e changes from θ_u to θ_b). The two forces also interact with each other: a continuing-operating firm that learns it is good tends, on the one hand, to create jobs because of higher θ^e(learning), on the other hand, to destroy jobs because of higher a (creative destruction). Since a significant part of the observed manufacturing job flows comes from continuing operating firms, in my model the value of θ_g, $\theta_u$and γ are assumed such that the force of creative destruction *dampens*, but never dominates job flows at continuing operating firms.

4.4. The Steady-State Failure Rates and the Size Distribution of Firms

Dunne, Roberts and Samuelson (1989) examine over 200, 000 plants that entered the U.S. manufacturing sector in the 1967-1977 period and find that younger plants display larger failure rates. This is also true in my model for firms aged between 0 and $\overline{a_u}^{ss}(D)$, among which the probability of exiting for an unsure firm equals the probability of learning that it is bad. According to the all-or-nothing learning and the large sample theorem, the failure rate of firms of age a equals:

$$\frac{f^{ss}(\theta_u,a)\cdot p\cdot(1-p_0)}{f^{ss}(\theta_u,a)+f^*(\theta_g,a)} = \frac{p\cdot(1-p_0)\cdot(1-p)^{a-1}}{p_0+(1-p_0)\cdot(1-p)^{a-1}}, \qquad 0 < a \leq \overline{a_u}^{ss}(D)$$

where $f^{ss}(\theta_u, a)$ is the steady-state measure of unsure firms of age a and $f^{ss}(\theta_g, a)$ the steady-state measure of good firms of age a. Apparently, the failure rate decreases with a. The negative relationship between failure rate and firm age comes from learning. Since more and more bad firms exit over time because of learning, the proportion of good firms increases so that the probability of exiting decreases as a cohort of firms grow old. .

It has also been documented that the industrial distribution of firm size is usually highly skewed toward smaller firms. With firm size represented by employment level, Figure 4 displays the steady-state industrial distribution of firm size implied by my model:

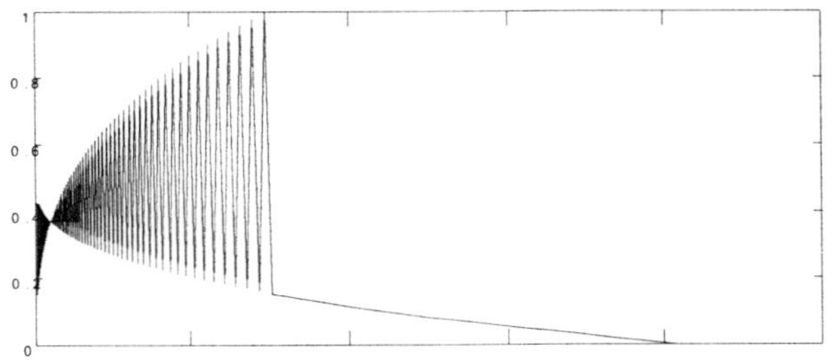

In Figure 4, the size distribution of firms is skewed toward small firms. In my model, firm-level employment depends positively both on vintage and on expected idiosyncratic productivity. A firm can be small because its vintage is old, or because it is still unsure whether it is good or bad. Since learning takes time, good firms are usually old and young firms are mostly unsure. This gives rise to Figure 4, in which a large proportion firms are small because they are either old with outdated vintages or are young but unsure. The big firms are *good firms that are also young,* which are only of a small group.[12]

[12]However, although the firm distribution is skewed toward young firms as documented empirically, it contradicts the fact that big firms are mostly old.

Table 5.

D	$f^{ss}(0, D)$	$\overline{a_g}^{ss}(D)$	$\overline{a_g}^{ss}(D) - \overline{a_u}^{ss}(D)$	Ratio of firms with θ_g
10000	62.0224	59	45	84.53%
9000	55.4686	57	45	84.10%
8000	52.3506	56	45	83.88%
7000	49.2998	55	45	83.66%

5. While Demand Fluctuates

This section extends the analysis into the response of the industry while demand fluctuates. Unfortunately, the endogenous state variable F is a high-dimensional object. The numerical solution of dynamic programming problems becomes increasingly difficult as the size of the state space increases. Ouyang (2006) follows Krusell and Smith (1998) by shrinking the state space into a limited set of variables and showing that these variables' laws of motion can approximate the equilibrium behavior of plants in the simulated time series. In this paper, I limit my analysis to comparative statics across steady states. Two interesting hypothesis arise: recessions feature a cleansing effect of potentially good firms, and recessions can be followed by a job-less recovery. [13]

5.1. The Co-movement of the Exit Margins

Table 2 summarizes statistics across steady states corresponding to different demand levels. Parameter values are as in Table 1.

Table 5 confirms proposition 1. Additionally, it displays the "insulation" effect: changes in demand are accommodated both by the exit margins and by the entry margin. In Table 5, as demand decreases, the entry size also decreases and the exit age of good firms becomes younger; but the difference in exit ages of good firms and unsure firms remain constant.

Proposition 1 and Table 5 suggests:

$$\frac{d(\overline{a_g}^*)}{d(D^*)} = \frac{d(\overline{a_u}^*)}{d(D^*)}$$

Hence, my comparative-statics exercise conjectures that the exit age of good firms and that of unsure firms co-move together while demand fluctuates; furthermore, their co-movements are of the same magnitude. [14]

5.2. The Scarring Effect of Recessions

What does the co-movement of exit ages imply? It implies that a drop in demand gives rise to a younger industrial structure, and hence a different firm distribution of idiosyncratic productivity. As shown in the last column of Table 5, the ratio of firms with θ_g, including

[13] The cleansing effect of potentially good firms is defined as a "scarring effect" and explored in Ouyang (2006).

[14] This conjecture is confirmed by the numerical exercise in Ouyang (2006).

those who have learned and those who have not, is lower at a low-demand steady state. Analytically, the steady-state ratio of firms with θ_g equals:

$$r_g^{ss}(D) = 1 - \frac{2}{2 - 2p_0 + pp_0\left(1 + \overline{a_u}^{ss}(D)\right) \cdot \overline{a_u}^{ss}(D) + 2pp_0\left(\overline{a_g}^{ss}(D) - \overline{a_u}^{ss}(D)\right)}$$

With $\overline{a_g}^{ss}(D) - \overline{a_u}^{ss}(D)$ independent of D but $\overline{a_u}^{ss}(D)$ increasing in D, $r_g^{ss}(D)$ increases in D.Hence, at a low-demand steady state, there are not only less *old* firms, but also less *good* firms. Ouyang (2006) defines the latter as the "scarring effect" of recessions.

The scarring effect stems from learning. New entrants begin unsure of their idiosyncratic productivity, although a proportion p_0 are truly good. Over time, more and more bad firms leave while good firms stay. Since learning takes time, the number of "potentially good firms" that realize their true idiosyncratic productivity depends on how many learning chances they have. If firms could live forever, eventually all the potentially good firms would get to realize their true idiosyncratic productivity. But a finite life span of unsure firms implies that if potentially good firms do not learn before age $\overline{a_u}^{ss}(D)$, they exit and thus forever lose the chance to learn. Therefore, $\overline{a_u}^{ss}(D)$ represents not only the exit age of unsure firms, but also the number of learning opportunities. A low $\overline{a_u}^{ss}(D)$ allows potentially good firms fewer chances to realize their true idiosyncratic productivity, so that the number of *old good firms* in operation after age $\overline{a_u}^{ss}(D)$ is also reduced.

Hence, the industry suffers from uncertainty; it tries to select out bad firms but the group of firms it clears at age $\overline{a_u}^{ss}(D)$ includes some firms that are truly good. The number of clearing mistakes the industry makes at $\overline{a_u}^{ss}(D)$ depends on the size of the unsure exit margin, which in turn depends on the value of $\overline{a_u}^{ss}(D)$. When a drop in demand reduces the value of $\overline{a_u}^{ss}(D)$, this reduces the number of learning opportunities, allows fewer good firms to become old and thus shifts the labor distribution toward bad firms.

With the all-or-nothing learning process, it can be shown that the number of potentially good firms that exit at $\overline{a_u}^{ss}(D)$ equals:

$$(1-p)^{\overline{a_u}^{ss}(D)} \cdot p_0$$

A drop in demand shifts both exit margins to younger ages. With the learning pace $p < 1$, a smaller $\overline{a_u}^{ss}(D)$ implies that more "potentially good firms" exit at the unsure firms' exit margin,which in turn, causes a smaller ratio of good firms in the industry.

Pre-Keynesian theorists like Hayek or Schumpeter argue that recessions are times of "cleansing", when outdated or relatively unprofitable techniques and products are pruned out of productive system. Caballero and Hammour (1994) formalize their idea by modeling the force of creative destruction with demand fluctuations. One objection to the cleansing view is that it implies countercyclical productivity, while average labor productivity is in fact procyclical. Ouyang (2006) follows the numerical approach in Krusell and Smith (1998) to explore a theory similar to the one presented in this paper, and finds that, with reasonable calibration, the scarring effect can dominate the cleansing effect and accounts for the observed pro-cyclical productivity.

5.3. The Slow Adjustment of Industrial Structure and the Jobless Recovery

The subsection deviates from the previous comparative statics and takes a first step to explore the transitory dynamics of industrial structure while demand fluctuates. To serve this purpose, it is necessary to introduce time indexes to the key variables. I let D_t, $f_t(0)$, $\overline{a_{gt}}$, and $\overline{a_{ut}}$ represent the period-t demand, entry size, exit age of good firms and that of unsure firms. Suppose that, in period t_0, the industry is at a steady state with demand D_{t_0}. Apparently,

$$\begin{aligned} f_{t_0}(0) &= f^{ss}(0, D_{t_0}), \\ \overline{a_{gt_0}} &= \overline{a_g}^{ss}(D_{t_0}), \\ \overline{a_{ut_0}} &= \overline{a_u}^{ss}(D_{t_0}). \end{aligned}$$

I introduce an *unexpected* once-and-for-all change in demand in period t_1: the demand level drops to D_{t_1} from D_{t_0}, with $D_{t_1} < D_{t_0}$.

According to the comparative statics, $f^{ss}(0, D_{t_1}) < f^{ss}(0, D_{t_0})$, $\overline{a_g}^{ss}(D_{t_1}) < \overline{a_g}^{ss}(D_{t_0})$ and $\overline{a_u}^{ss}(D_{t_1}) < \overline{a_u}^{ss}(D_{t_0})$. Figure 5 plots the two steady states together. The dashed line represents the firm distribution at the high-demand steady state, and the solid line represents that at the low-demand steady state. Note that the change in entry size is not shown in Figure 5. Since, at a steady state, all cohorts start their life cycle with the same number of firms, the size of entry matters only as a scale.

Now the question is, if all the firms observe the drop in demand and behave correspondingly, will the industry adjusts to the new steady-state structure instantaneously? In another word, what are the values of $f_{t_1}(0)$, $\overline{a_{gt_1}}$, and $\overline{a_{ut_1}}$?

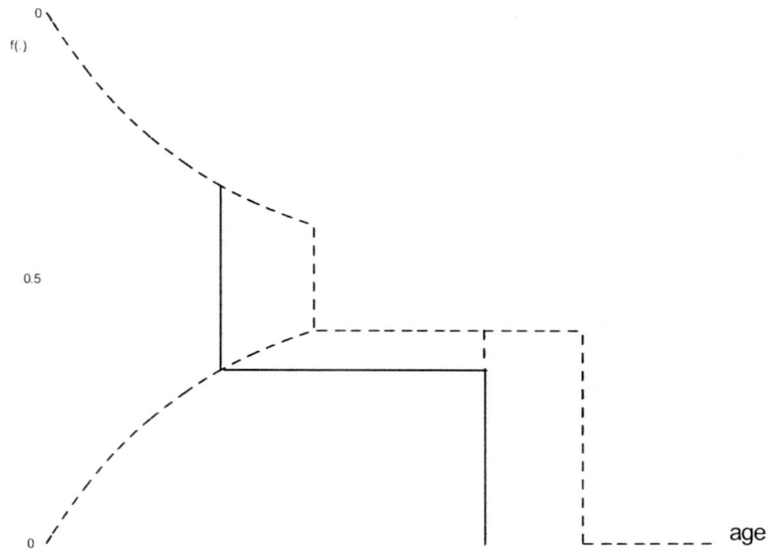

Figure 4. The high-demand and low-demand steady states.

If indeed $f_{t_1}(0) = f^{ss}(0, D_{t_1})$, $\overline{a_{gt_1}} = \overline{a_g}^{ss}(D_{t_1})$ and $\overline{a_{ut_1}} = \overline{a_u}^{ss}(D_{t_1})$, apparently all the unsure firms aged between $\overline{a_u}^{ss}(D_{t_1})$ and $\overline{a_u}^{ss}(D_{t_0})$ will exit as soon as they observe the drop in demand; so will the good firms aged between $\overline{a_g}^{ss}(D_{t_1})$ and $\overline{a_g}^{ss}(D_{t_0})$. How about the good firms aged between $\overline{a_u}^{ss}(D_{t_1})$ and $\overline{a_g}^{ss}(D_{t_1})$? As shown in Figure 5, some of them are included in the low-demand steady state, some others are not. However, *all of them* should stay because, according to the optimal rule to behave, good firms do not exit until $\overline{a_g}^{ss}(D_{t_1})$. This group of good firms, aged between $\overline{a_u}^{ss}(D_{t_1})$ and $\overline{a_g}^{ss}(D_{t_1})$ but not included in the low-demand steady state, are the "left-overs" from the high-demand steady state. Because of their existence, the period-$t_1$industrial output is higher, but the price is lower, than those at the low-demand steady state.

The numerical exercise in Ouyang (2006) suggests that $f_{t_1}(0) < f^{ss}(0, D_{t_1})$, $\overline{a_{gt_1}} < \overline{a_g}^{ss}(D_{t_1})$ and $\overline{a_{ut_1}} < \overline{a_u}^{ss}(D_{t_1})$. Both exit margins will over shift to younger ages. As demand stays at D_{t_1}, entrants keep coming in and incumbents keep aging. The "left-over" firms will gradually exit so that the industry eventually reaches the low-demand steady state.

The opposite holds for $D_{t_1} > D_{t_0}$. If demand jumps up instead in period t_1, the two exit margins will shift to older ages. In this case, no firms exit at the two margins in period t_1. Also because of the industrial structure at the previous low-demand steady state, there are no good firms older than $\overline{a_{gt_0}}$ and no unsure firms older than $\overline{a_{ut_0}}$. As demand stays at D_{t_1}, entrants keep coming in and incumbents keep aging. The industry reaches its high-demand steady state structure eventually.

Hence, I conclude that my model features slow adjustment in the industrial structure even if firms adjust instantaneously. The slow adjustment of the industrial structure can be applied to the "jobless recovery" observed following both the 1990-1991 recession and the 2001 recession. It has been reported that, although the economic slowdown that began in late 2000 has been relatively mild, the downturn in the labor market was severe and the recovery has been exceptionally slow, even slower to improve than in the 1990-91 episode. Significant increase in job creation and the total employment was not taking place as the economy recovers.[15]

What does my model say about the jobless recovery? There are two job-creation margins in my model: the entry margin and the positive learning margin by continuing-operating firms. A low-demand steady state features less entry and younger exit age of unsure firms. With unsure firms exiting at a younger age, the positive learning margin for job creation is not as strong as that at a high-demand steady state; or, in another word, there are less unsure firms learning to create jobs. Since the industry cannot adjust to the high-demand structure instantaneously, the positive learning margin stays weak even after the demand recovers. As shown in Table 1, over 90% of manufacturing job creation in the U.S. come from continuing-operating firms. My model suggests that, if the previous recession has significantly reduced the number of learning firms, the recovery can be "jobless".

6. Conclusion

This paper reviews two stylized facts on gross job flows. First, large and pervasive job flows exist in very narrowly defined industries, reflecting the importance of driving forces rising from idiosyncratic factors. Second, job-flow patterns differ significantly by plant age in both magnitudes and cyclical responses.

Motivated by these facts, I propose a theory combining the learning and the creative destruction forces. A simple "all-or-nothing" learning process is modeled in a vintage model of creative destruction: firms enter the industry with vintages and fixed efficiency; with the latter unobservable, they learn by extracting signals out of market outcomes. The creative

[15] See Bernanke (2003) and Schultze (2004), for example.

destruction force reallocates jobs into more advanced vintages while the learning force leads jobs to firms with higher idiosyncratic productivity. The steady state features declining firm failure rate with firm age and skewed firm size distribution to small size, both of which have been observed and documented empirically.

With such a framework, additional results arise. The comparative statics suggest that recessions cause both a cleansing effect as argued previously, and a scarring effect, under which the industry loses potentially good firms. Furthermore,my model suggests that a recovery can be jobless if the recession has significantly reduced the number of learning firms that create jobs.

References

Aghion, Philippe and Howitt, Peter. "A model of Growth Through Creative Destruction." *Econometrica,* March 1992, 60(2), pp. 323-351.

Aghion, Philippe and Howitt, Peter. "Growth and Unemployment." *The Review of Economic Studies*, July 1994, 61(3), pp. 477-494.

Aghion, Philippe and Saint-Paul, Gilles. "Virtues of Bad Times." *Macroeconomic Dynamics*, September 1998, 2(3), pp. 322-44.

Aw, Bee Yan; Chen, Xiaomin and Roberts, Mark J. "Firm-level Evidence on Productivity Differentials, Turnover, and Exports in Taiwanese Manufacturing." *Journal of Development Economics*, October 2001, 66(1), pp. 51-86.

Bahk, Byong-Hyong and Michael, Gort. "Decomposing Learning by Doing in New Plants." *The Journal of Political Economy*, 101(4). Aug.1993, pp. 561-583.

Baily, Martin Neil; Bartelsman, Eric J. and Haltiwanger, John. "Labor Productivity: Structural Change and Cyclical Dynamics." *The Review of Economics and Statistics*, August 2001, 83(3), pp. 420-433.

Baily, Martin Neil; Hulten, Charles. and Campbell, D. "Productivity Dynamics in Manufacturing Establishments." *Brookings Papers on Economic Activity: Microeconomics*. Brookings Institution. 1992.

Baldwin, John R. *The Dynamics of Industrial Competition.* Cambridge University Press, 1995.

Basu, Sustanto. "Procyclical Productivity: Increasing Returns or Cyclical Utilization?" *Quarterly Journal of Economics*, August 1996, 111(3), pp. 719-51.

Bernanke, Ben S. "The Jobless Recovery." Remarks at the Global Economic and Investment Outlook Conference, Carnegie Mellon University, Pittsburgh, Pennsylvania. November 6, 2003

Blanchard, Olivier and Pedro Portugal, "What Hides Behind an Unemployment Rate: Comparing Portuguese and U.S. Labor Markets." *the American Economic Review*, March 2001, 91(1), pp. 187-207.

Bowlus, Audra J. "Job Match Quality over the Business Cycle." *Panel Data and Labour Market Dynamics*, Amsterdam: North Holland, 1993, pp. 21-41.

Caballero, Ricardo J. and Hammour, Mohamad L. "The Cleansing Effect of Recessions." *The American Economic Review*, December 1994, 84(5), pp. 1350-68.

Caballero, Ricardo J. and Hammour, Mohamad L. "On the timing and Efficiency of Creative Destruction." *The Quarterly Journal of Economics*, August 1996, 111(3), pp. 805-52.

Campbell, Jeffrey R. and Fisher, Jonas D.M. "Idiosyncratic Risk and Aggregate Employment Dynamics." *The Review of Economic Dynamics*, 2004.

Carreira, Carlos and Paulino Teixeira. "Internal and External Restructuring over the Cycle: A Firm-based Analysis of Gross Flows and Productivity Growth." Mimeo, Universidade de Coimbra, 2006.

Davis, Steven J. and Haltiwanger, John. "Gross Job Flows." *Handbook of Labor Economics*, Amsterdam: North-Holland, 1999.

Davis, Steven J.; Haltiwanger, John and Schuh, Scott. *Job Creation and Job Destruction*, Cambridge, MIT Press,1996.

Davis, Steven J. and Haltiwanger, John. "Gross Job Creation, Gross Job Destruction, and Employment Reallocation." *The Quarterly Journal of Economics*, August 1992, 107(3), pp. 818-63.

Dunne, Timothy; Roberts, Mark J. and Samuelson, Larry. "The Growth and Failure of U.S. Manufacturing Plants." *The Quarterly Journal of Economics*, November 1989, 104(4), pp. 671-98.

Ericson, Richard and Pakes, Ariel. "Markov-Perfect Industry Dynamics: A Framework for Empirical Work." *The Review of Economic Studies,* January 1995, 62(1), pp. 53-82.

Foote, Christopher L. "Trend Employment Growth and the Bunching of firm Creation and Destruction." *The Quarterly Journal of Economics*. August 1998, 113(3), pp. 809-834.

Hall, Robert E. "Labor Demand, Labor Supply, and Employment Volatility." in Olivier J. Blanchard and Stanley Fischer, *NBER Macroeconomics Annual*. Cambridge, MA: MIT Press, 1991.

Hall, Robert E. "Lost Jobs." *Brookings Papers on Economic Activity*, 1995:1, pp. 221-256.

Lucas, Robert, E. "On the Size Distribution of Business Firms." *The Bell Journal of Economics*, Autumn1978, 9(2), pp. 508-523.

Lucas, Robert, E. *Models of Business Cycles,* Oxford: Basil Blackwell, 1987.

Jensen, J. Bradford; McGuckin, Robert H. and Stiroh, Kevin J. "The Impact of Vintage and Survival on Productivity: Evidence from Cohorts of U.S. Manufacturing Plants." Economic Studies Series Working paper 00-06, Census of Bureau, May 2000.

Jovanovic, Boyan. "Selection and the Evolution of Industry." *Econometrica,* May 1982, 50(3), pp. 649-70.

Krusell, Per. and Smith, Anthony A. Jr. "Income and Wealth Heterogeneity in the Macroeconomy." *The Journal of Political Economy*, 1998, 106(5), pp. 867-895.

Kydland, Finn E. and Prescott, Edward C, 1982. "Time to Build and Aggregate Fluctuations," *Econometrica*, vol. 50(6), pages 1345-70.

Mortensen, Dale and Pissarides,Christopher. "Job Creation and Job Destruction in the Theory of Unemployment." *The Review of Economic Studies,* July 1994, 61(3), pp. 397-415.

Moscarini, Giuseppe. "Skill and Luck in the Theory of Turnover." Mimeo, Department of economics of Yale University, February 2003.

Ouyang, Min. "The Scarring Effect of Recessions." Working paper, Department of economics of University of California at Irvine, February 2006.

Ouyang, Min. "Plant Life Cycle and Aggregate Employment Dynamics." Working paper, Department of economics of University of California at Irvine, June 2006.

Pries, Michael J. "Persistence of Employment Fluctuations: a Model of Recurring Firm Loss." *The Review of Economic Studies*, January 2004, 71(1), pp. 193-215.

Schultze, Charles L. "Offshoring, Import Competition, and the Jobless Recovery" The Brookings Institution Policy Brief #136. August 2004

Schumpeter, Joseph A. "Depressions." in Douglas Brown et al., *Economics of the Recovery Program,* New York, 1934, pp. 3-12.

In: Business Fluctuations and Cycles
Editor: T. Nagakawa, pp. 25-42
ISBN: 978-1-60021-503-2

Chapter 2

MACROECONOMIC STABILIZATION POLICY IN A HIGH-DIMENSIONAL KEYNESIAN BUSINESS CYCLE MODEL

Toichiro Asada*
Faculty of Economics, Chuo University
742-1 Higashinakano, Hachioji, Tokyo 192-0393, Japan

ABSTRACT

In this paper, we study the effect of macroeconomic stabilization policy by utilizing the analytical framework of the high-dimensional dynamic Keynesian model of the business cycle, which consists of a set of nonlinear differential equations with many endogenous variables. Endogenous variables in our model include both of private and public real debts, real national income, rate of employment, real capital stock, and real money supply. In our model, money supply, public debt, taxes and government expenditure are intimately related each other through the budget constraint of the 'consolidated government' including the central bank. We investigate the macroeconomic impact of fiscal stabilization policy with and without time lags in policy response analytically. It is shown that stability, instability, and cyclical fluctuations emerge according to the choice of the values of policy parameters, among others, the strength of the fiscal stabilization policy and the length of the policy lag.

Key words : Stabilization policy, High-dimensional Keynesian business cycle model, Budget constraint of government, Dynamic stability, Business cycle

JEL classification : C62, E31, E32, E52, E62

---

* E-mail : asada@tamacc.chuo-u.ac.jp

1. INTRODUCTION

In the 1940s and the 1950s, the 'Keynesian' theories of economic growth and economic fluctuations, which are based on Keynes(1936)'s vision on the working of the modern capitalist economy, flourished. A typical example is Harrod(1948), who stressed the disequilibrium and instability of the capital accumulation process. Harrod(1948) concentrated on the destabilizing positive feedback mechanism rater than the stabilizing negative feedback mechanism, and later his idea was formulated mathematically by Okishio(1993) and Nikaido(1996). Minsky(1986)'s 'financial instability hypothesis' is also based on such a Keynesian tradition of thinking. But, it seems that the mainstream macroeconomics after the 1970s discarded such a 'Keynesian' approach of disequilibrium dynamics. For example, even in a chapter on 'dynamic analysis of Keynesian model' in Sargent(1987) that is a representative textbook of the 'advanced Macroeconomics' in the 1980s, dynamic stability of the system is taken for granted, rather than proved. In Romer(1996) that is a typical textbook of Macroeconomics in the 1990s, the major part of the book is devoted to the interpretation of the recent mainstream approach of perfect equilibrium based on the dynamic optimization of a representative agent with perfect foresight or rational expectation. Recently, however, we experienced the revival of the economic approach that stresses the destabilizing positive feedback mechanism, mainly in the context of microeconomic analysis(cf. Arthur(1994), Agliardi(1998), and Rosser(1991)). Also in the field of macroeconomic dynamics, a research group of some theoretical economists including the author of this paper, led by Peter Flaschel and Carl Chiarella, has recently developed disequilibrium dynamic models of business cycles in the spirit of the Keynesian tradition with positive as well as negative feedback causal chains.[1]

In this paper, we study the effect of government's macroeconomic stabilization policy by utilizing the analytical framework of the 'high-dimensional dynamic Keynesian model' of the business cycle that is quoted in footnote 1. Endogenous variables in our model include both of private and public real debts, real national income, rate of employment, real capital stock, and real money supply. In our model, money supply, public debt, taxes and government expenditure are intimately related each other through the budget constraint of the 'consolidated government' including the central bank. We investigate the macroeconomic impact of fiscal stabilization policy analytically by means of an advanced mathematical method. It is shown that stability, instability, and cyclical fluctuations emerge according to the choice of the values of the policy parameters, among others, the strength of the fiscal stabilization policy and the length of the policy lag. In section 2, we formulate the basic model in this paper, and we provide a mathematical analysis as well as an economic interpretation of the solution of the basic model in sections 3 and 4. In section 5, we consider possibilities of some important extensions of the basic model. Economic meanings of the main symbols and some complicated mathematical formulae are given in the appendices. We hope that the model developed in

---

1 See, for example, Chiarella and Flaschel(2000), Chiarella, Flaschel, Groh and Semmler(2000), Asada, Chiarella, Flaschel and Franke(2003), Chiarella, Flaschel and Franke(2005), and Asada, Chen, Chiarella and Flaschel(2006). Their models are called the 'high-dimensional dynamic Keynesian models', which consist of the systems of nonlinear differential equations with many endogenous variables. Woodford(1988), Rose(1990), and Keen(2000) are based on related but somewhat different approaches.

this paper can provide some theoretical foundations for macroeconomic interpretation of the performances of recent U. S., Japanese, and other economies.

2. FORMULATION OF THE BASIC MODEL

The basic model in this paper consists of the following system of equations.[2]

$$\dot{d} = \phi(g(\beta y, \rho - \pi^e, d)) - s_f\{\beta y - i(\rho, d)d\} - \{g(\beta y, \rho - \pi^e, d) + \pi\}d \tag{1}$$

$$\dot{y} = \alpha[\phi(g(\beta y, \rho - \pi^e, d)) + v + (1 - s_r)\{\rho b + i(\rho, d)d\} - \{s_f + (1 - s_f)s_r\}\beta y - t_w - (1 - s_r)t_r] \ ; \ \alpha > 0 \tag{2}$$

$$\dot{e}/e = \dot{y}/y + g(\beta y, \rho - \pi^e, d) - n \tag{3}$$

$$\dot{m}/m = \mu - \pi - g(\beta y, \rho - \pi, d) \tag{4}$$

$$\dot{b}/b = \mu_B - \pi - g(\beta y, \rho - \pi^e, d) \tag{5}$$

$$\pi = f(e) + \pi^e \ ; \ f'(e) > 0, \ f(\bar{e}) = 0 \tag{6}$$

$$\rho = \rho(y, m) = \begin{cases} \rho_0 + (h_1 y - m)/h_2 & if \quad h_1 y - m \geqq 0 \\ \rho_0 & if \quad h_1 y - m < 0 \end{cases} \tag{7}$$

$$\mu m + \mu_B b = v + \rho b - (t_w + t_r) \tag{8}$$

$$\mu = \bar{\mu} > n \tag{9}$$

$$v = v_0 + \delta(\bar{e} - e) \ ; \ v_0 > 0, \ \delta \geqq 0 \tag{10}$$

$$\pi^e = \bar{\mu} - n \tag{11}$$

As for the list of the symbols, see **Appendix A**. Next, we shall explain how these equations can be derived.

If we assume that there is no issues of new shares and we neglect the repayment of the principal of private debt for the sake of simplicity, we can write the budget constraint of the private firms as follows.

$$\dot{D} = \phi(g)pK - s_f(rpK - iD) \ ; \ r = P/K \tag{12}$$

where $P =$ pre tax real profit and $r =$ pre tax rate of profit. On the other hand, by differentiating the definitional equation $d = D/pK$ with respect to time, we have

$$\dot{d}/d = \dot{D}/D - \dot{p}/p - \dot{K}/K = \dot{D}/D - \pi - g. \tag{13}$$

From equations (12) and (13) we obtain

$$\dot{d} = \phi(g) - s_f(r - id) - (g + \pi)d. \tag{14}$$

[2] This model is an adapted version of the model types presented in Asada(2006a, 2006b). A dot over a symbol denotes the derivative with respect to time.

Furthermore, we assume the following functional relationships for the determination of the variables i and g.

$$i = \rho + \xi(d) = i(\rho, d)\ ;\ \xi(d) \geqq 0,\ i_d = \xi'(d) > 0 \text{ for } d > 0,$$
$$i_d < 0 \text{ for } d < 0 \tag{15}$$

$$g = g(r, \rho - \pi^e, d)\ ;\ g_r = \partial g / \partial r > 0,\ g_{\rho-\pi} = \partial g / \partial (g - \pi^e) < 0,$$
$$g_d = \partial g / \partial d < 0 \tag{16}$$

Eq. (15) implies that the private and the public bonds are the imperfect substitutes, and the interest rate differentials reflect the difference of the 'degrees of the risk' of these assets. Eq. (16) is the investment function with debt effect, which can be derived from firms' optimizing behavior in the environment with both of Uzawa(1968)'s increasing cost and Kalecki(1937)'s increasing risk of investment(cf. Asada(1999), Asada and Semmler(1995)).

Next, we assume the following quantity adjustment process of the goods market disequilibrium following Keynesian tradition.

$$\dot{y} = \alpha(c + \phi(g) + v - y)\ ;\ c = C/K = (C_w + C_r)/K,\ \alpha > 0 \tag{17}$$

where $C_w =$ workers' real consumption expenditure, $C_r =$ capitalists' real consumption expenditure, and $c + \phi(g) + v$ becomes to be the effective demand per capital stock if we neglect the foreign trade for the sake of simplicity. As for the consumption functions of workers and capitalists, we follow Kalecki(1971)'s postulate of the two class economy. That is to say,

$$C_w = W - T_w = Y - P - T_w \tag{18}$$

$$C_r = (1 - s_r)\{(1 - s_f)P + \rho(B/p) + i(D/p) - T_r\} \tag{19}$$

where $W =$ pre tax real wage income. These equations say that workers spend all of their disposable income, and capitalists save a part of their disposable income. Substituting these equations into Eq. (17), we have

$$\dot{y} = \alpha[\phi(g) + v + (1 - s_r)(\rho b + id) - \{s_f + (1 - s_f)s_r\}r - t_w - (1 - s_r)t_r]. \tag{20}$$

For the pricing behavior of firms, we simply adopt the Kaleckian postulate of the mark up pricing in the imperfectly competitive economy, namely,

$$p = z(wN/Y) = zw/a\ ;\ z > 1 \tag{21}$$

where z is the average mark up, which is supposed to reflects the 'degree of monopoly' of the economy. In this case, we have

$$\beta = P/Y = (Y - W)/Y = 1 - (W/Y) = 1 - \{(w/p)N/Y\} = 1 - (1/z), \tag{22}$$

which means that the share of pre tax profit in national income also becomes a parameter that reflects the 'degree of monopoly'. Then, we have the following relationship, which means that the rate of profit is proportional to the rate of capacity utilization.

$$r = P/K = \beta Y/K = \beta y \tag{23}$$

Substituting equations (15), (16), and (23) into equations (14) and (20), we obtain equations (1) and (2).

Next, let us consider how to derive Eq. (3). Since we have

$$N = \frac{(Y/K)K}{Y/N} = yK/a \tag{24}$$

by definition, the rate of employment becomes

$$e = N/N_s = yK/aN_s, \tag{25}$$

from which we have the following equation.

$$\begin{aligned} \dot{e}/e &= \dot{y}/y + \dot{K}/K - \dot{N}_s/N_s - \dot{a}/a = \dot{y}/y + g - (n_1 + n_2) \\ &= \dot{y}/y + g - n \end{aligned} \tag{26}$$

Substituting equations (16) and (23) into Eq. (26), we obtain Eq. (3).

From the definitional relationships $m = M/pK$ and $b = B/pK$ we have the following two equations.

$$\dot{m}/m = \dot{M}/M - \dot{p}/p - \dot{K}/K = \mu - \pi - g \tag{27}$$

$$\dot{b}/b = \dot{B}/B - \dot{p}/p - \dot{K}/K = \mu_B - \pi - g \tag{28}$$

Substituting Eq. (16) into these two equations, we obtain equations (4) and (5).

As for the dynamic adjustment process of the labor market disequilibrium, we follow the standard hypothesis of expectation-augmented wage Phillips curve, i. e.,

$$\dot{w}/w = f(e) + n_2 + \pi^e \text{ ; } f'(e) > 0, \ f(\bar{e}) = 0 \tag{29}$$

On the other hand, it follows from the price equation (21) that

$$\pi = \dot{p}/p = \dot{w}/w - \dot{a}/a = \dot{w}/w - n_2. \tag{30}$$

From equations (29) and (30) we obtain a standard type of the expectation-augmented price Phillips curve (6).

Eq. (7) is a standard type of the 'LM equation' that describes the equilibrium condition for the money market, and we can derive it as follows. Following Asada, Chiarella, Flaschel and Franke(2003), let us specify the equilibrium condition for the money market as

$$M = h_1 pY + (\rho_0 - \rho)h_2 pK \text{ ; } h_1 > 0, \ h_2 > 0, \ \rho \geqq \rho_0 \geqq 0, \tag{31}$$

where the right hand side of this equation is a type of Keynesian nominal money demand function, and ρ_0 is the nonnegative lower bound of nominal interest rate of the government bond. Solving this equation with respect to ρ, we obtain Eq. (7).

We can derive Eq. (8) as follows. The budget constraint of the 'consolidated government' including the central bank, which says that the government deficit must be financed through the issue of new money or new bond, can be written as[3]

$$\dot{M} + \dot{B} = pG + \rho B - pT = pG + \rho B - p(T_w + T_r). \tag{32}$$

Dividing both sides of this equation by pK, we obtain Eq. (8).

---

[3] Eq. (32) is effective even in case of $\dot{M} < 0$ and/or $\dot{B} < 0$.

Eq. (9) specifies the monetary policy of the central bank, which is a quite simple 'monetarist rule' to keep the constant growth rate of nominal money supply through time. Eq. (10) specifies the government's fiscal stabilization policy rule. In case of $\delta>0,$ fiscal policy is counter-cyclical or 'Keynesian'. Eq. (11) describes the expectation formation hypothesis in our model. In section 3, it is shown that the rate of price inflation becomes $\bar{\mu}-n$ at the long run equilibrium point. Eq.(11) implies that the public's inflation expectation is correct in the long run. This expectation hypothesis is due to Stein(1971, 1982), and it was called 'quasi rational' expectation hypothesis by Asada(1991). This hypothesis may be rationalized if the behavior of the central bank is sufficiently credible, because of the following reasons.

Suppose that the central bank officially announces the long run equilibrium rate of inflation $\pi^*=\bar{\mu}-n$ as the target rate of inflation, and the public believes this announcement because the behavior of the central bank is supposed to be sufficiently 'credible'. In this case, the public will use this information to form their inflation expectation. In fact, this is the reason why the 'inflation targeting' by the central bank is effective in Krugman(1998)'s model.[4]

The system (1) – (11) is a complete system of equations, which determines the dynamics of eleven endogenous variables $(d,y,e,m,b,\pi,\rho,\mu_B,\mu,v,\pi^e)$. This system can be reduced to the following five-dimensional system of nonlinear differential equations, which may be called the 'fundamental dynamical system' of the basic model.[5]

$$\text{(i)}\quad \dot{d}=\phi(g(\beta y,\rho(y,m)-\bar{\mu}+n,d))-s_f\{\beta y-i(\rho(y,m),d)d\}$$
$$-\{g(\beta y,\rho(y,m)-\bar{\mu}+n,d)+f(e)+\bar{\mu}-n\}d=F_1(d,y,e,m)$$

$$\text{(ii)}\quad \dot{y}=\alpha[\phi(\beta y,\rho(y,m)-\bar{\mu}+n,d)+v_0+\delta(\bar{e}-e)+(1-s_r)\{\rho(y,m)b$$
$$+i(\rho(y,m),d)d-\{s_f+(1-s_f)s_r\}\beta y-t_w-(1-s_r)t_r]$$
$$=F_2(d,y,e,m,b\,;\alpha,\delta)$$

$$\text{(iii)}\quad \dot{e}=e[F_2(d,y,e,m,b\,;\alpha,\delta)/y+g(\beta y,\rho(y,m)-\bar{\mu}+n,d)-n]$$
$$=F_3(d,y,e,m,b\,;\alpha,\delta)$$

$$\text{(iv)}\quad \dot{m}=m[n-f(e)-g(\beta y,\rho(y,m)-\bar{\mu}+n,d)]=F_4(d,y,e,m)$$

$$\text{(v)}\quad \dot{b}=v_0+\delta(\bar{e}-e)+\rho(y,m)b-\bar{\mu}m-(t_w+t_r)-b[f(e)+\bar{\mu}-n$$
$$+g(\beta y,\rho(y,m)-\bar{\mu}+n,d)]=F_5(d,y,e,m,b\,;\delta) \tag{33}$$

This system is enough to determine the complicated interdependent dynamics of five important macroeconomic variables(real private debt, real national income, rate of employment, real money supply, and real public debt), some of which are divided by capital stock.

---

[4] See also Asada(2006a, 2006b).

[5] For simplicity, we assume that t_w and t_r are constant parameters following Chiarella and Flaschel(2000) and Asada, Chiarella, Flaschel and Franke(2003). In section 5, however, we introduce an alternative assumption of taxation.

3. NATURE OF THE LONG RUN EQUILIBRIUM SOLUTION

The long run equilibrium solution of the system (33), which satisfies the condition

$$\dot{d} = \dot{y} = \dot{e} = \dot{m} = \dot{b} = 0, \tag{34}$$

is determined by the following system of simultaneous equations.

(i) $n - s_f\{\beta y - i(\rho(y,m),d)d\} - \bar{\mu}d = 0$

(ii) $n + v_0 + (1-s_r)\{\rho(y,m)b + i(\rho(y,m),d) - \{s_f + (1-s_f)s_r\}\beta y$

$-t_r - (1-s_r)t_r = 0$

(iii) $g(\beta y, \rho(y,m) - \bar{\mu} + n, d) = n$

(iv) $e = \bar{e}$

(v) $v_0 + \rho(y,m)b - \bar{\mu}(m+b) - (t_w + t_r) = 0$ (35)

The equilibrium rate of employment (e^*) is determined by Eq. (35)(iv), and equilibrium values of other four variables (d^*, y^*, m^*, b^*) are determined simultaneously by other four equations in Eq. (35). This long run equilibrium solution has the following properties.

(1) The equilibrium rate of capital accumulation (g^*) is equal to the 'natural rate of growth' (n), which is the sum of the rate of growth of labor supply and the rate of growth of labor productivity.
(2) The equilibrium rate of employment (e^*) is equal to the 'natural rate of employment' $(\bar{e})$.
(3) The equilibrium rate of price inflation (π^*) is equal to the difference between the growth rate of nominal money supply and the natural rate of growth $(\bar{\mu} - n)$, which is also equal to the expected rate of price inflation (π^e).

These properties suggest that the long run equilibrium solution of this model has the typical 'classical' natures. In particular, the properties (1) and (2) say that the rate of growth and the rate of employment are determined independent of the monetary factors in long run equilibrium, which means that the 'long run neutrality of money' applies to this model. But, it is not correct to say that the monetary policy is irrelevant to the determination of the long run equilibrium. In fact, contrary to the first impression, the monetary policy can affect the nature of the long run equilibrium because of the following reason.

Since the nominal rate of interest of government bond has the nonnegative lower bound ρ_0, the expected real rate of interest must satisfy the following inequality.

$$\rho - \pi^e = \rho - \bar{\mu} + n \geqq \rho_0 - \bar{\mu} + n \tag{36}$$

The feasible range of the variables y and d is rather restricted, so that the relatively low value of the expected real rate of interest may be required to support the 'natural rate of growth'. The inequality (36) means, however, that the expected real rate of interest may be too high to support the natural rate of growth if the central bank chooses too small value of $\bar{\mu}$. This means that the target rate of price inflation announced by the central bank $(\bar{\mu} - n)$ may be too low to ensure the existence of the long run equilibrium. In this sense, the monetary policy is not neutral even in the long run.

In this paper, we *assume* that $\bar{\mu}$ is sufficiently high to ensure the existence of the economically meaningful long run equilibrium solution such that $d^* > 0,\ y^* > 0,\ m^* > 0,\ b^* > 0,$ and $\rho(y^*, m^*) > \rho_0$.[6]

4. STABILITY, INSTABILITY AND CYCLES : OUT OF STEADY STATE DYNAMICS

The long run equilibrium solution of this model is independent of the parameter values α and δ. But, in fact these parameter values can influence the nature of the out of steady state dynamics of the system. In this section, we study the local dynamics of the system by means of the linearization method. We can write the Jacobian matrix of the system (33) *at the equilibrium point* as follows.

$$J = \begin{bmatrix} F_{11} & F_{12} & -f'(\bar{e})d & F_{14} & 0 \\ \alpha G_{21} & \alpha G_{22} & -\alpha\delta & \alpha G_{24} & \alpha G_{25} \\ \bar{e}[\alpha G_{21}/y + g_d] & \bar{e}[\alpha G_{22}/y + H_{22}] & -\bar{e}\alpha\delta/y & \bar{e}[\alpha G_{24}/y + H_{24}] & \alpha G_{25}/y \\ -mg_d & -mH_{22} & -mf'(\bar{e}) & -mH_{24} & 0 \\ -bg_d & F_{52} & -\{\delta + bf'(\bar{e})\} & F_{54} & F_{55} \end{bmatrix} \tag{37}$$

The detailed expressions of the partial derivatives in this matrix are contained in **Appendix B**. Now, let us assume as follows.

Assumption 1.
$F_{11} < 0,\ F_{12} > 0,\ F_{14} > 0,\ G_{21} < 0,\ G_{22} > 0,\ H_{22} > 0,$ and $F_{55} < 0.$

In fact, these inequalities will be satisfied if $\phi'(n),\ g_r,\ |g_d|$ and h_2 are sufficiently large and $\bar{\mu} > \rho$ at the equilibrium point. In other words, **Assumption 1** will be satisfied if the sensitivity of investment adjustment cost, sensitivities of investment

---

[6] The situation such that $\rho = \rho_0$ is called the case of 'liquidity trap'. Therefore, the last inequality means that there is no liquidity trap at the long run equilibrium. For the extensive analyses of the case of liquidity trap, see Krugman(1998), Gong(2005), and Asada(2006a, 2006b).

activities with respect to the changes of the relevant variables, sensitivity of money demand with respect to the changes of the nominal rate of interest, and the growth rate of money supply are sufficiently large.

We can write the characteristic equation of the Jacobian matrix (37) as

$$\Delta(\lambda) = |\lambda I - J| = \lambda^5 + a_1\lambda^4 + a_2\lambda^3 + a_3\lambda^2 + a_4\lambda + a_5 = 0. \tag{38}$$

In particular, it is well known that the explicit expression of the coefficient a_1 is given by the following formula.

$$a_1 = -traceJ = -\underset{(-)}{F_{11}} + \alpha(\bar{e}\delta / y - \underset{(+)}{G_{22}}) + m\underset{(+)}{H_{24}} - \underset{(-)}{F_{55}} \tag{39}$$

It is also well known that the following set of inequalities is a set of the *necessary* (but not sufficient) conditions for the local stability of this five-dimensional system(cf. Gandolfo(1986)Chap. Chap. 16).

$$a_j > 0 \text{ for all } j \in \{1,2,\cdots,5\} \tag{40}$$

Proposition 1.

Suppose that $\delta < \underset{(+)}{G_{22}}\, y/\bar{e}.$ Then, the equilibrium point of the system (33) is unstable for all sufficiently large values of α under **Assumption 1**.

Proof.

In this case, the coefficient a_1 becomes negative for all sufficiently large values of α, which violates one of the necessary conditions for local stability (40).

ϒ

This proposition implies that the system becomes unstable if the fiscal policy is not sufficiently counter-cyclical(δ is small) and the adjustment speed in the goods market is sufficiently high(α is large).

Next, let us study the effect of the fiscal stabilization policy. For a while, we consider a special case of $s_r = 1.$ In this case, we have $G_{24} > 0$ and $G_{25} = 0,$ and the characteristic equation (38) is reduced to

$$\Delta(\lambda) = (\lambda - F_{55})|\lambda I - J_4| = 0, \tag{41}$$

where the matrix J_4 is defined as follows.

$$J_4 = \begin{bmatrix} F_{11} & F_{12} & -f'(\bar{e})d & F_{14} \\ \alpha G_{21} & \alpha G_{22} & -\alpha\delta & \alpha G_{24} \\ \bar{e}[\alpha G_{21}/y + g_d] & \bar{e}[\alpha G_{22}/y + H_{22}] & -\bar{e}\alpha\delta/y & \bar{e}[\alpha G_{24}/y + H_{24}] \\ -mg_d & -mH_{22} & -mf'(\bar{e}) & -mH_{24} \end{bmatrix} \tag{42}$$

Eq. (41) has a real root $\lambda_5 = F_{55} < 0,$ and other four roots are determined by the following equation.

$$\Delta_4(\lambda) = |\lambda I - J_4| = \lambda^4 + b_1\lambda^3 + b_2\lambda^2 + b_3\lambda + b_4 = 0 \tag{43}$$

The explicit expressions of the coefficients in this equation are given in **Appendix C**. It is well known that the equilibrium point of this system is locally stable *if and only if* the following set of inequalities is satisfied.[7]

$$b_j > 0 \text{ for all } j \in \{1,2,3,4\},\ \Phi = b_1 b_2 b_3 - b_1^2 b_4 - b_3^2 > 0 \tag{44}$$

Assumption 2.

The inequalities $A_3 > 0$ and $B_4 > 0$ are satisfied.

The explicit expressions of A_3 and B_4 are given in **Appendix C**. The inequality $A_3 > 0$ will be satisfied if the debt effect on investment expenditure $|g_d|$ is not extremely large. On the other hand, some additional conditions will be required to satisfy the inequality $B_4 > 0.$ It is worth noting that the values of A_3 and B_4 are independent of the parameter value $\delta \geqq 0,$ and their signs are determined independent of the parameter value $\alpha > 0.$

Proposition 2.

Suppose that $s_r = 1.$ Then, the equilibrium point of the system (33) is locally stable for all sufficiently large values of the fiscal policy parameter $\delta > 0$ irrespective of the value of the parameter $\alpha > 0$ under Assumptions 1 and 2.

Proof.

In this case, we have $b_4 > 0$ and all of the coefficients $b_j\ (j = 1,2,3)$ become linear increasing functions of $\delta.$ Furthermore, Φ becomes a cubic function of δ such that $\Phi = E_1\delta^3 + E_2\delta^2 + E_3\delta + E_4$ with $E_1 = A_1A_2A_3 > 0$ (cf. **Appendix C**). These properties imply that all of the inequalities (44) are satisfied for all sufficiently large values of $\delta > 0$ irrespective of the value of $\alpha > 0.$

ϒ

Proposition 3.

Proposition 2 applies even if $s_r < 1,$ as long as s_r is sufficiently close to 1.

---

[7] These inequalities are called the 'Routh-Hurwitz conditions for local stability' in case of the four-dimensional system of differential equations. See, for example, . Gandolfo(1966) Chap. 16, Asada and Yoshida(2003), Yoshida and Asada(2007), and Manfredi and Fanti(2004).

Proof.

This proposition follows from the continuity of the values of characteristic roots with respective to the coefficients of characteristic equation. ϒ

These propositions mean that the sufficiently strong counter-cyclical fiscal policy can stabilize the economy under some reasonable conditions even if the adjustment speed in the goods market (α) is so high that the economy is unstable in case of $\delta = 0$.

Now, suppose that the system is unstable at $\delta = 0$. In this case, the system is also unstable for all sufficient small values of $\delta > 0$ by continuity. Under the situation in which **Proposition 2** is applicable, however, the system becomes locally stable for all sufficiently large values of $\delta > 0$. In such a case, there exists at least one 'bifurcation point' $\delta_0 \in (0, +\infty)$, at which the qualitative property of the system changes discontinuously. It is evident that the real part of at least one root of the characteristic equation (43) becomes zero at such a bifurcation point. But, it follows from **Assumption 2** that $\Delta_4(0) = b_4 = B_4 > 0$, which means that the real root such that $\lambda = 0$ does not exist. Therefore, at the bifurcation point at least a pair of pure imaginary roots must exist. If there is only a pair of pure imaginary roots at $\delta = \delta_0$, this point is called the 'Hopf bifurcation point', and it is well known that there exists a family of non-constant closed orbits at some range of δ that is sufficiently close to the bifurcation point in this case.[8] If there are two pairs of pure imaginary roots at $\delta = \delta_0$, that point is not Hopf bifurcation point, and the existence of the closed orbits is not necessarily ensured. Even in this case, however, the existence of cyclical fluctuations is ensured at some parameter values δ which are sufficiently close to δ_0, because of the existence of (two pairs of) complex roots.

We have shown the existence of endogenous cyclical fluctuations at some parameter values of δ by assuming that $s_r = 1$, but the above reasoning applies even if $s_r < 1$ by continuity, as long as s_r is sufficiently close to 1. Thus, we have proved the following proposition.

Proposition 4.

Suppose that $s_r = 1$ or s_r is sufficiently close to 1. Then, there exist the endogenous cyclical fluctuations at some intermediate range of the fiscal policy parameter values $\delta > 0$ under Assumptions 1 and 2.

---

8 See, for example, Gandolfo(1986) Chap. 25 and Lorenz(1993) Chap. 3.

5. Some Extensions of the Model

Finally, we shall consider four natural extensions of the basic model in this paper. First, we consider the effect of policy lag on the dynamic stability/instability of the system. The simplest way to introduce policy lag into our model is to replace Eq. (10) with the following set of equations(cf. Yoshida and Asada 2007).

$$v = v_0 + \delta(\bar{e} - e^*) \ ; \ \delta \geqq 0 \tag{45}$$

$$\dot{e}^* = (1/\varepsilon)(e - e^*) \ ; \ \varepsilon > 0 \tag{46}$$

where e^* is interpreted as the rate of employment that is *expected* by the policy maker(government), and ε is considered to be the policy lag. This modified system becomes six-dimensional model of nonlinear differential equations rather than five-dimensional model, and the five-dimensional basic model can be considered to be a special case of $\varepsilon = 0$. After tedious calculation, we can prove that the increase of the policy lag ε tends to destabilize the system.[9]

Second, let us consider more realistic treatment of the expectation formation hypothesis. Asada(2006a, 2006b) introduced the following type of the expectation formation hypothesis.

$$\dot{\pi}^e = \gamma\{\theta(\bar{\mu} - n - \pi^e) + (1-\theta)(\pi - \pi^e)\} \ ; \ \gamma > 0, \ 0 \leqq \theta \leqq 1 \tag{47}$$

This hypothesis may be called the 'mixed expectation hypothesis', because this is a mixture of backward-looking(adaptive) and forward-looking expectations. We can consider that the parameter θ is a measure of the 'credibility' of the inflation targeting of the central bank. If $\theta = 0,$ the public does not believe the announcement by the central bank, and in this case the inflation expectation becomes purely 'adaptive' or 'backward-looking'. If θ is close to 1, the public believes that the inflation targeting by the central bank is highly credible. If we replace Eq. (11) with Eq. (47), the system becomes six-dimensional. The system becomes even seven-dimensional if we introduce both of policy lag and mixed expectation hypothesis. By using simpler versions of the model, Asada(2006 a, 2006b) showed that high value of γ combined with sufficiently small value of θ tends to destabilize the economy.

Third possibility of the extension of the model is to introduce variable tax-capital ratio. In the basic model, we assumed that $t_w = T_w / K$ and $t_r = T_r / K$ are constant to simplify our analysis. An alternative more natural formulation of taxation rule may be as follows.

$$t_w = T_w / K = \tau_w W / K = \tau_w (1-\beta) Y / K = \tau_w (1-\beta) y \ ; \ 0 < \tau_w < 1 \tag{48}$$

$$\begin{aligned} t_r &= T_r / K = \tau_r \{(1 - s_f)(P/K) + \rho(B/pK) + i(D/pK)\} \\ &= \tau_r \{(1-s_f)\beta y + \rho b + id\} \ ; \ 0 < \tau_r < 1 \end{aligned} \tag{49}$$

[9] See Yoshida and Asada(2007) for the extensive analysis of policy lag in a similar but simplified version of the model.

In this case, the model becomes more complicated even if such a model is still tractable, because t_w and t_r are no longer constant.

Fourth possibility of the extension will be to introduce the endogenous determination of the 'natural rate of growth'. As the experiences of the U. S., Japanese, and other economies suggest, it is very likely that the growth rate of labor supply and/or the rate of technical progress decline(increase) if the rate of employment decreases(increases). This hypothesis can be formulated as

$$n = n(e)\ ;\ n'(e) > 0,\ n(\bar{e}) = \bar{n} > 0. \tag{50}$$

This model is, so to speak, a Keynesian endogenous growth model with variable rate of employment, which is in contrast with the neoclassical full employment endogenous growth models.[10] We can easily see, however, that the qualitative conclusion about stability/instability is not much affected as long as the value of $n'(\bar{e})$ is not extremely large.[11]

ACKNOWLEDGMENT

The author is grateful to Chuo University for the financial support of this research.

APPENDIX A : LIST OF THE SYMBOLS

A – 1. Variables

$D =$ nominal stock of firms' private debt. $K =$ real capital stock. $p =$ price level. $d = D / pK =$ private debt-capital ratio. $Y =$ real output(real national income). $y = Y / K =$ output-capital ratio, which is supposed to be proportional to 'rate of capacity utilization' of the capital stock. $g = \dot{K} / K =$ rate of capital accumulation. $\phi(g) =$ adjustment cost function of investment that was introduced by Uzawa(1969) with the properties $\phi'(g) \geqq 1, \quad \phi''(g) \geqq 0.$ $I = \phi(g)K =$ real private investment expenditure. $\rho =$ nominal rate of interest of public bond. $i =$ nominal rate of interest that is applied to firms' private debt. $\pi = \dot{p} / p =$ rate of price inflation. $\pi^e =$ expected rate of price inflation. $\rho - \pi^e =$ expected real rate of interest of public bond. $G =$ real government expenditure. $v = G / K.$ $B =$ nominal stock of public debt(public bond). $b = B / pK =$ public debt-capital ratio. $T_w =$ real income tax on workers. $t_w = T_w / K.$ $T_r =$ real income tax on capitalists. $t_r = T_r / K.$ $N =$ labor employment. $N_s =$ labor

[10] Pally(1996) develops another type of Keynesian endogenous growth model. For the neoclassical endogenous growth models, see Barro and Sala-i-Martin(1995).

[11] Another important extension will be to reconsider the problem of stabilization policy in a context of the open economy. Asada, Chiarella, Flaschel, and Franke(2003) will provide a foundation of such an analysis.

supply. $e = N/N_s =$ rate of employment = 1 – rate of unemployment. $n_1 = \dot{N}_s/N_s =$ growth rate of labor supply>0. $a = Y/N =$ average labor productivity. $n_2 = \dot{a}/a =$ growth rate of average labor productivity (rate of technical progress)$\geqq 0$. $n = n_1 + n_2 =$ 'natural' rate of growth (or 'potential' rate of growth)>0. $M =$ nominal money supply. $m = M/pK =$ money-capital ratio. $\mu = \dot{M}/M =$ growth rate of nominal money supply. $\mu_B = \dot{B}/B =$ growth rate of nominal public debt.

A – 2. Parameters

$\beta =$ share of pre tax profit in national income $(0<\beta<1)$. $s_f =$ rate of internal retention of firms $(0< s_f \leqq 1)$. $s_r =$ capitalists' propensity to save $(0< s_r \leqq 1)$. $\alpha =$ adjustment speed in the goods market. $\bar{e} =$ 'natural' rate of employment = 1 – 'natural' rate of unemployment $(0<\bar{e}<1)$. $\rho_0 =$ nonnegative lower bound of ρ. h_1 and h_2 are positive parameters of money demand function. $v_0 =$ constant part of v. $\delta =$ measure of the strength of counter-cyclical fiscal stabilization policy.

APPENDIX B : PARTIAL DERIVATIVES[12]

$$F_{11} = \partial F_1/\partial d = (\underset{(+)}{\phi'(n)} - d)\underset{(-)}{g_d} - \bar{\mu} + s_f(\underset{(+)}{i_d}\, d + i).$$

$$F_{12} = \partial F_1/\partial y = \beta\{(\underset{(+)}{\phi'(n)} - d)\underset{(+)}{g_r} - s_f\} + (1-d)(\underset{(+)}{\phi'(n)} - d)\underset{(-)}{g_{\rho-\pi}}\,\underset{(+)}{\rho_y} + s_f\,\underset{(+)}{\rho_y}\, d.$$

$$F_{14} = \partial F_1/\partial m = (\underset{(+)}{\phi'(n)} - d + s_f d)\underset{(-)}{g_{\rho-\pi}}\,\underset{(-)}{\rho_m}.$$

$$G_{21} = \partial\left(\frac{F_2}{\alpha}\right)/\partial d = \underset{(+)}{\phi'(n)}\,\underset{(-)}{g_d} + (1-s_f)(\underset{(+)}{i_d}\, d + i).$$

$$G_{22} = \partial\left(\frac{F_2}{\alpha}\right)/\partial y = \beta[\underset{(+)}{\phi'(n)}\,\underset{(+)}{g_r} - \{s_f + (1-s_f)s_r\}] + \{\underset{(+)}{\phi'(n)}\,\underset{(-)}{g_{\rho-\pi}} + (1-s_r)(b+d)\}\underset{(+)}{\rho_y}.$$

$$G_{24} = \partial\left(\frac{F_2}{\alpha}\right)/\partial m = \{\underset{(+)}{\phi'(n)}\,\underset{(-)}{g_{\rho-\pi}} + (1-s_r)(b+d)\}\underset{(-)}{\rho_m}.$$

$$G_{25} = \partial\left(\frac{F_2}{\alpha}\right)/\partial b = (1-s_r)\rho \geqq 0.$$

$$H_{22} = \beta\,\underset{(+)}{g_r} + \underset{(-)}{g_{\rho-\pi}}\,\underset{(+)}{\rho_y}. \quad H_{24} = \underset{(-)}{g_{\rho-\pi}}\,\underset{(-)}{\rho_m} > 0.$$

---

[12] In these expressions, we have $\rho_y = h_1/h_2 > 0$ and $\rho_m = -1/h_2 < 0$.

$$F_{52} = \partial F_5 / \partial y = b\{\beta \underset{(+)}{g_r} + (1 + \underset{(-)}{g_{\rho-\pi}}) \underset{(+)}{\rho_y}\}.\ F_{54} = \partial F_5 / \partial m = b(1 + \underset{(-)}{g_{\rho-\pi}}) \underset{(-)}{\rho_m}.$$

$$F_{55} = \partial F_5 / \partial b = \rho - \bar{\mu}.$$

APPENDIX C : COEFFICIENTS OF THE CHARACTERISTIC EQUATION[13]

$$b_1 = -traceJ_4 = -\underset{(-)}{F_{11}} - \alpha \underset{(+)}{G_{22}} + \bar{e}\alpha\delta / y + m \underset{(+)}{H_{24}} = A_1\delta + B_1 = b_1(\delta),$$

$$A_1 = \bar{e}\alpha / y > 0.$$

$b_2 =$ sum of all principal second-order minors of J_4

$$= \alpha \begin{vmatrix} F_{11} & F_{12} \\ G_{21} & G_{22} \end{vmatrix} + \bar{e} \begin{vmatrix} F_{11} & -f'(\bar{e})d \\ \alpha G_{21} / y + g_d & -\alpha\delta / y \end{vmatrix} - m \begin{vmatrix} F_{11} & F_{14} \\ g_d & H_{24} \end{vmatrix}$$

$$- \alpha\bar{e}\delta \begin{vmatrix} G_{22} & 1 \\ \alpha G_{22} / y + H_{22} & \alpha / y \end{vmatrix} - \alpha m \begin{vmatrix} G_{22} & G_{24} \\ H_{22} & H_{24} \end{vmatrix} - \bar{e}m \begin{vmatrix} -\alpha\delta / y & \alpha G_{24} / y + H_{24} \\ f'(\bar{e}) & H_{24} \end{vmatrix}$$

$$= A_2\delta + B_2 = b_2(\delta),\quad A_2 = \bar{e}\alpha(-\underset{(-)}{F_{11}} / y + \underset{(+)}{H_{22}} + m \underset{(+)}{H_{24}} / y) > 0.$$

$b_3 = -$ (sum of all principal third-order minors of J_4)

$$= \alpha\bar{e}m \begin{vmatrix} G_{22} & -\delta & G_{24} \\ \alpha G_{22} / y + H_{22} & -\alpha\delta / y & \alpha G_{24} / y + H_{24} \\ H_{22} & f'(\bar{e}) & H_{24} \end{vmatrix}$$

$$+ \bar{e}m \begin{vmatrix} F_{11} & -f'(\bar{e})d & F_{14} \\ \alpha G_{21} / y + g_d & -\alpha\delta / y & \alpha G_{24} / y + H_{24} \\ g_d & f'(\bar{e}) & H_{24} \end{vmatrix} + \alpha m \begin{vmatrix} F_{11} & F_{12} & F_{14} \\ G_{21} & G_{22} & G_{24} \\ g_d & H_{22} & H_{24} \end{vmatrix}$$

$$- \alpha\bar{e} \begin{vmatrix} F_{11} & F_{12} & -f'(\bar{e})d \\ G_{21} & G_{22} & -\delta \\ \alpha G_{21} / y + g_d & \alpha G_{22} / y + H_{22} & -\alpha\delta / y \end{vmatrix} = A_3\delta + B_3 = b_3(\delta),$$

$$A_3 = \bar{e}\alpha\{(m / y)(-\underset{(-)}{F_{11}} \underset{(+)}{H_{24}} + \underset{(+)}{F_{14}} \underset{(-)}{g_d}) - \underset{(-)}{F_{11}} \underset{(+)}{H_{22}} + \underset{(+)}{F_{12}} \underset{(-)}{g_d}\}.$$

[13] All of A_j, B_j, and E_j in this appendix $(j = 1,2,3,4)$ are independent of the parameter value δ.

$$b_4 = \det J_4 = -\alpha \bar{e} m \begin{vmatrix} F_{11} & F_{12} & -f'(\bar{e})d & F_{14} \\ G_{21} & G_{22} & -\delta & G_{24} \\ \alpha G_{21}/y + g_d & \alpha G_{22}/y + H_{22} & -\alpha\delta/y & \alpha G_{24}/y + H_{24} \\ g_d & H_{22} & f'(\bar{e}) & H_{24} \end{vmatrix}$$

$$= -\alpha \bar{e} m \begin{vmatrix} F_{11} & F_{12} & -f'(\bar{e})d & F_{14} \\ G_{21} & G_{22} & -\delta & G_{24} \\ 0 & 0 & -f'(\bar{e}) & 0 \\ g_d & H_{22} & f'(\bar{e}) & H_{24} \end{vmatrix} = \alpha \bar{e} m f'(\bar{e}) \begin{vmatrix} F_{11} & F_{12} & F_{14} \\ G_{21} & G_{22} & G_{24} \\ g_d & H_{22} & H_{24} \end{vmatrix}$$

$$= \alpha \bar{e} m f'(\bar{e})(\underset{(-)}{F_{11}}\, \underset{(+)}{G_{22}}\, \underset{(+)}{H_{24}} + \underset{(+)}{F_{12}}\, \underset{(+)}{G_{24}}\, \underset{(-)}{g_d} + \underset{(+)}{F_{14}}\, \underset{(+)}{H_{22}}\, \underset{(-)}{G_{21}} - \underset{(+)}{F_{14}}\, \underset{(+)}{G_{22}}\, \underset{(-)}{g_d} - \underset{(+)}{F_{12}}\, \underset{(-)}{G_{21}}\, \underset{(+)}{H_{24}}$$

$$- \underset{(-)}{F_{11}}\, \underset{(+)}{H_{22}}\, \underset{(+)}{G_{24}}) = B_4.$$

$$\Phi = b_1 b_2 b_3 - b_1^{\,2} b_4 - b_3^{\,2} = E_1\delta^3 + E_2\delta^2 + E_3\delta + E_4 = \Phi(\delta),\ E_1 = A_1 A_2 A_3.$$

REFERENCES

[1] Agliardi, E. (1998). *Positive Feedback Economics*, Macmillan, London.

[2] Arthur, B.(1994). *Increasing Returns and Path Dependence in the Economy*. The University of Michigan Press, Ann Arbor.

[3] Asada(1991). "On a Mixed Competitive-Monopolistic Macrodynamic Model in a Monetary Economy." *Journal of Economics / Zeitschrift für Nationalökonomie* 54-1, pp. 33-53.

[4] Asada, T.(1999). "Investment and Finance : A Theoretical Approach." *Annals of Operations Research* 89, pp. 75-87.

[5] Asada, T.(2006a). "Inflation Targeting Policy in a Dynamic Keynesian Model with Debt Accumulation : A Japanese Perspective." in : C. Chiarella, P. Flaschel, R. Franke and W. Semmler (eds.) *Quantitative and Empirical Analysis of Nonlinear Dynamic Macromodels,* Elsevier, Amsterdam, pp. 517-544.

[6] Asada, T.(2006b). "Stabilization Policy in a Keynes-Goodwin Model with Debt Accumulation." *Structural Change and Economic Dynamics* 17, pp. 466-485.

[7] Asada, T., P. Chen, C. Chiarella and P. Flaschel(2006). "Keynesian Dynamics and the Wage-price Spiral : A Baseline Disequilibrium Approach." *Journal of Macroeconomics* 28, pp. 90-130.

[8] Asada, T., C. Chiarella, P. Flaschel, and R. Franke(2003). *Open Economy Macrodynamics : An Integrated Disequilibrium Approach*. Springer-Verlag, Berlin.

[9] Asada, T. and W. Semmler(1995). "Growth and Finance : An Intertemporal Model." *Journal of Macroeconomics* 17, pp. 623-649.

[10] Asada, T. and H. Yoshida(2003). "Coefficient Criterion for Four-dimensional Hopf Bifurcations : A Complete Mathematical Characterization and Applications to Economic Dynamics." *Chaos, Solitons and Fractals* 18, pp. 525-536.

[11] Barro, R. J. and Sala-i-Martin, X.(1995). *Economic Growth.* McGraw-Hill, New York.

[12] Chiarella, C. and P. Flaschel(2000). *The Dynamics of Keynesian Monetary Growth : A Macrofoundations*. Cambridge University Press, Cambridge, U. K.

[13] Chiarella, C., P. Flaschel and R. Franke(2005). *Foundations for a Disequilibrium Theory of the Business Cycle : Qualitative Analysis and Quantitative Assessment*. Cambridge University Press, Cambridge, U. K.

[14] Chiarella, C., P. Flaschel, P. Groh and W. Semmler(2000). *Disequilibrium, Growth, and Labor Market Dynamics*. Springer-Verlag, Berlin.

[15] Gandolfo, G.(1986). *Economic Dynamics*(Third Edition). Springer-Verlag, Berlin.

[16] Gong, G.(2005). "Modeling Stabilization Policies in a Financially Unstable Economy." *Metroeconomica* 56, pp. 281-304.

[17] Harrod, R. F.(1948). *Towards a Dynamic Economics*. Macmillan, London.

[18] Kalecki, M.(1937). "The Principle of Increasing Risk." *Economica* 4, pp. 440-447.

[19] Kalecki, M.(1971). *Selected Essays on the Dynamics of the Capitalist Economy.* Cambridge University Press, Cambridge, U. K.

[20] Keen, S.(2000). "The Nonlinear Economics of Debt Deflation." in : W. A. Barnett, C. Chiarella, S. Keen, R. Marks and H. Schnabl (eds.) *Commerce, Complexity, and Evolution*, Cambridge University Press, Cambridge, U. K., pp. 83-110.

[21] Keynes, J. M.(1936). *The General Theory of Employment, Interest and Money.* Macmillan, London.

[22] Krugman, P.(1998). "It's Baaack : Japan's Slump and the Return of the Liquidity Trap." *Brookings Papers on Economic Activity* 2, 137-205.

[23] Lorenz, H. W.(1993), *Nonlinear Dynamical Economics and Chaotic Motion*(Second Edition). Springer-Verlag, Berlin.

[24] Manfredi, P. and L. Fanti(2004). "Cycles in Dynamic Economic Modelling." *Economic Modelling* 21, pp. 573-594.

[25] Minsky, H. P.(1986). *Stabilizing an Unstable Economy.* Yale University Press, New Haven.

[26] Nikaido, H.(1996). *Prices, Cycles, and Growth.* The MIT Press, Cambridge, Massachusetts, U. S. A.

[27] Okishio, N.(1993). *Essays on Political Economy.* P. Flaschel and M. Krüger (eds.) Peter Lang, Frankfurt am Main.

[28] Pally, T.(1996). "Growth Theory in a Keynesian Mode : Some Keynesian Foundations for New Endogenous Growth Theory." *Journal of Post Keynesian Economics* 19, pp. 113-135.

[29] Romer, P.(1996). *Advanced Macroeconomics*. McGraw-Hill, New York.

[30] Rose, H.(1990). *Macroeconomic Dynamics.* Basil Blackwell, Oxford.

[31] Rosser, Jr., J. B.(1991). *From Catastrophe to Chaos : A General Theory of Economic Discontinuities.* Kluwer Academic Publishers, Boston.

[32] Sargent, T. J.(1987). *Macroeconomic Theory*(Second Edition). Academic Press, San Diego.

[33] Stein, J. L.(1971). *Money and Capacity Growth.* Columbia University Press, New York.

[34] Stein, J. L.(1982). *Monetarist, Keynesian and New Classical Economics.* Basil Blackwell, Oxford.

[35] Uzawa, H.(1969). "Time Preference and the Penrose Effect in a Two-class Model of Economic Growth." *Journal of Political Economy* 77, pp. 628-652.

[36] Woodford, M.(1988). "Expectations, Finance and Aggregate Instability." in : M. Kohn and S. C. Tsiang (eds.) *Finance Constraints, Expectations, and Macroeconomics*, Clarendon Press, Oxford, pp. 230-261.

[37] Yoshida, H. and T. Asada(2007). "Dynamic Analysis of Policy Lag in a Keynes-Goodwin Model : Stability, Instability, Cycles and Chaos." *Journal of Economic Behavior and Organizatio,* 62, pp. 441-469.

In: Business Fluctuations and Cycles
Editor: T. Nagakawa, pp. 43-66
ISBN 978-1-60021-503-3

Chapter 3

DURATION DEPENDENT MARKOV-SWITCHING VECTOR AUTOREGRESSION PROPERTIES, BAYESIAN INFERENCE AND APPLICATION TO THE ANALYSIS OF THE U.S. BUSINESS CYCLE

Matteo M. Pelagatti*
Department of Statistics
Università degli Studi di Milano-Bicocca
Via Bicocca degli Arcimboldi, 8, 20126 Milano, Italy

Abstract

Duration dependent Markov-switching VAR (DDMS-VAR) models are time series models with data generating process consisting in a mixture of two VAR processes. The switching between the two VAR processes is governed by a two state Markov chain with transition probabilities that depend on how long the chain has been in a state. In the present paper we analyze the second order properties of such models and propose a Markov chain Monte Carlo algorithm to carry out Bayesian inference on the model's unknowns.

The methodology is then applied to the analysis of the U.S. business cycle. The model replicates rather well the NBER dating, and we find strong evidence against duration dependence in expansion phases. As for contractions, there is a very weak evidence in favor of duration dependence. This uncertainty is, however, coherent with the low number of recessions (seven) present in our dataset.

1. Introduction and motivation

Since the path-breaking paper of Hamilton (1989), many applications of the Markov switching autoregressive model (MS-AR) to business cycle analysis have demonstrated its potential, particularly in dating the cycle in an "objective" way. The basic MS-AR model has, nevertheless, some limitations: (i) it is univariate, (ii) the probabilities of transition from one state to the other (or to the other ones) are constant over time, iii) it is not capable of

*E-mail address: matteo.pelagatti@unimib.it

generating spectra with peaks at business cycle frequencies. Since business cycles are fluctuations of the aggregate economic activity, involving many macroeconomic variables at the same time[1], point (i) is not a negligible weakness. The multivariate generalization of the MS model was carried out by Krolzig (1997), in his excellent monograph on the MS-VAR model and by Kim and Nelson (1999) in their outstanding book on state-space models with Markov-Switching.

As far as point (ii) is concerned, it may be reasonable to believe that the probability of exiting a contraction is not the same at the very beginning of this phase as after several months. Some authors, such as Diebold and Rudebusch (1990), Diebold et al. (1993) and Watson (1994) have found evidence of duration dependence in the U.S. business cycles, and therefore, as Diebold et al. (1993) point out, the standard MS model results, in this framework, miss-specified. In order to face this limitation, Durland and McCurdy (1994) introduced the (univariate) duration-dependent Markov switching autoregression, recently further developed by Lam (2004), designing an involved alternative filter for the unobservable state variable. In the present article the duration-dependent switching model is generalized in a multivariate manner, and it is shown how standard tools related to the MS-AR model, such as Hamilton's filter and Kim's smoother (Kim, 1994) can be used to model duration dependence. Indeed, the filter proposed by Durland and McCurdy (1994) may be shown to be equivalent to Hamilton's filter calculated for a more general Markov chain. While Durland and McCurdy (1994) carry out their inference on the model by exploiting maximum likelihood estimation, we relay on Bayesian inference using Markov chain Monte Carlo (MCMC) techniques. The advantages of this technique are at least threefold: (a) it does not relay on asymptotics[2], and in latent variable models, where the unknowns are many, "asymptopia" may be quite far away, (b) inference on latent variables is not conditional on the estimated parameters (like in MLE), (c) since inference on Markov-switching (MS) models is notoriously rather sensitive to the presence of outliers, the possibility of using prior distributions on the parameters may limit their damages, making the estimates more robust.

The only existing work dealing with multivariate MS models with duration dependence is that of Kim and Nelson (1998). Our approach differs from their in two ways. They implement a common MS factor model, generalizing Stock and Watson (1991), while we use a MS-VAR framework. As in Kim and Nelson (1998), we carry out inference using Bayesian Gibbs sampling techniques, but while they relay on the single-move Gibbs sampler [3], the use of our extended state-space Markov chain allows us to exploit the more efficient multi-move Gibbs sampler of Carter and Kohn (1994), which generates the state variables in a block.

---

[1]The NBER Business Cycle Dating Committee defines a recession as "a significant decline in economic activity spread across the economy, lasting more than a few months, normally visible in real GDP, real income, employment, industrial production, and wholesale-retail sales" (*http://www.nber.org/cycles.html/*).

[2]Actually MCMC techniques do relay on asymptotic results, but the size of the sample is under control of the researcher and some diagnostics on convergence are available. Here it is meant that the reliability of the inference does not depend on the sample size of the real-world data.

[3]They state: "Due to the time-varying nature of the transition probabilities, S_t, $t = 1, 2, \ldots, T$ [i.e. the hidden Markov chain], cannot be generated as a block [...] Each S_t should be generated one at a time conditional on $S_{j \neq t}$, $j = 1, 2, \ldots, T$, and on other variates. It is straightforward to modify Albert and Chib's (1993) procedure to achive this goal."

As far as point (iii) is concerned, the analysis of the second order properties of DDMS-VAR models carried out in this paper reveals that these processes may generate spectra with peaks in business cycle frequencies, similar to the typical spectral shapes of many (detrended) economic variables. This is an important improvement with respect to standard MS models, since for many empirical economists the business cycle should have period in the range 1.5-8 years (see King and Watson, 1996; Baxter and King, 1999; Christiano and Fitzgerald, 2003; Valle e Azevedo et al., 2006, among the others).

The paper is organized as follows: the duration-dependent Markov switching VAR model (DDMS-VAR) is defined in section 2., its second order properties are derived in section 3., while the MCMC-based Bayesian inference is explained in section 4., and an application of the model to the U.S. business cycle is carried out in section 5.. Since a user fiendly freeware package for modelling with DDMS-VAR models has been written by the author, in the appendix we include a short guide to this software.

2. The model

The duration-dependent MS-VAR model[4] is defined by

$$\begin{aligned} \boldsymbol{y}_t = \boldsymbol{\mu}_0 + \boldsymbol{\mu}_1 S_t + \boldsymbol{A}_1(\boldsymbol{y}_{t-1} - \boldsymbol{\mu}_0 - \boldsymbol{\mu}_1 S_{t-1}) + \dots \\ + \boldsymbol{A}_p(\boldsymbol{y}_{t-p} - \boldsymbol{\mu}_0 - \boldsymbol{\mu}_1 S_{t-p}) + \varepsilon_t \end{aligned} \tag{1}$$

where $\boldsymbol{y}_t$ is a vector of observable variables, S_t is two state $\{0, 1\}$ Markov chain with time varying transition probabilities, $\boldsymbol{A}_1, \dots, \boldsymbol{A}_p$ are coefficient matrices of a stable VAR process, and ε_t is a gaussian (vector) white noise with covariance matrix $\boldsymbol{\Sigma}$.

As in Durland and McCurdy (1994), in order to allow for duration dependence, the pair (S_t, D_t) is considered, where D_t is the duration variable defined by

$$D_t = \begin{cases} 1 & \text{if } S_t \neq S_{t-1} \\ D_{t-1} + 1 & \text{if } S_t = S_{t-1} \text{ and } D_{t-1} < \tau \\ D_{t-1} & \text{if } S_t = S_{t-1} \text{ and } D_{t-1} = \tau \end{cases} . \tag{2}$$

It easy to see that (S_t, D_t) is also a Markov chain, since conditionally on (S_{t-1}, D_{t-1}), (S_t, D_t) is independent of (S_{t-k}, D_{t-k}) with $k = 2, 3, \dots$. An example of a possible sample path of (S_t, D_t) is shown in table 1. The value τ is the maximum that the duration

Table 1. A possible realization of the process (S_t, D_t).

t	1	2	3	4	5	6	7	8	9	10	11	12
S_t	1	1	1	1	0	0	0	1	0	0	0	0
D_t	3	4	5	6	1	2	3	1	1	2	3	4

variable D_t can reach and must be fixed *a priori* so that the Markov chain (S_t, D_t) be

[4]Using Krolzig's terminology, we are defining a duration dependent MSM(2)-VAR, that is, Markov-Switching in Mean VAR with two states. More flexible models, in which also the covariance matrix and the VAR coefficients vary, are possible, but usually not very useful in Business cycle analysis. In fact, such models tend to pick other features of the data (outliers, structural changes) rather than contractions and expansions.

defined on the finite state space

$$\{(0,1),(1,1),(0,2),(1,2),\ldots,(0,\tau),(1,\tau)\}. \tag{3}$$

When $D_t = \tau$, only four events are given non-zero probabilities:

$$\begin{array}{ll}(S_t = i, D_t = \tau)|(S_{t-1} = i, D_{t-1} = \tau) & i = 0,1 \\ (S_t = i, D_t = 1)|(S_{t-1} = j, D_{t-1} = \tau) & i \neq j, \quad i,j = 0,1.\end{array}$$

with the following interpretation: when the economy has been in state i at least τ times, the additional periods in which the state remains i influence no more the probabilities of transition. Thus, the transition matrix $\boldsymbol{P}$ has the form[5]

$$\begin{bmatrix} 0 & p_{0|1}(1) & 0 & p_{0|1}(2) & \cdots & 0 & p_{0|1}(\tau-1) & 0 & p_{0|1}(\tau) \\ p_{1|0}(1) & 0 & p_{1|0}(2) & 0 & \cdots & p_{1|0}(\tau-1) & 0 & p_{1|0}(\tau) & 0 \\ p_{0|0}(1) & 0 & 0 & 0 & \cdots & 0 & 0 & 0 & 0 \\ 0 & p_{1|1}(1) & 0 & 0 & \cdots & 0 & 0 & 0 & 0 \\ 0 & 0 & p_{0|0}(2) & 0 & \cdots & 0 & 0 & 0 & 0 \\ 0 & 0 & 0 & p_{1|1}(2) & \cdots & 0 & 0 & 0 & 0 \\ \vdots & \vdots & \vdots & \vdots & \ddots & \vdots & \vdots & \vdots & \vdots \\ 0 & 0 & 0 & 0 & \cdots & p_{0|0}(\tau-1) & 0 & p_{0|0}(\tau) & 0 \\ 0 & 0 & 0 & 0 & \cdots & 0 & p_{1|1}(\tau-1) & 0 & p_{1|1}(\tau) \end{bmatrix}$$

where $p_{i|j}(d) = \Pr(S_t = i|S_{t-1} = j, D_{t-1} = d)$.

As pointed out by Hamilton (1994, section 22.4), it is always possible to write the likelihood function of $\boldsymbol{y}_t$, depending only on the state variable at time t, even though in the model a p-order autoregression is present; this can be done using the extended state variable $S_t^* = (D_t, S_t, S_{t-1}, \ldots, S_{t-p})$, which comprehends all the possible combinations of the states of the economy in the last p periods. In Table 2 the state space of non-negligible states[6] S_t^*, with $p = 4$ and $\tau = 5$, is shown. If $\tau \geq p$ the number of non-negligible states is given by $u = 2(2^p + \tau - p - 1)$. The transition matrix $\boldsymbol{P}^*$ of the Markov chain S_t^* is a rather sparse $(u \times u)$ matrix, having a maximum number 2τ of independent non-zero elements.

Along the lines of Kim and Nelson (1998), in order to reduce the number (2τ) of elements in $\boldsymbol{P}^*$ to be estimated, a more parsimonious Probit specification was used[7]. Consider the linear model

$$Z_t = [\beta_1 + \beta_2 D_{t-1}]S_{t-1} + [\beta_3 + \beta_4 D_{t-1}](1 - S_{t-1}) + \epsilon_t \tag{4}$$

with $\epsilon_t \sim \mathcal{N}(0,1)$, and Z_t latent variable defined by

$$\begin{array}{l}\Pr(Z_t \geq 0|S_{t-1}, D_{t-1}) = \Pr(S_t = 1|S_{t-1}, D_{t-1}) \\ \Pr(Z_t < 0|S_{t-1}, D_{t-1}) = \Pr(S_t = 0|S_{t-1}, D_{t-1}).\end{array}$$

[5]The transition matrix is designed so that the elements of each column sum to one. Our transition matrix is the transpose of the usual transition matrix in Markov chain literature.

[6]"Negligible states" stands here for 'states always associated with zero probability'. For example the state $(D_t = 5, S_t = 1, S_{t-1} = 0, S_{t-2} = s_2, S_{t-3} = s_3, S_{t-4} = s_4)$, where s_2, s_3 and s_4 can be either 0 or 1, is negligible as it is not possible for S_t to have been 5 periods in the same state, if the state at time $t-1$ is different from the state at time t.

[7]Durland and McCurdy (1994) considered a Logit specification, but the Probit model turns out to be somewhat simpler in a Bayesian framework.

Table 2. State space of $S_t^* = (D_t, S_t, S_{t-1}, \ldots, S_{t-p})$ for $p = 4, \tau = 5$.

	D_t	S_t	S_{t-1}	S_{t-2}	S_{t-3}	S_{t-4}		D_t	S_t	S_{t-1}	S_{t-2}	S_{t-3}	S_{t-4}
1	1	0	1	0	0	0	17	2	0	0	1	0	0
2	1	0	1	0	0	1	18	2	0	0	1	0	1
3	1	0	1	0	1	0	19	2	0	0	1	1	0
4	1	0	1	0	1	1	20	2	0	0	1	1	1
5	1	0	1	1	0	0	21	2	1	1	0	0	0
6	1	0	1	1	0	1	22	2	1	1	0	0	1
7	1	0	1	1	1	0	23	2	1	1	0	1	0
8	1	0	1	1	1	1	24	2	1	1	0	1	1
9	1	1	0	0	0	0	25	3	0	0	0	1	0
10	1	1	0	0	0	1	26	3	0	0	0	1	1
11	1	1	0	0	1	0	27	3	1	1	1	0	0
12	1	1	0	0	1	1	28	3	1	1	1	0	1
13	1	1	0	1	0	0	29	4	0	0	0	0	1
14	1	1	0	1	0	1	30	4	1	1	1	1	0
15	1	1	0	1	1	0	31	5	0	0	0	0	0
16	1	1	0	1	1	1	32	5	1	1	1	1	1

It's easy to show that

$$p_{1|1}(d) = \Pr(S_t = 1|S_{t-1} = 1, D_{t-1} = d) = 1 - \Phi(-\beta_1 - \beta_2 d)$$
$$p_{0|0}(d) = \Pr(S_t = 0|S_{t-1} = 0, D_{t-1} = d) = \Phi(-\beta_3 - \beta_4 d)$$

where $d = 1, \ldots, \tau$, and $\Phi(.)$ is the standard normal cumulative distribution function. Now four parameters completely define the transition matrix $\boldsymbol{P}^*$.

3. Second order properties of the model

The second order properties of a non-linear, non-gaussian process are by no means exhaustive in describing its behavior, nevertheless there are good reasons for studying the cross- and auto-covariance structure and spectrum of such time series models. From a practical point of view, practitioners usually analyze the features of economic time series by means of sample second order moments; furthermore important concepts like business cycle, seasonality, etc. are (implicitly or explicitly) defined in the frequency domain.

For the purpose of this section, it is convenient to use the VAR representation of a Markov chain (Hamilton, 1994, p.679). Let X_t be a Markov chain with state space $\{1, 2, \ldots, N\}$ and transition matrix $\boldsymbol{P}$. If we define the random vector

$$\xi_t = \begin{cases} (1, 0, 0, \ldots, 0, 0)' & \text{for } X_t = 1 \\ (0, 1, 0, \ldots, 0, 0)' & \text{for } X_t = 2 \\ \vdots & \vdots \\ (0, 0, 0, \ldots, 1, 0)' & \text{for } X_t = N-1 \\ (0, 0, 0, \ldots, 0, 1)' & \text{for } X_t = N \end{cases}$$

it is straightforward to check that $\mathrm{E}[\boldsymbol{\xi}_{t+1}|\boldsymbol{\xi}_t, \boldsymbol{\xi}_{t-1}, \ldots] = \mathrm{E}[\boldsymbol{\xi}_{t+1}|\boldsymbol{\xi}_t] = \boldsymbol{P}\boldsymbol{\xi}_t$. This last consideration let us represent the Markov chain as

$$\boldsymbol{\xi}_{t+1} = \boldsymbol{P}\boldsymbol{\xi}_t + \boldsymbol{v}_{t+1}, \tag{5}$$

with $\boldsymbol{v}_t$ martingale difference sequence with respect to the σ-algebra generated by $\{X_t, X_{t-1}, \ldots\}$. If we can observe a vector $\boldsymbol{y}_t$, which takes the value z_i, $i = 1, 2, \ldots, N$ when X_t is in its i-th state, $\boldsymbol{y}_t$ has the representation

$$\boldsymbol{y}_t = \boldsymbol{Z}\boldsymbol{\xi}_t$$

with $\boldsymbol{Z} = [z_1, \ldots, z_N]$.

The following proposition that holds in this more general setting will be useful in determining the properties of the DDMS-VAR model.

Proposition 1 *Let $\{X_t\}$ be an ergodic Markov chain with state space $1, 2, \ldots, N$, let $\boldsymbol{P} = \{\Pr(X_{t+1} = i|X_t = j)\}$ be its transition matrix and $\boldsymbol{\pi}$ the vector of ergodic probabilities. Then*

$$\mathrm{E}[\boldsymbol{y}_t] = \boldsymbol{Z}\boldsymbol{\pi} \tag{6}$$

$$\mathrm{Cov}[\boldsymbol{y}_t, \boldsymbol{y}_{t-k}] = \boldsymbol{Z}[\boldsymbol{P}^k \mathrm{diag}(\boldsymbol{\pi}) - \boldsymbol{\pi}\boldsymbol{\pi}']\boldsymbol{Z}' \tag{7}$$

Proof. Using the VAR representation of the Markov chain the expectation of $\boldsymbol{y}_t$ is just

$$\boldsymbol{\mu} = \mathrm{E}[\boldsymbol{y}_t] = \boldsymbol{Z}\mathrm{E}[\boldsymbol{\xi}_t] = \boldsymbol{Z}\boldsymbol{\pi}.$$

For the cross-covariance function we have

$$\begin{aligned}
\mathrm{E}[(\boldsymbol{y}_t - \boldsymbol{\mu})(\boldsymbol{y}_{t-k} - \boldsymbol{\mu})'] &= \mathrm{E}[(\boldsymbol{Z}\boldsymbol{\xi}_t - \boldsymbol{Z}\boldsymbol{\pi})(\boldsymbol{Z}\boldsymbol{\xi}_{t-k} - \boldsymbol{Z}\boldsymbol{\pi})'] \\
&= \boldsymbol{Z}\mathrm{E}[(\boldsymbol{\xi}_t - \boldsymbol{\pi})(\boldsymbol{\xi}'_{t-k} - \boldsymbol{\pi}')]\boldsymbol{Z}' \\
&= \boldsymbol{Z}\mathrm{E}[(\boldsymbol{\xi}_t\boldsymbol{\xi}'_{t-k}) - \boldsymbol{\pi}\boldsymbol{\pi}']\boldsymbol{Z}' \\
&= \boldsymbol{Z}[\boldsymbol{P}^k\mathrm{E}(\boldsymbol{\xi}_{t-k}\boldsymbol{\xi}'_{t-k}) - \boldsymbol{\pi}\boldsymbol{\pi}']\boldsymbol{Z}' \\
&= \boldsymbol{Z}[\boldsymbol{P}^k \mathrm{diag}(\boldsymbol{\pi}) - \boldsymbol{\pi}\boldsymbol{\pi}']\boldsymbol{Z}'
\end{aligned}$$

■

The DDMS-VAR model has the representation

$$\boldsymbol{y}_t = \boldsymbol{Z}\boldsymbol{\xi}_t + \boldsymbol{w}_t \tag{8}$$

where $\boldsymbol{w}_t$ is a stable VAR(p) process. The Markov chain driving $\boldsymbol{\xi}_t$ is here (S_t, D_t) defined in the previous section and the matrix $\boldsymbol{Z}$ has the form

$$\boldsymbol{Z} = \mathbf{1}'_\tau \otimes \left[\boldsymbol{\mu}_0 \,|\, \boldsymbol{\mu}_0 + \boldsymbol{\mu}_1\right] \tag{9}$$

with $\mathbf{1}_\tau$ vector of ones of dimension τ. The matrix $\boldsymbol{Z}$ associates the mean vector $\boldsymbol{\mu}_0$ to the states for which $S_t = 0$ (odd states in Table 2) and $\boldsymbol{\mu}_0 + \boldsymbol{\mu}_1$ to the sates for which $S_t = 1$ (even states in Table 2).

Since $\boldsymbol{\xi}_t$ and $\boldsymbol{w}_t$ are independent processes, the cross-covariance function of $\boldsymbol{y}_t$ is just the sum of the cross-covariance functions of $\boldsymbol{\xi}_t$ and of $\boldsymbol{w}_t$. Being the latter well known, we concentrate on the former and suppose that $\boldsymbol{w}_t$ in (8) is identically zero. Thus, in the following we assume

$$\boldsymbol{y}_t = \boldsymbol{Z}\boldsymbol{\xi}_t.$$

The correlation structure of $\boldsymbol{y}_t$ is given by the following proposition.

Proposition 2 (Cross-correlation function of a DDMS process) *Under the hypotheses of Proposition 1, the correlation of any element of $\boldsymbol{y}_t$ with any element of $\boldsymbol{y}_{t-k}$, with $\boldsymbol{Z}$ as in (9), is given by*

$$\mathrm{Corr}(y_{i,t}, y_{j,t}) = \frac{\boldsymbol{\zeta}'\left[\boldsymbol{P}^k \mathrm{diag}(\boldsymbol{\pi}) - \boldsymbol{\pi}\boldsymbol{\pi}'\right]\boldsymbol{\zeta}}{\boldsymbol{\zeta}'\left[\mathrm{diag}(\boldsymbol{\pi}) - \boldsymbol{\pi}\boldsymbol{\pi}'\right]\boldsymbol{\zeta}} \qquad \forall i, j = 1, 2, \ldots, K \tag{10}$$

where $\boldsymbol{\zeta}$ is a 2τ-vector of one of the two following forms

$$\boldsymbol{\zeta} = (1, 0, 1, 0, \ldots 1, 0)' \text{ or } \boldsymbol{\zeta} = (0, 1, 0, 1, \ldots 0, 1)'.$$

Thus, all the auto-correlation and cross-correlation functions are equal and independent of the choice of $(\mu_{i,0}, \mu_{i,1})$, $i = 1, \ldots, K$.

Proof. Since correlations are invariant with respect to translations of the random variables, let's consider the variables

$$\tilde{y}_{i,t} = y_{i,t} - \mu_{i,0} = (\mu_{i,0}, \mu_{i,0} + \mu_{i,1}, \ldots, \mu_{i,0}, \mu_{i,0} + \mu_{i,1})\boldsymbol{\xi}_t - \mu_{i,0} = \mu_{i,1}\boldsymbol{\zeta}'\boldsymbol{\xi}_t$$

with $\boldsymbol{\zeta}' = (0, 1, 0, 1, \ldots 0, 1)$. Using proposition 1, we have

$$\begin{aligned}\mathrm{Corr}(\tilde{y}_{i,t}, \tilde{y}_{j,t-k}) &= \frac{\mu_{i,1}\mu_{j,1}\boldsymbol{\zeta}'\left[\boldsymbol{P}^k \mathrm{diag}(\boldsymbol{\pi}) - \boldsymbol{\pi}\boldsymbol{\pi}'\right]\boldsymbol{\zeta}}{\sqrt{\mu_{i,1}^2\boldsymbol{\zeta}'\left[\mathrm{diag}(\boldsymbol{\pi}) - \boldsymbol{\pi}\boldsymbol{\pi}'\right]\boldsymbol{\zeta} \cdot \mu_{j,1}^2\boldsymbol{\zeta}'\left[\mathrm{diag}(\boldsymbol{\pi}) - \boldsymbol{\pi}\boldsymbol{\pi}'\right]\boldsymbol{\zeta}}} \\ &= \frac{\boldsymbol{\zeta}'\left[\boldsymbol{P}^k \mathrm{diag}(\boldsymbol{\pi}) - \boldsymbol{\pi}\boldsymbol{\pi}'\right]\boldsymbol{\zeta}}{\boldsymbol{\zeta}'\left[\mathrm{diag}(\boldsymbol{\pi}) - \boldsymbol{\pi}\boldsymbol{\pi}'\right]\boldsymbol{\zeta}}.\end{aligned}$$

The proof still holds if we take $\tilde{y}_{i,t} = y_{i,t} - \mu_{i,0} - \mu_{i,1} = -\mu_{i,1}\boldsymbol{\zeta}'\boldsymbol{\xi}_t$ with $\boldsymbol{\zeta}' = (1, 0, 1, 0 \ldots 1, 0)$. ■

Since the autocorrelation of the DDMS process is a complicated function of the elements of $\boldsymbol{P}$, which in the Probit specification are functions of the parameters β_i, $i = \{1, 2, 3, 4\}$, we will rely on numerical computations to study the behavior of the relative spectral density[8].

Figure 1 shows the spectra of some symmetric DDMS models. The effect of β_1 $(= -\beta_3)$ on the spectrum may be seen in the first panel of the figure, while the consequences of changing β_2 $(= -\beta_4)$ are evident in the second panel. It is interesting to notice that the DDMS model is capable of a wide range of cyclical behaviors.

[8]The existence of the spectral density is guaranteed by the geometric convergence of the Markov chain.

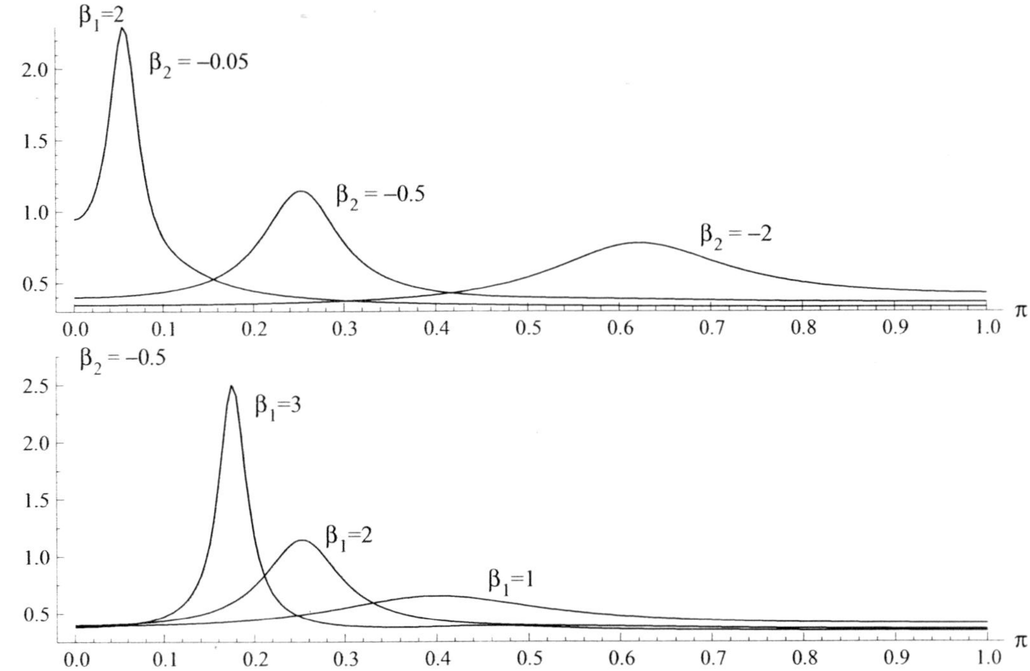

Figure 1. Spectra of symmetrical DDMS: $\beta_1 = -\beta_3$ and $\beta_2 = -\beta_4$.

Even more interesting is the behavior of asymmetric DDMS's. As figure 2 illustrates, asymmetric DDMS's can have multi-modal spectra. This feature seems particularly useful, since (detrended) economic time series having estimated spectra with most of the power concentrated around frequency zero and a local maximum at business cycle frequencies are not rare[9].

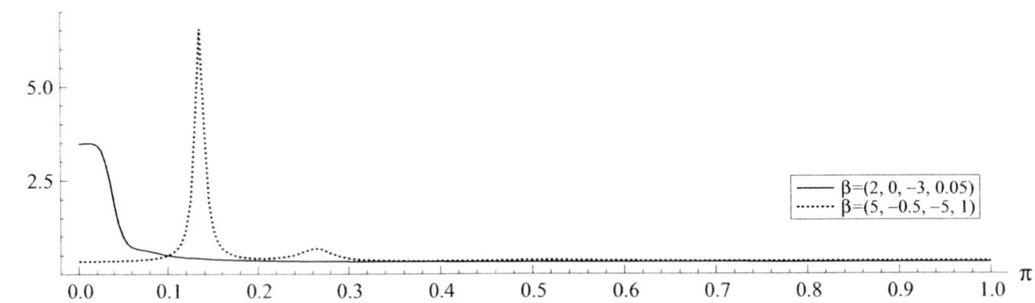

Figure 2. Spectra of asymmetrical DDMS.

[9]This feature may be clearly seen, for example, in the spectrum (here not reported) of the U.S. employment data used later in this paper.

4. Bayesian inference on the model's unknowns

In this section it is shown how to carry out Bayesian inference on the model's unknowns

$$\boldsymbol{\theta} = (\boldsymbol{\mu}, \boldsymbol{A}, \boldsymbol{\Sigma}, \boldsymbol{\beta}, \{(S_t, D_t)\}_{t=1}^{T}),$$

where $\boldsymbol{\mu} = (\boldsymbol{\mu}_0', \boldsymbol{\mu}_1')'$ and $\boldsymbol{A} = (\boldsymbol{A}_1, \ldots, \boldsymbol{A}_p)$, using MCMC methods.

4.1. Priors

In order to exploit conditional conjugacy, we use the prior joint distribution [10]

$$p(\boldsymbol{\mu}, \boldsymbol{A}, \boldsymbol{\Sigma}, \boldsymbol{\beta}, (S_0, D_0)) = p(\boldsymbol{\mu})p(\boldsymbol{A})p(\Sigma)p(\boldsymbol{\beta})p(S_0, D_0),$$

where

$$\begin{aligned} \boldsymbol{\mu} &\sim \mathcal{N}(\boldsymbol{m}_0, \boldsymbol{M}_0), \\ \text{vec}(\boldsymbol{A}) &\sim \mathcal{N}(\boldsymbol{a}_0, \boldsymbol{A}_0), \\ p(\boldsymbol{\Sigma}) &\propto |\boldsymbol{\Sigma}|^{-\frac{1}{2}(\text{rank}(\boldsymbol{\Sigma})+1)}, \\ \boldsymbol{\beta} &\sim \mathcal{N}(\boldsymbol{b}_0, \boldsymbol{B}_0), \end{aligned}$$

and $p(S_0, D_0)$ is a probability function that assigns a prior probability to every element of the state-space of (S_0, D_0). Alternatively it is possible to let $p(S_0, D_0)$ be the ergodic probability function of the Markov chain $\{(S_t, D_t)\}$.

4.2. Gibbs sampling in short

Let $\boldsymbol{\theta}_i$, $i = 1, \ldots, I$, be a partition of the set $\boldsymbol{\theta}$ containing all the unknowns of the model, and $\boldsymbol{\theta}_{-i}$ represent the set $\boldsymbol{\theta}$ without the elements in $\boldsymbol{\theta}_i$. In order to implement a Gibbs sampler to sample from the joint posterior distribution of all the unknowns of the model, it is sufficient to find the full conditional posterior distribution $p(\boldsymbol{\theta}_i|\boldsymbol{\theta}_{-i}, \boldsymbol{Y})$, with $\boldsymbol{Y} = (\boldsymbol{y}_1, \ldots, \boldsymbol{y}_T)$ and $i = 1, \ldots, I$. A Gibbs sampler step is the generation of a random variate from $p(\boldsymbol{\theta}_i|\boldsymbol{\theta}_{-i}, \boldsymbol{Y})$, $i = 1, \ldots, I$, where the elements of $\boldsymbol{\theta}_{-i}$ are substituted with the most recent sampled values of the relative variates. Since, under mild regularity conditions, the Markov chain defined for $\boldsymbol{\theta}^{(i)}$, where $\boldsymbol{\theta}^{(i)}$ is the value of $\boldsymbol{\theta}$ generated at the ith iteration of the Gibbs sampler, converges to its stationary distribution, and this stationary distribution is the "true" posterior distribution $p(\boldsymbol{\theta}|\boldsymbol{Y})$, it is sufficient to fix an initial burn-in period of M iterations, such that the Markov chain may virtually "forget" the arbitrary starting values $\boldsymbol{\theta}^{(0)}$, to sample from (an approximation of) the joint posterior distribution. The values obtained for each element of $\boldsymbol{\theta}$ are samples from the marginal posterior distribution of each parameters.

4.3. Gibbs sampling steps

Step 1. Generation of $\{S_t^*\}_{t=1}^{T}$

We use an implementation of the multi-move Gibbs sampler originally proposed by Carter and Kohn (1994) and Fruwirth-Schnatter (1994), which, suppressing the conditioning on

[10] $p(\bullet)$ denotes a generic density or probability function.

the other parameters from the notation, exploits the identity

$$p(S_1^*,\ldots,S_T^*|\boldsymbol{Y}_T)=p(S_T^*|\boldsymbol{Y}_T)\prod_{t=1}^{T-1}p(S_t^*|S_{t+1}^*,\boldsymbol{Y}_t),\tag{11}$$

with $\boldsymbol{Y}_t=(\boldsymbol{y}_1,\ldots,\boldsymbol{y}_t)$.

Let $\hat{\boldsymbol{\xi}}_{t|r}$ be the vector containing the probabilities of S_t^* being in each state (the first element is the probability of being in state 1, the second element is the probability of being in state 2, and so on) given $\boldsymbol{Y}_r$ and the model's parameters. Let $\boldsymbol{\eta}_t$ be the vector containing the likelihood of each state given $\boldsymbol{Y}_t$ and the model's parameters, whose generic element is

$$(2\pi)^{-n/2}|\boldsymbol{\Sigma}|^{-1/2}\exp\left\{-\frac{1}{2}(\boldsymbol{y}_t-\hat{\boldsymbol{y}}_t)'\boldsymbol{\Sigma}^{-1}(\boldsymbol{y}_t-\hat{\boldsymbol{y}}_t)\right\},$$

where

$$\hat{\boldsymbol{y}}_t=\boldsymbol{\mu}_0+\boldsymbol{\mu}_1S_t+\boldsymbol{A}_1(\boldsymbol{y}_{t-1}-\boldsymbol{\mu}_0-\boldsymbol{\mu}_1S_{t-1})+\ldots+\boldsymbol{A}_p(\boldsymbol{y}_{t-p}-\boldsymbol{\mu}_0-\boldsymbol{\mu}_1S_{t-p})$$

changes value according to the state of S_t^*.

The filtered probabilities of the states can be calculated using Hamilton's filter

$$\hat{\boldsymbol{\xi}}_{t|t}=\frac{\hat{\boldsymbol{\xi}}_{t|t-1}\odot\boldsymbol{\eta}_t}{\hat{\boldsymbol{\xi}}_{t|t-1}'\boldsymbol{\eta}_t}$$

$$\hat{\boldsymbol{\xi}}_{t+1|t}=\boldsymbol{P}^*\hat{\boldsymbol{\xi}}_{t|t}$$

with the symbol $\odot$ indicating elementwise multiplication. The filter is completed with the prior probabilities vector $\hat{\boldsymbol{\xi}}_{1|0}$, that, as already remarked, can be set equal to the vector of ergodic probabilities of the Markov chain $\{S_t^*\}$.

In order to sample from the distribution of $\{S_t^*\}_1^T$ given the full information set $\boldsymbol{Y}_T$, we exploit the result

$$\begin{aligned}\Pr(S_t^*=j|S_{t+1}^*=i,\boldsymbol{Y}_t) &= \frac{\Pr(S_{t+1}^*=i|S_t^*=j)\Pr(S_t^*=j|\boldsymbol{Y}_t)}{\sum_{j=1}^m\Pr(S_{t+1}^*=i|S_t^*=j)\Pr(S_t^*=j|\boldsymbol{Y}_t)}\\ &= \frac{p_{i|j}\hat{\xi}_{t|t}^{(j)}}{\sum_{j=1}^m p_{i|j}\hat{\xi}_{t|t}^{(j)}},\end{aligned}$$

where $p_{i|j}$ is the transition probability of moving to state i from state j (element (i,j) of the transition matrix $\boldsymbol{P}^*$) and $\xi_{t|t}^{(j)}$ is the j-th element of vector $\boldsymbol{\xi}_{t|t}$. In matrix notation the same can be written as

$$\hat{\boldsymbol{\xi}}_{t|(S_{t+1}^*=i,\boldsymbol{Y}_T)}=\frac{\boldsymbol{p}_{i\cdot}\odot\hat{\boldsymbol{\xi}}_{t|t}}{\boldsymbol{p}_{i\cdot}'\hat{\boldsymbol{\xi}}_{t|t}}\tag{12}$$

where $\boldsymbol{p}_{i\cdot}'$ denotes the i-th row of the transition matrix $\boldsymbol{P}^*$.

Now all the probability functions in equation (11) have been given a form, and the states can be generated starting from the filtered probability $\hat{\boldsymbol{\xi}}_{T|T}$ and proceeding backward

$(T-1,\ldots,1)$, using equation (12) where i is to be substituted with the last generated value s^*_{t+1}.

Once a set of sampled $\{S^*_t\}^T_{t=1}$ has been generated, it is automatically available a sample for $\{S_t\}^T_{t=1}$ and $\{D_t\}^T_{t=1}$.

The advantage of using the described multi-move Gibbs sampler, compared to the single move Gibbs sampler that can be implemented as in Carlin et al. (1992), or using the software BUGS[11], is that the whole vector of states is sampled at once, improving significantly the speed of convergence of the Gibbs samper's chain to its ergodic distribution. Kim and Nelson (1999, section 10.3), in their monograph on state-space models with regime switching, use a single-move Gibbs sampler (12000 sample points) to achieve (almost) the same goal as in this paper, but the slow convergence properties of the single-move sampler do not give evidence in favour of the reliability of their estimates.

Step 2. Generation of $(\boldsymbol{A},\boldsymbol{\Sigma})$

Conditionally on $\{S_t\}^T_{t=1}$ and $\boldsymbol{\mu}$ equation (1) is just a multivariate normal (auto-)regression model for the variable $\boldsymbol{y}^*_t = \boldsymbol{y}_t - \boldsymbol{\mu}_0 - \boldsymbol{\mu}_1 S_t$, whose parameters, given the discussed prior distribution, have the following posterior distributions, known in literature. Let $\boldsymbol{X}$ be the matrix, whose t^{th} column is

$$\boldsymbol{x}_{\bullet t} = \begin{pmatrix} \boldsymbol{y}^*_t \\ \boldsymbol{y}^*_{t-1} \\ \vdots \\ \boldsymbol{y}^*_{t-p} \end{pmatrix},$$

for $t=1,\ldots,T$, and let $\boldsymbol{Y}^* = (\boldsymbol{y}^*_1,\ldots,\boldsymbol{y}^*_T)$.

The posterior for $(\text{vec}(\boldsymbol{A}),\boldsymbol{\Sigma})$ is, suppressing the conditioning on the other parameters, the normal–inverse Wishart distribution

$$\begin{aligned}
&p(\text{vec}(\boldsymbol{A}),\boldsymbol{\Sigma}|\boldsymbol{Y},\boldsymbol{X}) = p(\text{vec}(\boldsymbol{A})|\boldsymbol{\Sigma},\boldsymbol{Y},\boldsymbol{X})p(\boldsymbol{\Sigma}|\boldsymbol{Y},\boldsymbol{X})\\
&p(\boldsymbol{\Sigma}|\boldsymbol{Y},\boldsymbol{X}) \text{ density of a } \mathcal{IW}_k(\boldsymbol{V},n-m)\\
&p(\text{vec}(\boldsymbol{A})|\boldsymbol{\Sigma},\boldsymbol{Y},\boldsymbol{X}) \text{ density of a } \mathcal{N}(\boldsymbol{a}_1,\boldsymbol{A}_1),
\end{aligned}$$

with

$$\begin{aligned}
\boldsymbol{V} &= \boldsymbol{Y}^*\boldsymbol{Y}^{*\prime} - \boldsymbol{Y}^*\boldsymbol{X}'(\boldsymbol{X}\boldsymbol{X}')^{-1}\boldsymbol{X}\boldsymbol{Y}^{*\prime}\\
\boldsymbol{A}_1 &= (\boldsymbol{A}_0^{-1} + \boldsymbol{X}\boldsymbol{X}'\boldsymbol{\Sigma}^{-1})^{-1}\\
\boldsymbol{a}_1 &= \boldsymbol{A}_1[\boldsymbol{A}_0^{-1}\boldsymbol{a}_0 + (\boldsymbol{X}\otimes\boldsymbol{\Sigma}^{-1})\text{vec}(\boldsymbol{Y})].
\end{aligned}$$

Step 3. Generation of $\boldsymbol{\mu}$

Conditionally on $\boldsymbol{A}$ and $\boldsymbol{\Sigma}$, by multiplying both sides of equation (2.) times

$$\boldsymbol{A}(\mathrm{L}) = (\boldsymbol{I} - \boldsymbol{A}_1\mathrm{L} - \ldots - \boldsymbol{A}_p\mathrm{L}^p),$$

[11] *http://www.mrc-bsu.cam.ac.uk/bugs/*

where L is the lag operator, we obtain

$$\boldsymbol{A}(\mathrm{L})\boldsymbol{y}_t = \boldsymbol{\mu}_0\boldsymbol{A}(1) + \boldsymbol{\mu}_1\boldsymbol{A}(\mathrm{L})S_t + \boldsymbol{\varepsilon}_t,$$

which is a multivariate normal linear regression model with known variance $\boldsymbol{\Sigma}$, and can be treated as shown in step 2., with respect to the specified prior for $\boldsymbol{\mu}$.

Step 4. Generation of $\boldsymbol{\beta}$

Conditionally on $\{S_t^*\}_{t=1}^T$, consider the probit model described in section 2.. Albert and Chib (1993) have proposed a method based on a data augmentation algorithm to draw from the posterior of the parameters of a probit model. Given the parameter vector $\boldsymbol{\beta}$ of last Gibbs sampler iteration, generate the latent variables $\{S_t^\bullet\}$ from the respective truncated normal densities

$$\begin{aligned} Z_t|(S_t = 0, \boldsymbol{x}_t, \boldsymbol{\beta}) &\sim \mathcal{N}(\boldsymbol{x}_t'\boldsymbol{\beta}, 1)\mathbb{I}_{(-\infty,0)} \\ Z_t|(S_t = 1, \boldsymbol{x}_t, \boldsymbol{\beta}) &\sim \mathcal{N}(\boldsymbol{x}_t'\boldsymbol{\beta}, 1)\mathbb{I}_{[0,\infty)} \end{aligned}$$

with

$$\begin{aligned} \boldsymbol{\beta} &= (\beta_1, \beta_2, \beta_3, \beta_4)' \\ \boldsymbol{x}_t &= (S_{t-1}, D_{t-1}, (1 - S_{t-1}), (1 - S_{t-1})D_{t-1})' \end{aligned} \tag{13}$$

and $\mathbb{I}_{\{\cdot\}}$ indicator function used to denote truncation.

With the generated Z_t's the Probit regression equation (4) becomes, again, a normal linear model with known variance.

The former Gibbs sampler steps were numbered from 1 to 4, but any ordering of them would eventually bring to the same ergodic distribution.

5. Duration dependence in the U.S. business cycle

Inspired by the seminal work of Burns and Mitchell, the NBER Business Cycle Dating Committee today primarily looks at four key monthly indicators: i) industrial production (IP), ii) employees on nonagricultural payrolls (EMPL), iii) manufacturing and trade sales in million of year 2000 dollars (SALES), iv) personal income less transfer payments in billions of year 2000 dollars (INCOME). Therefore, the model and the inference illustrated in the previous sections have been applied to 100 times the difference of the logarithm of these time series dating from February 1959 to April 2006. Following Chauvet and Hamilton (2005) we carried out the same analysis also substituting the employees on nonagricultural payrolls with the total civil employment series, since the former has been noticed to lag the business cycle, especially in recent times (cf. Stock and Watson, 1991; Chauvet, 1998). Since the results concerning duration dependence are virtually the same, we report only this second analysis.

The model estimated on these data is a DDMS-VAR(1) with diagonal autoregressive matrix and $\tau = 60$ (5 years). The choice of using the DDMS alone as the only common dynamic factor is justified by the fact that the estimates of the cospectral densities for each pair of time series have very similar behaviors. Excluding the duration dependence feature, our model is similar to the one of Chauvet and Hamilton (2005) [12].

The inference on the model unknowns is based on a Gibbs sample of 21,000 points, the first 1,000 of which were discarded. The autocorrelations and the kernel density estimates for each parameter are available from the author on request. All the correlations die out before the 100th lag, thus the choice of a burn-in sample of 1,000 points seems quite reasonable.

Summaries of the marginal posterior distributions are shown in Table 3, while in Figure 3 the probability of recession resulting from the model is compared with the official NBER dating: the signal "probability of being in recession" extracted by our model matches the official dating rather well (Table 4), and is much less noisy than the signal extracted univariately[13]. NBER's trough dates seem to be matched more frequently by the model than the peaks. The dates in which our dating differ form NBER are those with contraction probabilities very close to 0.5, that is, with greatest uncertainty about the active state. Figure 3 is very similar to Figure 8 in Chauvet and Hamilton (2005), indicating that neither the duration dependence feature nor the smooth transition from one state to the other have a great influence in the signal extraction [14].

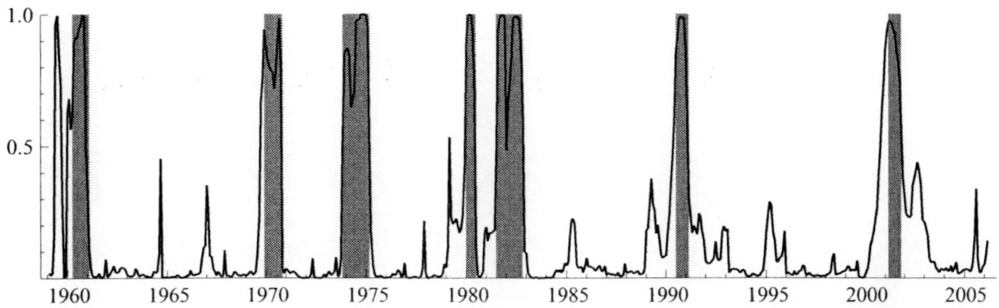

Figure 3. (Smoothed) probability of recession (line) and NBER dating (gray shade)

Figure 4 shows how the duration of a state (contraction or expansion) influences the transition probabilities. Expansion phases are surely not duration dependent, while the evidence for duration dependence of contractions is very weak. In fact, the 95% credible interval of the "Contraction$_0$" parameter in Table 3 includes zero, and the Savage-Dickey density ratio (Bayes factor) for testing the absence of duration dependence in a contraction state is 18.8. This uncertainty about the presence of duration dependence in business cy-

[12]They allow for some smoothness in the change of regimes, while in our model the change is abrupt.

[13]Here not reported.

[14]The results of Chauvet and Hamilton (2005) are based on the same dataset as ours ending on January 2004. They perform (approximate) ML estimation for a common factor model with common factor given by

$$F_t = \mu_0 + \mu_1 S_t + \phi F_{t-1} + \eta_t,$$

$\eta_t \sim N(0, \sigma_\eta^2)$ and idiosyncratic components given by AR(1) processes.

Table 3. Description of the prior and posterior distributions of the model parameters.

	Prior		Posterior				
Parameter	mean	var	mean	s.d.	2.5%	50%	97.5%
AR coefficients							
IP	0.0	1.0	0.087	0.041	0.007	0.087	0.167
EMPL	0.0	1.0	-0.227	0.041	-0.307	-0.227	-0.147
INCOME	0.0	1.0	0.096	0.043	0.014	0.096	0.181
SALES	0.0	1.0	-0.240	0.037	-0.312	-0.240	-0.167
μ_0 (mean in state 0)							
IP	-0.4	1.0	0.450	0.055	0.359	0.445	0.571
EMPL	-0.1	1.0	0.187	0.018	0.159	0.185	0.225
INCOME	-0.1	1.0	0.348	0.032	0.298	0.345	0.421
SALES	-0.3	1.0	0.422	0.051	0.339	0.418	0.528
μ_1 (mean increment from state 0 to state 1)							
IP	0.8	1.0	-1.029	0.165	-1.328	-1.039	-0.674
EMPL	0.3	1.0	-0.240	0.041	-0.324	-0.238	-0.163
INCOME	0.5	1.0	-0.451	0.074	-0.608	-0.447	-0.317
SALES	0.7	1.0	-0.838	0.155	-1.155	-0.837	-0.533
$\mu_0 + \mu_1$ (mean in state 1)							
IP	0.4	1.4	-0.579	0.193	-0.911	-0.597	-0.132
EMPL	0.2	1.4	-0.052	0.046	-0.142	-0.053	0.043
INCOME	0.4	1.4	-0.102	0.084	-0.270	-0.102	0.071
SALES	0.4	1.4	-0.416	0.173	-0.754	-0.420	-0.036
β (probit coefficients)							
Constant_0	1.5	2.2	1.268	0.417	0.456	1.264	2.095
Duration_0	0.0	1.0	-0.043	0.058	-0.181	-0.034	0.046
Constant_1	-1.5	2.2	-2.010	0.369	-2.776	-1.989	-1.368
Duration_1	0.0	1.0	0.008	0.015	-0.012	0.006	0.035

Table 4. Business cycle turning points: NBER dating vs. DDMSVAR dating.

Start of contraction			End of contraction		
NBER	DDMSVAR	Diff.	NBER	DDMSVAR	Diff.
Apr 1960	Feb 1960	-2	Feb 1961	Dec 1960	-2
Dec 1969	Nov 1969	-1	Nov 1970	Nov 1970	0
Nov 1973	Dec 1973	+1	Mar 1975	Apr 1975	+1
Jan 1980	Feb 1980	+1	Jul 1980	Jul 1980	0
Jul 1981	Sep 1981	+2	Nov 1982	Dec 1982	+1
Jul 1990	Jul 1990	0	Mar 1991	Mar 1991	0
Mar 2001	Dec 2000	-3	Nov 2001	Dec 2001	+1

cles is mirrored in the scientific literature of the last 30 years. In fact, McCulloch (1975) concludes that business cycles are duration independent, Diebold and Rudebusch (1990), Durland and McCurdy (1994) and Mills (2001) find duration dependence only in contraction phases, Sichel (1991) and Zuehlke (2003) observe duration dependence in post-war contractions and pre-war expansions, while Lam (2004) concludes that both contractions and expansions are duration dependent. The models and datasets used by the different authors differ significantly, and this is certainly a cause for the variability of the conclusions, but it is also true that the samples used for this issue include a small number of cycles (in our case just seven contractions and eight expansions), and this makes the conclusions intrinsically unstable and sensitive to other sources of variability (model and sample selection, and type of inference). Furthermore, in much of the cited literature the inference on duration dependence was conditional on some predetermined dating of the business cycle. In our work, the inference on business cycle phases and on duration dependence is carried out simultaneously. This adds variability to our results, but in principle there is no good reason for excluding uncertainty about the state of the cycle, when testing for duration dependence.

6. Conclusions

We proposed the DDMS-VAR process and showed how this process is able to generate sample paths reproducing the stylized facts noticed in empirical business cycle analysis. We derived the second order properties of this class of processes and revealed how well these models match the empirical features found in many macroeconomic time series.

A Gibbs sampling algorithm for carrying out Bayesian inference on the model unknowns has been developed and implemented in a user friendly software package freely available from the author's web site (cf. Appendix).

Applied to four U.S. time series concerning production, employment, sales and personal income, the model proved to have good capabilities of discerning recessions and expansions: the probabilities of recession tend to assume extremely low or high values. The resulting dating of the U.S. business cycle phases turned out to be very close to the official one as determined by the pool of experts of the NBER.

The Gibbs sampling approach developed for the DDMS-VAR modelling of the business

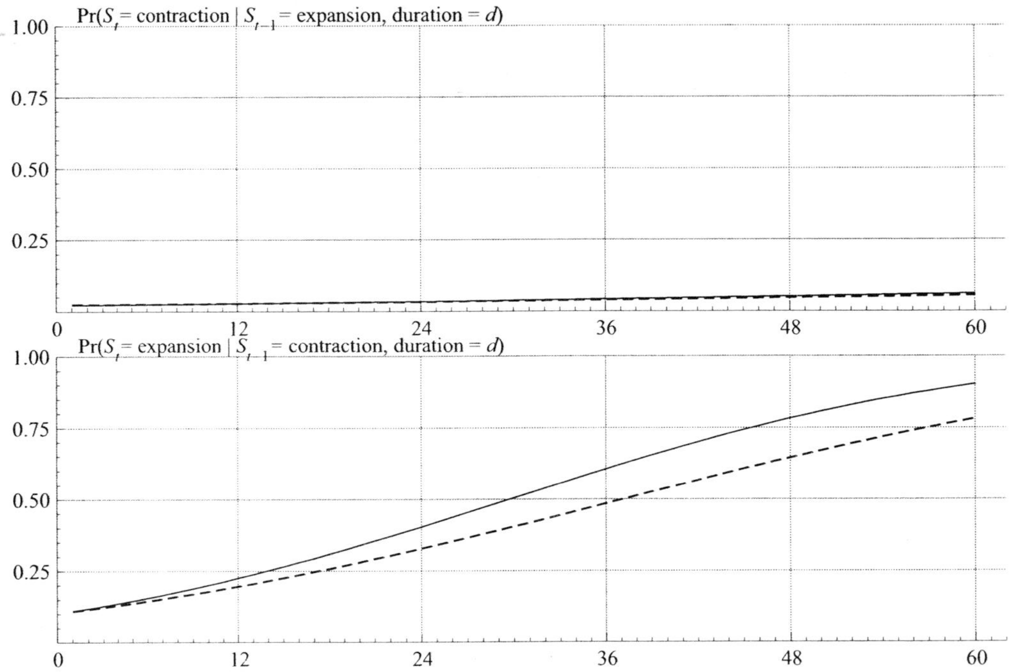

Figure 4. Mean (solid), median (dash) of the posterior distribution of the probability of moving a) from a recession into an expansion after d months of recession b) from an expansion into a recession after d months of expansion

cycle has many advantages but also drawbacks: the former are that (i) it allows prior information to be exploited, (ii) it avoids the computational problems pointed out by Hamilton (1994, p. 689) that can arise with maximum likelihood estimation, (iii) it does not relay on asymptotic inference (see note 2), (iv) the inference on the state variables is not conditional on the set of estimated parameters. The big disadvantage is a long computation time, and sometimes some numerical instability.

As far as duration-dependence is concerned, we found no evidence of this feature in expansions and a very weak evidence in contraction phases. We argued that the weakness in the latter result, compared to previous studies, may be attributed to the fact that our inference on duration dependence incorporates the uncertainty about the dating of the business cycle, while in other analyses in literature tests are conditional on a given classification of the states. Furthermore, the seven contraction phases in our dataset may not be enough for building reliable tests on duration dependence.

References

Albert J.H. & Chib S. (1993). Bayesian analysis of binary and polychotomous responce data. *Journal of the American Statistical Association*, 88, 669–679.

Baxter M. & King R.G. (1999). Measuring business cycles: approximate band pass filters for economic time series. *Review of Economics and Statistics*, 81 (4), 575–593.

Carlin B.P., Polson N.G. & Stoffer D.S. (1992). A Monte Carlo approach to nonnormal and nonlinear state-space modeling. *Journal of the American Statistical Association*, 87, 493–500.

Carter C.K. & Kohn R. (1994) On Gibbs sampling for state space models. *Biometrika*, 81, 541–553.

Chauvet M. (1998). An economic characterization of business cycle dynamics with factor structure and regime switches. *International Economic Review*, 39, 969–996.

Chauvet M. & Hamilton J.D. (2005). Dating business cycle turing points. Working Paper.

Christiano, L. & Fitzgerald T. (2003). The band-pass filter. *International Economic Review*, 44, 435-65.

Diebold F. & Rudebusch G. (1990). A nonparametric investigation of duration dependence in the American business cycle. *Journal of Political Economy*, 98, 596–616.

Diebold F., Rudebusch G. & Sichel D. (1993). Further evidence on business cycle duration dependence. In: Stock J. & Watson M. (Eds.), *Business Cycles, Indicators and Forcasting* (pp. 255–280). Chicago: University of Chicago Press.

Doornik J.A. (2001). *Ox. An object-oriented matrix programming language*. London: Timberlake Consultants Ltd.

Durland J. & McCurdy T. (1994). Duration-dependent transitions in a Markov model of U.S. GNP growth. Journal of Business and Economic Statistics 12, 279–288.

Fruwirth-Schnatter S. (1994). Data augmentation and dynamic linear models. *Journal of Time Series Analysis*, 15, 183–202.

Hamilton J.D. (1989). A new approach to the economic analysis of nonstationary time series and the business cycle. *Econometrica*, 57, 357–384.

Hamilton J.D. (1994). *Time series analysis*. Priceton: Princeton University Press.

Kim C.J. (1994). Dynamic linear models with Markov-switching. *Journal of Econometrics*, 60, 1–22.

Kim C.J. & Nelson C.R. (1998). Business cycle turning points, a new coincident index, and test for duration dependence based on a dynamic factor model with regime switching. *Review of Economics and Statistics*, 80 (2), 188–201.

Kim C.J. & Nelson C.R. (1999). *State-space models with regime switching: classical and Gibbs-sampling approches with applications*. Cambridge: MIT Press.

King R.G. & Watson M.W. (1996). Money, prices, interest rates and the business cycle. *Review of Economics and Statistics*, 78 (1), 35–53.

Krolzig H.M. (1997). *Markov-switching vector autoregressions. Modelling, statistical inference and application to business cycle analysis* . Berlin: Springer-Verlag.

Lam P.-S. (2004). A Markov-Switching Model of GDP Growth with Duration Dependence. *International Economic Review*, 45 (1), 175–204.

Maheu J.M. & McCurdy T.H. (2000a). Identifying Bull and Bear Markets in Stock Returns. *Journal of Business and Economic Statistics* , 18 (1), 100-112.

Maheu J.M. & McCurdy T.H. (2000b). Volatility dynamics under duration-dependent mixing. *Journal of Empirical Finance*, 7, 345–372.

Maheu J.M. & McCurdy T.H. (2002). Nonlinear Features of Realized FX Volatility. *Review of Economics and Staistics*, 84 (4), 668–681.

McCulloch H.J. (1975). The Monte Carlo Cycle in Business Activity. *Economic Inquiry*, 13, 303–312.

Mills T.C. (2001). Business cycle asymmetry and duration dependence: an international perspective. *Journal of Applied Statistics*, 28 (6), 713-724.

Sichel D.E. (1991). Business cycle duration dependence: a parametric approach. *Review of Economics and Statistics*, 73, 254–256.

Stock J.H. & Watson M.W. (1991). A Probability Model of the Coincident Economic Indicators. In K. Lahiri & G.H. Moore (Eds.), *Leading Economic Indicators: New Approahces and Forecasting Records* , Cambridge: Cambridge University Press.

Valle e Azevedo J., Koopman S.J. & Rua A. (2006). Tracking the business cycle of the Euro area: a multivariate model-based band-pass filter. *Journal of Business and Economic Statistics*, 24 (3), 278–290.

Watson J. (1994). Business cycle durations and postwar stabilization of the U.S. economy. *American Economic Review*, 84, 24–46.

Zuehlke T.W. (2003). Business Cycle Duration Dependence Reconsidered. *Journal of Business and Economic Statistics* , 21 (4), 564–569.

APPENDIX

A The DDMSVAR package

DDMSVAR for Ox[15] is a software for time series modeling with DDMS-VAR processes that can be used in three different ways: (i) as a menu driven package [16], (ii) as an Ox object class, (iii) as a software library for Ox. The DDMSVAR software is freely available [17] at the author's internet site[18]. In this section I give a brief description of the software and in next section I illustrate its use with a real-world application.

A1. OxPack version

The easiest way to use DDMSVAR is adding the package to OxPack giving DDMSVAR as class name. The following steps must be followed to load the data, specify the model and estimate it.

Formulate

Open a database, choose the time series to be modelled and give them the Y variable status. If you wish to specify an initial series of state variables, this series has to be included in the database and, once selected in the model variables' list, give it the State variable init status; otherwise DDMSVAR assigns the state variable's initial values automatically.

Model settings

Chose the order of the VAR model (p), the maximal duration (tau), which must be at least[19] 2, and write a comma separated list of percentiles of the marginal posterior distributions, that you want to read in the output (default is 2.5,50,97.5).

Estimate/Options

At the moment only the illustrated Gibbs sampler is implemented. Choose the data sample and press Options.... The options window is divided in three areas.

ITERATIONS

Here you choose the number of iteration of the Gibbs sampler, and the number of burn in iteration, that is, the amounts of start iterations that will not be used for estimation, because

[15]Ox (Doornik, 2001) is an object-oriented matrix programming language freely available for the academic community in its console version.

[16]If run with the commercial version of Ox (OxProfessional).

[17]The software is freely available and usable (at your own risk). Please cite the present article in any work in which the DDMSVAR software is used.

[18]*www.statistica.unimib.it/utenti/p_matteo/*

[19]If you wish to estimate a classical MS-VAR model, choose tau = 2 and use priors for the parameters β_2 and β_4 that put an enormous mass of probability around 0. This will prevent the duration variable from having influence in the probit regression. The maximal value for tau depends only on the power of your computer, but have care that the dimensions of the transition matrix $u \times u$ don't grow too much, or the waiting time may become unbearable.

too much influenced by the arbitrary starting values. Of course the latter must be smaller than the former.

PRIORS & INITIAL VALUES

If you want to specify prior means and variances of the parameters to be estimated, do it in a .in7 or .xls database following these rules: prior means and variances for the vectorization of the autoregressive matrix $\boldsymbol{A} = [\boldsymbol{A}_1, \boldsymbol{A}_2, \ldots, \boldsymbol{A}_p]$ must be in fields with names mean_a and var_a; prior means and variances for the mean vectors $\boldsymbol{\mu}_0$ and $\boldsymbol{\mu}_1$ must be in fields with names mean_mu0, var_mu0, mean_mu1 and var_mu1; the fields for the vector $\boldsymbol{\beta}$ are to be named mean_beta and var_beta. The file name is to be specified with extension. If you don't specify the file, DDMSVAR uses priors that are vague for typical applications.

The file containing the initial values for the Gibbs sampler needs also to be a database in .in7 or .xls format, with fields a for $\text{vec}(\boldsymbol{A})$, mu0 for $\boldsymbol{\mu}_0$, mu1 for $\boldsymbol{\mu}_1$, sigma for $\text{vech}(\boldsymbol{\Sigma})$ and beta for $\boldsymbol{\beta}$. If no file is specified, DDMSVAR assigns initial values automatically.

SAVING OPTIONS

In order to save the Gibbs sample generated by DDMSVAR, specify a file name (you don't need to write the extension, at the moment the only format available is .in7) and check Save also state series if the specified file should contain also the samples of the state variables. Check Probabilities of state 0 in *filename.ext* to save the smoothed probabilities $\{\Pr(S_t = 0|\boldsymbol{Y}_T)\}_{t=1}^T$ in the database from which the time series are taken.

Program's Output

Since Gibbs sampling may take a long time, after five iterations the program prints an estimate of the waiting time. The user is informed of the progress of the process every 100 iterations.

At the end of the iteration process, the estimated means, standard deviations (in the output named standard errors), percentiles of the marginal posterior distributions are given.

The output consists also of a number of graphs:

1. probabilities of S_t being in state 0 and 1,

2. mean and percentiles of the transition probabilities distributions with respect to the duration,

3. autocorrelation function of every sampled parameter (the faster it dies out, the higher the speed of the Gibbs sampler in exploring the posterior distribution's support, and the smaller the number of iteration needed to achieve the same estimate's precision),

4. kernel density estimates of the marginal posterior distributions,

5. Gibbs sample graphs (to check if the burn in period is long enough to ensure that the initial values have been "forgot"),

6. running means, to visually check the convergence of the Gibbs sample means.

A2. The DDMSVAR() object class

The second simplest way to use the software is creating an instance of the object DDMSVAR and using its member functions. The best way to illustrate the most relevant member functions of the class DDMSVAR is showing a sample program and commenting it.

```
#include "DDMSVAR.ox" main() {
    decl dd = new DDMSVAR();

    dd->LoadIn7("USA4.in7");
    dd->Select(Y_VAR, {"DLIP", 0, 0, "DLEMP", 0, 0,
                       "DLTRADE", 0, 0, "DLINCOME",0 ,0});
    dd->Select(S_VAR,{"NBER", 0, 0});
    dd->SetSelSample(1960, 1, 2001, 8);

    dd->SetVAROrder(0);
    dd->SetMaxDuration(60);
    dd->SetIteration(21000);
    dd->SetBurnIn(1000);
    dd->SetPosteriorPercentiles(<0.05,50,99.5>);
    dd->SetPriorFileName("prior.in7");
    dd->SetInitFileName("init.in7");
    dd->SetSampleFileName("prova.in7",TRUE);

    dd->Estimate();

    dd->StatesGraph("states.eps");
    dd->DurationGraph("duration.eps");
    dd->Correlograms("acf.eps", 100);
    dd->Densities("density.eps");
    dd->SampleGraphs("sample.eps");
    dd->RunningMeans("means.eps");
}
```

dd is declared as instance of the object DDMSVAR. The first four member functions are an inheritance of the class Database and will not be commented here[20]. Notice only that the variable selected in the S_VAR group must contain the initial values for the state variable time series. Nevertheless, if no series is selected as S_VAR, DDMSVAR calculates initial values for the state variables automatically.

`SetVAROrder(const iP)` sets the order of the VAR model to the integer value `iP`.

`SetMaxDuration(const iTau)` sets the maximal duration to the integer value `iTau`.

[20] See Doornik (2001).

`SetIteration(const iIter)` sets the number of Gibbs sampling iterations to the integer value `iIter`.

`SetBurnIn(const iBurn)` sets the number of burn in iterations to the integer value `iBurn`.

`SetPosteriorPercentiles(const vPerc)` sets the percentiles of the posterior distributions that have to be printed in the output. `vPerc` is a row vector containing the percentiles (in %).

`SetPriorFileName(const sFileName)`,
`SetInitFileName(const sFileName)` are optional; they are used to specify respectively the file containing the prior means and variances of the parameters and the file with the initial values for the Gibbs sampler (see the previous subsection for the format that the two files need to have). If they are not used, priors are vague and initial values are automatically calculated.

`SetSampleFileName(const sFileName, const bSaveS)` is optional; if used it sets the file name for saving the Gibbs sample and if `bSaveS` is `FALSE` the state variables are not saved, otherwise they are saved in the same file `sFileName`. `sFileName` does not need the extension, since the only available format is .in7.

`Estimate()` carries out the iteration process and generates the textual output (if run within GiveWin-OxRun it does also the graphs). After 5 iteration the user is informed of the expected waiting time and every 100 iterations also about the progress of the Gibbs sampler.

`StatesGraph(const sFileName)`,
`DurationGraph(const sFileName)`,
`Correlograms(const sFileName, const iMaxLag)`,
`Densities(const sFileName)`,
`SampleGraphs(const sFileName)`,
`RunningMeans(const sFileName)` are optional and used to save the graphs described in the last subsection. `sFileName` is a string containing the file name with extension (.emf, .wmf, .gwg, .eps, .ps) and `iMaxLag` is the maximum lag for which the autocorrelation function should be calculated.

A3. DDMSVAR software library

The last and most complicated (but also flexible) way to use the software is as library of functions. The DDMS-VAR library consists in 25 functions, but the user need to know only the following 10. Throughout the function list, it is used the notation below.

p	scalar	order of vector autoregression (VAR(p))
tau	scalar	maximal duration (τ)
k	scalar	number of time series in the model

T	scalar	number of observations of the k time series
u	scalar	dimension of the state space of $\{S_t^*\}$ ($u = 2(2^p + \tau - p - 1)$)
Y	$(k \times T)$	matrix of observation vectors ($\boldsymbol{Y}_T$)
s	$(T \times 1)$	vector of current state variable (S_t)
mu0	$(k \times 1)$	vector of means when the state is 0 ($\boldsymbol{\mu}_0$)
mu1	$(k \times 1)$	vector of mean-increments when the state is 1 ($\boldsymbol{\mu}_1$)
A	$(k \times pk)$	VAR matrices side by side ($[\boldsymbol{A}_1, \ldots, \boldsymbol{A}_p]$)
Sig	$(k \times k)$	covariance matrix of VAR error ($\boldsymbol{\Sigma}$)
SS	$(u \times p{+}2)$	state space of the complete Markov chain $\{S^*\}$ (tab. 2)
pd	(tau $\times$ 4)	matrix of the probabilities $[p_{00}(d), p_{01}(d), p_{10}(d), p_{11}(d)]$
P	$(u \times u)$	transition matrix relative to SS ($\boldsymbol{P}^*$)
xi_flt	$(u \times T{-}p)$	filtered probabilities ($[\hat{\boldsymbol{\xi}}_{t\|t}]$)
eta	$(u \times T{-}p)$	matrix of likelihoods ($[\eta_t]$)

ddss(p,tau)
Returns the state space SS (see table 2).

A_sampler(Y,s,mu0,mu1,p,a0,pA0)
Carry out step 2. of the Gibbs sampler, returning a sample point from the posterior of vec($\boldsymbol{A}$) with a0 and pA0 being respectively the prior mean vector and the prior precision matrix (inverse of covariance matrix) of vec ($\boldsymbol{A}$).

mu_sampler(Y,s,p,A,Sig,m0,pM0)
Carry out step 3. of the Gibbs sampler, returning a sample point from the posterior of $[\boldsymbol{\mu}_0', \boldsymbol{\mu}_1']'$ with m0 and pM0 being respectively the prior mean vector and the prior precision matrix (inverse of covariance matrix) of $[\boldsymbol{\mu}_0', \boldsymbol{\mu}_1']'$.

probitdur(beta,tau)
Returns the matrix pd containing the transition probabilities for every duration $d = 1, 2, \ldots, \tau$.

$$\text{pd} = \begin{pmatrix} p_{0|0}(1) & p_{0|1}(1) & p_{1|0}(1) & p_{1|1}(1) \\ p_{0|0}(2) & p_{0|1}(2) & p_{1|0}(2) & p_{1|1}(2) \\ \vdots & \vdots & \vdots & \vdots \\ p_{0|0}(\tau) & p_{0|1}(\tau) & p_{1|0}(\tau) & p_{1|1}(\tau) \end{pmatrix}.$$

ddtm(SS,pd)
Puts the transition probabilities pd into the transition matrix relative to the chain with state space SS.

ergodic(P)
Returns the vector xi0 of ergodic probabilities of the chain with transition matrix P.

msvarlik(Y,mu0,mu1,Sig,A,SS)
Returns eta, matrix of $T - p$ columns of likelihood contributions for every possible state

in SS.

ham_flt(xi0,P,eta)
Returns xi_flt, matrix of $T - p$ columns of filtered probabilities of being in each state in SS.

state_sampler(xi_flt,P)
Carry out step 1. of the Gibbs sampler. It returns a sample time series of values drawn from the chain with state space SS, transition matrix P and filtered probabilities xi_flt.

new_beta(s,X,lastbeta,diffuse,b,B0)
Carry out step 4. of the Gibbs sampler. It returns a new sample point from the posterior of the vector β, given the dependent variables in X, where the generic row is given by (13). If diffuse$\neq 0$, a diffuse prior is used.

The functions of this library may be used also to carry out maximum likelihood estimation of the parameter of the DDMS-VAR model with minimum effort: an example program is available from the author.

In: Business Fluctuations and Cycles
Editor: T. Nagakawa, pp. 67-112
ISBN: 978-1-60021-503-2

Chapter 4

INFLATION, UNEMPLOYMENT, LABOR FORCE CHANGE IN EUROPEAN COUNTIES

Ivan O. Kitov
Institute for the Dynamics of the Geospheres,
Russian Academy of Sciences, Moscow, Russia

ABSTRACT

Linear relationships between inflation, unemployment, and labor force are obtained for two European countries - Austria and France. The best fit models of inflation as a linear and lagged function of labor force change rate and unemployment explain more than 90% of observed variation (R^2>0.9). Labor force projections for Austria provide a forecast of decreasing inflation for the next ten years. In France, inflation lags by four years behind labor force change and unemployment allowing for an exact prediction at a four-year horizon. Standard error of such a prediction is lower than 1%. The results confirm those obtained for the USA and Japan and provide strong evidences in favor of the concept of labor force growth as the only driving force behind unemployment and inflation.

INTRODUCTION

Current discussions around the Phillips curve are even more active and extensive than 30 years ago, with a full set of models exploring various assumptions on the real forces behind inflation. There is no unique and comprehensive model, however, which is able to explain all observations relevant to inflation in developed countries.

There are three principal ways to follow in the discussion on sources of inflation. The first way is to continue the investigation of inflation in the framework of the Phillips curve (PC). The second is to admit that there is no real driving force behind inflation except unpredictable exogenous shocks of unknown origin such as productivity or supply shocks in modern real business cycle (RBC) models. The third is to abolish the current paradigm and to use a different mechanism driving inflation and unemployment together, which is based on natural first principles (theoretical foundations), and validated by observations (empirical foundations). This paper adds to the development of the third concept using labor force change as the driving force behind both inflation and unemployment.

Conventional economists running along the first wide avenue are numerous and represent a good part of the theoretical power elaborating monetary policies of central banks in developed countries. In fact, the Phillips curve allows for a feasible monetary policy due to the assumption that there is an interaction between monetary controllable impulses or exogenous shocks and variables describing real economy such as real GDP, output gap, marginal cost, labor cost share, etc. (Unemployment is missing in this list of the variables associated with real economy because, according to our concept, it does not belong). In the absence of such an interaction, no monetary policy is necessary with inflation completely reflecting money growth in developed economies, as mentioned in the Robert Lucas' Nobel Prize Lecture (Lucas, 1995). The money supply is an arbitrary choice of central banks, which does not influence any real economic variable. In the framework of the conventional Phillips curves, however, inflation is not neutral. relative to the performance of real economies and central banks that have to balance smoothing of price fluctuations and losses in real economic growth. These are only assumptions, however, not confirmed by empirical evidences to the extent adopted in hard sciences. Statistical inferences supporting the PC assumptions are not objective links or trade-offs between involved economic variables but non-zero correlation. See, for example, Ang *et al.* (2005), Ball (2000), Ball and Mankiw (2002), Ball *et al.* (2005), Stock and Watson (1999, 2002a, 2002b, 2003, 2005), Gali and Gertler (1999), Gali, Gertler, and Lopez-Salido (2001, 2005), Sbordone (2002, 2005), Rasche and Williams (2005), Piger and Rasche (2006), among others, where the statistical character of the links between inflation and many other economic and financial parameters is the primary objective. These authors have successfully found that functional dependencies between inflation and studied parameters unpredictably vary through time.

Despite similar outcomes sought under the PC approach one can distinguish several "schools of thought" elaborating various approaches both empirical and theoretical. There is a large group of economists who adopted numerous techniques of econometrics, which link inflation to their own lagged values and some measures of real activity, which differ from unemployment as originally introduced by A.W. Phillips. In the simplest approximation, a NAIRU concept has been elaborated by Gordon (1988, 1998), Steiger, Stock, and Watson (1997a, 1997b), Ball and Mankiw (2002), among many others, in order to improve the original model. More complicated econometric PC models include hundreds of variables related to real activity aggregated in few indices, as presented by Marcellino *et al.* (2001), Stock and Watson (1999, 2002a, 2002b, 2003), Ang *et al.* (2005), Canova (2002), Hubrich (2005).

Another conventional approach is associated with the accelerationist or "expectation augmented" Phillips curve allowing only for backward-looking expectations (Friedman 1968, Phelps 1967). Despite the Lucas (1976) and Sargent (1971) critique and failure to predict actual observations in the USA and other developed countries during the 1970s and 1980s, the model has survived and is often used by central bankers in the elaboration of actual monetary policy (Rudd and Whelan, 2005).

Fast growing in number and evolving in theoretical diversity is the group related to the New Keynesian Phillips Curve (NKPC) based on rational expectations not on lagged inflation. The expectations are usually modeled by a random price adjustment process, and thus intrinsically related to real marginal cost. In the most recent models developed by Gali and Gertler (1999), Gali, Gertler, and Lopez-Salido (2001, 2005), Sbordone (2002, 2005), among others, unit labor marginal cost is used as a marginal cost proxy. A hybrid model including lagged and future inflation values, various parameters related to real activity, and exogenous shocks, monetary and price ones, is also considered as an alternative to the pure cases of conventional PC or NKPC models with various degree of success (Rudd and Whelan, 2005).

One can also distinguish a group of economists applying a modern behavioral approach in order to explain the price adjustment process - Akerlof (2002), Mankiw (2001), Mankiw and Reis (2002), Ball *et al.* (2005), among others. In this framework, sticky prices used by the NKPC group are replaced with "sticky" information. This makes individual decisions on price change, i.e. on overall inflation when aggregated over the whole economy, to be imperfect due to imperfection in processing of available information. Effectively, it means that the inflation expectations resulted from the imperfect information processing are not "rational" and do not meet axiomatic requirements of rational expectations used by the NKPC.

In practice, the conventional explanation of the price inflation lacks empirical justification extended beyond autoregressive properties of inflation itself, and is also theoretically challenged by modern growth models insisting on independence of real economic performance on monetary issues, as introduced by Kydland and Prescott (1982). The real business cycle theory implies that variations in real economies are almost completely described by exogenous shocks in productivity and supply. Money is absent in RBC models or artificially introduced in some of them-Gavine and Kydland (1996) and Prescott (2004). Numerous econometric studies confirm the RBC assumption on money neutrality by statistical inferences; Atkeson and Ohanian (2002), Piger and Rasche (2005), Rasche and Williams (2005), among many others, have found that AR models explain evolution of inflation almost completely, with a marginal improvement from usage of real economic variables being only a statistical and transient one.

A study of inflation and unemployment as economic variables driven solely by labor force change has been carried out by Kitov (2006a, 2006b, 2006c) for the two largest economies – the USA and Japan. The study has revealed linear relationships between inflation, unemployment and labor force. In the USA, the linear relationships are also characterized by time lags with the change in labor force leading inflation and unemployment by two and five years, respectively. In Japan, labor force change, unemployment and inflation evolve synchronously. The revealed linear link allows a partial inflation control and provides clear foundations for a reasonable economic policy related to inflation and unemployment.

In this paper, the same approach linking inflation and unemployment to labor force change is applied to Austria and France. The reminder of the paper is organized in four sections. Section 1 briefly presents data sources and the model. Data on inflation, unemployment, and labor force for European countries is available from various sources. This diversity creates a number of problems but allows for an indirect estimation of the uncertainty related to various data series.

Section 2 is devoted to Austria as a country with elaborated statistics providing a long time series with changing definitions and procedures. The changes are well documented and clear in corresponding curves. The importance of information on definitions and procedures for a successful modelling is illustrated and discussed.

Inflation and unemployment in France are considered in Section 3. The country represents an economy with a size in between those of the USA and Austria. The case of France is of a large importance for our concept because of the outstanding changes related to the rules of the European Monetary Union fixing allowed inflation to figures near 2%. The limitation violates the partition of labor force change into inflation and unemployment, which was natural for France and observed since the 1960s. An elevated unemployment is observed as a response to the fast growth in labor force started in 1996 and the fixed inflation. Section 4 discusses principal findings of the study and concludes.

1. Data Sources and the Model

The principal source of information relevant to the study is the OECD database (http://www.oecd.org/scripts/cde) which provides comprehensive data sets on labor force, unemployment, working age population, and participation rate. National statistical sources are used for obtaining original data on inflation (CPI and GDP deflator) and corroborative data on unemployment and labor force. As a rule, the data are available at the Eurostat web-site (http://epp.eurostat.cec.eu.int). An extended set of data on economic and population variables in Austria is obtained by the courtesy of Austrian national Bank employees[14].

In some cases, readings associated with the same variable but obtained from different sources do not coincide. This is due to different approaches and definitions applied by corresponding agencies. Diversity of definitions is accompanied by a degree of uncertainty related to corresponding measurements. For example, figures related to labor force are usually obtained in surveys covering population samples of various sizes: from 0.2 per cent to 3.3 per cent of total population (Eurostat, 2002). The uncertainty associated with such measurements cannot be easily estimated but certainly affects reliability of the inflation/labor force linear relationship (Kitov, 2006a, 2006c).

When using the term "accuracy" we refer not to the absolute difference between measured and actual values but to some estimated uncertainty of measurements. This uncertainty might be roughly approximated by variations in a given parameter between consequent surveys or between different agencies. For example, the US Census Bureau (2002) gives a very low measurement related uncertainty for the annual population estimates. At the same time, some micro-surveys conducted after decennial censuses indicate the presence of deviations from the census enumerated values as large as 5 per cent in some age groups (West and Robinson, 1999). Such errors are far above those garantied by pure statistical approach used in the evaluation of survey/census results. Therefore, one can consider the uncertainty of several percent as the one characterizing the population estimates during and between censuses, at least in some age groups. Survey reported uncertainties are just a formal statistical estimate of the internal consistency of the measurements. (It is worth noting that population related variables could be potentially measured exactly because they are countable not measurable). In any case, the

[14] The author thanks Dr. Gnan from the OeNB for providing an extensive data set for Austria.

discrepancy between model predicted values and corresponding measurements has to be considered in the framework of measurements uncertainty.

The model, which we test in the study, links inflation and unemployment to labor force change rate. It is important to use the rate of growth not increment as a predictor in order to match dimension of inflation and unemployment, which are defined as rates as well. An implicit assumption of the model is that inflation and unemployment do not depend directly on parameters describing real economic activity (Kitov, 2006a). Moreover, inflation does not depend on its own previous and/or future values because it is completely controlled by a variable of different nature.

As defined in Kitov (2006a), inflation and unemployment are linear and potentially lagged functions of labor force:

$$\pi(t)=A_1 dLF(t-t_1)/LF(t-t_1)+A_2 \quad (1)$$

$$UE(t)=B_1 dLF(t-t_2)/LF(t-t_2)+B_2 \quad (2)$$

where $\pi(t)$ is the inflation at time t (represented by some standard measure such as GDP deflator or CPI), $UE(t)$ is the unemployment at time t (which is also potentially represented by various measures), $LF(t)$ is the labor force at time t, t_1 and t_2 are the time lags between the inflation, unemployment, and labor force, respectively, A_1, B_1, A_2, and B_2 are country specific coefficients, which have to be determined empirically. The coefficients may vary through time for a given country as different measures (or definitions) of the studied variables are used.

Linear relationships (1) and (2) define inflation and unemployment separately. These variables are two indivisible features of a unique process, however. The process is the labor force growth, which is accommodated in real economies though two channels. The first channel is the increase in employment and corresponding change in personal income distribution (PID). All persons obtaining new paid jobs or their equivalents presumably change their incomes to some higher levels. There is an ultimate empirical fact, however, that the US PID does not change with time in relative terms, i.e. when normalized to the total population and total income (Kitov, 2005b). The increasing number of people at higher income levels, as related to the new paid jobs, leads to a certain disturbance in the PID. This over-concentration (or over-pressure) of population in some income bins above its neutral value must be compensated by such an extension in corresponding income scale, which returns the PID to its original density. Related stretching of the income scale is called inflation (Kitov, 2006a). The mechanism responsible for the compensation and the income scale stretching, obviously, has some positive relaxation time, which effectively separates in time the source of inflation, i.e. the labor force change, and the reaction, i.e. the inflation.

The second channel is related to those persons in the labor force who failed to obtain a new paid job. These people do not leave the labor force but join unemployment. Supposedly, they do not change corresponding PID because they do not change their incomes. Therefore, total labor force change equals unemployment change plus employment change, the latter process expressed through lagged inflation. In the case of a "natural" behavior of an economic system, which is defined as a stable balance of socio-economic forces in corresponding society, the partition of labor force growth between unemployment and inflation is retained through time and the linear relationships hold separately. There is always a possibility, however, to fix one of the two dependent variables. For example, central banks are able to fix inflation rate by monetary means. Such a violation of the natural economic behavior would undoubtedly distort the partition of the labor force change – the portion previously accommodated by inflation would be redirected to unemployment. To account for this effect one should to use a generalized relationship as represented by the sum of relationships (1) and (2):

$$\pi(t)+UE(t)= A_1dLF(t-t_1)/LF(t-t_1)+B_1dLF(t-t_2)/LF(t-t_2)+A_2+B_2 \quad (3)$$

Equation (3) balances labor force change, inflation and unemployment, the latter two variables potentially lagging by different times behind the labor force change. The importance of this generalized relationship is demonstrated in this paper on the example of France.

For the USA, there has been no need so far to apply relationship (3) because corresponding monetary policies and other potential sources of disturbance do not change the natural partition of labor force change, as observed since the late 1950s. Coefficients in relationships (1) and (2) specific for the USA are as follows: A_1=4, A_2=-0.03, t_1=2 years (GDP deflator as a measure of inflation), B_1=2.1, B_2=-0.023, t_2=5 years.

For Japan, A_1=1.77, A_2=-0.003, t_1=0 years (GDP deflator as a measure of inflation) (Kitov, 2006b). The labor force change rate measured in Japan is negative since 1999 and corresponding measures of inflation, GDP deflator and CPI, are negative as well. There is no indication of any recovery to positive figures any time soon if to consider the decrease in working age population and participation rate as observed in Japan from 1999.

The formal statistical assessment of the linear relationships carried out by Kitov (2006d) for the USA indicates that root mean square forecasting error (RMSFE) at a two-year horizon for the period between 1965 and 2002 is only 0.8%. This value is superior to that obtained with any other inflation model by almost a factor of 2, as presented by Stocks and Watson (1999, 2005), Atkeson and Ohanian (2001), Ang *et al.* (2005), Marcellino *et al.* (2005). When the entire period is split into two segments before and after 1983, the forecasting superiority is retained with RMSFE of 1.0% for the first (1965-1983) and 0.5% for the second (1983-2002) sub- period. In a majority of inflation models, the turning point in 1983 is dictated by inability to describe inflation process with one set of defining parameters. Therefore, special discussions are devoted to statistical, economic, and/or financial justification of the split and the change in parameters (see Stock and Watson, 2005). Our model denies the existence of any change in the US inflation behavior around 1983 or in any other point after 1960. Every inflation reading is completely defined by the labor force change occurred two years before.

The linear relationships between inflation, unemployment, and labor force change perform excellent for the two largest world economies during a long period. These relationships are expected to be successful for other developed economies with similar socio-economic organization. European countries provide a variety of features related to inflation and unemployment as one can conclude from the economic statistics provided by OCED and Eurostat. This diversity includes periods of very high inflation accompanied by high unemployment, periods of low inflation and unemployment, and other combinations complicated by transition periods. It is a big challenge for any theory of inflation to explain these empirical facts.

Currently, the diversity resulted in a well-recognized and thoroughly discussed failure of conventional economics to provide a consistent and reliable description covering the past 50 years and all developed countries. As a consequence, the current monetary policy of the European Central Bank is based mainly on invalidated assumptions and subjective opinions of economists and central bankers, but not on a robust model predicting inflation behavior under different conditions. In the USA, the current (and historical!) practice aimed at inflation control, as implemented by the Federal Open Market Committee, definitely, has no visible influence on the observed inflation, if labor force change is the driving force.

2. AUSTRIA

The first country to examine is Austria. It provides an example of a small economy in terms of working age population. At the same time, the Austrian economy is characterized by a long history of measurements and availability of time series and descriptive information relevant to the concept under study.

Austria has been demonstrating an excellent economic performance since 1950 and is characterized by an average per capita GDP annual increment of $467 (Geary-Khamis PPP - The Groningen Growth and Development Center and Conference Board, 2006) for the period between 1950 and 2005. This value is very close to that for the USA ($480) and Japan ($485) (Kitov, 2006e). Such a good performance distinguishes Austria from a raw of relatively weak performances of larger European economies such as France ($406), the UK ($378), Italy ($405), and Sweden ($381) during the same period.

It was discussed in Kitov (2006a, 2006b, 2006d) that data quality is the principal characteristic defining the success of any attempt of modelling inflation and unemployment as a function of labor force change. There are two main sources of uncertainty in the data related to our study. The first source is associated with measurement errors. It is a more important issue for the accuracy of labor force surveys, which usually provide original data on unemployment and labor force. In the surveys, measurement accuracy depends on sampling and nonsampling errors. The former is estimated using population coverage and some standard statistical principles, and the latter is more difficult to evaluate (CB, 2002).

The second source of uncertainty is important for both labor force, including unemployment as a constituent part, and inflation measurements and is associated with variations in definitions given to these economic variables. The definitions are often revised and modified, sometimes dramatically, as one can judge from the description given by the OECD (2005). When applied to labor force, such revisions introduce severe breaks in corresponding time series associated with the change in units of measurements. (In physics, it would have been practically impossible to obtain any reliable empirical relationship if measurement units had varied in such uncontrollable way as in economics.) Moreover, European countries have implemented the changes at different times creating asynchronous breaks. Modifications of methodologies and procedures related to inflation measurements are accompanied by introduction of new measures such as harmonized index of consumer prices (Eurostat, 2006a). The latter index has replaced the old CPI definition in official statistics of European countries.

Therefore, we start with a detailed description of the data obtained for Austria. We use six sources providing annual readings for CPI, GDP deflator, population estimates, unemployment rate, participation rate, and labor force level: Eurostat, OECD, AMS (Arbeitsmarktservice) Österreich (http://www.ams.or.at), HSV (Hauptverband der Sozialversicherungtraeger) Österreich (http://www.hsv.or.at), Statistik Austria (http://www.statistik.at), and the Österreichische Nationalbank (ÖNB – http://www.oenb.at). These sources estimate the same variables in different ways. Comparison of equivalent (by title) time series allows a quantitative evaluation of differences between them. The main purpose of such a cross-examination is twofold: 1) demonstration of the discrepancy between the series as a quantitative measure of the uncertainty in corresponding parameters and 2) determination of the degree of similarity between the series. The estimated uncertainty puts a strong constraint on the level of confidence related to statistical estimates using the data sets. One cannot trust any statistical inference with a confidence level higher than allowed by the uncertainty. On the other hand, equivalent time series obtained according to various definitions (procedures, methodologies, samples, etc.) of the same parameter represent different portions of some actual value of the parameter. For example, various definitions of employment are aimed at obtaining the number of those persons who work for pay or profit. The persons are the only source of goods and services sold for money. The definitions are designed in a way for corresponding estimates to approach the actual value. If consistent and successful, the definitions always provide close to constant and different estimates of the portions of the actual value. Thus, the estimates are scalable - one can easily compute values according to all definitions having only one of them. In this sense, various definitions and related estimates are exchangeable in the framework of the linear relationship between inflation, unemployment, and labor force.

Three different definitions of inflation rate are presented in Figure 1: CPI and GDP deflator as obtained using prices expressed in national currency (national accounts -NAC), and GDP deflator estimated using the Austrian shilling/Euro exchange rate (Euro accounts - EUR). The latter variable is characterized by the largest variations. The curves corresponding to the inflation measurements represented by the NAC CPI and NAC GDP deflator are closer (correlation coefficient of 0.92 for the period between 1961 and 2004), but differ in amplitude and timing of principal changes. There are periods of an almost total coincidence, however. The EUR GDP deflator series is characterized by correlation coefficients 0.86 and 0.82 as obtained for the NAC GDP deflator and CPI, respectively. Therefore, one can expect a better exchangeability between the NAC CPI and NAC GDP deflator than that in the two other combinations. Since the middle 1970s, inflation in Austria has a definition-independent tendency to decrease. The last 25 years are characterized by annual inflation rates below 5% for the NAC representations.

Standard labor force surveys conducted in Europe cover small portions of total population (Eurostat, 2006b). Levels of labor force and unemployment are estimated using specific weights (population controls) for every person in the survey to compute the portion of population with the same characteristics as the person has. Population controls or population portions in predefined age-sex-race bins are primarily obtained during censuses, which theoretically cover entire population.

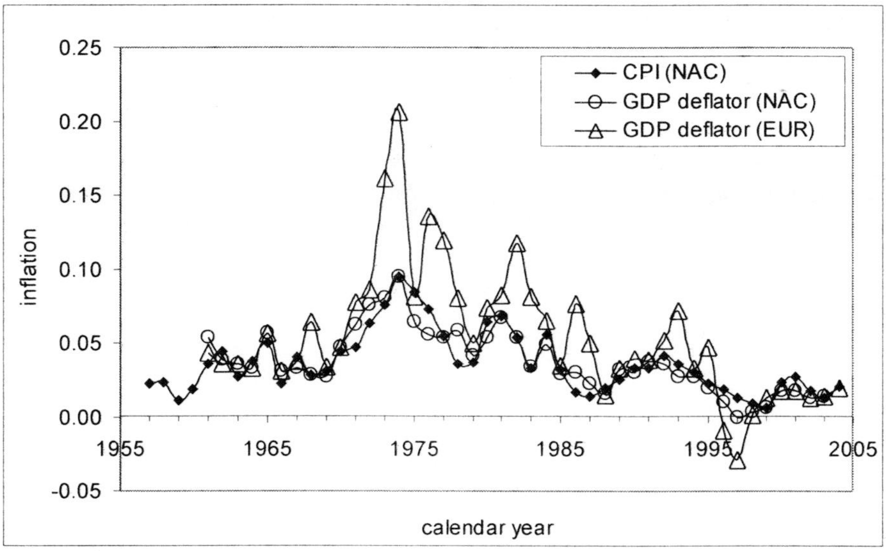

Figure 1. Comparison of three variables representing inflation in Austria: GDP deflator determined using national currency (NAC) and Euro (EUR), and CPI determined by using national currency. The GDP deflator curves coincide since 2000. Inflation volatility is much lower when it is represented in national currency. Correlation coefficients for the period between 1961 and 2004: CPI NAC/GDP deflator NAC - 0.92; CPI NAC/GDP deflator EUR - 0.82; GDP deflator NAC/GDP deflator EUR - 0.86.

Between censuses, i.e. during postcensal periods, estimated figures are used as obtained by the population components change: births, deaths, net migration, as, for example, reported by the US Census Bureau (2002). Because of low accuracy of postcensal estimates, every new census reveals some "error of the closure", i.e. the difference between pre-estimated and census enumerated values. To adjust to new population figures, the difference is proportionally distributed over the years between the censuses; similar to the procedures applied by the US Census Bureau (2004). Such population revisions may be as large as several percent. Thus, when using some current figures of labor force and unemployment, one has to bear in mind that the figures are prone to further revisions according to the censuses to come.

Figure 2 illustrates the differences in population revision procedures between OECD and Statistik Austria (NAC): two curves represent the rate of change in the population of 15 years of age and over in Austria. Between 1960 and 1983, the curves coincide since OECD uses the national definition. After 1983, the curves diverge, with the OECD curve being almost everywhere above that corresponding to the national approach. There are three distinct spikes in the OECD curve: between 1990 and 1993 and in 2002, which are related to population revisions. As explained by OECD (2005), "From 1992, data are annual averages. Prior to 1992, data are mid-year estimates obtained by averaging official estimates at 31 December for two consecutive years". And - "From 2002, data are in line with the 2001 census". The 2002 revision impulsively compensates the difference between OECD and Statistik Austria accumulated during the previous 20 years: the populations in 1982 and 2002 coincide. Such step adjustments are observed in the USA population data as well (Kitov, 2006a). They introduce a significant deterioration in statistical estimates, but are easily removed by a simple redistribution as demonstrated by Kitov (2006d). Sometimes such step adjustments are confused with actual changes in the economic variables under stud. One has to be careful to distinguish between actual changes and artificial corrections usually associated with the years of census or large revisions in definitions.

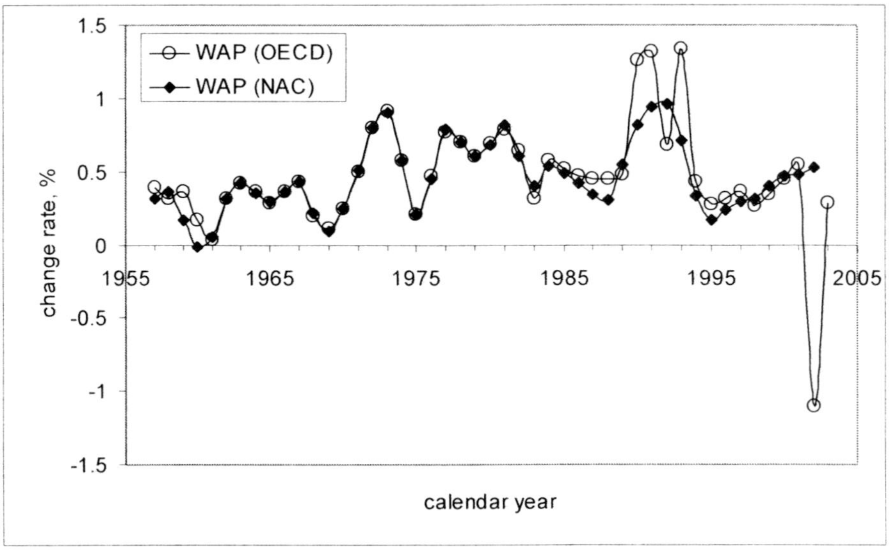

Figure 2. Comparison of the rate of change in working age population (aged 15 and over) in Austria as determined by the OECD and national statistics (NAC). Notice the spikes in the OECD curve related to step adjustments according to population surveys.

The national estimates in Figure 2 are visually smoother indicating some measures applied to distribute the errors of the closure and other adjustments over the entire period. In average, the population over 15 years of age in Austria has been changing slowly so far – at an annual rate below 0.5% - with occasional jumps to 0.7% - 1.0%. Such weak but steady growth supports, however, a gradual increase in labor force and prevents deflationary periods.

The level of labor force can be represented as a product of total population and corresponding participation rate (LFPR) both taken in some predefined age range. There is no conventional definition concerning the age range, however. Popular is an open range above 15 years of age and that between 15 and 64 years. The OECD series using the former definition is presented in Figure 3. OeNB (2005) provides another measure of LFPR - "the fraction of the working-age population that is employed or seeking employment", also presented in Figure 3. The curves have been evolving more or less synchronously, with the OECD curve well above that reported by the OeNB.

The LFPR is responsible for a substantial part of the labor force total change: ~ 8% increase from 1976 to 1996, i.e. 0.4% per year. The current LFPR value of about 59%, as reported by the OECD, is historically high. One can hardly expect a further increase in LFPR. A decrease is more probable, as some other developed countries demonstrate.

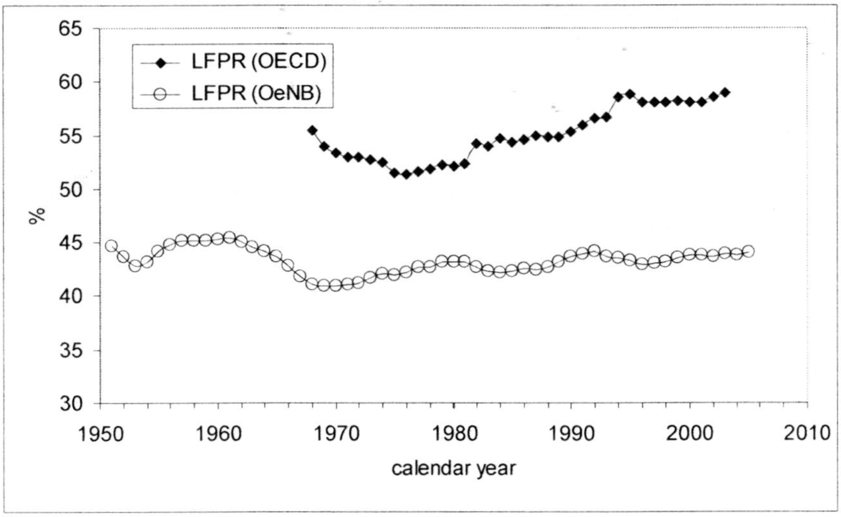

Figure 3. Labor force participation rate (LFPR) in Austria as determined by OECD and obtained from the OeNB. A weak tendency to growth was observed in the beginning of the 2000s.

The rate of labor force growth was very low in Austria during the last 10 years, as Figure 4 demonstrates. There are three labor force time series displayed, as estimated by the OECD, Eurostat, and NAC. The Eurostat series is represented by civilian labor force. Prior to 1994, armed forces were included in the civilian labor force (CLF), in services. The NAC readings include the estimates of employment made according to the HSV definition and those of unemployment level made by AMS (Statistik Austria, 2005). Both agencies base their estimates on administrative records. Thus, their approach has been undergoing weaker changes in definitions and procedures since the 1960s compared to that adopted by the OECD and Eurostat.

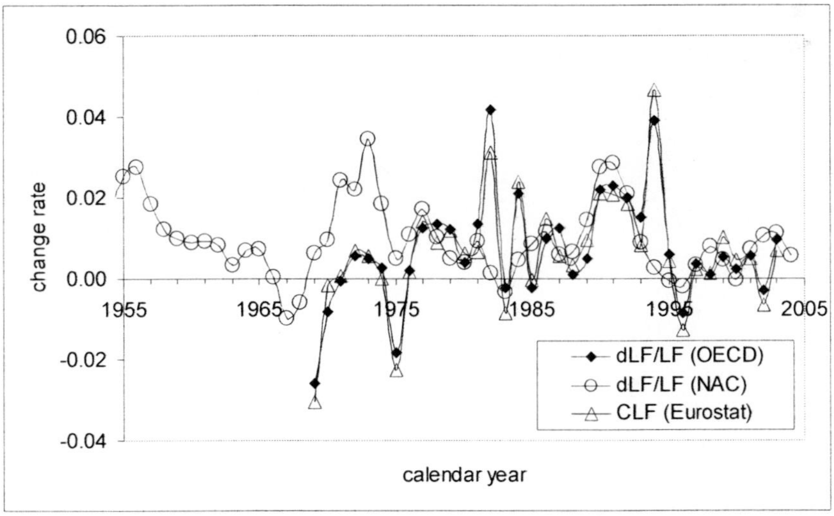

Figure 4. Comparison of labor force change rate estimates as reported by OECD, NAC, and Eurostat. Notice the smoothness of the NAC curve.

The curves in Figure 4 have inherited the features, which are demonstrated by corresponding working age populations in Figure 2. The OECD curve is characterized by several spikes of artificial character, as discussed above. The Eurostat curve is similar to that reported by the OECD with minor deviations probably associated with differences between LF and CLF. The NAC LF curve is smoother. It demonstrates a period of a slow growth with a high volatility in the 1970s, a period with an elevated growth with a high volatility between 1981 and 1995, and again a slow growth period with a low volatility during the last ten years (from 1995 to 2005). The second period is characterized by significant changes in the labor force definition - both for employment and unemployment (OECD, 2005):

- "In 1982, re-weighting of the sample was made, due to an underestimation of persons aged 15 to 29 years.
- In 1984, the sample was revised and a change occurred in the classification of women on maternity leave: they were classified as unemployed before 1984 and as employed thereafter.
- In 1987, a change occurred in the definition of the unemployed where non-registered jobseekers were classified as unemployed if they had been seeking work in the last four weeks and if they were available for work within four weeks. In previous surveys, the unemployment concept excluded most unemployed persons not previously employed and most persons re-entering the labor market.
- Employment data from 1994 are compatible with ILO guidelines and the time criterion applied to classify persons as employed is reduced to 1 hour. "

Therefore, one can expect some measurable changes in the units of the labor force measurements during the period between 1982 and 1987 and in 1994. The latter change is potentially the largest since the time criterion dropped from 13 hours, as had been defined in 1974, to 1 hour. For the sake of consistency in definitions and procedures, the NAC labor force is used as a predictor in this study. The OECD labor force time series is also used in few cases to illustrate that the definitions provide similar results. For the labor force series, quantitative statistical estimates of similarity (such as correlation) are worthless due to the spikes in the OECD time series.

There are three curves associated with unemployment estimates for Austria shown in Figure 5, as defined by the national statistics approach (AMS), Eurostat, and OECD. It is illustrative to trace changes in the definitions used by the institutions over time. Currently, OECD and Eurostat use very similar approaches. There was a period between 1977 and 1983 when OECD adopted the national definition, which was different from the one used by Eurostat. During a short period between 1973 and 1977, the three time series were very close to each other. A major change in all three series occurred between 1982 1987 according to the changes in definitions, as described above. Therefore, the unemployment curves in Figure 5 are characterized by two distinct branches: a low (~2%) unemployment period between 1960 and 1982 and a period of an elevated unemployment (~4% for the OECD and Eurostat, and ~6.5% for the AMS) since 1983.

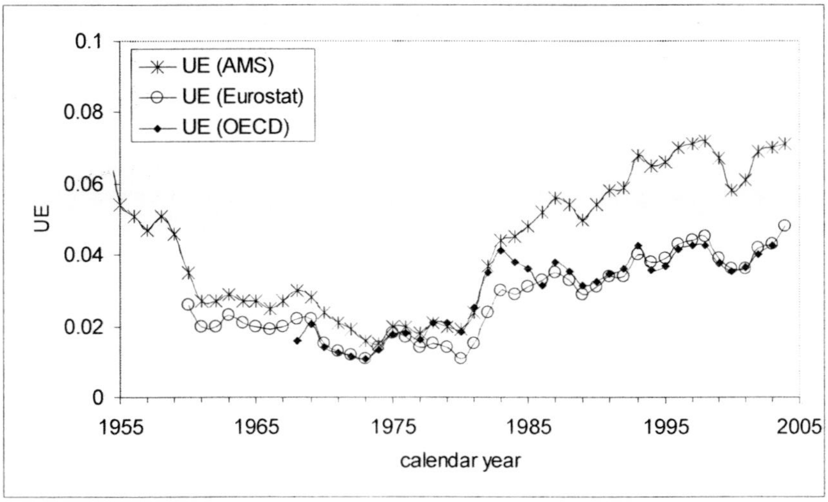

Figure 5. Estimates of unemployment rate in Austria according to definitions given by the AMS, Eurostat, and OECD.

The switches between various definitions, as adopted by the OECD, also do not facilitate obtaining of a unique relationship between labor force change and unemployment. The AMS definition based on administrative records might be the most consistent among the three, but it definitely differs from the definition recommended by the International Labor Organization, as adopted in European countries (Statistik Austria, 2005). We use the national and OECD time series to represent unemployment in the linear relationship linking it to labor force.

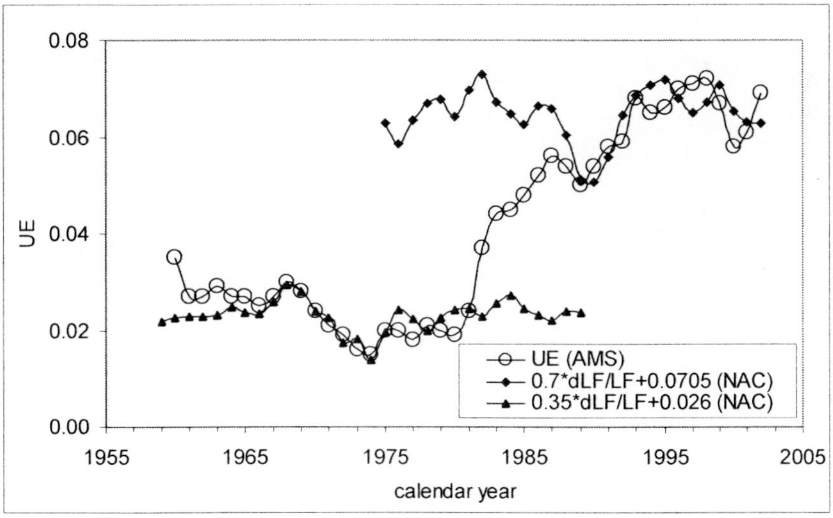

Figure 6. Comparison of the observed (AMS) and predicted by the linear relationships (shown in lower right corner of the panel) using the NAC (AMS+HSV) labor force and the AMS unemployment rate. Changes in the unemployment and labor force definitions between 1983 and 1987 make it impossible to fit the unemployment curve during this period. Otherwise, the predicted curve is in a good agreement with the measured one.

The above discussion explains why one cannot model the whole period by a unique linear relationship. There was a period of substantial changes in units of measurement between 1982 and 1987. Therefore, we model the Austrian unemployment (*UE*) during the periods before 1982 and after 1986 separately. The period between 1982 and 1987 is hardly to be matched by a linear relationship. Results of the modeling are presented in Figure 6, where the AMS unemployment curve is matched by the following relationships:

$$UE(t)=0.35*dLF(t)/LF(t)+0.0260 \ (t<1982) \quad (4)$$

$$UE(t)=0.70*dLF(t)/LF(t)+0.0705 \ (t>1986) \quad (5)$$

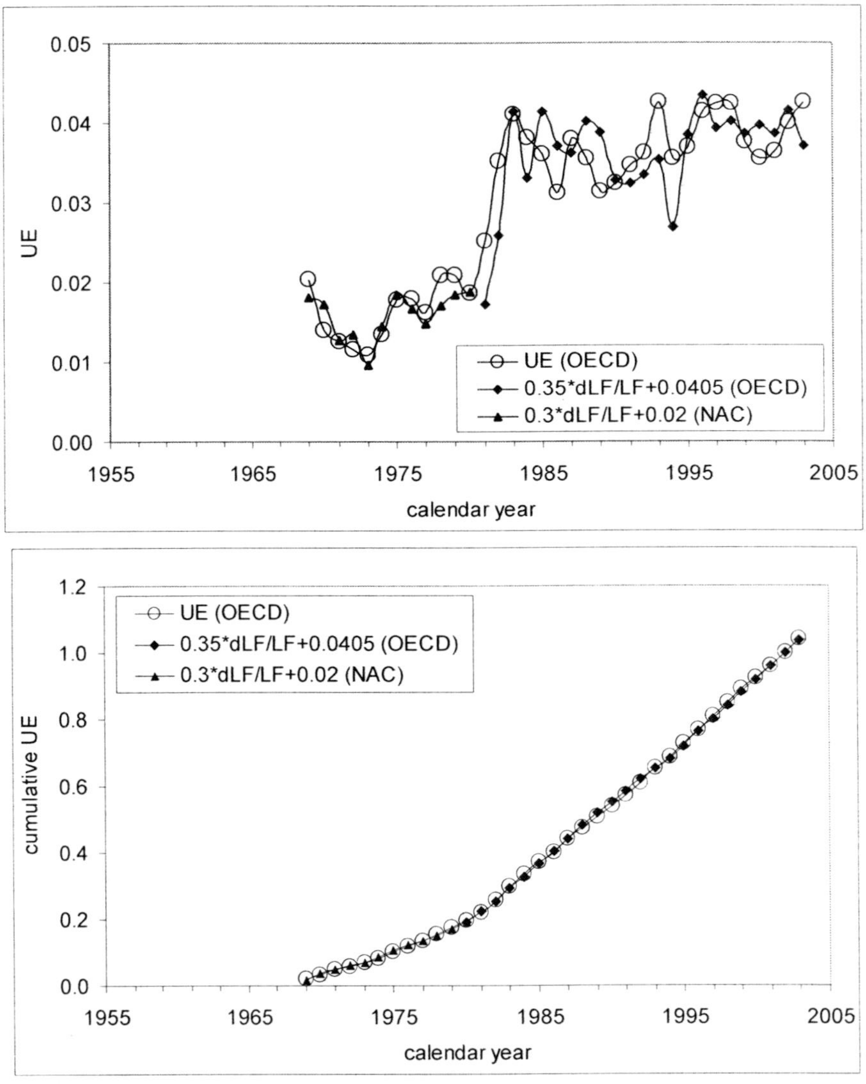

Figure 7. Comparison of the observed (OECD) and predicted (AMS before 1980 and OECD after 1980) unemployment rate in Austria. The upper frame displays annual readings and the lower one – cumulative unemployment since 1968. Notice a major change in unemployment definition between 1981 and 1984 (OECD, 2005)

The NAC labor force time series is used for the prediction with no time lead ahead of the unemployment. The absence of any lag might be presumed as a natural behavior of labor force and unemployment as one of the labor force components, but labor force change in the US leads unemployment by 5 years. Hence, processes behind labor force change and unemployment growth are different. Coefficients in relationships (4) and (5) provide the best visible fit between the observed and predicted curves. From the Figure and the relationships, one can conclude that there was a step change in the unemployment average level from approximately 0.03 during the years before 1982 to 0.07 for the period after 1986. In addition, the linear coefficient has doubled indicating a higher sensitivity of the unemployment to the labor force change under the new definitions introduced between 1982 and 1987.

The annual OECD unemployment readings presented in Figure 7 vary by less than 1%, if to exclude a short period between 1980 and 1983, when changes in definitions resulted in a step-like unemployment increase. Duration of this period of changing definitions is different from that related to the NAC unemployment according to the timing of the changes as adopted by AMS and OECD. This jump in the unemployment rate from 2% to 4% during the two years between 1981 and 1983 is not well modeled. Otherwise, the following relationships are used to match the observed unemployment readings:

$$UE(t)=0.35*dLF(t)/LF(t)+0.0405 \quad (t\geq 1983) \qquad (6)$$

$$UE(t)=0.30*dLF(t)/LF(t)+0.020 \quad (t\leq 1980) \qquad (7)$$

For the period before 1980, the NAC labor force readings are used, and the OECD labor force is used after 1981. We combined the labor force data sets in order to demonstrate their exchangeability in the description of the unemployment. Cumulative curves in the lower panel of Figure 7 illustrate the quality of the overall match between the measured and predicted values. The cumulative curves are very sensitive to the intercepts in relationships (6) and (7) as they are summed through time. Therefore, the intercepts 0.0405 and 0.020 are significant to the last digits. Potential variation in the linear coefficients in (6) and (7) is not so well resolved.

Amplitude of the variations in the unemployment during the entire period except the short period between 1980 and 1983 is so low that makes the prediction according to (6) and (7) of a limited reliability. To obtain a more reliable prediction, the unemployment has to undergo an actual (not definition related) change at an annual rate of several percent, what would have been a big surprise for Austria with its stable socio-economic conditions and demographic structure. The agreement observed between the cumulative curves also is not statistically significant since it just reflects the unchanging unemployment and labor force growth rates during the two separately modeled periods.

These results can be interpreted, however, as an indication of a weak dependence of the unemployment on the labor force change. The latter is transmitted only by one third into the unemployment as the linear coefficients 0.30 and 0.35 indicate. These transmission coefficients are an order of magnitude smaller than that for the USA (Kitov, 2006a). The difference is of a potential importance because labor force participation rate and unemployment in both countries are close.

Table 1 consistently lists results of linear regression analysis carried out in the study for various measures of unemployment and inflation with labor force as a predictor, as obtained for Austria. First row of the Table presents standard deviation (stdev) as obtained for the OECD readings of unemployment in Austria during the period between 1983 and 2003.

Table 1. Results of linear regression analysis for Austria

Period	Dependent variable	Predictor	A	B	R^2	stdev
1983-2003	annual UE (OECD)					0.0036
1983-2003	annual UE (OECD)	annual dLF(t)/LF(t) (OECD)	1.03 (0.020)	0.026 (0.007)	0.11	0.0035
1983-2003	cumulative UE (OECD)	cumulative dLF(t)/LF(t) (OECD)	1.00 (0.006)	0.010 (0.003)	0.99 9	0.007
1965-2003	annual GDP deflator (NAC)					0.022
1965-2003	annual GDP deflator (NAC)	annual dLF(t)/LF(t) (NAC)	0.880 (007)	0.005 (0.003)	0.81	0.010
1965-2003	annual GDP deflator (NAC)	2-year moving average dLF(t)/LF(t) (NAC)	0.95 (0.07)	0.003 (0.003)	0.85	0.009
1965-2003	2-year moving average GDP deflator (NAC)	2-year moving average dLF(t)/LF(t) (NAC)	0.93 (0.06)	0.003 (0.002)	0.88	0.007
1960-2003	cumulative GDP deflator (NAC)	cumulative dLF(t)/LF(t) (NAC)	1.03 (0.004)	0.003 (0.005)	0.99 9	0.011
1965-2003	annual CPI (NAC)					0.022
1965-2003	annual CPI (NAC)	annual dLF(t)/LF(t) (NAC)	0.76 (0.10)	0.010 (0.004)	0.60	0.014
1965-2003	annual CPI (NAC)	2-year moving average dLF(t)/LF(t) (NAC)	0.85 (0.10)	0.006 (0.004)	0.64	0.013
1965-2003	2-year moving average CPI (NAC)	2-year moving average dLF(t)/LF(t) (NAC)	0.83 (0.09)	0.007 (0.004)	0.72	0.011
1965-2003	annual GDP deflator (Eurostat)					0.046
1965-2003	annual GDP deflator (Eurostat)	annual dLF(t)/LF(t) (NAC)	0.82 (0.10)	0.010 (0.007)	0.66	0.027
1965-2003	annual GDP deflator (Eurostat)	2-year moving average dLF(t)/LF(t) (NAC)	0.88 (0.10)	0.008 (0.007)	0.68	0.027
1965-2003	2-year moving average GDP deflator (Eurostat)	2-year moving average dLF(t)/LF(t) (NAC)	0.87 (0.07)	0.008 (0.005)	0.78	0.02
1965-2003	annual GDP deflator (NAC)					0.022
1965-2003	annual GDP deflator (NAC)	annual dLF(t)/LF(t)-UE(t) (NAC)	0.89 (0.06)	0.04 (0.03)	0.86	0.008
1965-2003	annual GDP deflator (NAC)	2-year moving average dLF(t)/LF(t)-UE(t) (NAC)	0.89 (0.06)	0.004 (0.003)	0.86	0.008
1965-2003	2-year moving average GDP deflator (NAC)	2-year moving average dLF(t)/LF(t)-UE(t) (NAC)	0.91 (0.05)	0.003 (0.002)	0.91	0.007

The standard deviation is 0.0036. Second and third rows present regression coefficients with their standard errors, R^2, and stdev as obtained for the OECD unemployment between 1983 and 2003 with a predictor computed by relationship (6) with the OECD labor force readings. (A linear regression analysis for the whole period between 1969 and 2003 would be meaningless because of the artificial change in the predicted curve around 1982.) For the annual *UE* readings after 1983, R^2 is very low (0.11) and stdev=0.0035, i.e. marginally lower than stdev for the *UE* series itself. For the cumulative curves during the same period, R^2=0.999 and stdev=0.007. Therefore, relationships (4) through (7) are accurate one but not reliable. In fact, only large and synchronized in time and amplitude actual changes can provide a more reliable evidence for the model. Inflation in Austria provides a variable with higher fluctuations to predict.

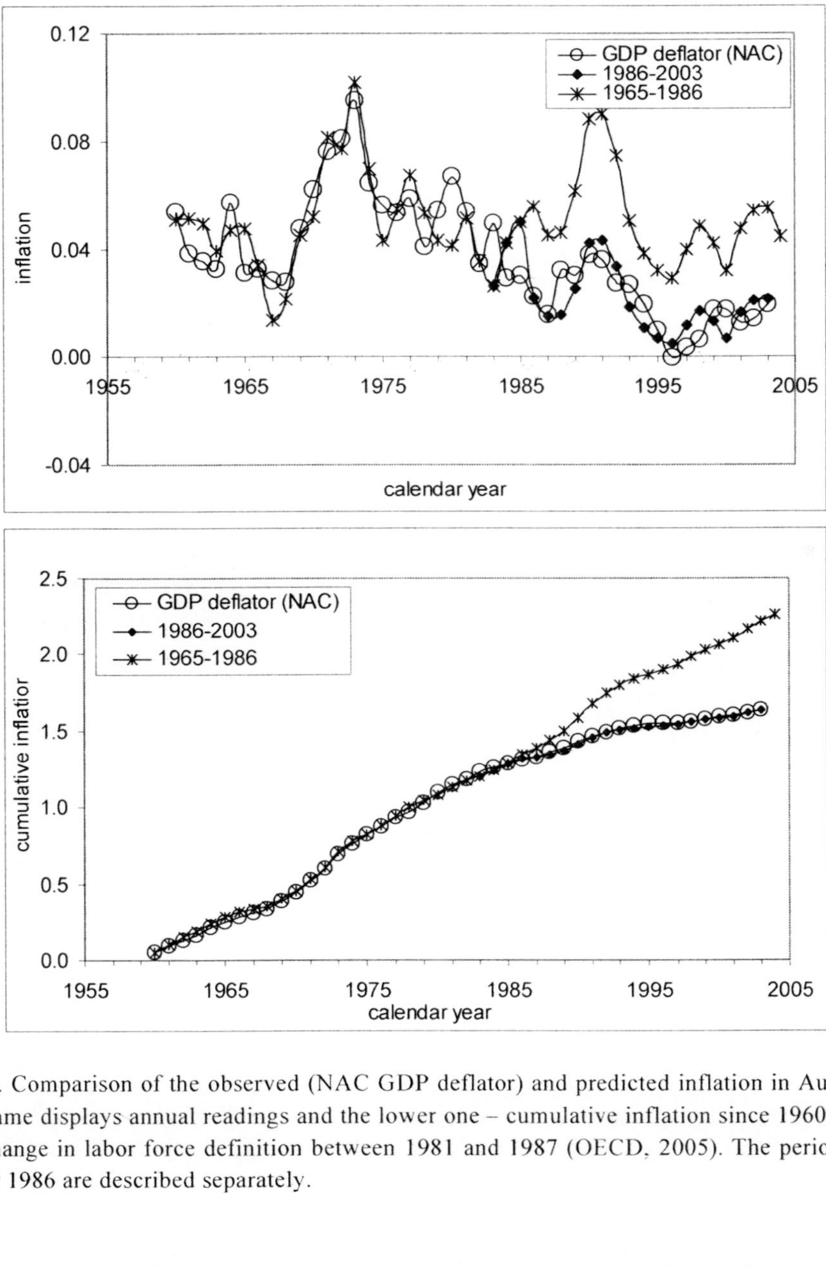

Figure 8. Comparison of the observed (NAC GDP deflator) and predicted inflation in Austria. The upper frame displays annual readings and the lower one – cumulative inflation since 1960. Notice a major change in labor force definition between 1981 and 1987 (OECD, 2005). The periods before and after 1986 are described separately.

Figure 8 depicts observed and predicted, annual and cumulative, inflation values in Austria for the period between 1960 and 2003. As mentioned above, there was a significant change in the labor force (employment and unemployment separately) statistics in the 1980s. Thus, the two different periods are described by two different linear relationships without any time lag between variables. The GDP deflator, as determined by the national statistics approach, represents inflation. Labor force is also taken according to the NAC (AMS+HSV) definition. The relationships predicting inflation are as follows:

$$\pi(t)=2.0*dLF(t)/LF(t)+0.033 \; (1960\leq t \leq 1985) \qquad (8)$$

$$\pi(t)=1.25*dLF(t)/LF(t)+0.0075 \; (t\geq 1986) \qquad (9)$$

Coefficients in the relationships are obtained by fitting the cumulative curves over the entire period, with 1986 being the point where relationship (8) is replaced by relationship (9). Ratio of the linear coefficients in (8) and (9) is 2/1.25=1.6 and the intercept dropped from 0.033 to 0.0075. The change in the linear coefficients is consistent with the changes in the definition of labor force in between 1982 and 1987 – gradually more and more persons were counted in as employed and unemployed with a substantial increase in the labor force level. The increase resulted in corresponding growth in annual increments and the decrease in the linear coefficient (or sensitivity) in relationship (9). Thus, the sensitivity of the inflation to the new measure of labor force (or new units of measurement) in Austria decreased. This does not mean that the observed inflation path has changed, but, if to use relationship (8) for the second period, the inflation would be overestimated, as shown in Figure 8. The deviation between the two predicted curves after 1986 demonstrates the importance of the changes in definition for quantitative modeling of economic parameters.

The two predicted curves are in a good agreement with the actual inflation readings within relevant periods. A prominent feature is an almost complete coincidence between 1968 and 1975, when the highest changes in the inflation rate were observed: from 0.027 in 1968 to 0.095 in 1973, and back to 0.056 in 1975. Conventional inflation models, including the Phillips curve, the NKPC or any other model using autoregressive properties of inflation, fail to describe such a dynamic behavior as a rule. They require introduction of some artificial, i.e. based on various invalidated assumptions, features such as structural breaks. Another opportunity used in conventional models is to split corresponding time series into two segments before and after such inflation peak, as was observed in Austria in 1973. Our model describes the whole period without any difficulty and the best description of the inflation is achieved during the period of the largest changes. This provides the best evidence of an adequate modeling by relationship (8).

Similar conclusion is valid for the period after 1987, where an excellent timing and amplitude correspondence is observed between the measured inflation and that predicted according relationship (9). In addition, there is a transition period between 1982 and 1987, where neither of relationships (8) and (9) is expected to be accurate due to the reported changes in the labor force definition.

A quantitative measure of the agreement between the observed and predicted curves is provided by a linear regression analysis. Table 1 lists standard deviation for the NAC GDP deflator time series between 1965 and 2003, stdev=0.022 (2.2%). The inflation computed according to (8) and (9) is used as a predictor and results in R^2= 0.81 and stdev=0.01 (1%). Hence, the prediction based on the labor force explains 81% of variation in the original inflation series. Standard deviation could be considered as an equivalent of root mean square forecasting error (RMSFE) – for "in-sample" forecasts in the case of Austria. For the USA, R^2=0.62 and stdev=0.014 for the original annual readings of GDP deflator and labor force covering the same period (Kitov, 2006d). Perhaps, the Austrian labor force and inflation measurements are characterized by a higher accuracy.

A number of simple measures is proposed by Kitov (2006d) in order to improve the quality of labor force measurements and to obtain more reliable statistical estimates. Due to the lack of information on quantitative characteristics of the revisions applied to the Austrian labor force series, similar to that available for the USA, we cannot correct for probable step revisions. Thus, a natural next step is to apply a moving average technique. A two-year moving average suppresses the noise associated with the labor force measurements and also removes the shift in timing between the inflation and labor force readings - by definition, annual values of labor force correspond rather to July than to December. Averaging over two years effectively moves the center of the measurement period to December. Table 1 represents the results of a linear regression when two-year moving average is applied to the labor force and inflation. Averaging of the labor force solely before usage in relationships (8) and (9), results in R^2=0.85 and stdev=0.009. When both variables are averaged in two-year windows, R^2=0.88 and stdev=0.007. These results quantitatively evidence an excellent predictive power of relationship (8) and (9) over the entire period between 1965 and 2003. If to recall that the period between 1983 and 1986 is poorly modeled due to the turbulence in the labor force definitions, one can expect that further improvements in the accuracy of the labor force measurements are possible, which might lead to a higher confidence as presented by statistical estimates.

Regression of the cumulative curves is characterized by R^2=0.999 and stdev=0.0011. Thus, one can precisely replace the inflation cumulative curve or, in other words, inflation index with that obtained from the labor force measurements. This substitution is a reciprocal one– it is possible to exactly estimate the total increase in the labor force between 1965 and 2003 by measuring the GDP inflation.

Currently, inflation is Austria, as represented by the NAC GDP deflator, is close to 2%, as explicitly defined by the monetary policy adopted by the European System of Central Banks (ECB, 2004) and correspondingly by the Austrian National Bank (OeNB, 2005). The inflation obeys the revealed dependence on the labor force change as well. Hence, the new monetary policy oriented to price stability does not disturb the relationship describing the last 40 years of the Austrian inflation.

Linear relationship (9) obtained for the current period implies that one per cent of the labor force change produces inflation of 2%=1.25%+0.75%, where 0.75% is the persistent inflation level, i.e. the inflation existing even when no labor force change is observed. Thus, an annual change in labor force of +1% produces the OeNB's target inflation.

Obviously, labor force change in Austria is affected not only by the OeNB's monetary policy. There are demographic, social, political, economic processes behind the change. Therefore, it is probable that the labor force will change in future in a way not matching the target inflation. In the case of a decrease in the labor force, a deflationary period is probable starting from -0.6% annual labor force change rate, as relationship (9) defines: 1.25*(-0.006) +0.0075=0.

Labor force participation rate is stable in Austria during the last ten years and close to 59% (the OECD definition). If this tendency holds in future, the labor force will be defined by the level of the population of 15 years of age and above. Statistics Austria (2006) provides a good population projection and corresponding approximation for this variable as a sum of the population aged between 15 and 60 years and that above 60 years as presented separately:

Year	**From 15 to 60 years of age**	**>60 years of age**	**Total**
2004	5059	1789	6848
2010	5112	1928	7040
2015	5120	2053	7173

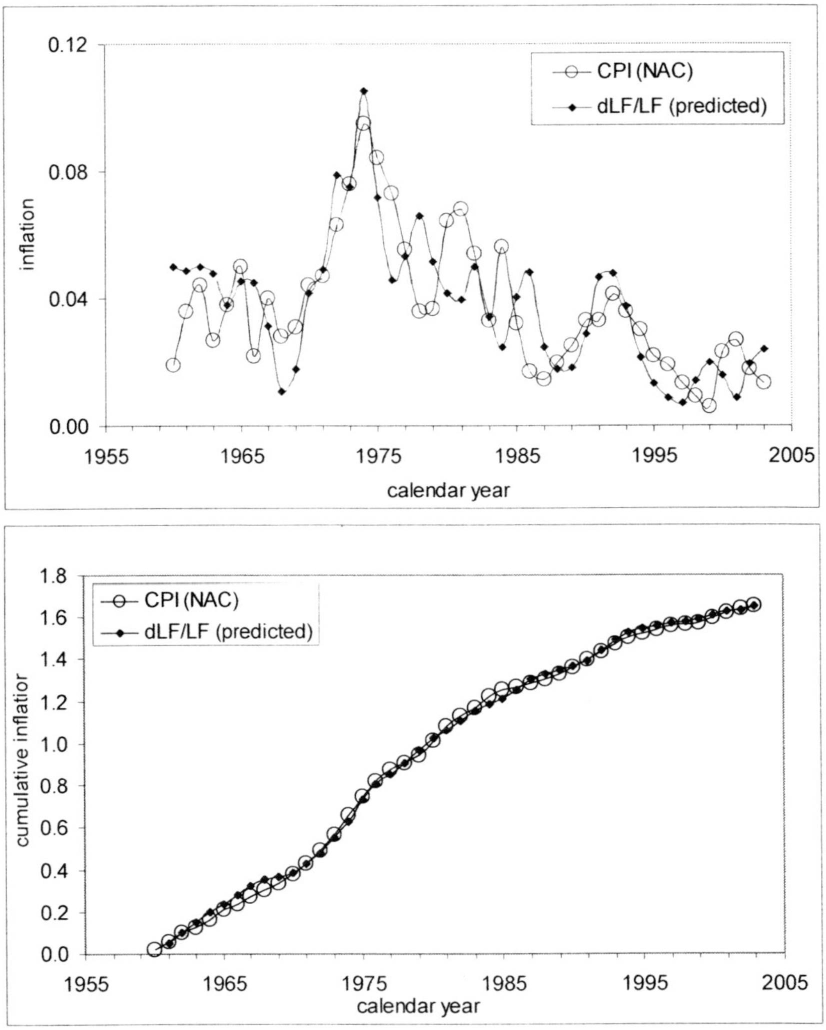

Figure 9. Comparison of the observed (NAC CPI) and predicted inflation in Austria. The upper frame displays annual readings and the lower one – cumulative inflation since 1960. Notice a major change in labor force definition between 1981 and 1987 (OECD, 2005). The periods before and after 1986 are described separately.

The population above 15 years of age will grow by 2.8% between 2004 and 2010 and by another 1.9% during the following five years. The mean growth rate of 0.4% per year provides a 1.2% inflation growth rate during the next ten years. The value is below the 2% target and the Austrian monetary authorities have to provide an approximately 0.8% average annual growth in the participation rate, i.e. from 59% in 2005 to 67% in 2015. Otherwise, the target inflation rate will not be matched.

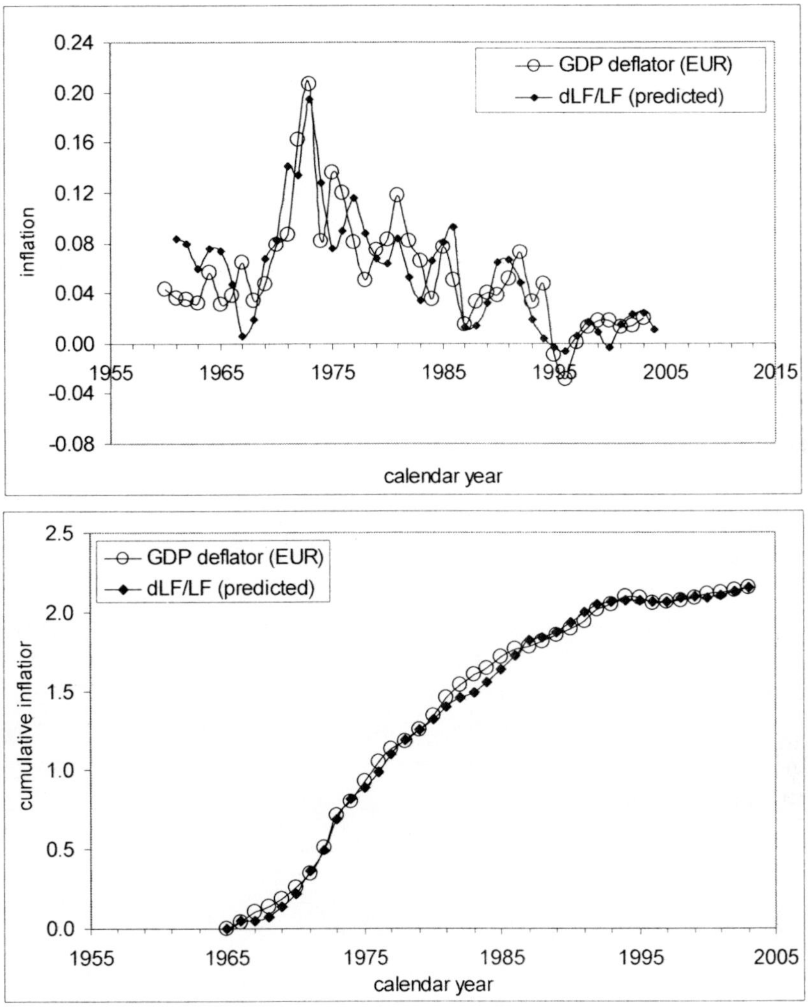

Figure 10. Comparison of the observed (EUR GDP deflator) and predicted inflation in Austria. The upper frame displays annual readings and the lower one – cumulative inflation since 1965. Notice a major change in labor force definition between 1981 and 1987 (OECD, 2005). The periods before and after 1986 are described separately.

Figures 9 and 10 show the results of a similar analysis for the other two measures of inflation: the NAC CPI and the GDP deflator calculated at the exchange rate to Euro. The NAC CPI readings are very close to those obtained for the NAC GDP deflator. Therefore, coefficients in relationship (1) are also close: A_1=2, A_2=0.0315 before 1986, A_1=1.35, A_2=0.0095 after 1986. The linear relationships for the EUR GDP deflator readings are characterized by larger coefficients: A_1=4, A_2=0.047 before 1986, A_1=2.5, A_2=0.00 after 1986. Results of the regression analysis are presented in Table 1.

The CPI time series is characterized by stdev=0.022 for the period between 1965 and 2003, which is equal to the standard deviation related to the NAC GDP deflator series. At the same time, a linear regression of the CPI NAC against the predicted inflation results in a lower R^2=0.60 and larger stdev=0.014. Therefore, even small differences between the GDP deflator and CPI, as defined by correlation coefficient 0.92, result in a large difference in statistical estimates.

The Eurostat GDP deflator demonstrates a higher scattering: stdev=0.046 for the period between 1965 and 2003. Correspondingly, R^2=0.66 and stdev=0.027, i.e. much poorer than the results shown by the NAC GDP deflator. Especially, it concerns the high standard deviation, which is by a factor of 2.5 larger than that for the NAC GDP deflator. However, if normalized to standard deviation of corresponding inflation series, i.e. to 0.014/0.022=0.64 and 0.027/0.046=0.59, the relative volatility does not differ much in the cases of the NAC and Eurostat GDP deflators. The two-year moving average technique provides a gradual improvement on the results of the regression of the annual values, as presented in Table 1.

It is confirmed above that both inflation and unemployment in Austria are linear functions of labor force change rate with no time lag. There is no need to apply generalized relationship (3) to the data in order to balance some potential disturbances, which might be induced by the ESCB fixed inflation rate. Relationships (1) and (2) work excellent separately and its sum should also work well. There is another issue associated with usage of (3), however. Measurement errors make prediction of the annual time series unreliable during the periods of weak changes in defining parameters, i.e. when the change in labor force is lower than the accuracy of the labor force measurements. In such a situation, the observed change is statistically insignificant, as we have obtained for the unemployment. Relationship (3) provides a potential way to improve the match. All the involved variables have almost independent measurement errors. Thus, one can expect an additional destructive interference of the errors when the variables are used together, such as relationship (3) defines.

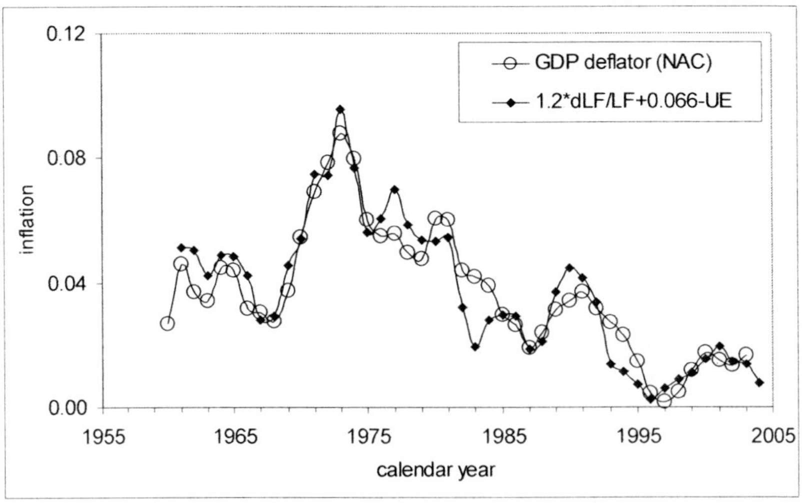

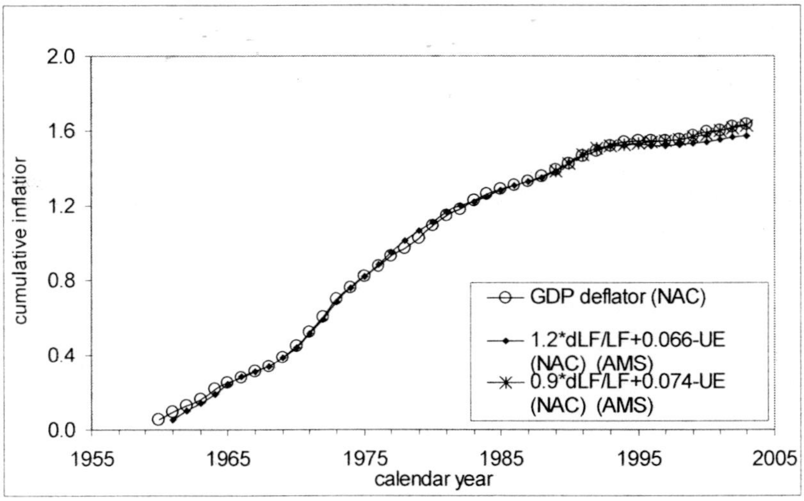

Figure 11. Comparison of the observed (NAC GDP deflator) and predicted inflation in Austria. The upper frame displays annual readings and the lower one – cumulative inflation since 1960. The predicted inflation is a linear function of the labor force change and unemployment as defined by relationship (3). Notice the absence of the major change in 1986 due to effective compensation of the labor force change by the unemployment. There is a slight discrepancy started in 1994 with corresponding change in linear coefficient and intercept, as described by the relationships in the lower right corner of the lower frame.

Figure 11 displays the observed and predicted inflation. The former is presented by the NAC GDP deflator. The latter is obtained using relationship (3) with coefficients computed for the case of the predictor based on the NAC (AMS+HSV) labor force and the AMS unemployment. This representation of inflation is less sensitive to the changes in the unemployment and labor force definitions. In fact, the unemployment is a part of the labor force and any change in unemployment is automatically included into the labor force change, but the changes in the unemployment and employment definitions are not synchronized. The latter observation makes the changes in the labor force and unemployment also to be asynchronous. In any case, the agreement between the predicted and observed curves is remarkable over the whole interval between 1965 and 2003.

There is a small deviation starting in 1994, however, as the cumulative curves in Figure 11 show. One can explain the discrepancy as associated with the change in the employment definition in 1994 - the time criterion was decreased to 1 hour, as mentioned above. Obviously, the change resulted in the increase of the overall labor force level and corresponding change rate. In addition, the labor force survey procedures, including population coverage and timing, were changed and Statistik Austria became responsible for the labor force estimates in line with the Eurostat and ILO definitions since 1994 (Statistik Austria, 2004). These modifications could result in the observed change of the inflation sensitivity to the labor force change due to the introduction of new units of measurements. So far, the inflation in Austria (in all the three representations) was modeled for the period after 1986 separately. The difference between units of measurement in the 7-year long interval between 1987 and 1994 and during the nine years after 1994 was so weak that is could not be resolved using the short intervals. The difference was balanced in (9), i.e. a small overestimation of inflation in the first interval was compensated by a small underestimation during the second period. The generalized approach has a higher resolution because of longer baselines: 29 years between 1965 and 1994 and 9 years between 1994 and 2003. Therefore, the deviation between two branches has been revealed and successfully modeled by the introduction of new coefficients in the generalized linear relationships after 1994:

$$\pi(t)=1.2*dLF(t)/LF(t)-UE(t)+0.066 \quad (1965\leq t\leq 1994) \qquad (10)$$

$$\pi(t)=0.9*dLF(t)/LF(t)-UE(t)+0.0074 \quad (t\geq 1995) \qquad (11)$$

The predicted values of inflation according to relationships (10) and (11) with the NAC labor force and the AMS unemployment are used as a predictor for a linear regression of the NAC GDP readings. For the annual readings between 1965 and 2003, Table 1 lists the following values: R^2=0.86 and stdev=0.008. This is an outstanding result considering the uncertainty associated with the measurement of the inflation, labor force, and unemployment. The predictor explains 86% of inflation variation including the periods of high and low inflation, and the periods of intensive growth and decrease of the inflation, as presented in Figure 11. The choice of 1965 is arbitrary and an extension of the period to 1960 does not change R^2 much - it drops to 0.84. Standard error of the regression is only 0.008. The slight improvement in statistical description related to usage of (3) instead of (1), as expressed by R^2 increase from 0.81 to 0.86 for the annual readings, is apparently related to a stabilizing role of the unemployment readings. Averaging in two-year moving windows provides almost no additional improvement in statistical estimates. When the predicted values are averaged, R^2=0.87 and stdev=0.008. When both observed and predicted readings are averaged, R^2=0.91 and stdev=0.007. In any case, generalized relationship (3) provides a very accurate description of inflation in Austria between 1960 and present.

In this Section, we have scrupulously considered details of the procedures related to measurements in order to obtain the best agreement between the observed and predicted values. As a result we have obtained a very accurate, in statistical sense, description of unemployment and inflation in Austria during the last 45 years. In addition, a prediction of inflation for the next ten years has been computed using population projections provided by Statistik Austria. We have also learned several important lessons for future investigations:

- Data related to labor force and unemployment needs special consideration because of numerous revisions of definitions and procedures.
- There is not break or any other discontinuity in inflation behavior around its peak and trough values. Linear dependence of inflation and unemployment on labor force change is very consistent and reliable over time.
- The larger is the amplitude of inflation (unemployment) change the better is its prediction based on labor force change. An alternative opportunity to increase resolution is to improve accuracy of corresponding measurements.
- The GDP deflator is the best representation of inflation, at least in Austria and the USA.

- The generalized linear relationship linking together inflation, unemployment, and labor force potentially provides an additional improvement in prediction of inflation.
- Quantitatively, the best fit model of inflation in Austria is characterized by R^2=0.86 and RMSFE=0.008, as obtained for the period between 1965 and 2003.

Concluding this Section, it is worth noting that Austria provides a good opportunity not only to model the dependence between inflation, unemployment, and labor force change, but also evaluate consistency of various definitions of the studied variables. Despite the documented changes in units of measurements, the variables do not lose their intrinsic links persistent through the last 45 years. There is no reason to think that these bounds will disappear in the near future.

3. France

France is characterized by an outstanding productivity and has the largest GDP per working hour among large developed economies, as presented by the Groningen Growth and Development Center and Conference Board (2006). At the same time, real economic performance in France is far from a stellar one during the last twenty-five years with the mean annual real GDP growth of 2%. Therefore, France is an example of an economy different in many aspects from those in the USA, Japan, and Austria. This is especially important for the concept we examine. Linear relationships (1) and (2) with country specific coefficients are supposed to be intrinsic ones to any developed economy and to express deep socio-economic bounds between people. In turn, the linear relationship for inflation does not depend on such parameters of real economy as output gap, marginal labor cost, and so on.

OECD (2005) provides relatively long time series for the variables involved in the study: GDP deflator (between 1971 and 2004), CPI based on the national currency (between 1956 and 2004), labor force level (between 1956 and 2004), unemployment rate (between 1960 and 2004), working age population (between 1960 and 2004), and labor force participation rate (from 1960 to 2004). Inflation estimates are also available at the web-sites of Eurostat- the Euro based CPI between 1979 and 2005, and at the National Institute for Statistics and Economic Studies (INSEE)- http://www.incee.fr.

There are three different measures of inflation in France shown in Figure 12: the OECD CPI, the CPI based on the Euro, and the OECD GDP deflator. The time series for CPI and GDP deflator published by the INSEE (2006) almost coincide with those provided by OECD and Eurostat and start from 1983 as a rule. Therefore, they are not presented in the Figure. The OECD GDP deflator and CPI inflation are very similar with only relatively small discrepancies during some short intervals. These curves show a high inflation rate between 1975 and 1985 and a gradual decrease to the current level close to 2%.

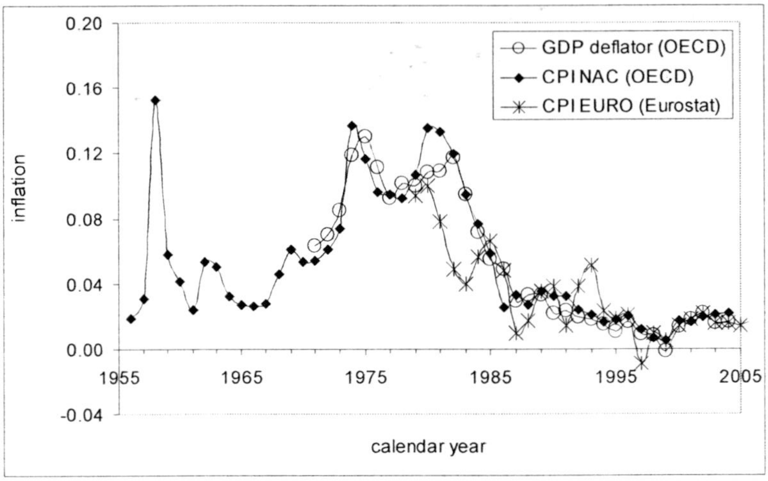

Figure 12. Comparison of various measures of inflation in France. There are three time series: GDP deflator and CPI based on national currency obtained from the OECD web-site and CPI inflation based on the exchange rate to Euro, as given by Eurostat. The GDP deflator and CPI NAC time series start from 1971 and 1956, respectively. The CPI EURO starts from 1979.

Only two measures of inflation from the three available are modeled in the study. The Eurostat CPI based on the Euro is limited in time and volatile due to the exchange rate fluctuations. So, this time series is neglected. GDP deflator is probably the best variable reflecting inherent links between inflation and labor force change, as found for the USA, Japan, and Austria. So, our primary goal is to model the GDP deflator provided by the OECD. The OECD CPI time series is also predicted for a comparison. CPI is of a lower interest for our study because it hardly represents a valid economic parameter to model in our framework.

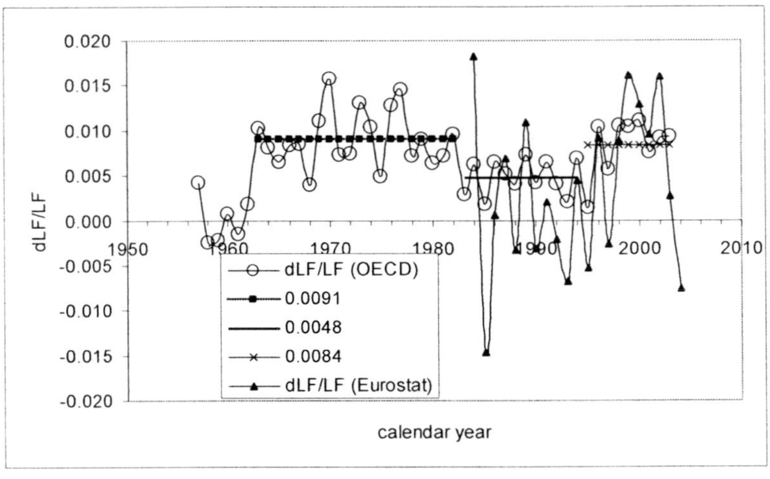

Figure 13. Labor force change rate in France as given by the OECD and Eurostat. The OECD time series starts from 1956 and the Eurostat's one - in 1983. The latter curve is characterized by higher fluctuations. The mean growth rates of the OECD labor force are also shown for three different periods as defined in the text. Notice a period of strong growth started in 1996.

Figure 13 displays the principal variable of the model – labor force change rate, *dLF/LF*, in France for the period between 1956 and 2004. The Eurostat web-site also publishes time series for the number of unemployed (1983 through 2004) and employed (1978 through 2004) separately. The sum of the two series gives a labor force estimate between 1983 and 2004 also presented in Figure 13. Because of the limited interval spanned by the Eurostat labor force series and its high volatility of unknown origin only the OECD labor force readings are used to predict unemployment and inflation rate.

The OECD labor force series can be split into several distinct periods. From 1958 to 1963, a very low and even negative change rate was observed, which is potentially associated with statistical definitions or methodology of measurements in the past. From 1963 through 1981, a strong labor force growth was measured with the mean annual rate of +0.94%. A relatively slow growth between 1982 and 1995 with the mean annual rate of +0.48% is followed by a new period of a strong growth started in 1996 with the mean annual rate of +0.84%. According to the linear relationships under study, inflation and unemployment have to evolve in the same way. It is interesting that the recent increase in the labor force has not been accompanied by any visible change in the inflation, as Figure 12 evidences.

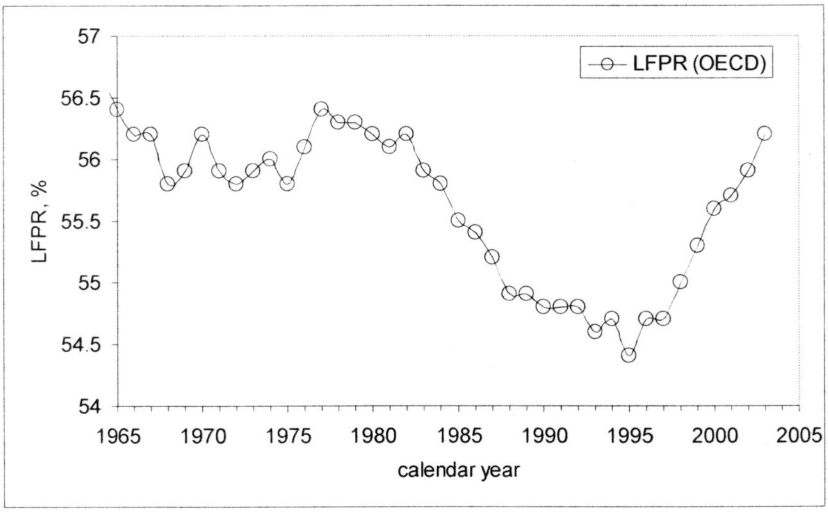

Figure 14. Labor force participation rate in France as defined by OECD for the population above 15 years of age. There was a long period of a gradual decrease in LFPR between 1975 and 1995 when the lowermost level was measured -54.4%. In 1996, a period of strong growth started with the average annual increment of ~0.2%. In 2004, the LFPR reached 55.7%.

Taking into consideration a gradual decrease in the rate of working-age population growth in France (OECD, 2006), one can expect an intensive growth of labor force participation rate (LFPR) started in 1996 to be responsible for the rapid increase in the labor force. Figure 14 proves that the expected strong growth in the LFPR has been an actual and consistent one since 1996. During the previous forty years, the participation rate in France was as low as 55% compared to 59% in the USA and above 60% in Japan. So, it is natural that the participation rate in France has started to grow at some point.

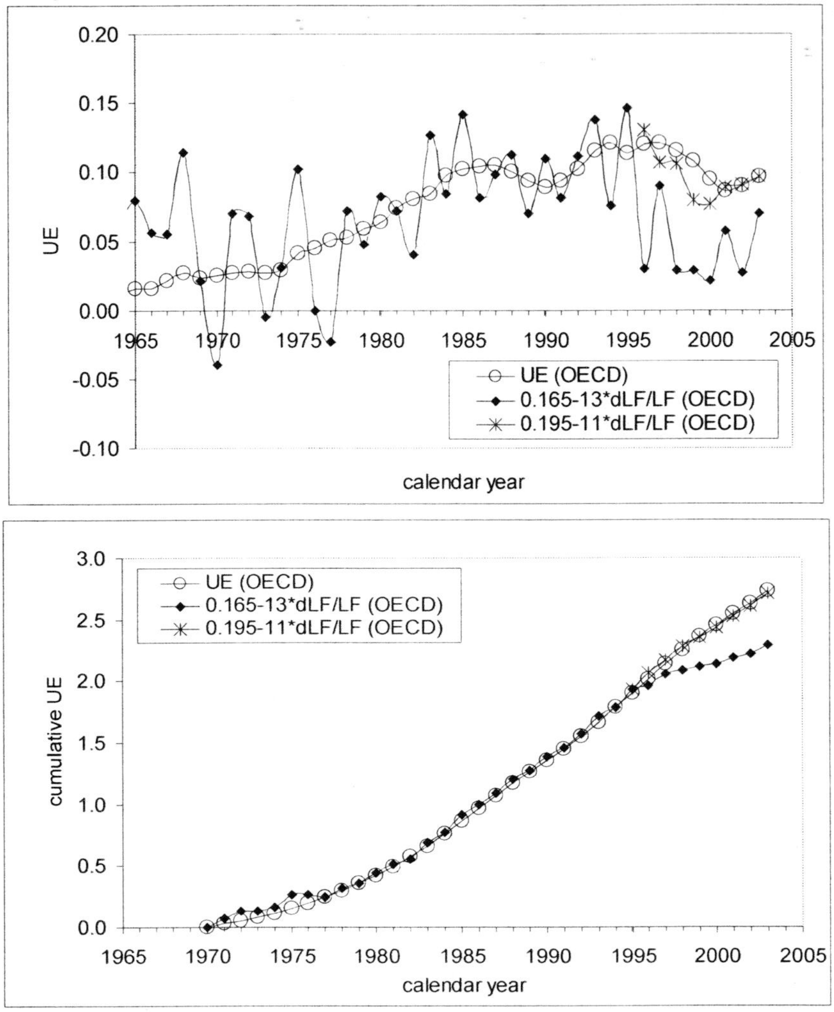

Figure 15. Comparison of the observed and predicted unemployment in France: the upper frame for the annual readings and the lower for the cumulative values of the unemployment since 1970. There is no time lag between the unemployment and labor force change. Notice the discrepancy started in 1996 – the year when the labor force participation rate started to grow fast, and two years after the Banque de France obtained a new status and introduced a new monetary policy - price stability. The predicted unemployment is about twice as low as the observed one, as presented in the upper panel. The period after 1996 can be described by a different dependence of the unemployment on the labor force with a higher intercept (0.195) and a lower (in absolute value) linear coefficient (-11), as given in the legend. Results of corresponding regression analysis are given in Table 2.

The current period of the labor force growth almost coincides with the establishment of a new entity of the French national bank, Banque de France, as an independent monetary authority having a fixed target value of inflation rate. In 1993, the European System of Central Banks (ESCB) cardinally changed its approach to inflation managing – the main target is currently to reach price stability at a level near 2% of annual growth (ECB, 2004). Whatever reasons are put forth to justify the new approach they are not theoretically and empirically sound, i.e. there are no reliable evidences for the assumptions underlying the current concepts of inflation to be valid. The most recent models rely on exogenous shocks as the driving force behind inflation (Rudd and Whelan, 2005; GG (1999); Gali *at al.*, 2002, 2005; Hall, 2005). Such shocks are inherently unpredictable and uncontrollable in time and amplitude. So, the approach based on an aggregated opinion of central bankers and economists is barely valid in view of unpredictable exogenous shocks. Our concept provides a clear understanding of the nature of these exogenous forces and thus a control over unemployment and inflation.

For France, as for the US, Japan, and Austria we use the same procedure to fit annual and cumulative inflation and unemployment readings by linear functions of labor force change rate. The most sensitive to coefficients in relationship (1) is a cumulative curve. Even a small systematic error in predicted amplitude cumulates to a high value when aggregated over thirty-five years. Predicted and measured annual and cumulative curves for the OECD unemployment rate between 1970 and 2004 are presented in Figure 15.

The predicted curve in Figure 15a is obtained from the OECD labor force change rate and shows large-amplitude fluctuations around the measured unemployment curve. This is a result of a very large coefficient in the relationship between $UE(t)$ and $dLF(t)/LF(t)$:

$$UE(t)=0.165-13*dLF(t)/LF(t) \qquad (12)$$

Linear coefficient in (12) amplifies labor force change and any measurement error in the labor force by a factor of 13. This coefficient is also a negative one, i.e. any increase in labor force is converted in a synchronized (no time lag between the labor force and the unemployment change) and 13-time amplified drop of the unemployment rate in France. On the other hand, in the absence of any growth in the labor force the unemployment rate reaches a 16.5% level. (The high sensitivity of the unemployment to the labor force change provides a good opportunity to control the unemployment through a reasonable labor market policy. At the same time, the high sensitivity demands any such a policy to be thoroughly and deeply discussed before implementation.) From 1970 through 1995, there is a good agreement between the observed and predicted curves. The period before 1970 is neglected in the study. As we have learned from the case of Austria, the earlier period is characterized by some changes in the methodology of labor force survey and/or the definitions of labor force itself. The model period after 1970 is also in line with many other studies devoted to the modeling of various Phillips curves in European countries, where the period before 1970 is rarely covered (see Angelini *et al.* (2001); Canova, F., (2002), Cristadoro *et al.* (2001); Espasa *et al.* (2002); Gali *et al.* (2001), Ihrig and Marquez (2003); Marcellino *et al.* (2001); Hubrich (2005), among others).

The observed unemployment curve gradually elevates from 3% in 1970 to almost 10% in 2004, with the predicted curve fluctuating around the observed one with an amplitude reaching 0.1. In 1996, a sudden drop in the predicted curve started a major deviation from the measured curve. The predicted curve falls from 10% in 1996 to 4% in 2003. It is possible to compute the total number of unemployed people who could get paid jobs under the theoretical curve in excess of the measured number: 4%*27,000,000~1,000,000 per year. Thus, approximately one million less than expected persons have job in France every year since 1996.

There are three potential explanations of the deviation. The first one is associated with a probable change in unit of measurements, as has been found for Austria. There is no documented change in the labor force and unemployment definitions in the 1990s in France, however. Therefore, this explanation is not working for France. The second possibility is that coefficients in relationship (12) were changed in 1996 by some external forces to new values, but the linear link to labor force is retained. We have discussed such a situation is Section 1 and suggested that generalized relationship (3) has to replace individual relationships (1) and (2). We will examine this assumption in detail later on. The third explanation is that there is no linear relationship between unemployment, inflation, and labor force and the deviation started in 1996 is unpredictable and spontaneous.

A standard linear regression analysis is carried out for the period between 1970 and 1995. The OECD unemployment rate is a dependent variable and the theoretical curve is used as a predictor. Table 2 lists some results of the analysis. The measured time series is characterized by stdev=0.032. As expected from the high volatility in the annual readings of the predictor (see Figure 15a) corresponding regression gives R^2=0.48 with stdev=0.023. Hence, the annual time series is poorly predicted.

Figure 15b represents a cumulative view on the predicted and observed unemployment in France. This view emphasizes the deviation started in 1996. The cumulative curves provide a good way to demonstrate that the oscillations in the predicted curve are induced by some uncorrelated measurement errors, not by actual change. At the same time, the curves definitely show some problematic years in the beginning of the period. Overall, the curves almost coincide and confirm the reliability of the linear relationship between *UE(t)* and *dLF(t)/LF(t)*. A linear regression of the cumulative curves gives R^2=0.998 and stdev=0.028.

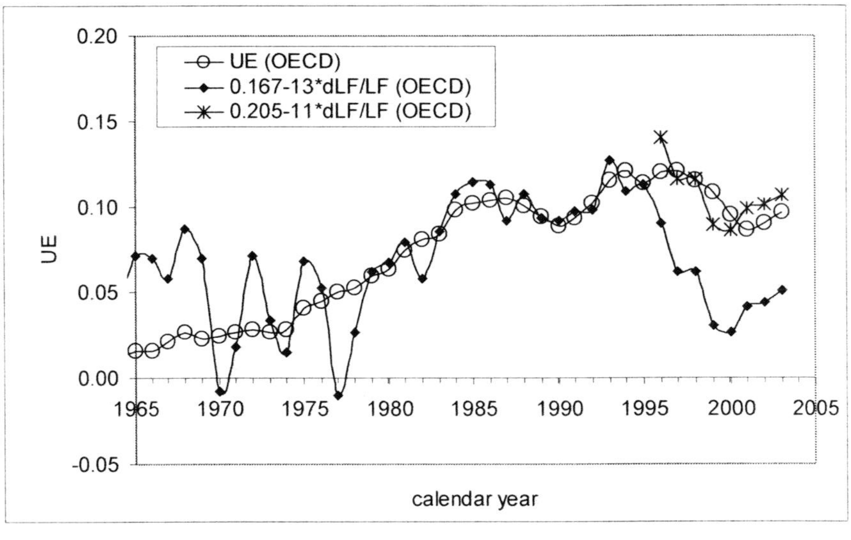

Figure 16. Same as in Figure 15a, but with the predicted curve smoothed by a 2-year moving average. There is a better agreement between the observed and predicted time series, especially between 1978 and 1995. Notice a slightly higher intercept 0.167 instead of 0.165 for the annual readings in Figure 15.

Table 2. Results of linear regression analysis for France

Period	Dependent variable	Predictor	A	B	R^2	stdev
1970-1995	annual unemployment (OECD)					0.032
1970-1995	annual unemployment (OECD)	annual dLF(t)/LF(t) (OECD)	0.45 (0.10)	0.04 (0.008)	0.48	0.023
1970-1995	annual unemployment (OECD)	2-year moving average dLF(t)/LF(t) (OECD)	0.71 (0.08)	0.02 (0.006)	0.75	0.016
1970-1995	annual unemployment (OECD)	5-year moving average dLF(t)/LF(t) (OECD)	1.00 (0.07)	0.000 (0.005)	0.90	0.010
1970-1995	cumulative unemployment (OECD)	cumulative dLF(t)/LF(t) (OECD)	1.01 (0.009)	0.04 (0.001)	0.99 8	0.028
1971-1999	GDP deflator (OECD)					0.042
1971-1999	annual GDP deflator (OECD)	annual dLF(t-4)/LF(t-4) (OECD)	0.48 (010)	0.03 (0.008)	0.47	0.031
1971-1999	annual GDP deflator (OECD)	2-year moving average dLF(t-4)/LF(t-4) (OECD)	0.74 (0.08)	0.01 (0.006)	0.74	0.022
1971-1999	annual GDP deflator (OECD)	3-year moving average dLF(t-4)/LF(t-4) (OECD)	0.94 (0.06)	0.001 (0.004)	0.91	0.013
1971-1999	annual GDP deflator (OECD)	7-year moving average dLF(t-4)/LF(t-4) (OECD)	1.09 (0.07)	0.01 (0.005)	0.89	0.014
1977-1999	7-year moving average GDP deflator (OECD)	7-year moving average dLF(t-4)/LF(t-4) (OECD)	0.97 (0.03)	0.001 (0.003)	0.97	0.006
1970-1999	CPI inflation (OECD)					0.043
1970-1999	annual CPI inflation (OECD)	annual dLF(t-4)/LF(t-4) (OECD)	0.50 (010)	0.03 (0.008)	0.48	0.031
1970-1999	annual CPI inflation (OECD)	2-year moving average dLF(t-4)/LF(t-4) (OECD)	0.81 (0.09)	0.01 (0.007)	0.74	0.022
1970-1999	annual CPI inflation (OECD)	3-year moving average dLF(t-4)/LF(t-4) (OECD)	1.00 (0.08)	0.000 (0.006)	0.85	0.017
1977-1999	annual CPI inflation (OECD)	7-year moving average dLF(t-4)/LF(t-4) (OECD)	1.15 (0.09)	0.01 (0.007)	0.83	0.018
1971-1999	GDP deflator (OECD)					0.042
1971-2004	annual GDP deflator (OECD)	annual dLF(t-4)/LF(t-4)-UE(t-4) (OECD)	0.89 (0.06)	0.004 (0.004)	0.88	0.014
1971-2004	annual GDP deflator (OECD)	2-year moving average dLF(t-4)/LF(t-4)-UE(t-4) (OECD)	0.91 (0.06)	0.003 (0.004)	0.87	0.015
1971-2004	annual GDP deflator (OECD)	3-year moving average dLF(t-4)/LF(t-4)-UE(t-4) (OECD)	0.97 (0.05)	0.000 (0.003)	0.93	0.011
1971-2004	annual GDP deflator (OECD)	7-year moving average dLF(t-4)/LF(t-4)-UE(t-4) (OECD)	1.03 (0.05)	0.003 (0.004)	0.93	0.011
1977-2004	7-year moving average GDP deflator (OECD)	7-year moving average dLF(t-4)/LF(t-4)-UE(t-4) (OECD)	0.99 (0.02)	0.000 (0.001)	0.99	0.004

Moving average is thoroughly used in this study in order to obtain a better agreement between the observed and predicted curves. This technique effectively suppresses the noise associated with measurement errors. Figure 16 displays the annual measured curve and that obtained by a 2-year moving average as applied to the predictor. There is a significant improvement in the predictive power of relationship (12), especially between

1978 and 1995 - the curves practically coincide. The improved overall agreement is also reflected in a higher R^2=0.75 and lower stdev=0.016, as presented in Table 2. When a 5-year moving average is applied to the predictor, R^2 increases to 0.90 and stdev falls to 0.010. Hence, moving average is very efficient in noise suppression and provides an explanation of about 90% of variation in the unemployment rate. One can not expect any further improvement beyond the level associated with some intrinsic measurement uncertainty, however. More accurate measurements of the labor force are necessary for obtaining a higher correlation between the observed and predicted time series.

According to relationship (2), inflation is also a linear function of labor force change. Figure 17 illustrates the fit between observed (the OECD GDP deflator) and predicted inflation. Figure 17a compares the measured annual values to those obtained according to the following relationship:

$$\pi(t)=17*dLF(t-4)/LF(t-4)-0.063 \quad (13)$$

where $\pi(t)$ is the inflation at time t, $LF(t-4)$ is the labor force four years before. Thus, there is a four years lag in France between the labor force change and corresponding reaction of the inflation. The linear coefficient 17 indicates that the inflation is aslo very sensitive to the labor forced change. The intercept -0.063 means that a positive labor force change rate has to be retained in order to avoid deflation. The threshold for a deflationary period is a labor force change rate of 0.0037(=0.063/17) per year. Actual change rate was consistently higher than the threshold value over the studied period, as Figure 13 demonstrates.

The predicted inflation has been rapidly increasing since 2000 according to the labor force increase started in 1996 and the four-year lag. The observed inflation has been fluctuating near 2% since 1995, however. This inflation rate is the one defined by the ECB (2004) and Banque de France (2005) as the target of monetary policy. Therefore, one might suppose that the observed inflation is fixed by some special measures applied by the ESCB such as a monetary supply constrained to real GDP growth plus 2%. The effect of the inflation rate fixed by force is expressed in the observed deviation of the predicted unemployment and inflation from those measured in France. The unemployment reacts immediately to the labor force increase started in 1996. The inflation reacts four years later. In the absence of the fixed inflation rate or price stability, the observed inflation and unemployment would follow their predicted paths: in 2004, 9% inflation would be accompanied by 4% unemployment.

Since the discrepancy between the observed and measured inflation starts in 2000, a linear regression analysis is carried out for the period between 1971 and 1999. The GDP deflator is a dependent variable and a predictor is obtained according to relationship (13). Some results of the analysis are presented in Table 2. Standard deviation of the actual time series for the studied period is 0.042. The regression of the annual readings is characterized by R^2=0.47 and stdev=0.031. R^2 is a low one and close to that obtained for the unemployment. In both cases, the reason for the low correlation is low accuracy of labor force measurements accompanied by the high sensitivity of the predicted values to the labor force change rate.

Moving average provides a more accurate representation of the labor force change rate. For the four-year lag, as observed in France, even a 7-year moving window applied to the predictor does not include the labor force readings contemporaneous to the predicted inflation. Therefore, the lag guarantees a natural "out-of-sample" inflation forecast at various time horizons - from 1 year to 4 years. Table 2 lists standard errors (deviations) and R^2, which are obtained by linear regressions with various moving averages. Obviously, the larger is forecasting horizon, i.e. the shorter is corresponding averaging window, the larger is the forecast uncertainty. On the other hand, there must be some optimal width of moving windows. For a very wide window, the readings at the left (early) side of the window introduce some additional noise rather than improve the modeled leading value. In fact, for a 2-year moving average applied to the predicted inflation R^2=0.74 and stdev=0.022, for a 3-year window R^2=0.91 and stdev=0.013, and for a 7-year window R^2=0.89 with stdev=0.014. So, the best result is obtained for the 3-year moving average, which explains 91% of variation in the original inflation time for the period between 1971 and 1999. Figure 17b demonstrates the outstanding predictive power of the 3-year moving average.

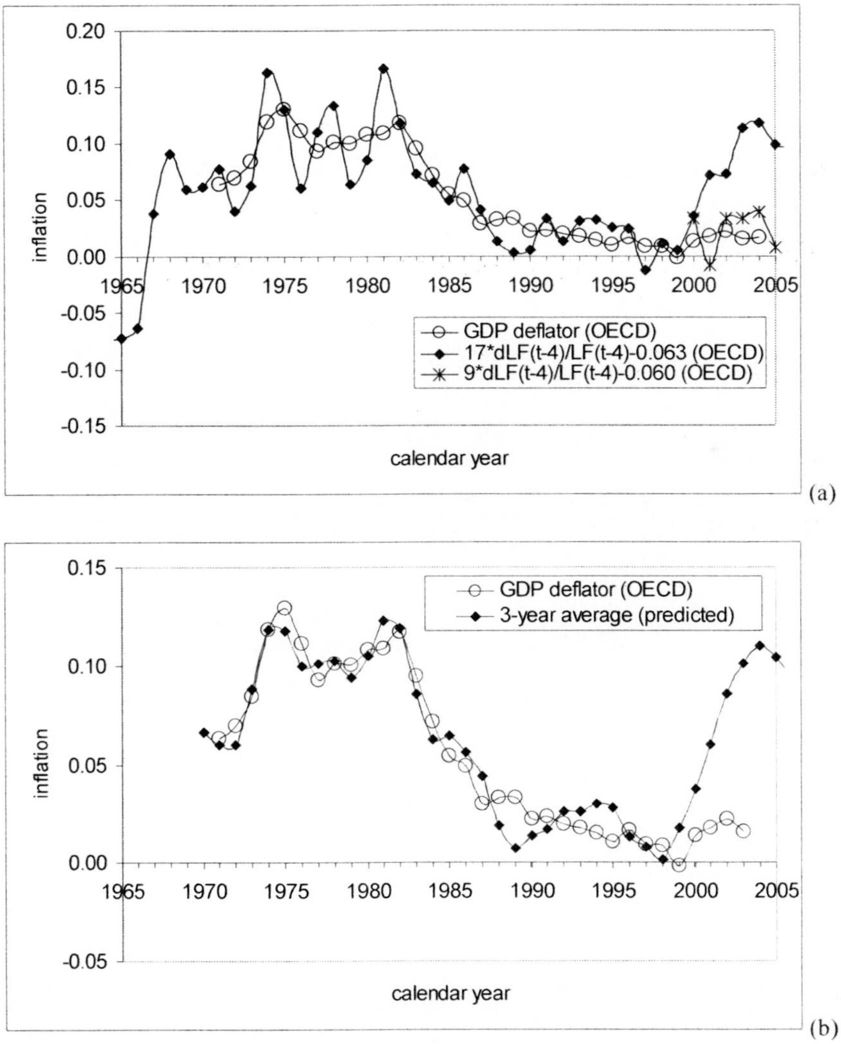

Figure 17. Continued on next page.

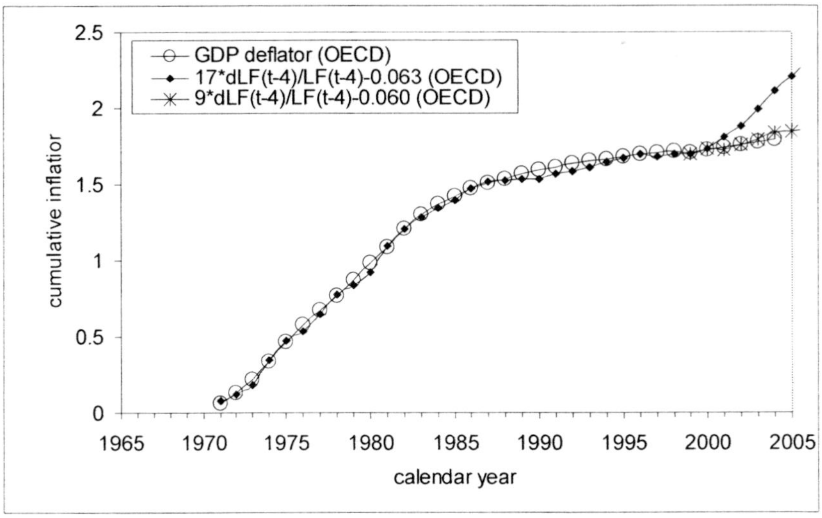

(c)

Figure 17. Comparison of the observed and predicted inflation, as defined by the relationship given in the text and in the legend (OECD GDP deflator) in France: a) annual readings, b) real annual readings and predicted readings smoothed by a 3-year moving average, c) cumulative inflation since 1970. The inflation lags by four years behind the labor force change. Notice the discrepancy started in 2000 – four years after the start of the labor force. The predicted inflation oscillates around 10% after 2000. The period after 1999 can be described by a different dependence of the GDP deflator on the labor force with a slightly larger intercept (-0.060 instead of -0.063) and a much lower linear coefficient (9 instead of 17), as given in the legend.

One can potentially reach an additional improvement on the results obtained with the 3-year moving average by using more powerful techniques for noise suppression. This is not the purpose of this study, however. We just reveal inherent links between unemployment, inflation, and labor force at a high level of confidence, as represented by R^2. Further improvements in R^2 related to the annual readings above 0.91 hardly deserve any additional effort and potentially fall into a conflict with the level of uncertainty in the inflation and labor force measurements.

In our framework, the residual difference between the observed and predicted readings is related solely to measurement errors. In France, labor force is measured with an uncertainty, which is not appropriate to the modeling of the more accurately measured unemployment and inflation. One-year long measuring baseline is not enough for obtaining a reliable estimate of labor force change rate. Moving average takes an advantage of a longer baseline for the calculation of the change rate and provides a substantial increase in the predictive power of relationships (12) and (13). Therefore, a longer basic time unit will potentially result in a higher accuracy of corresponding measurements and in a better correlation between the modeled variables. Table 2 supports this assumption by an example of a regression of 7-year moving averages of the observed and predicted inflation: R^2=0.97 and stdev=0.006. Hence, if to replace the current one-year basic interval with a seven-year long one, the inflation prediction would be as accurate as 0.006 for the period between 1971 and 1999. The same effect might be obtained by improvements in the current measuring procedures, however. There is a direct trade-off between the efforts invested in such improvements and the accuracy of predicted inflation and unemployment. Since the problem of low measurement accuracy is a resolvable one we leave it to appropriate agencies.

Figure 17c compares two cumulative curves as obtained for the measured and predicted inflation. There is a good agreement during the years between 1971 and 1999. We do not provide in Table 2 statistical estimates for the cumulative curves of inflation in France. Obviously, R^2 has to be very close to 1.0 and standard deviation is similar to that for the case of the annual readings. The cumulative curves evidence that the labor force cumulative change provides a precise measure of the inflation index growth and vice versa.

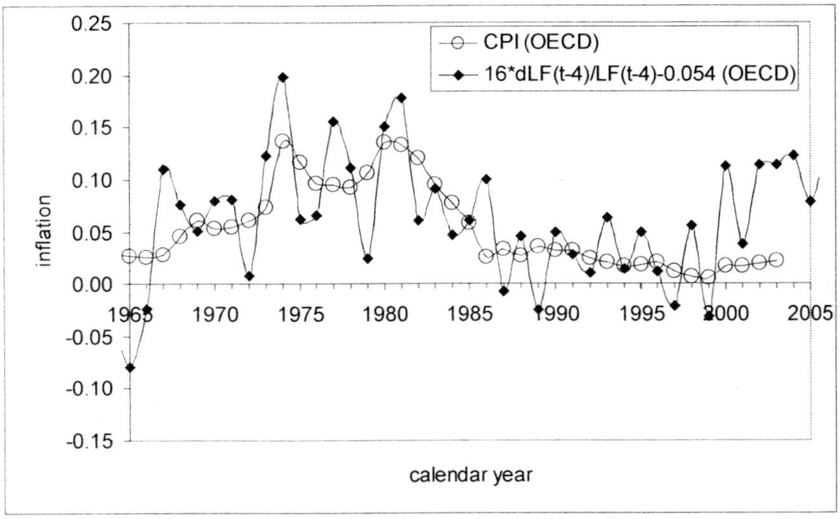

(a)

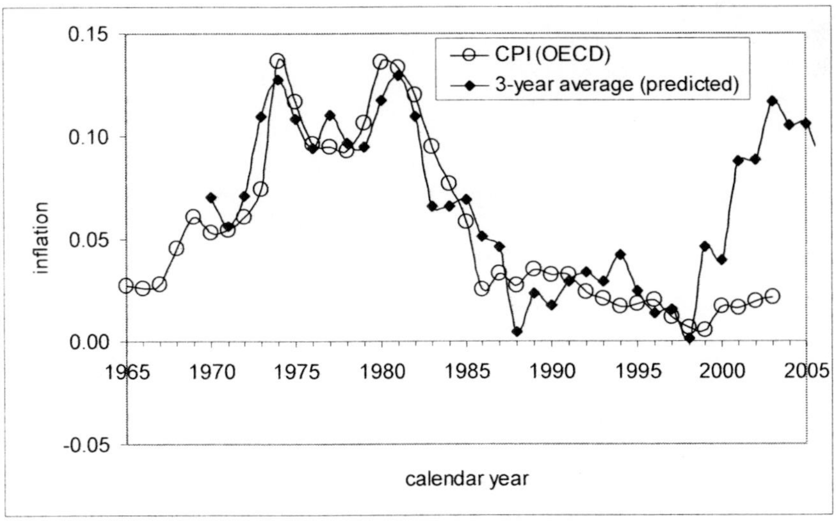

(b)

Figure 18. Continued on next page.

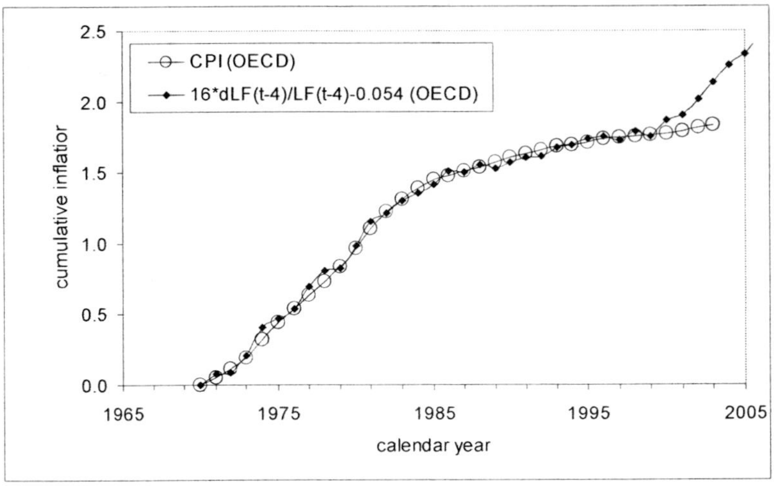

(c)

Figure 18. Same as in Figure 17, for the observed inflation expressed by the OECD CPI.

Figure 18 and Table 2 represent results of a similar analysis as applied to the OECD CPI inflation. The actual time series is characterized by standard deviation of 0.043 for the period between 1971 and 1999, which is just marginally higher than that for the OECD deflator during the same period. The best predictor for the annual readings is also obtained with a 3-year moving average: R^2=0.85 and stdev=0.017. These values indicate a slightly lower predictive power of the labor force change rate compared to that obtained for the GDP deflator. This is a common situation for the countries studied so far. GDP deflator is a consistently better measure of inflation as related to labor force change rate. Caveats in CPI definition and measuring procedures are well known and have been actively discussed since the Boskin's report (1998). Obviously, the problems associated with the uncertainty in CPI measurement lead to the poorer performance of the labor force as a predictor.

Having discussed the potentially resolvable problems associated with the uncertainty in labor force measurements, we start to tackle the problem associated with the discrepancy between the observed and predicted curves. This problem is a critical one for the concept. Potentially, the discrepancy is associated with the new monetary policy first applied by the Banque de France in the beginning of the 1990s. The policy of a constrained money supply, if applied, could obviously disturb relationships (12) and (13). New coefficients in the linear relationships are computed and presented in relevant Figures for the periods after 1995 for the unemployment after 1999 for the inflation, respectively. The coefficients are unreliable, however, due to the shortness of observations, but definitely different from the old ones. Probably, one could conclude that the Banque de France has created some new links between the unemployment, inflation, and labor force.

Our assumption is a different one. Money supply in excess of that related to real GDP growth is completely controlled by the demand of growing labor force because the excess is always accommodated in a developed economy through employment growth, which causes inflation. The latter serves as a mechanism which effectively returns personal income distribution (normalized to total population and nominal GDP growth) in the economy to its original shape (Kitov, 2006a,d). The relative amount of money that the economy needs to accommodate a given relative labor force increase through employment is constant through time in corresponding country but varies among developed countries. This amount has to be supplied to the economy, however. Central banks are responsible for this process. In the USA and Japan, central banks provide adequate procedures for money supply and individual dependence on labor force change does not vary with time both for inflation and unemployment. The ESCB limits money supply to achieve price stability. In Austria, it does not affect the individual linear relationships because actual money supply almost equals the amount required by the observed labor force growth. For France, the labor force growth is so intensive that demands a much larger money input for creation of an appropriate number of new jobs. The 2% artificial constraint on inflation (and thus money supply) disturbs relationships (12) and (13). The labor force growth induces only an increase in employment, which accommodates the given 2% inflation instead of the 9% predicted inflation. Those people who enter the labor force in France in excess of that allowed by the target inflation have no choice except to join "the army of unemployed". Hence, when inflation is fixed, the difference between observed and predicted change in the inflation must be completely compensated by an equivalent change in unemployment in excess of the predicted one. Generalized relationship (3) mathematically describes this assumption.

For France, generalized relationship is obtained as a sum of (12) and (13), which gives the following equation:

$$\pi(t)= 4*dLF(t-4)/LF(t-4)-UE(t-4)+0.095 \quad (1971<t<2004) \qquad (14)$$

where the intercept 0.095 is slightly different from that obtained as a straight sum of corresponding free terms: 0.165-0.063=0.102. The difference is dictated by the fit of the cumulative curves presented in Figure 19, which illustrates results of the generalized approach. It is important to emphasize that relationship (14) is valid for the entire interval where the OECD GDP deflator readings are available.

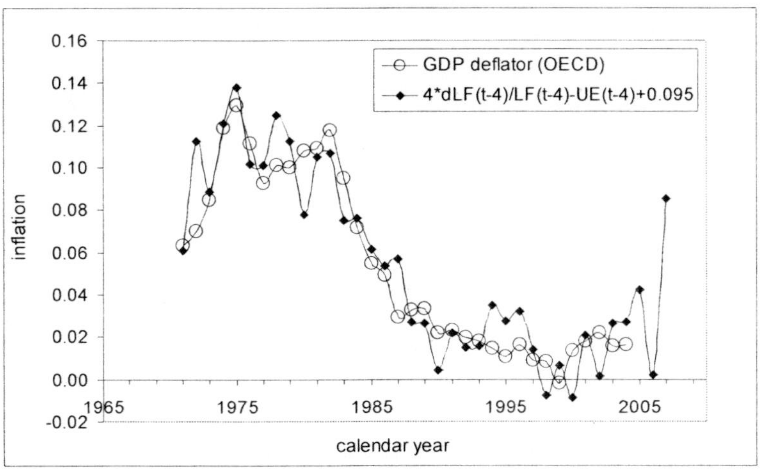

(a)

Figure 19. Continued on next page.

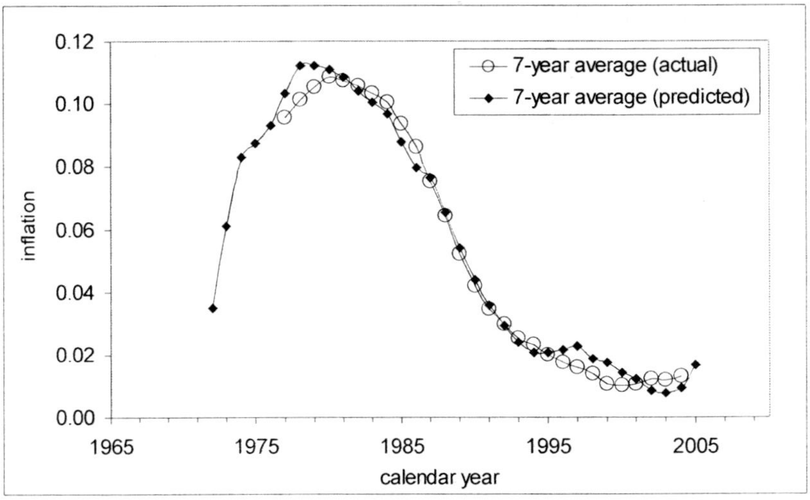

(b)

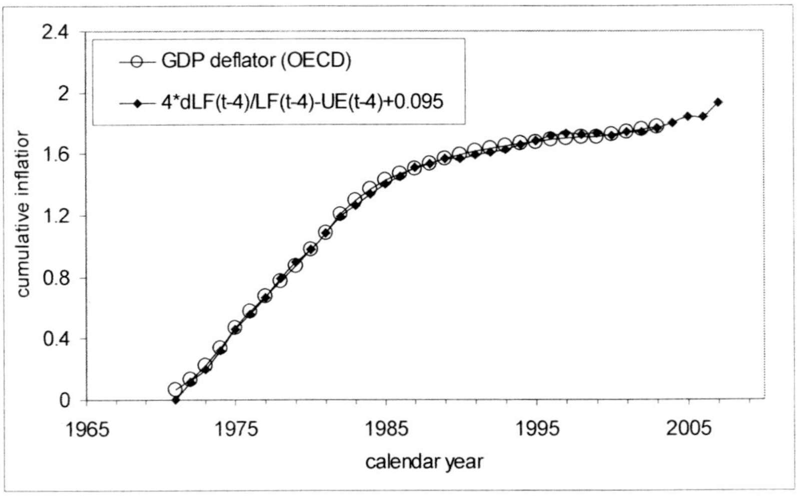

(c)

Figure 19. Comparison of the observed and predicted inflation in France a) annual readings, b) real annual readings and predicted readings smoothed by a 7-year moving average, c) cumulative inflation since 1970. The predicted inflation is a linear function of the labor force change and unemployment. There is no discrepancy starting in 2000.

Annual readings are presented in Figure 19a. A linear regression of the observed inflation against that predicted according to (14) is characterized by an outstanding for annual curves R^2=0.88 and stdev=0.014. Moving averages of the predictor provide an additional improvement on the annual results: for a 2-year moving average R^2=0.89 and stdev=0.015, for a 3-year moving average R^2=0.93 and stdev=0.011, and for a 7-year moving average R^2=0.93 and stdev=0.011 as well. These values are the best we have obtained for France so far. They explain the inflation to the extent beyond which measurement uncertainty should play a key role. Practically, there is no room for any further improvements in R^2 given the current time series. The regression results also undoubtedly prove the success of the generalized approach.

The 7-year averages displayed in Figure 19b give an additional visual evidence of the excellent predictive power of relationship (14). A linear regression of these averages during the period between 1977 and 2004 is characterized by R^2=0.99 and stdev=0.004. We have already discussed the importance of a substantial reduction in the uncertainty of the labor force measurements. The 7-year moving averages provide a good approximation of the results one can potentially obtain from the improved labor force measurements. A standard error of prediction of 0.004 and even lower might be obtained at a four-year horizon for inflation forecasts in France. Figure 19c shows cumulative curves and provide a prediction of the GDP deflator index four years beyond 2004. One can expect a slight increase in the inflation during the years if labor force estimates for the years between 2001 and 2004 are accurate. Unfortunately, the estimates are prone to potential adjustments in future than new data from the next census will be available.

In this Section, we have successfully modeled unemployment and inflation in France as a linear and lagged function of labor force change rate for a relatively long period. The unemployment is characterized by a very high and negative sensitivity to the labor force change rate, i.e. even a small increase in the labor force level leads to a substantial drop of the unemployment rate. Both variables evolve synchronously. The inflation lags four years behind the labor force change and also is very sensitive to it. This lag provides a basis for an out-of-sample inflation forecast at a four-year horizon with an accuracy of 1.0% for the whole period between 1971 and 2004. (A detailed study of the properties of GDP deflator and CPI forecast in France at various time horizons will be presented in a paper, which is currently under preparation.)

The lags and sensitivities found for the unemployment and inflation in France are quite different from those obtained for the USA, Japan, and Austria. The latter two countries are characterized by the absence of any time lags and low sensitivities. In the USA, inflation lags by two and unemployment by five years behind labor force change, with sensitivities much lower than those in France. Apparently, the variety of lags is the source of the problems with Phillips curves of various kinds. In France, inflation lags by four years behind unemployment, and in the USA - leads by three years. Nevertheless, the Phillips curve in its original form does exist because both variables are linear functions of labor force change and thus also can be linked by a linear dependence.

The high sensitivities of the inflation and unemployment to the labor force change in France require very accurate labor force measurements for a reliable modeling. Unfortunately, the OECD labor force time series does not meet this requirement and only poor statistical results are obtained for annual readings. The best agreement between observed and predicted time series is obtained with a moving average technique applied to the labor force values. For the period between 1971 and 1996, linear regression analysis provides as high values of R^2 as 0.9 for the unemployment and 0.91 for the GDP deflator for 5-year and 3-year moving average of the labor force, respectively. Corresponding standard deviations (errors) are as low as 0.010 and 0.013, respectively

As a result we have obtained a very accurate description of unemployment and inflation in France during the last 35 years. In contrast to Austria, a prediction of inflation for the next four years has been computed using only past readings of the labor force. No population projections are necessary for the inflation forecast at a four-year horizon. At longer horizons, one can use labor force forecasts. Accuracy of such long-term unemployment and inflation forecasts is proportional to the accuracy of the labor force predictions. Monetary policy of the ECB is also an important factor for the forecast because of its influence on the partition of the labor force growth between inflation and unemployment. The sum of these two variables is always a linear function of the labor force change, however. Therefore, it is for the ECB and Banque de France to decide on the partition of the labor force growth into unemployment and inflation. There is no opportunity to compensate the past high unemployment by freeing monetary supply. To achieve the predicted 4% unemployment rate a further intensive growth in labor force is necessary. Otherwise, the unemployment will be retained at its current level.

4. Conclusion

It is demonstrated at a very high level of confidence that Austria and France are characterized by linear relationships between inflation and unemployment from one side and labor force change from the other side. The best predictions explain more than 90% of observed variation in unemployment and inflation in both countries. The residual variation can hardly be explained using the data available due to intrinsic uncertainty in corresponding measurements. The relationships contain lags associated with some dynamic processes of internal transformations induced by labor force change. These lags are large and distinct in France and in the USA representing strong evidence in favor of the assumption that labor force change is the only driving force behind inflation and unemployment. This linear dependence on labor force provides a new approach to the conventional Phillips curve linking inflation and unemployment. The relationship between inflation and unemployment does exist, but the unemployment in many cases lags or leads the inflation by several years, introducing confusion in standard econometric analysis. The conventional Phillips curve does not allow inflation to lead unemployment, as it happens in the USA.

Among economic and econometric models explaining behavior of inflation and linking it to various economic parameters, including those related to behavioral characteristics of human beings, there is no one which would explain the whole variety of empirical facts. What the models lack is first principles when a simple and measurable variable drives other economic parameters. In such a case the whole set of observations aligns in a clear pattern with obvious links. In hard sciences, this is a standard situation. In economics, such first principles connecting measurable economic variables are absent so far. The new concept fills this lacuna, putting forth population characteristics as the only parameter defining all the studied macro and microeconomic characteristics.

Other concepts meet inevitable obstacles due to misspecification of actual relationships: measurable variables are substituted with unobserved or immeasurable variables. For inflation, the NKPC ends with a marginal cost which is unobservable, accelerationists rely on some natural (but theoretically undefined and empirically unobservable) level of unemployment, and "behaviorists" demand some mechanism of imperfect information processing. In fact, marginal cost, which in practice is often represented by a unit labor cost, is not only unobservable but also unpredictable in the NKPC framework as associated with exogenous productivity and supply shocks. A natural level of unemployment, which can also vary through time, seems to be rather an additional degree of freedom in the Phillips curve than a measurable parameter.

Similar problems arise in the real business cycle where real economic growth is determined mostly by exogenous productivity and supply shocks. The only positive features known about the shocks are that they are random, persistent in time, and characterized by decaying amplitude during the last 25 years. No explanation of the shocks' nature is given as to what actually leaves the question of the real growth driving force open.

All these problems have been successfully overcome in the population related models. At the same time, the developed concept does not contradict to the conventional consideration. Let us try to reverse some statements of the NKPC approach and assume that inflation is driven by some exogenous force and evolves according to some strict relationships (for example, according to the linear lagged equations obtained in this study). In a given developed country, which undergoes a permanent real and nominal economic growth, the creation and extinction of firms, change in labor force quantity, and age structure, one can always distinguish in the set of existing firms a subset of firms. This phemomena can set new prices according to some "expected" inflation change, some firms, which are able only to match previous inflation values, and some firms, which can not change prices at all. In practice, more than three groups can be distinguished and the distribution of the firms against price setting capabilities is more or less continuous. The distribution may have various shapes with only one requirement that the integral price change over the firms has to give the observed inflation value (for the sake of simplicity we presume here real economic growth to be zero). In other words, the firms are allowed to change the prices according to the inflation rate driven by the exogenous force represented by labor force change and do that through a "monopolistic competition process" whatever it means. In the framework of the NKPC, the distribution is used to estimate rigidity of nominal marginal cost. If the distribution does not change fast in time, the rigidity might be close to a constant one and the NKPC model fits the observations to the extent nominal marginal cost is represented by unit labor cost. Same is valid for sticky prices, sticky information, labor market imperfectness, etc. Corresponding characteristics can be easily obtained from the observed behavior but are only derivatives not the driving forces.

Advantages of the labor force change as the driving force for inflation are as follows:

1. What guarantees increasing accuracy of fit with development of more accurate methodology and procedures.
2. Meets requirement of the fixed personal income distribution because it directly follows from the internal redistribution in the PID.
3. Represents a part of a broader economic concept based on population characteristics.

There is a standard scientific problem associated with the applicability of some empirical relationship to a broader set of problems both in a logical and historical sense. In philosophy of science, this area of applicability can be reformulated in the principle of falsifiability, i.e. a possibility to find an example when a given relationship does not hold. In other words, this principle confines the area of applicability, where the relationship can be verified and validated. A fame example in physics is the Newton's second law, which needs to be reformulated for speeds approaching the light speed.

In economics, such a distinct point in time between periods where a given relationship holds and is not applicable is usually absent due to unidirectional evolution in time. There is no possibility to repeat the past events or to re-measure economic variables of interest if they were not measured at proper time. Thus, empirical relationships in economics lack the beginning time, as a rule. Actually, necessary observations are not conducted in a methodologically appropriate manner due to the absence of contemporaneous demand. Despite a huge amount of economic information both qualitative and quantitative accurate measurements of some fundamental economic variables are very limited in time and accuracy.

France is currently enjoying a low inflation rate due to the limitations induced by the European Monetary Union in the field of monetary policy. Due to strict rules France does not allow its people to get into employment and occupy their otherwise available positions in the personal income distribution. Money supply in the country does not meet the requirements of the natural employment growth associated with the observed labor force growth. The people entering the French labor force are forced to become unemployed. The principal question is – does it affect real economic growth? In the case of a natural behavior, i.e. the one not restricted by external non-economic rules similar to those superimposed on economies of socialist countries, real growth of an economy does not depend on inflation and vise versa. When monetary authorities artificially suppress inflation by a restricted money input one can expect a diminishing real economic growth due to the increase in unemployment above its natural level and corresponding decrease in labor force. If the labor force growth is independent, less people obtain paid jobs. Total production suffers, the economy slows down, and the personal income distribution is disturbed. All these effects are obviously country-dependent due to variation in sensitivity to inflation and unemployment resulting from labor force change. The driving force behind the sensitivities is apparently personal income distribution.

There are four countries studied so far - the USA, Japan, Austria, and France. The results obtained in the study indicate the existence of a linear link between principal economic parameters: inflation, unemployment, and labor force. However, there are many developed countries not yet studied, however. As we have learned already, every country potentially represents a unique case with specific sensitivities and lags to be determined empirically. Problems related to measurement uncertainty, especially in labor force, raise additional difficulties for the study. Therefore, future work will be focused on the largest economies such as the UK, Germany, Italy, Switzerland, Canada, etc. Results of individual cases should provide an extended basis for a comparative analysis, which may potentially help to understand the mechanisms responsible for varying sensitivities and lags.

REFERENCES

Akerlof, G., (2002). "Behavioral Macroeconomics and Macroeconomic Behavior". *American Economic Review* **92**, 411-433.

Ang, A., G. Bekaert, and M. Wei. (2005). "Do Macro Variables, Asset Markets, or Surveys Forecast Inflation Better?" manuscript, Columbia University.

Angelini, E., Henry, J. & Mestre, R. (2001). "Diffusion index-based inflation forecasts for the euro area", *ECB Working Paper* **61**, European Central Bank.

Atkeson, A., Ohanian, L.E., (2001), "Are Phillips curves useful for forecasting inflation?", *Federal Reserve Bank of Minneapolis Quarterly Review*, **25**(1), 2–11.

Ball, L., (2000). "Near Rationality and Inflation in Two Monetary Regimes". *NBER Working Paper* No. **7988**.

Ball, L., Mankiw, N.G., (2002). "The NAIRU in theory and practice", *Journal of economic Perspectives.*

Ball, L., Mankiw, N.G., Teis, R., (2005). "Monetary Policy for Inattentive Economies". *Journal of Monetary Economics* **52**, 703-725.

Friedman, M., (1968). "The Role of Monetary Policy", American Economic Review 58, 1-17.

Banque de France, (2005). "1993 A Landmark Reform Grants the Bank Independence", http://www.banque-france.fr/gb/instit/histoire/histor5.htm

Boskin, M.J., Dulberger, E.R., Gordon, R.J., Griliches, Z., Jorgenson, D.W., (1998). „ Consumer prices, consumer price index, and the cost of living" , *Journal of economic perspectives*, **12**(1), 3-26.

The Conference Board and Groningen Growth and Development Centre, (2006). Total Economy Database, May 2006, *http://www.ggdc.net"*

Canova, F., (2002). "G7 inflation forecasts", *ECB Working Paper* **151**, European Central Bank.

Census Bureau, (2002). "The Current Population Survey: Design and Methodology", Technical paper 63RV, Washington, U.S. Census Bureaus and Bureau of Labor statistics, March 2002. http://www.census.gov/prod/2002pubs/tp63rv.pdf

Census Bureau, (2004). "National Intercensal Estimates (1990-200)", *http://www.census.gov/popest/archives/methodology/intercensal_nat_meth.html*

Cristadoro, R., Forni, M., Reichlin, L. & Veronese, G., (2001). "A core inflation index for the euro area", *Temi di Discussione* **435**, Banca d'Italia.

Espasa, A., Senra, E. & Albacete, R. (2002). "Forecasting inflation in the European Monetary Union: A disaggregated approach by countries and by sectors", *European Journal of Finance* **8**(4): 402–421.

Eurostat, (2006a). "Harmonized Indices of Consumer Prices", http://epp.eurostat.ec.
europa.eu/portal/page?_pageid=1996,45323734&_dad=portal&_schema=PORTAL&screen=welcomeref&open=/&product=EUROIND_CP&depth=2

Eurostat, (2006b). "The European Labor Force Survey", *http://forum.europa.eu.int/irc /dsis/employment/info/data/eu_lfs/index.htm*

European Central Bank, (2004). "The Monetary Policy of the ECB", *http://www.ecb.int/pub/pdf/other/monetarypolicy2004en.pdf*

Gali, J., Gertler, M., (1999). "Inflation Dynamics: a Structural Econometric Approach". *Journal of Monetary Economics* **44**(2), 195-222.

Gali, J., Gertler, M., Lopez-Salido, D., (2001). "European Inflation Dynamics". *European Economic Review* **45**(7), 1237-1270.

Gali, J., Gertler, M., Lopez-Salido, D., (2005). "Robustness of the Estimates of the Hybrid New Keynesian Phillips Curve". *Journal of Monetary Economics* **52**, 1107-1118.

Gavin, W.T., Kydland, F., (1996). "Endogenous Money Supply and the Business Cycle". *FRB Working Paper* **9605**.

Gordon, R.J., (1988). "The role of wages in the inflation process", *American Economic Review, Papers and Proceedings*, **78**, 276-283.

Gordon, R.J., (1998)."Foundations of the goldilocks economy: supply shocks and the time-varying NAIRU", *Brookings papers on economic activity*, **2**, 297-346.

Groningen Growth and Development Centre and the Conference Board, (2006). Total Economy Database, May 2006, http://www.ggdc.net

Hall, R., (2005). "Separating the Business Cycle from Other Economic Fluctuations", in The Greenspan Era: Lessons for the Future, Federal Reserve Bank of Kansas City, pp. 133-179, August 2005.

Hubrich, K., (2005). "Forecasting euro area inflation: Does aggregating forecasts by HICP component improve forecast accuracy?", *International Journal of Forecasting* **21**(1): 119–136.

Ihrig, J., Marquez, J., (2003). "An empirical analysis of inflation in OECD countries", Board of Governors of the FRS, *International Finance Discussion Paper* n. **765**.

INSEE, (2006). "Consumer Price Index History", Table. *http://www.insee.fr/en/indicateur/indic_cons/french-cpi-history.asp#autres_bases*

Kitov, I., (2005a). "A model for microeconomic and macroeconomic development," *Working Papers* **05**, ECINEQ, Society for the Study of Economic Inequality.

Kitov, I., (2005b). "Modelling the overall personal income distribution in the USA from 1994 to 2002," *Working Papers* **07**, ECINEQ, Society for the Study of Economic Inequality.

Kitov, I., (2006a). "Inflation, Unemployment, Labor Force Change in the USA". *Working Papers* **28**, ECINEQ, Society for the Study of Economic Inequality.

Kitov, I., (2006b). "The Japanese economy". Available at SSRN: *http://ssrn.com/abstract=886663.*

Kitov, I., (2006c). "GDP growth rate and population". *Working Papers* **42**, ECINEQ, Society for the Study of Economic Inequality.

Kitov, Ivan, (2006d)." Exact prediction of inflation in the USA". Available at SSRN: *http://ssrn.com/abstract=916060.*

Kitov, Ivan, (2006e)." Real GDP per capita in developed countries". Available at SSRN: *http://ssrn.com/abstract=886666.*

Kydland, F., Prescott, E., (1982). "Time to Build and Aggregate Fluctuations". *Econometrica* **50** (November), 1345-1370.

Kydland, F., (2004). "Quantitative Aggregate Theory". *Nobel Prize Lecture*, December 8, 2004.

Lucas, R., (1976). "Econometric Policy Evaluation: A Critique". *Carnegie-Rochester Series on Public Policy*, **1**, 19-46.

Lucas, R., (1995). "Monetary Neutrality", Prize Lecture, *http://nobelprize.org/economics/laureates/1995/lucas-lecture.pdf*

Mankiw, N.G., (2001). "The Inexorable and Mysterious Trade-off Between Inflation and Unemployment". *The Economic Journal* **111**, C45-C61.

Mankiw, N.G., Reis, R., (2002). "Sticky Information versus Sticky prices: a Proposal to Replace the New Keynesian Phillips Curve". *Quarterly Journal of Economics* **117**, 1295-1328.

Marcellino, M., (2002). "Forecasting EMU macroeconomic variables", *Discussion Paper* **3529**, CEPR.

Marcellino, M., Stock, J. H, Watson, M. W., (2001). "Macroeconomic forecasting in the Euro area: country specific versus area-wide information", *IGIER Working paper* **201**, http://www.igier.uni-bocconi.it/

Marcellino, M., Stock, J. H, Watson, M. W., (2005). "A comparison of direct and iterated multistep AR methods for forecasting macroeconomic time series", *Journal of Econometrics*, forthcoming.

OECD, (2005). "Methodological Notes related to the OECD publication "Labor Force Statistics 1984-2004 – 2005 Edition", 24-Aug-2005, http://www.oecd.org/dataoecd/35/3/2771299.pdf

OECD, (2006). "Corporate Database Environment. Labour Databases", *http://www1.oecd.org/scripts/cde/*

OeNB, (2005). "The Eurosystem's definition of price stability", Table, *http://www.oenb.at/en/geldp_volksw/geldpolitik/ziele/definition/the_eurosystems_definition_of_price_stability.jsp*

OeNB, (2006). "Economic and Industry Indicators", Table, *http://www.oenb.at/isaweb/report.do?lang=EN&report=7.1*

Piger, J. M., Rasche, R. H., (2006). "Inflation: do expectations trump the gap?," *Working Papers* 2006-013, Federal Reserve Bank of St. Louis

Phelps, E., (1967). "Phillips Curve, Expectations of Inflation, and Optimal Inflation over Time". *Economica* **135**, 254-281.

Prescott, E., (2004). "The Transformation of Macroeconomic Policy and Research". *Nobel Prize Lecture*, December 8, 2004.

Rasche, R. H., Williams, M. M., (2005). "The effectiveness of monetary policy," *Working Papers* 2005-048, Federal Reserve Bank of St. Louis.

Rudd, J., Whelan, K., (2005). "New tests of the New Keynesian Phillips Curve. *Journal of Monetary Economics*", forthcoming.

Sargent, T., (1971). "A Note on the 'Accelerationist' Controversy". *Journal of Money, Credit, and Banking* **3**, 721-725.

Sbordone, A., (2002). "Prices and Unit Labor Cost: a New Test of Price Stickiness". *Journal of Monetary Economics* **49**(2), 265-292.

Sbordone, A., (2005). "Do Expected Future Marginal Costs Drive Inflation Dynamics?" *Journal of Monetary Economics* **52**, 1183-1197.

Staiger, D., Stock, J. H., Watson, M. W., (1997a). "How precise are estimates of the natural rate of unemployment?", in C.Romer and D.Romer (eds.): Reducing Inflation, Chicago, University of Chicago Press.

Staiger, D., Stock, J. H., Watson, M. W., (1997b). "The NAIRU, unemployment and monetary policy", *Journal of Economic Perspectives*, **11**, 33-49.

Statistik Austria, (2005). "Standard-Dokumentation. Metainformationen (Definitionen, Erläuterungen, Methoden, Qualität) zur Mikrozensus ab 2004Arbeitskräfte- und Wohnungserhebung", *http://www.statistik.at/standarddokumentation/008863.pdf#pagemode=bookmarks*

Statistik Austria, (2006). "Statistische Uebersichten. Kapitel 15. Beschaeftigung und Arbeitsmarkt". *http://www.statistik.at/statistische_uebersichten/deutsch/k15.shtml*

Stock, J. H., Watson, M. W., (1999). Forecasting inflation, *Journal of Monetary Economics* **44**: 293–335.

Stock, J. H., Watson, M. W., (2002a). "Forecasting using principal components from a large number of predictors", *Journal of the American Statistical Association* **97**: 1167–1179.

Stock, J. H., Watson, M. W., (2002b). "Macroeconomic forecasting using diffusion indices", *Journal of Business and Economic Statistics* **20**(2): 147–162.

Stock, J.H., Watson, M.W., (2003), "Forecasting output and inflation: The role of asset prices," *Journal of Economic Literature* **41**:788-829.

Stock, J. H., Watson, M. W., (2005). "Has Inflation Become Harder to Forecast," manuscript, http://ksghome.harvard.edu/~JStock/papers.htm

West, K.K., Robinson, J.G., (1999)."What Do We Know About the Undercount of Children?", US Census Bureau, Population Division *working paper* **39**, Issued August 1999. *http://www.census.gov/population/www/documentation/twps0039/twps0039.html*

In: Business Fluctuations and Cycles
Editor: T. Nagakawa, pp. 113-136
ISBN 978-1-60021-503-3

Chapter 5

THE NON-MARKET SECTOR IN EUROPE AND IN THE UNITED STATES: UNDERGROUND ACTIVITIES AND HOME PRODUCTION*

Francesco Busato[1] ***and Bruno Chiarini***[2†]
[1]Columbia University
[2]University of Napoli "Parthenope", Studi Economici, Via Medina 40, 80133 Napoli, Italy

Abstract

This paper suggests that the "home production" and the "underground" sectors are two crucial phenomena for properly understanding the European and the United States business cycles. These sectors spell out the labor reallocation mechanism between market and non-market sectors, and rely upon two important and distinguishing aspects: a different degree of family institutionalization and the incentive for individuals and firms to seek tax-free income. The analysis is fruitfully carried out by reviewing two broad classes of multi-sector dynamic general equilibrium model incorporating different informal sectors. It is surprising, but the literature on the role of informal sectors in macromodels is not large, although their implications are extremely relevant.

Journal of Economic Literature Classification Numbers: E320, E260, J22, H200.

Keywords: Two-sector Dynamic General Equilibrium Model, Underground Economy, Propagation of Shocks, Taxation.

1. Introduction

In the industrialized countries, along with the official (market) activity sector, other informal activities often flourish. As a matter of fact, in the United States (US hereafter) economy

*We have benefited from the comments and suggestions of John Donaldson, Edmund Phelps, Elisabetta Marzano and Guido Rey, and we thank the participants in the seminars at various Universities.
†E-mail address: bruno.chiarini@uniparthenope.it

the household sector is sizeable both in terms of input used in this sector and in terms of home-production output. The evidence for many European economies indicates large and increasing black markets for both labor forces and output. Despite these evidence, informal sectors have only recently been incorporated into macroeconomic models, and we are not aware of contributions drawing comparative implications. [1]

This is somewhat surprising, since the different structure of the European and the US non market sectors may represent one of the most important distinctive characteristics of their business cycles, and provide a more careful explanation of the unemployment experiences. In fact, several features characterizing the informal sector offers an additional explanation for the European and US labor market differentials (unemployment, wages, rigidities etc.).[2] The relation between market and underground activities deserve some attention, as well.

This paper compares the household production with the underground sector as two cases in point of non-market sectors. These two informal sectors provide useful insights concerning the inputs' allocation between the corresponding labor markets (the official and the unofficial). There are many candidate factors capable to enhance agents' willingness to shift resources out of market activity. The excess of tax burden and social security contributions is at the heart of both informal sectors. The tax policy and enforcement policies measure the opportunity cost of engaging in nonmarket activities and may generate a further distinction between United States and European economies in terms of labor market and business cycle features.

An informal sector is an important flexibility-enhancing instrument available in economies with high distortionary taxation. The paper reviews the literature comparing the characteristics and the performance of two classes of dynamic general equilibrium models of the US economy and European Economy (EE hereafter), where an explicit formalization of a nonmarket sector is included. The paper highlights the common features and the differences between underground activities and home production, and underlines the corresponding economic mechanisms by relying on numerical simulations.

Both the US and the EE are characterized by a remarkable burden of taxation and a large and increasing share of the informal economy. In this context agents reallocate resources from the market to either the home production sector or to the underground sector. The choice of the destination sector depends on the social structure and several institutional factors. The first aspect is related to the *stability of family* as an institution, while the *laws' enforceability* accounts for the second distinguishing element.[3] The family model is

[1]Here we are not discussing whether informal sectors are a burden to society or, on the contrary, are a source of economic strength, nether we make effort to measure the social or welfare costs of these informal sectors. Moreover, we are concerned with the size of the underground economy as encompassing those activities which are otherwise legal but go unreported or unrecorded.

[2]Among the labor market features used by an extensive literature with different theoretical and empirical frameworks, to investigate on the differences between the US and European economies, we quote the role stressed for employment protection systems, benefit replacement rates and benefit duration, active labor market policies, union density and coverage; payroll tax rate, participation rates of marred women, the the hours worked and the employment rates of prime-age men. It is surprising that in general schemes as well as in the Europe versus North America analysis, which use the above arguments, the underground economy and home production are not involved in these frameworks.

[3]The enforceability may be defined as a probability be forced to effectively pay the tax rates and a severe surcharge tax, after being discovered violating the law.

crucial since it characterizes the domestic allocation of labor between genders and, within the family, the willingness of its components to accept any kind of informal and temporal job. Informal activities are different whether the family context is highly institutionalized or not.

A key feature *common* to both the EE and US economies is that the non market sectors enhance the ability and willingness of agents to substitute into and out of market activity. In particular, there are more opportunities for for allocating labor services, for undertaking risk sharing (on the household side), and for smoothing production and profits (on the firms' side). Allocating their time between market and nonmarket activities, rather than simply between labor and leisure as in the canonical model, agents produce significant phenomena and business cycle issues that traditional schemes often time neglect.

Differences between these two classes of models concern the tradeability of the produced commodity, the source of the resources used for financing investments, and the cyclicality of labor services allocated to the two non market sectors. More precisely, there are five main differences: the response to economic policies, the commodities' number and their substitutability, the financing of capital investment, the insurance opportunities offered by the second sector, and the different cyclical properties between home production and underground activities.

The remainder of this paper is organized as follows. Section 2 reviews a set of stylized facts on the role and the features of the burden of taxation in US and European countries, and the characteristics of the informal sectors in the two economies. Section 3 reviews two dynamic general equilibrium models with, respectively, an underground sector and a home production sector. Section 4 reviews differences and similarities of the two model's solutions. In Section 5, using taxation experiments, we show the reallocation mechanism generated by the models. Section 6 concludes the papers.

2. Stylized Facts

2.1. Burden of Taxation and Informal Sector's Size

The literature on the informal sector argues that the increase in taxation and social security contributions is responsible for the increase of the size of the informal sectors observed in US and European economies.[4] Here we review characteristics and sizes of the burden of taxation and document the size of the informal sectors in the two economies.

Although there may exist some methodological problem in comparing tax systems, [5] the following figures show a high level of tax burden as common characteristic between the two economies. They indicate, however, remarkable differences. As tax-to-GDP ratio, the burden of taxation in EE stood at almost 41% in 1999. About 11 percentage points higher than in the United States. If taxes are defined as income taxes and the social contributions

[4]See Schneider and Enste (2000) and the papers quoted therein and McGrattan, Rogerson and Wright (1997). Of course, the informal sector may be explained also by institutional mechanisms such as labor market regulations, but the burden of taxation remain the main reason to push firms and workers to develop an informal sector.

[5]The sources are OECD (1999; 2001) and Joumard (2002).

over the labor cost, this percentage reaches 46.4% in Italy, 51.3% in Germany, 48.1 in France and 30.3% in United Kingdom. Between 1985 and 2002, the general government current tax receipts (which excludes capital receipts) for the EU ranges from 41.8 to 43.9 per cent of the nominal GDP. In the US in the same period, this percentage is between 28.7 to 30.8. The tax mix is also very different. Most EU countries rely heavily on social security contributions. In 1999 these are about 32% of total tax revenue whereas US social contribution reaches 24% of the total revenue. The average effective tax rate on labor in Europe is about 15 percentage points higher than in the US.

The tax wedge on labor is one of the distinctive features. Labor income is heavily taxed in many European countries such as Italy, France, Belgium Austria. Moreover, as stressed recently from an Oecd study, both the average and marginal tax wedges on labor are high. In 2000, the EU area reported an *average effective* tax wedge on labor (personal income tax plus employee's social security contributions plus employer's social security contribution) of 40%. This figure in the United States is about 30%. An analogous picture is valid for the *marginal* tax wedge on labor. These features, in particular the high marginal tax wedges on labor, affect the participation rate and the working hours and, as stressed by several studies, [6] in systems where taxes are levied on households, discourage the other family members from taking on a job.

This creates an incentive for many family members to stay outside the official labor market. This kind of behavior characterizes pensioners and older workers, unemployed young adults and spouses of low-income earners. **Table 1** reports the marginal effective tax rate on additional income for different family types. This is the amount of earnings which are taxed away via income taxes or mean testing procedures and cancellation of benefits.

Table 1. Marginal Effective Tax Rates on Additional Income

Principal E.	Full-time			Unemployed		Part-time
Secondary E.	Full-time	Part-time	NE	Full-time	Part-time*	NE
France	28	38	76	29	30	69
Germany	51	50	80	31	19	115
Italy	33	25	63	37	19	84
Spain	23	19	78	23	19	77
EU	35	31	77	38	38	107
US	19	11	68	20	0	102

Table 1. All numbers in the Table are in percentages; "Principal E": principal earner of wage income; "Secondary E": secondary earner of wage income; "NE": non-employed; (*) Employed without benefit entitlements. Source: Joumard (2002) and OECD (1999).

High marginal effective tax rates over a range of earnings imply a low incentive to earn in that range. This could reduce hour of work and earnings without affecting the net income. The effect on the official labor market of tax and benefit systems may be relevant, reducing the work incentives, preventing formal part-time work and thereby encouraging nonmarket

[6] See Joumard (2002) and the works quoted therein.

labor supply and labor demand. Underground and home production phenomena may be an explanatory factor when the structure of social security contributions and income taxation produce an high marginal effective tax rate on the other family members earning.

This is particularly true when taxation is levied on couples rather than individual basis, though the family structure is much more complex in many of the EU countries. It is not a case that both many of the EU countries and the US have the joint as the unit of taxation (France; Germany; US; Spain; Portugal; Switzerland) and others (Italy; Netherlands; Denmark; Canada) with individual basis have full transfer of basic relief (tax paid by one partner is dependent on the income of the other).[7] These aspects of tax structure and benefits are important in a policy area that has been completely neglected such as the nonmarket sector consequences.[8]

Finally, statutory rates on corporate profits are somewhat high and broadly the same in the major OECD countries. Effective corporate tax rate ranges from 37% of Italy to about 40% in Germany. A bit lower figure is imposed in the US. Of course the corporate tax follows alternative complicated approaches. The tax structure applied to net income may be graduated on income or may be a unique flat rate tax applied to net capital income. The important point here is that high rates encourage individuals and firms to seek tax-free income.

2.2. The Informal Sector in US and EE

2.2.1. The United States and the Size of Home Production

The US non market sector is characterized by a large home production, while underground activities account for a small share of GDP. In particular, Greenwood, Rogerson, and Wright (1995) document that investment in household capital is larger than that in market capital by about 15 percent. More importantly, household production generates a sizeable portion of aggregate output. For example, Eisner (1988) reports that home production constitutes between 20 and 50 percent of the value of gross national product, and Bonke (1992) estimates that the value of household production is around 40 to 50 percent of GNP in most western countries. In addition, several studies indicate that a typical North-American married couple allocates a large size of its discretionary time to work in household production activities.[9] This quantity is close to the time that it does working for paid compensation. [10]

A large body of literature introduce a household production sector into a stochastic growth model, mainly for the US economy. Benhabib, Rogerson, and Wright (1991), Greenwood and Hercowitz (1991), and Greenwood, Rogerson, and Wright (1995) find that introducing a household production sector into an otherwise standard closed economy business cycle model, improves the ability of the model to explain the volatility of output, the relative volatilities of output, consumption, investment, and hours, the correlation between

[7]See OECD (1997).

[8]On the contrary, the importance between marginal tax rates and poverty trap, in-work benefit, and family taxation have been extensively investigated. See, OECD (1997).

[9]In particular, Juster and Stafford (1991) find that a typical married US couple spends 25 percent of their time working at home while allocating 33 percent of their time on market activities.

[10]Benhabib, Rogerson and Wright (1991) indicate that the output of the household sector may be as much as half that of the market sector.

hours and productivity, and the correlation between the investments in home and market capital. Einarsson and Marquis (1997)resolve some drawbacks of the canonical home production model. They demonstrate that casting the home production mechanism into an endogenous growth model, it is possible to generate comovement between employment and output across the market and the home sectors, even with a single technology shock to market production. McGrattan, Rogerson, and Wright (1997) estimate a model with a household production sector to study the impact of different types of fiscal policies. Their results suggest that the model has considerably different implications for fiscal policies than those of the standard model. Rupert, Rogerson and Wright (2000) include home production into the standard life cycle model, and show that there exist a downward bias in the estimates of the intertemporal substitution elasticities obtained with the standard model and Baxter and Jermann (1999) use home production to solve the excess sensitivity of consumption puzzle. Gomme, Kydland and Rupert (2001) introduce home production in a time-to-build technology, improving the ability of the model in matching the comovement of sectoral investments. Perli (1998) presents a business cycle model with the home production, showing that this provides an indeterminate equilibrium. In this case, cycles may be driven by self-fulfilling expectations.

Canova and Uribe (1997) construct an international business cycle model with a household production sector and show that the model can generate some important features of the data as household production provides important channels for transmitting business cycles between countries. The main focus was to examine the ability of dynamic equilibrium models to account for the business cycle behavior of the labor market, while augmented with an household production sector.[11] In this context, a non-market sector appears to be a relevant *shock absorber*, for it is able to influence the ability and willingness of individuals to substitute into and out of market activity.

In the US the shadow economy constituted between only 3.6 and 4.2 percent of GNP in 1970. In 1990 this share reached about 7 percent and, in 1998 it was estimated to about 8 percent. Although it may appear relevant, these estimates represent the smallest hidden economy size in the OECD countries. [12]

2.2.2. The European Economies and the Size of Underground Economy

In the **EE**, the picture is different. Household production sector appears relatively smaller in size (in terms of hours allocated to household activities) compared to the US. This appearance is due to a different degree of institutionalization of the family in US and EE. The EE home production is as sizeable as the US, but its cost for the family is lower than US. In the United States, there exists a high degree of de-institutionalization of the traditional family model: this means that the family model is characterized by high divorce rates, high proportion of live births outside marriage, while unemployed young adults do not remain close to their families. In the majority of the couples both spouses have jobs.

On the contrary, in many European countries, in particular in Southern Europe (Greece,

[11] Quoting Gronau (1986), "the greatest contribution of the theory of home production in the past decade was in its service to the better understanding of consumption behavior and changes in labor supply over the business cycle".

[12] See, Schneider and Schneider and Enste (2000).

Italy, Spain and France) the family model is more traditional, with a domestic division of labor between genders and within the family. Adult children (who often continue to live with their parents) and older parents are taken care of within the same home. These countries share in common a lower rate both of divorce and birth of births outside marriage. In more than half of all couples only the husband has a job while pensioners, women and young adults have a high willingness to accept any kind of temporary and informal job.

One of the main difference between these two household (society) models seems to be the work/job sharing arrangement between spouses. Both members have a regular job in the North-American society, while only one (usually the husband) has a regular job in more than half of southern European couples. Hence young pensioners, women and young unemployed have a high willingness to accept any kind of informal and temporary job. Underground or informal activities are more relevant, in this context, than home production activities.[13]

We may draw two implications. First, home production is quite costly in the US where both components of a couple work in the majority of marriages. In this case, under certain conditions, it may pay to substitute market with nonmarket jobs. Conversely, in EE where a large share of families only the husband works, the home production is much cheaper. The second implication from the different family structure is the high degree of EE family institutionalization, which tends to tie together several members, along with higher average and marginal effective tax rates, make many of them prone to look for black jobs.

In the EE countries, there exist a pernicious effect, because under the current tax system, the probability to be detected is negligible for a firm. This means that firms have a strong incentive to shift a part of their labor demand on the shadow economy. European non-market sector is determined by underground activities, which represent a large part of GNP. Schneider and Enste (2000), show that the size of underground economic activity is quite large and increasing in many countries. In particular, several Southern European countries have underground economies almost one-third as large as officially measured GNP. For instance, Greece has a share of the hidden economy of official GNP of about 27-30 percent. Estimations for Italy range from 20 to 27 percent while for Spain this range is 16-23 percent and Belgium of 21-23 percent of GNP. The importance of the hidden activities is shown also for several northern countries such as Norway, Sweden and Denmark (about 17-18 percent), but also France and Germany report relevant estimation (close to 15 percent).

The literature demonstrates that there can be interesting interactions between underground and market activity and that these interactions cannot be neglected in analyzing the European countries. Loayza (1996) and Sarte (2000) model the connection between the informal sector and the formal one, drawing interesting macroeconomic implications using AK growth models. Ihrig and Moe (2001) develop a dynamic model of a representative agent's decision to accumulate capital and to work in both the sectors with the aim of studying the role of government taxation policies on the underground sector. These authors, simulating their simple dynamic model, show that lowering tax rates as opposed to increasing the enforcement of tax policies, play a larger role in determining a country's standard of living. The results support the view of the informal sector as an important source of subsistence and as a relatively easy way to expand employment during recessions. These works

[13] See, Jurado Guerrero and Naldini (1997) and Gallie and Paugam (2000).

refer to developing countries but they are interesting also for many developed countries with a sizeable underground sector. Busato and Chiarini (2004) incorporating an underground sector in a dynamic general equilibrium model, improve the fit of the model to the Italian data, especially along several important labor market dimensions. They show that underground activities offer risk sharing opportunities by allowing households to smooth income through a proper labor allocation between the two sectors. Conesa, Diaz-Moreno and Galdon-Sanchez (2001) analyze the role of underground activities as an explanation of differences in registered aggregate fluctuations. The quantitative implications of the model show a substantial improvement in capturing the cyclical behavior of the economy.

3. Non-Market Sector in Dynamic Equilibrium Models

3.1. The Underground Economy

In order to describe the working of the reallocation mechanism, this section reviews an underground economy model set up by Busato and Chiarini (2004). In this model there exist three agents: the firm, the consumer-worker-investor, and the government.[14] In addition there are two sectors: the market and the underground sector, and there is a homogenous consumption good. In this context, agents are subject to distortionary taxation, but they can use the underground sector to evade taxes, while optimally allocating labor across sectors. In addition, the consumer-worker-investor is consistent with the traditional family model suitable to represent many European countries cases.

Each firm $i \in [0, 1]$ produces final output by using two different technologies, one associated with the market, y^i_{mt}, and the other with the non-market sector, y^i_{ut}.[15]

$$y^i_{mt} = \lambda^m_t \left(k^i_t\right)^\alpha \left(\theta^i_t n^i_t\right)^{1-\alpha} \text{ and } y^i_{ut} = \lambda^u_t (1 - \theta^i_t) n^i_t, \tag{1}$$

where the market output, y^i_{mt}, is the result of capital, k^i_t, and market labor, $n^i_{mt} \equiv \theta^i_t n^i_t$, applied to a Cobb-Douglas technology. Next, θ^i_t $(0 < \theta^i_t < 1)$ denotes the share of labor demand allocated by $i - th$ firm to the market sector. The non-market output, y^i_{ut}, is produced with a production function which uses only non-market labor, $n^i_{ut} \equiv (1 - \theta^i_t) n^i_t$.[16] Finally, λ^m_t and λ^u_t denote sectoral stochastic productivity shocks.

Following Prescott and Mehra (1980), we assume that each firm solves a myopic profit maximization problem, on a period-by-period basis, subject to a technological constraint, and to the possibility that it may be discovered producing in the unofficial economy, convicted of tax evasion and subject to a penalty surcharge.

[14]The model presented here resembles that in Busato and Chiarini (2004).

[15]This technology specification is equivalent to a more general set-up where both production functions use capital and labor, for example $y^i_{mt} = M_t \left(k^i_t\right)^\alpha \left(n^i_{mt}\right)^{1-\alpha}$ and $y^i_{ut} = Z_t \left(k^i_{ut}\right)^\beta \left(n^i_{ut}\right)^{1-\beta}$. From Uzawa (1965) and Lucas (1988) if $\beta < \alpha$ we can set the smaller elasticity to zero without loss of any generality. Since underground activities are labor intensive, we can simplify the model, and preserving the main economic intuition, by assuming that underground sector produces using only labor. We anticipate that in a Rational Expectations Equilibrium (REE) firms use both technologies (for a formal proof see Busato and Chiarini (2004))

[16]We could imagine that the same firm produces in the market economy in the day, while in the underground economy by night.

Firms are subject to distortionary taxation, which is partially evaded by allocating resource to the underground (and untaxed by definition) sector. Market-produced revenues, $q_t^m(1-t_t)y_{mt}^i$, are taxed at the stochastic corporate rate t_t, where q_t^m denotes the price of market-produced good. Firms do not pay taxes on non-market produced revenues, $q_t^u y_{ut}^i$, where q_t^u is the price of non-market-produced commodity. Firms, however, may be discovered evading, with probability $p \in (0,1)$, and forced to pay the stochastic tax rate, t_t, increased by a surcharge factor, $s > 1$, applied to the standard tax rate. Note that since the market-produced and the non-market produced goods are identical, in a REE they must have the same price.

Since $q_t = 1$ holds in the equilibrium, we can impose it along the solution. In the first case (firm is discovered,with probability p), revenues, denoted as $y_{D,t}^i$, are:

$$y_{D,t}^i = (1-t_t)y_{mt}^i + (1-st_t)y_{ut}^i$$

In the second case (firm is not discovered, with probability $1-p$), revenues equal:

$$y_{ND,t}^i = (1-t_t)y_{mt}^i + y_{ut}^i$$

To compute total expected revenues, we apply linear projection, and we have $E\left(y_t^i|\mathcal{I}_t\right) = py_{D,t}^i + (1-p)\,y_{ND,t}^i$, where E denotes an expectation operator conditional on information set $\mathcal{I}_t$. Simplifying, we rewrite $E\left(y_t^i|\mathcal{I}_t\right) = (1-t_t)y_{mt}^i + (1-pst_t)y_{ut}^i$, where $(1-pst_t) > 0$ ensures that a firm cannot go bankrupt.

The cost of renting capital equals its marginal productivity r_t, net of capital depreciation, δ. The cost of market labor is represented by the wage paid for hours worked, augmented by social security stochastic tax rate, t_t, which, for simplicity, is assumed equal to social security tax rate. We denote the former as $w_t^m = (1+t_t)w_t$, where w_t is pre-tax wage, while the cost of non-market labor equals the pre-tax wage, i.e. $w_t^u = w_t$.

To introduce a traditional family model, with a domestic division of labor between genders and within the family, we suppose that the economy is populated by a continuum of consumers, uniformly distributed over the unit interval. Each consumer works in only one of the two sectors. They receive incomes that are functions of the sectoral, idiosyncratic, shocks. Within the economy there exist extended families, exogenously determined and of fixed size. We assume that family members have perfect information concerning each other's idiosyncratic shocks to each sector. For simplicity suppose there exists one family, which is composed by two working individuals, Mr. κ and Miss. l[17]. Without loss of generality, we assume that Mr. κ works in market sector, while Miss. l works in the non-market sector.

Since Mr. κ and Miss. l belong to the same family, it is sensible to assume that their preferences do not differ significantly. We assume therefore, that they have the same utility function for consumption. The heterogeneity, however, concerns their labor supply, which is consistent with the fact they work in different sectors. This theoretical family structure is a reasonable approximation of a traditional family with a high degree of institutionalization. To model their preferences for consumption and labor, we generalize the structure presented

[17]We choose to restrict the analysis to one family to keep notation simple. The size and the number of the extended family can easily be enlarged.

by Busato and Chiarini (2004), which derives from Cho and Rogerson's (1988) extended family labor supply model. Precisely, we specify instantaneous utility function as follows:

$$U(c_t^{\kappa}, c_t^{l}, l_t^{\kappa}, l_t^{l}) = \varphi u(c_t^{\kappa}) + (1-\varphi)u(c_t^{l}) - v\left(l_t^{\kappa}\right)l_t^{l} - \mu(l_t^{l}) \tag{2}$$

where $u(c_t^{\kappa})$ and $u(c_t^{l})$ represent utility from Mr. κ and Miss l consumption, and $v(l_t^{\kappa})l_t^{l}$ describes the disutility of working in both sectors. We interpret the last term, $\mu(l_t^{l})$, as reflecting the idiosyncratic cost of working in the non-market sector. This cost may be associated in particular with the lack of any social and health insurance in the non-market sector. Finally, φ and $(1-\varphi)$ denote the relative weights of Mr. κ and Miss l utility function.

An aspect of primary interest in our labor market is workers' labor supply in the two sectors of the economy. Mr. κ, which works in the market sector, supplies l_t^{κ}, and receive a wage $w_t^{\kappa} = w_t(1-\tau)$, where τ is the tax rate on wage income. Miss l, who works in the other sector, offers l_t^{l}, and earns a wage $w_t^{l} = w_t$. The family budget constraint is

$$w_t(1-\tau)l_t^{\kappa} + w_t l_t^{l} + R_t K_t^{tot} = C_t^{tot} + X_t^{tot} \tag{3}$$

where $C_t^{tot} = c_t^{\kappa} + c_t^{l}$ and X_t^{tot} represents total consumption and total investment by the family, respectively. Eventually they pool their savings together, and rent the grand total, X_t^{tot}, to the firms, which capital stock evolves according to a standard capital accumulation constraint, $K_{t+1}^{tot} = (1-\delta)K_t^{tot} + X_t^{tot}$, where δ denotes the exogenous and constant depreciation rate.

In this context we introduce a Risk Sharing Contract, defined as follows.

Definition 1 (Risk Sharing Contract) *The contract has three features:*

1. $l_t^{\kappa} = \theta_t L_t$ *and* $l_t^{l} = (1-\theta_t)\,L_t$. *Mr.* κ *and Miss.* l *pool together their labor supplies,* L_t, *then they allocate a share* θ_t *to market sector, and the remaining* $1-\theta_t$ *to non-market sector.*

2. *The extended family chooses total consumption* C_t^{tot}*.Then Mr.* κ *and Miss.* l *consumption will be* $c_t^{\kappa} = \omega C_t^{tot}$ *and* $c_t^{l} = (1-\omega)C_t^{tot}$.[18]

3. *We assume that agents accept the contract, that it holds for each period in time, and that it is incentive compatible and perfectly enforceable*[19].

Readers unfamiliar with Contract Theory would call it a "marriage" contract. Since we are not interested in studying consumption reallocation, we assume that family member undertake a Perfect Risk Sharing scheme that allows each consumer to have the same consumption profile.

[18]In this way individual consumption is disentangled from individual income. It may be interesting to note that this is the argument behind the risk sharing and consumption literature (see Deaton, 1992 for a survey). In that context, optimal risk sharing is induces by financial market completeness. In our model, the insurance comes from the real sector.

[19]By definition, an implicit contract will need to be sustained as an equilibrium in the interaction between the parties (Salanie', 1997). The contract we present in this model has the very simple goal to provide insurance against production idiosyncratic risk. For this reasons we assume that agents accept the contract.

Definition 2 (Perfect Risk Sharing) *After entering the contract, consumers agree on a perfect risk sharing scheme, in the sense that they set ratio between marginal utilities equal to a constant, i.e.* $\frac{u'_{\kappa}(C_{\kappa,t})}{u'_{l}(C_{l,t})} = \frac{\phi_{\kappa}}{\phi_{l}}$*.Since* $u'_{\kappa}(c_t^{\kappa}) = u'_{l}(c_t^{\kappa}) = u'(C_t)$*, we have* $c_t^{\kappa} = \frac{\phi_{\kappa}}{\phi_{l}} c_t^{l}$*. Assuming, that both consumers have the same weight within the family, we can set* $\phi_{\kappa} = \phi_{l}$*, and therefore* $c_t^{\kappa} = c_t^{l}$*. The PRS is defined in the sense of the two consumers enjoying the same consumption profile, smoothed on period by period basis. In terms of total consumption, we have* $c_t^{\kappa} = c_t^{l} = \frac{1}{2}C_t^j$*, where* C_t^j *represents consumption chosen by j-th household at time t.*

The contract has the simple goal to pool together labor supply, and income insuring the family against idiosyncratic shocks.[20]

To complete the description of extended family behavior, we specify the functional forms for (2), consistent with the Risk Sharing Contract and the Perfect Risk Sharing scheme. In particular, preferences of j-th consumer or family, are described by the following function, where total labor supply is normalized to unity ($n_t = 1$):

$$\mathcal{U}^j = \sum_{t=0}^{\infty} \beta^t u^j(c_t^j, n_{mt}^j, n_{ut}^j).$$

In particular, the instantaneous utility function (separable between consumption and labor) is specified as follows:

$$u^j(c_t^j, n_{mt}^j, n_{ut}^j) \equiv \frac{(c_t^j)^{1-q} - 1}{1-q} - h\frac{(\theta_t^j)^{1+\gamma}}{1+\gamma}(1-\theta_t^j) - f\frac{(1-\theta_t^j)^{1-\eta}}{1-\eta}, \qquad (4)$$

where c_t^j denotes consumption profile of consumer j, θ_t^j her market labor supply, and $1 - \theta_t^j$ her non-market labor supply.[21] The second term, $h\frac{(\theta_t^j)^{1+\gamma}}{1+\gamma}(1-\theta_t^j)$, represents the overall disutility of working, while the last term, $f\frac{(1-\theta_t^j)^{1-\eta}}{1-\eta}$, reflects the idiosyncratic cost of working in the underground sector. In particular, this cost may be associated with the lack of any social and health insurance in the underground sector. To have a well behaved utility function, we assume that $h, f \geq 0$, $\gamma, \eta > -1$, that all the parts of the momentary utility function are well behaved[22].

The representative household, next, faces the following budget constraint:

$$w_t(1-\tau_t)\theta_t^j + w_t(1-\theta_t^j) + R_t k_t^j = c_t^j + x_t^j,$$

[20]Note that in this paper we do not consider strategic interaction among agents. It is clear, however, that this would be a natural development of the structure presented here.

[21]To represent consumer behavior in this environment, we refer to Cho and Cooley (1994) family labor supply model. They distinguish labor supply with regard to an intensive (the hours worked), and an extensive margin (the employment margin). In our model we reinterpret these two dimensions as representing worker's labor supply in the regular and in the underground sectors

[22]Restriction on the utility function to make the inter-temporal optimization problem well defined are derived in Busato and Chiarini (2004).

where x_t denotes investment at time t. Notice that in this model capital stock is not taxed. If it were, it should be necessary to allow for the possibility of deducing depreciated capital from taxable income, since this in one of the reasons behind the existence of an underground sector. Finally, investment increases the capital stock according to a standard state equation:

$$k_{t+1} = (1 - \delta)k_t + x_t.$$

3.2. The Household Production Economy

Enforcement of tax policies plays a large role in determining resources reallocation. The enforceability rules in the EE are weak. This has led us to introduce a tax-evasion model into the general equilibrium economy described above. Enforceability in US economy is stronger than in the European economy and we stylize this fact, assuming that the probability to be detected in US is equal to one. In this case, the expected revenues $(1 - p)\, y^i_{ND,t} = 0$. In the following model for the US economy we, therefore, do not specify an underground sector.

As well as underground activities, household production is a large part of the economic activity.[23] More importantly, the addition of household production influences the ability and willingness of individuals to substitute into and out of market activities.[24] In this sense home production is similar to underground activities, even though movitations for shifting resources to one or the other sector are different, and are detailed below. To carry out a consistent comparison between these two nonmarket activities, it is necessary to present a home production model augmented with distortionary taxation. This section reviews a home production model such as that of McGrattan, Rogerson and Wrigth (1997).

Consider first the corporate sector. The i-th firm, $i \in [0, 1]$, is characterized by production technologies for the market and the non-market sectors that display constant returns to scale, and which are specified as follows:

$$y^i_{mt} = \lambda^m_t \left(k^i_{mt}\right)^{\alpha} \left(n^i_{mt}\right)^{1-\alpha} \quad \text{and} \quad y^i_{ht} = \lambda^h_t \left(k^i_{ht}\right)^{\beta} \left(n^i_{ht}\right)^{1-\beta}, \tag{5}$$

where employment supplied to the market n^i_m and the capital stock k^i_m produce market output y^i_m, whereas employment supplied in the home sector n^i_h and home capital sector k^i_h produce home output y^i_h. Maximization implies factor prices equal marginal product because of the constant returns to scale.

Next, assume that consumers are infinitely lived and homogenous, and total population is normalized to unity. The $j \in [0, 1]$ household has preferences over stochastic processes for aggregate consumption flow, c^j_t, and leisure, ℓ^j_t, described by the following utility function:

[23] Home production has been part of standard labor paradigm. Fundamental references include Becker (1965), Pollak and Watcher (1975), and Gronau (1986)). Only recently has been introduced into macro models. However, the literature is quite large: see Benhabib, Rogerson and Wright (1991) for a survey, or among the many Rios Rull (1993), McGrattan, Rogerson and Wright (1992), Fisher (1992), Fung (1992), Perli (1998), Gomme, Kydland and Rupert (2001).

[24] As reported in Greenwood, Rogerson and Wrigth (1993), a typical family spends almost as much time in production activities such as cooking, cleaning, and so on, as it does working for salary.

$$\mathcal{U}^j = \sum_{t=0}^{\infty} \beta^t u^j(c_t^j, \ell_t),$$

where the instantaneous utility is assumed to be a constant relative risk aversion transformation of a Cobb-Douglas function,

$$u^j(c_t^j, \ell_t^j) \equiv \frac{\left(c_t^q \ell_t^{1-q}\right)^{1-\rho} - 1}{1-\rho},$$

where leisure in this context is an aggregate of total available time normalized to unity, market hours n_{mt}, and non-market hours n_{ht}: $\ell_t^j = 1 - n_{mt}^j - n_{ht}^j$. Consumption, next, is an aggregate of private consumption c_{pt}^j, and government consumption c_{gt}^j:

$$c_t = \left\{\phi_1 (c_{pt}^j)^{e_1} + (1-\phi_1)(c_{gt}^j)^{e_1}\right\}^{\frac{1}{e_1}}, \tag{6}$$

where $\phi_1 \in (0,1)$, and the parameter $e_1 \leqq 1$ is the household willingness to substitute between the two types of consumption goods. Private consumption itself is an aggregate of market consumption c_{mt}^j, and non-market consumption c_{ht}^j:

$$c_{pt} = \left\{\phi_2 (c_{mt}^j)^{e_2} + (1-\phi_2)(c_{ht}^j)^{e_2}\right\}^{\frac{1}{e2}}, \tag{7}$$

where notation is analogous to that of (6). Next, feasibility in the market sector is ensured by the following equation:

$$c_{mt} + x_t = (1-\tau_{ht})\, w_t h_{mt} + (1-\tau_{kt})\, r_t k_{mt} + \delta \tau_{kt} k_{mt} + T_t, \tag{8}$$

where τ_{ht} and τ_{kt} are the stochastic taxes on capital and labor, w_t and r_t are the marginal prices for capital and labor, and T_t is a lump-sum transfer. Following McGrattan, Rogerson and Wright (*1997*) we assume that the depreciated capital is tax deducible, for which reason it is added up to the income side of previous equation.

The fiscal authority faces a budget constraint:

$$c_{gt} = h_{mt}\tau_{ht} w_t + \tau_{kt} r_t k_{mt} - \delta \tau_{kt} k_{mt} - T_t.$$

Notice that the transfer T_t ensures that the government balances its budget in each point in time, given realization of stochastic tax rates (τ_{ht} and τ_{kt}) and of ν_t (defined below). In addition, notice that the home capital stock is not subject to taxation, at least in the basic formulation of the model.[25] Finally, it is assumed that government consumption is a stochastic process given by:

$$c_{gt} = \nu_t y_t,$$

where ν_t is a random variable and y_t is the aggregate output.

Finally, let aggregate capital stock, k_t, evolving according the following:

[25]In a policy experiment presented below the possibility of taxing home capital stock is taken into account.

$$k_{t+1} = (1 - \delta)k_t + x_t,$$

where $k_t = k_{mt} + k_{ht}$.

4. Two Mechanisms for Risk Hedging and Optimal Labor Allocation

First notice that, technically speaking, both the home production model and the underground economy model, are characterized by three agents: a large number of myopic firms, a large number of identical infinitely-lived and forward looking households, and the government. In addition there are two sectors: the market and the nonmarket sector. Differences between these two classes of models concern, however, the tradeability of the produced commodity, the origin of resources used for financing investments, and the cyclicality of labor services allocated to the two non market sectors. We outline five issues: the reaction to policy distortions, the commodities' number and their substitutability, the financing of capital investment, the insurance opportunities offered by the second sector, and the different cyclical properties between home production and underground activities.

4.1. Risk Sharing and Labor Flexibility

In both the models, agents are more willing to shift resources out of market activity in response to policy distortions. Thus, in home production and underground economy models, policies do not affect only total hours worked but also how hours are allocated between the market and the nonmarket sectors.[26] In these models there exist a high degree of *flexibility* of the labor inputs. However, whereas in the home production labor flexibility involves the labor supply, in the underground economy it is a key feature of both firms' labor demand and households' labor supply.

4.2. Consumption Goods and their Substitutability

In the home production class of models there exist two goods, denoted as market and nonmarket commodities, each of which is produced with a sector specific technology. In addition, the preference specification allows for different degrees of substitutability between market and non-market goods.[27]

In the model with underground sector there exists only one homogenous good, which is produced using two different technologies: one associated with market sector, and the other with underground sector. In this environment it is natural to focus on the case of perfect substitutability between market-produced final output and underground-produced one. This

[26] This aspect has also important development implications. In fact as agents change their allocation of time spent in market and nonmarket work, differences in output per person will be due to both differences in capital and in market hours per worker. See Parente, Rogerson and Wright (1999).

[27] It is customary, in this literature, to consider the version with perfect substitutability as the benchmark simulated economy.

latter issue, however, can be generalized, developing underground models with two goods and relative prices.

4.3. Investments Financing

The home production model shows that only market-produced goods can be consumed and invested, either into market capital or into non-market capital. There are no uses for home production output other than consumption - it cannot be sold or transformed into capital, for example, the way that market-produced output can. In the underground economy model, however, there exists only one capital stock (invested in the market sector), but market and non-market-produced output can be transformed into market capital and, in our simple version, without any adjustment cost. The underground sector offers an additional channel for financing capital stock accumulation, and an additional dimension along which firms can employ the available labor supply.[28] While home production model is a legitimate two sector model, the underground economy model could be more appropriately defined as a *two technology model*, since the same good is produced using two different technologies.

Notice that, when households shift working time in the home sector, in general they decrease the marginal product of capital in the market sector, thereby causing a change in the desired allocation of capital across the two sectors: agents will invest more in the home sector. In the model of underground economy presented above, when agents draw working time out of market sector to the underground economy the product of capital falls but there is not change in the capital allocation across sectors.

4.4. Production and Consumption Smoothing

Notice that an underground sector offers profit smoothing opportunities for firms, and insurance opportunities for consumers. More precisely, firms can smooth their profits by a proper allocation of labor demand between the two sectors, on a period by period base. In addition, consumers can smooth not only consumption, by substituting over time consumption and investments, but they can also smooth income, by allocating their labor supply across sectors, on a period by period base. In the model with underground sector consumers have two sources of income, which, being countercyclical, offer insurance against bad times. This mechanism is absent in models with home production.

4.5. Cyclical Properties of Labor Services

Finally, Ingram, Kocherlakota and Savin (1997) find that hours spent in home production are acyclical whereas other studies find that home hours are countercyclical.[29] It is important to notice that this implies that during recessions home production models predict that workers may adjust by switching into leisure, whereas a model with underground activities predicts a switch into underground activities. Difference is that in our class of model, non-market income increases during recessions, mitigating slumps, by offering insurance

[28] Technically speaking, the specification of consumer intertemporal feasibility constraint, equation (3), incorporates this feature.

[29] Benhabib, Rogerson and Wright (1991), Greenwood, Rogerson, Wright (1995), Canova and Ubide (1997), Blankenau and Ayhan Kose (2002).

Table 2. Underground Activity Model

q	η	h	f	γ	α	δ
1.0	0.62	6.0	1.0	2.0	.36	.025
s	p	β	t, τ	$\bar{\theta}$	ρ_m, ρ_z	σ_m, σ_z
1.30	.03	0.98	.275	.735	.95	.712

Table 2. According to the Italian Tax Law (Legislative Decree 471/97, Section 13, paragraph 1) the surcharge s equals 30 or 200 percent of the statutory tax rate. We present results just for the first value. The standard deviations of innovation, σ_m, σ_z, are defined as percentages.

opportunities to household. Again this mechanism is not present in home production models.

5. The Reallocation Mechanism: A Fiscal Policy Experiment

RBC models with fiscal policy do a good job in matching some observed comovements in the data. In the set up considered by this model taxes affect labor and consumption allocations, and stimulate production and labor demand in the informal sector. Because it seems that government taxation plays a relevant role in the allocation of output and labor input between these sectors, our interest in this analysis is motivated by the desire to assess its empirical implications in term of resource reallocation in economies with an informal sector. In particular, we investigate how changes in corporate and personal income taxes affects production and labor allocation between the market and the non-market sector.

5.1. Calibration

The underground-activity model is calibrated for the Italian economy though the analysis can be generalized to a large number of European countries which present a sizeable underground sector.[30] The calibration is based on the seasonally adjusted ISTAT series from 1970:1 to 1996:4, expressed in constant 1995 prices, and on a set of underground output estimations provided by Bovi (1999). More details are presented in Busato and Chiarini (2004). For convenience, calibrated parameters are presented in **Table 2**.

The home production model is, instead, calibrated for the US economy. The parameters' estimated are taken from McGrattan, Rogerson and Wright (1997), with use procedure presented in McGrattan (1994). Parameters are included in **Table 3**.[31]

5.2. Taxation and Household Production

To have an idea of the dimension of the taxation impact on the relationship between the household production and the market sector, we may imagine to eliminate distortionary

[30]Countries like Belgium, Denmark, Greece , Portugal and Spain have a large share of the underground sector. See, Schneider and Enste (2000).

[31]There is an important difference between the two calibrations. Busato and Chiarini (2004) calibrate tax rate relying on the statutory tax rates, while McGrattan Rogerson and Wright (1997) use effective tax rates.

Table 3. Home Production Model

q	e_1	e_2	b	b_1	b_2	b_3	b_4
5.27	0.62	6.0	.448	0.00	.385	.020	.525
a_1	a_2	a_3	a_4	τ_k	τ_n	δ	
1.00	.485	0.21	.234	0.57	0.23	0.22	

Table 3. Source: McGrattan, Rogerson and Wright (1997).

taxation in the US market sector, setting in the home production model of Section 6, $\tau_{ht} = \tau_{kt} = 0$. A further experiment is accomplished introducing taxation over non-market activities.

According to McGrattan, Rogerson and Wright estimates, the effect of eliminating distortionary taxation in the market sector is quite remarkable: output increases by 43 percent, market consumption increases by 47 percent, market investment increases by 87 percent, market hours increase by 22 percent, and the stock market capital more than double. In the home sector, however, the picture is reversed for all variables but capital, which increases by 34 percent. In other words, there is a shift in labor from the home sector to the market sector, while capital stock increases in both sectors.[32]

The second experiment concerns the introduction of a tax on the home production capital. In order to do this, the feasibility constraint (6) should be rewritten as follows:

$$c_{mt} + x_t = (1 - \tau_{ht})\, w_t h_{mt} + (1 - \tau_{kt})\, r_t k_{mt} + \delta \tau_{kt} k_{mt} + T_t - \tau_p k_n, \tag{9}$$

where τ_p can be interpreted as a residential "property tax". When τ_p is set different from zero, all variables are lower with the exception of market consumption. With respect to the base case ($\tau_p = 0$),the latter rise ranges from 3 to 7 per cent, whereas home production and (since home capital is produced in the market) market production fall from 1.2 to 2 per cent. Of course home capital stock, being the taxed factor, falls. However, since a property tax does not affect labor/leisure choice, market capital/labor ratio does not change. Moreover, the reduction of capital stock is associated to a large reduction in investment, and, by this end, there is an increase in market consumption. The labor input reduces slightly in home production sector while in the market sector the fall ranges from 1.24 to 2 per cent. The simulations show that in this economy there may be frequent and relevant opportunities from substituting between market and home goods.

5.3. Taxation and Underground Activities

In Figure 1 (Tax Cuts on the Income and the Corporate Tax Rates) the square line represents market output, the line with circles denotes total output, the line with triangles represents non-market output, and the dotted line represents the tax rate profile.

[32]Notice that a model that ignores the home production sector has different production. See for example the contribution of McGRattan (1994), where market sector fluctuations are much larger that in a model augmented with an household production sector.

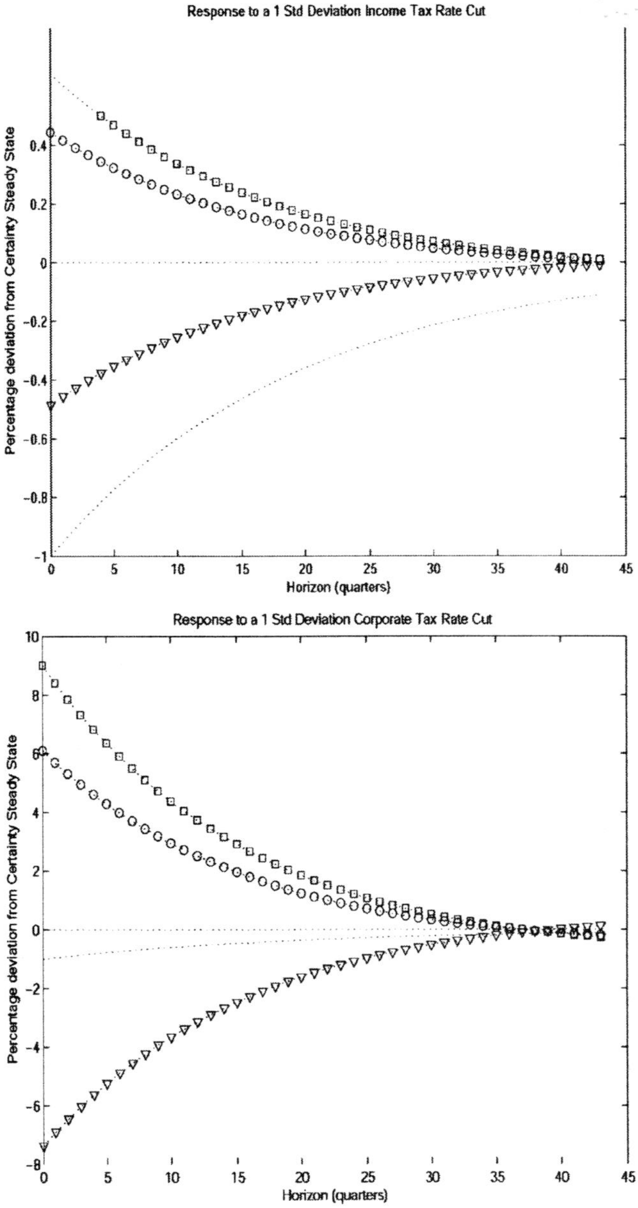
Response to a 1 Std Deviation Income Tax Rate Cut
Percentage deviation from Certainty Steady State
Horizon (quarters)
Response to a 1 Std Deviation Corporate Tax Rate Cut
Percentage deviation from Certainty Steady State
Horizon (quarters)

Figure 1.

Here we give a brief insight of the allocation mechanism in the underground model of Section 5 performing an impulse-response analysis cutting income and corporate tax rates. A cut in the corporate tax rates, remarkably increases production and labor input in the market sector ($\frac{\Delta y_m}{y_m} = +8\%$), while reduces labor and production in the underground sector. In particular, production activity in the underground economy falls by more than six percent ($\frac{\Delta y_u}{y_u} = -6.5\%$). Notice, however, that the fall in the unreported activities thwarts to some degree the expansion effects of the tax cut. The positive impact on output and income taxation induces firms and households to work less in the underground sector highlighting a strong reallocation effect between the two economies.

The reaction of the economic system is diminished when the model is subject to a cut to personal income taxes. In particular, we have that $\frac{\Delta y_m}{y_m} = -0.5\%$ and $\frac{\Delta y_u}{y_u} = +0.6\%$. Both impact responses are smaller than those of standard RBC models without the underground sector. That is because the consumers can reallocate consumption and labor intra-temporally within the two sectors, reducing the loss generated by the fiscal policy. More precisely, they shift resources from the underground to the market sector.

While taxes causes a distortion in the formal sector in both the US and European economies, driving a remarkable reallocations of inputs and outputs between sectors, the existence of different informal sectors have an equally important effects on the labor market and the economy. These effects, possibly, create different cyclical and welfare implications. These models can be extended in different directions but, if one wishes to study the labor market structure and the cyclical properties of these economies and perform comparative analysis, the informal sectors cannot be neglected.

6. Conclusions

This paper suggests that home production and underground sectors are two crucial phenomena for properly understanding the European and United States economies. These sectors spell out the mechanism of reallocation of the labor input and production between market and nonmarket sector and rely upon two important and distinguishing aspects: a different degree of family institutionalization and the incentive for individuals and firms to seek tax-free income. This is fruitfully done reviewing two dynamic general equilibrium models incorporating different informal sectors and attributing their differences to the EE and US economies tax enforceability rules and family features. It is surprising, but the literature on the role of informal sectors in macromodels is not large, although their implications are extremely relevant.

The review of these models provide important policy implications. **First**, our analysis support the long-held view that the rise of the tax and social security burdens is the most important cause of the increase of informal activity. Experiments carried out in McGrattan, Rogerson and Wright (1997) and Busato and Chiarini (2004) provide empirical support to this analysis. Taxes distort production and labor choices stimulating production and labor supply in the untaxed sector of the economy. **Second**, the effects of these reallocation mechanisms may hamper, to some degree, the effectiveness of a fiscal contraction policy. This happens because the underground and the home production sectors offer to the agents a channel through which they may reallocate their resources, avoiding (at least partially) the fiscal policy effects.**Third**, since the size of unrecorded activity is relevant, it may distort our understanding of the business cycle, raising difficulties for policy analysis. **Fourth**, the informal sectors are features of the labor markets that may help to understand many of their dynamic phenomena.

References

[1] Becker G. S., 1965, A Theory of Allocation of Time, *Economic Journal,* **75**, 493-517

[2] Basu S., K. Miles and J Fernald, *Are Technology Improvements Contractionary?* 1999 manuscript.

[3] Baxter M. and R. King, 1993, Fiscal policy in general equilibrium, *American Economic Review* **83**, 315-334.

[4] Baxter M. and Jermann U.J. 1999, Household production and the excess sensitivity of consumption to current income, *American Economic Review,* **89**, 902-920.

[5] Benhabib J., R. Rogerson and R. Wright R., 1991, Homework in Macroeconomics: Household Production and Aggregate Fluctuations, *Journal of Political Economy* **99**, 1166-1187.

[6] Blankenau W. and Ayhan Kose M. 2002, *How different is the cyclical behavior of home production across countries?* IMF,Washington.

[7] Bonke J. 1992, Distribution of economic resources: implications of including household production, *Review of Income and Wealth,* **38**, 281-293.

[8] Bovi M., 1999, Un miglioramento del metodo di Tanzi per la stima dell'economia sommersa in Italia, ISTAT, *Quaderni di Ricerca* **2**, 5-51.

[9] Braun R.A., 1994, Tax Disturbances and Real economic Activity in the Postwar United States, *Journal of Monetary Economics* **33**, 441-62.

[10] Burnside C., M. Eichembaum and S.T.Rebelo, 1995, Capital Utilization and Returns to Scale, *NBER Macroeconomics Annual*, MIT Press, 67-110.

[11] Busato F. and B. Chiarini, 2004, Market and Underground Activities in a Two Sector Dynamic Equilibrium Model, *Economic Theory* **23**, 831 861.

[12] Campbell J.Y.,1994, Inspecting the mechanism, *Journal of Monetary Economics* **33**, 463-506.

[13] Canova, F. and A.J. Ubide, 1995. Household Production and International Business Cycles, *CEPR Discussion Papers* **1113**, C.E.P.R. Discussion Papers

[14] Chang, Gomes, Schorfeide, 2001, Learning by Doing as Propagation Mechanism, forthcoming *American Economic Review*

[15] Chiarini B. and P. Piselli, 2000, Aggregate Fluctuation in a Unionized Labor Market, *Working Paper* **2**, University of Naples Istituto Universitario Navale, *http://economia.uninav.it/ise/wp.htm*

[16] Christiano L. and M. Eichembaum, 1992, Current Real Business Cycle theory and aggregate labour market fluctuations, *American Economic Review* **82**, 430-450.

[17] Cho J.O. and T. F. Cooley, 1995, The Business Cycle with Nominal Contracts, *Economic Theory* **6**, 13-33.

[18] Cho J.O. and T.F. Cooley, 1994, Employment and Hours over the Business Cycle, Journal of Economics, *Dynamics and Control* **18**, 411-432.

[19] Cho J.O. and R. Rogerson, 1988, Family Labour Supply and Aggregate Fluctuations, *Journal of Monetary Economics* **21**, 233-245.

[20] Cogley T. and J.M. Nason, 1995, Output Dynamics in Real Business Cycle Models, *American Economic Review* **85**, 492-511.

[21] Conesa J., C.D. Moreno and J. Galdon, 2001, *Spanish Economic Review*, 2001, 3, pp. 41-53

[22] Danthine J.P. and J.B. Donaldson, 2001, Output Dynamics in Real Business Cycle Models, *Decentralizing the Stochastic Growth Model*, mimeo, Columbia University

[23] Deaton A., 1992, *Understanding Consumption,* Oxford: Oxford University Press.

[24] Edelberg W, M. Eichenbaum, J. Fisher, 1999, Understanding the Effects of a Shock to Government Purchases, *Review of Economic Dynamics*, **2**, 1, 166-206

[25] Einarsson T. and M.H. Marquis, 1997, Home production with endogenous growth, *Journal of Monetary Economics*, **39**, 551-569.

[26] Feige E.L., 1989, The Underground Economies. *Tax Evasion and Information Distortion*, (Cambridge University Press; Cambridge).

[27] Fiorito R. and T. Kollintzas, 1994, Stylized facts of Business Cycles in the G7 from a Real Business Cycles Perspective, *European Economic Review* **38**, 235-269.

[28] Fisher J.D.M., 1992, *Relative Prices, Complementarities and Comovements*, Manuscript, Northwester University Reproduced

[29] Francis N. and V. Ramey 2002, Is the Technological Driven Business Cycle Hypothesis Dead?, *NBER Working Paper*, **8726**

[30] Fung S., 1992, Inflation, *Taxation and Home Production in a Real Business Cycle Model*, manuscript University of Western Ontario.

[31] Gali J., 1999, Technology, Employment, and the Business Cycle: Do Technology Shocks Explain Aggregate Fluctuations, *American Economic Review*, **89**, 249-271.

[32] Giles D, 1999, Measuring the Hidden Economy: Implications for Econometric Modelling, *Economic Journal*, **109**, 456, 370-80.

[33] Gomme P., Kydland F. and Rupert P., 2001, Time-to-build and household production, *Journal of Political Economy* forthcoming.

[34] Greenwood J. and Z. Hercowitz, 1991, The Allocation of Capital and Time over the Business Cycle, *Journal of Political Economy* **99**, 1188-1214.

[35] Gronau, R, 1986, Home Production-A Survey, *Handbook of labor economics,* **1**, 273-304

[36] Ihrig J. and Moe K.S. 2001, *Lurking in the Shadows: the Informal Sector and Government Policy,* Board of Governors of the Federal Reserve System, June.

[37] Ingram B.F., Kocherlakota N.R. and Savin N.E. (1997), Using Theory for Measurement: an Analysis of the Cyclical Behavior of Home Production, *Journal of Monetary Economics*, **40**, 435-456.

[38] Juster F.T. and Stafford F.P. 1991, The Allocation of Time: Empirical Findings, Behavioral Models, and Problems of Measurement, *Journal of Economic Literature*, **29**, 471-522.

[39] Joumard I. 2002, Tax Systems in European Union Countries, *Oecd Economic Studies*, **34**, 91-151.

[40] King R.G., C.I. Plosser and S.T. Rebelo, 1988a, Production, Growth and Business Cycles: I. The Basic Neoclassical Model, *Journal of Monetary Economics,* **21**, 195-232.

[41] King R.G., C.I. Plosser and S.T. Rebelo, 1988b, Production, Growth and Business cycles: II New directions, *Journal of Monetary Economics* **21**, 309-342.

[42] King R.G. and S.T. Rebelo, 1999, Resuscitating Real Business Cycles, in Taylor J.B. and Woodford M. (eds.), *Handbook of Macroeconomics* Vol.1 (Elsevier Science, Amsterdam).

[43] Hansen G.D., 1985, Indivisible Labour and Supply and the Business Cycle, *Journal of Monetary Economics* **16**, 309-327.

[44] Hodrick. R. J and E. Prescott, 1997, Postwar U.S. Business Cycles: An Empirical Investigation, *Journal of Money, Credit, and Banking,* **29**, 1, 1-16.

[45] Ingram B.F., N.R. Kocherlakota and N.E. Savin, 1994, Explaining Business Cycles. A Multiple-Shock Approach, *Journal of Monetary Economics* **34**, 415-428.

[46] Loayza N. 1996, The Economics of the Informal Sector: a Simple Model and some Empirical Evidence from Latin America, *Carnegie-Rochester Conference Series on Public Policy,* **45**, 129-162.

[47] Lucas R.E.Jr., 1988, On the Mechanics of Development Planning, *Journal of Monetary Economics* **22**, 3-42.

[48] Mare' M., 1996, L'evasione in Italia e nei paesi OECD: Evidenze Empiriche, Determinanti ed Effetti Economici, *Moneta e Credito* **49**, 393-443.

[49] McGrattan E.R., 1994, The Macroeconomic Effects of Distortionary Taxation, *Journal of Monetary Economics* **33**, 559-71.

[50] McGrattan E.R., R. Rogerson and R. Wright, 1997, An Equilibrium Model of the Business Cycle with Household Production and Fiscal Policy, *International Economic Review* **38**, 267-90.

[51] Olson M., 1982, Environmental Indivisibilities and Information Costs: Fanaticism, Agnosticism, and Intellectual Progress, The American Economic Review, *Papers and Proceedings of the Ninety-Fourth Annual Meeting of the American Economic Association*, **72**, 2, 262-266.

[52] OECD, 1997 *Job Strategy: Making Work to Pay. Taxation, benefits, Employment and Unemployment*, Paris.

[53] OECD 1999 *Benefit System and Work Incentives*, Paris.

[54] OECD, 2001 *Revenue Statistics* 1965-2000, Paris.

[55] OECD, 2001 *Taxing Wages* 1999-2000, Paris.

[56] Parente S.L., R. Rogerson and R. Wright, 1999, Household production and development, Fed Bank of Cleveland, *Economic Review*, **35**, 21-35.

[57] Perli R., 1998, Increasing Returns, Home Production and Persistence of Business Cycles, *Journal of Economic Dynamics and Control*, vol. 22 (April 1998), pp. 519-43.

[58] Pollak R.A, M.L. Watcher, 1975, The Relevance of the Household Production and its Implications for the Allocation of Time, *Journal of Political Economy*, **83**, 255-77

[59] Prescott E. C. and R. Mehra, 1980, Recursive Competitive Equilibrium: the Case of Homogenous Household, *Econometrica*, 1365-79

[60] Ramey V.A. and M.D. Shapiro, 1997, Costly Capital Reallocation and the Effects of Government Spending, *NBER Working Paper Series*, *http://www.nber.org/papers/w6283*

[61] Rios-Rull, J.V., 1993, Working in the Market, Working at Home, and the Acquisition of Skills: A General-Equilibrium Approach, *American Economic Review,* **83**, 4, 893-907

[62] Salanie' B., 2001, *The Economics of Contracts,* The MIT Press eds.

[63] Sarte P-D. 2000, Informality and Rent-seeking Bureaucracies in a Model of long-run Growth, *Journal of Monetary Economics*, **46**, 173-197.

[64] Shea J., 1998, What Do Technology Shocks Do?, *NBER Macroeconomics Annual*, 275- 310.

[65] Stadler G.W., 1994, Real Business Cycle, *Journal of Economics Litterature* XXXII, 1750-1783.

[66] Schneider F. and D. Enste, 2000, Shadow Economies: Size, Causes, and Consequences, *Journal of Economic Literature* **XXXVIII**, 77-114.

[67] Spiro P. 1994, *The Underground Economy: Toward a More Balanced View of Alternative Methodologies Canadian Business Economics* , **2**, 4, 18-21.

[68] Stokey N. and R.E. Lucas with E.C. Prescott, 1989, *Recursive Methods in Economics Dynamics*, (Harvard University Press; Cambridge MA).

[69] Tanzi V., 1983, The Underground Economy in the United States: Annual Estimates, 1930-80, *International Monetary Fund Staff Papers,* **30**, 2, 283-305.

[70] Tanzi V., 1980, Inflationary Expectations, Economic Activity, Taxes, and Interest Rates, *The American Economic Review*, **70**, 1, 12-21.

[71] Thomas J.J., 1992, Informal Economic Activity in London School of Economics, *Handbooks in Economics,* (Harvester Wheatsheaf; London).

[72] Thomas J.J., 1999, Quantifying the Black Economy: 'Measurement Without Theory' Yet Again?, *Economic Journal* **109**, 381-89.

[73] Uhlig H., 1999, A Toolkit for Analyzing Nonlinear Dynamic Stochastic Models Easily, in R. Marimon and A. Scott (eds) *Computational Methods for the Study of Dynamic Economies*, (Oxford University Press; Oxford).

[74] Uzawa H., 1965, Optimal Technical Change in an Aggregative Model of Economic Growth, *International Economic Review* **6**, 18-31.

In: Business Fluctuations and Cycles
Editor: T. Nagakawa, pp. 137-169
ISBN: 978-1-60021-503-3

Chapter 6

HOW MUCH DO TRADE AND FINANCIAL LINKAGES MATTER FOR BUSINESS CYCLE SYNCHRONIZATION?

Alicia García Herrero and Juan M. Ruiz[1]
Department of International Economics
Bank of Spain, Madrid, Spain

ABSTRACT

We estimate a system of equations to analyze whether trade and financial linkages influence business cycle synchronization directly or indirectly. We use a small, open economy (Spain) as benchmark for the results, instead of the US as generally done in the literature. Neither trade nor financial linkages are found significant in directly influencing business cycle synchronization. Only the similarity in productive structure appears to foster economic integration, after controlling for common policies. Trade linkages are found to increase output synchronization indirectly, by contributing to the similarity of productive structures, which might point to the prevalence of intra-industry trade. The positive influence of financial linkages on output synchronization is even more indirect, by fostering trade integration and, thereby, a more similar productive structure. The net effects of both trade and financial linkages on business cycle synchronization are found statistically significant, but economically very small.

Keywords: business cycle synchronization, trade linkages, financial linkages, productive structure, integration.

JEL classification: E32, F41, F12, E44.

---

[1] Mailing Address: Bank of Spain, Dept. of International Economics (ERI), Alcalá 48, 28014 Madrid, Spain. Authors' e-mail addresses are *alicia.garcia-herrero and jruiz* (please add @bde.es at the end to complete the address). We thank Andrew Rose and participants at the 6th ETSG conference for comments. The opinions expressed herein are those of the authors and not necessarily those of the Bank of Spain. Updated versions of this paper can be found at *http://www.eco.uc3m.es/jruiz/research.htm*

1. INTRODUCTION

The last few years have witnessed increasing economic globalization stemming from a very rapid growth in trade and financial linkages, among other factors. At least at first sight, one would be tempted to think that tighter trade and financial linkages contribute to the synchronization of business cycles. However, there is neither a clear *a priori* in the theoretical literature nor a consensus in the empirical work. In fact, they generate both demand and supply reactions, which may counteract each other. In addition, it is not even clear whether business cycle synchronization has increased over time. It very much depends on how synchronization is measured and which countries are considered.

The issue is relevant for several reasons. First, if business cycles are more synchronized, the transmission of shocks across countries will be stronger and faster. This could be an important rationale in favor of international policy coordination. Second, business cycles synchronization has profound implications for the design and functioning of common currency areas. Third, if the business cycle in a country is mainly driven by external factors, such as trade and financial linkages, domestic policies aimed at economic stabilization are bound to have a smaller impact. In the same vein, if trade linkages lead to business cycle synchronization, external demand will not manage to dampen economic fluctuations, but quite the opposite. This implies that exchange rate policy will be unlikely to play an important role in boosting demand at times of low economic activity.

This paper contributes to the empirical literature mainly in two ways. First, most of the existing studies analyze the issue estimating a reduced-form equation. However, there are a number of interrelations between trade linkages, financial integration and business cycle synchronization, which need to be taken into account so that the results are meaningful. We, therefore, use a system of equations to analyze the issue.

Second, many studies suffer from the lack of bilateral data to measure financial linkages and use aggregate financial stocks or flows. This, which measures financial integration with the rest of the world, can hardly explain business cycle co-movements between two countries. Those studies which use bilateral data generally take the US or a group of big economies as a benchmark to measure business cycle synchronization. Such a large economy, or area, influences other countries through many channels other than trade and financial linkages, which is bound to bias the estimated coefficients. To minimize this problem, we use a small open economy, namely Spain, as a benchmark.

From our empirical exercise, we obtain several conclusions: First, trade or financial linkages only influence the synchronization of business cycles through their effect on the similarity of economic structure. Second, the synchronization of output increases as economic structures become more similar —suggesting the prevalence of sectoral shocks in the last 15 years—, and as macroeconomic policies become more synchronized. Third, more trade integration *increases* the similarity of productive structures (which might point to intra-industry trade), and thus leads to *higher* business cycle synchronization. The *total effect* of trade integration on the similarity of productive structures turns out to be positive, but economically small. Fourth, the net effect of financial linkages on output synchronization is also indirect, positive, and very small: its fostering of trade linkages is reflected in its positive effect on the similarity of productive structures, and thus on the correlation of cycles.

Perhaps the more important conclusion of the exercise, however, is our finding that, even though these indirect effects of trade and financial integration over business cycle synchronization are statistically significant, they are not very relevant economically. The effect of a similar productive structure or synchronized macro policies seems economically more relevant in influencing the synchronization of cycles.

The rest of the paper is organized as follows: the next section reviews recent literature on the relationship between trade and financial integration and business cycle synchronization; section 3 outlines the main theoretical predictions and the estimation strategy; section 4 presents the empirical results and section 5 concludes.

2. Related Literature

Although the synchronization of business cycles has been extensively analyzed in the literature, there is no clear picture of whether it has increased over time, even less so of its determinants.

The conflicting evidence on the trend of synchronization over time may be attributed to the country coverage, the sample period and/or the econometric technique applied. On the one hand, Helbling and Bayoumi (2003) find decreasing synchronization between the US and rest of G-7 countries, Heathcote and Perri (2003a,b) report a similar result between the US and an aggregate of Europe, Japan and Canada. On the other hand, Kose et al (2003b) show an increasing co-movement between individual advanced countries and world (G-7) aggregates. With a broader perspective, Bordo and Helbling (2003) find increased synchronization over the last 125 years for 16 industrial countries. In the same vein, using dynamic factor models, Stock and Watson (2003),[2] Helbling and Bayoumi (2003) and Lumsdaine and Prasad (2003) show strong evidence of a common factor driving business cycles in advanced countries. However, with a similar methodology but for a sample of sixty countries, Kose, Otrok and Whiteman (2003) find that the common component (the so-called "world factor") is less important in developing countries.

There are also large differences in how synchronization is measured. Kose et al (2003b) use correlations of output and consumption of countries with respect to aggregate consumption and output of G-7 countries. They complement it with dynamic factor models to look for common components and assess whether the importance of the common component has increased over time, signaling a stronger synchronization. Heathcote and Perri (2003b) split the sample in two equal-length periods and measure cross-regional correlations of the log-difference of US GDP with that of an aggregate of Europe, Japan and Canada. They also propose and use a measure of correlation that corrects for the existence of high conditional volatility, based on Loretan and English (2000). Helbling and Bayoumi (2003) employ various indicators of synchronization, including a binary indicator of expansions and recessions; correlation coefficients and detrended series.[3] They finally use dynamic factor models to assess what is the role of common components on output synchronization. Finally,

[2] In particular, they find that find that this common component has become more important to explain G-7 business cycles after 1984 than between 1960 and 1983

[3] Detrending is done using Baxter and King (1999) band-pass filter to eliminate low- and high-frequency components to keep business cycle components defined as those between 6 and 32 quarters. An alternative method used is log first differences.

Imbs (2004b) measures synchronization by using cross-country correlations of band-pass series of quarterly GDP over the last 20 years.

Moving to the potential channels of synchronization we focus on this study, namely trade and financial linkages, neither the theoretical nor the empirical literature offer a definitive answer on their impact on synchronization. Regarding trade, Kose and Yi (2001) suggest that higher trade integration might lead to more or less synchronization of cycles, depending on the nature of trade and the type of shocks. Countries will become more synchronized if there is an increase of intra-industry trade and industry-specific shocks are the main drivers of business cycles. However, if there is more inter-industry trade, then industry-specific shocks would reduce the co-movement of output in both countries. Empirical studies find that higher trade integration increases cross-country output correlations, especially among advanced economies [Frankel and Rose (1998), Clark and van Wincoop (2001), Imbs (2004a, 2004b)], possibly reflecting increased intra-industry trade rather than inter-industry trade.

Measures of trade linkages also differ across studies. Some of the earlier studies used aggregate measures of trade openness (i.e., trade integration instead of trade linkages between two countries). This is obviously less appropriate to investigate the determinants of business cycle synchronization between two countries. As for bilateral trade relations, some authors have used *de jure* measures namely restrictions to trade, such as import duties [IMF WEO (2002)]. The most common *de facto* measure is the sum of exports and imports between two countries, divided by GDP [IMF WEO (2002), Imbs (2004b)], or over the ratio of the product of GDPs divided by world output, to make it independent of country size (Clark and van Wincoop (2001)). Another alternative, non-standard measure is the dispersion between two countries' goods prices [IMF WEO (2002)]. More details on these measures will be offered in Section 3, since we shall be using them in our study.

As for financial linkages, there is some evidence of a positive relationship between financial integration and business cycle co-movements both in output and consumption in the case of advanced economies (Imbs 2004a,b) but not so for developing economies (Kose, Prasad and Terrones (2003b)). In addition, these results are challenged by potential reverse causality. In fact, Heathcote and Perri (2003b) propose that higher financial integration may arise as a result of less correlated real shocks, since the gains from asset trade are bigger. By fostering financial flows, financial integration would dampen GDP correlations more than the reduction implied by the lower correlation of shocks

The measures of financial linkages also differ.[4] As for trade linkages, earlier studies used aggregate measures rather than bilateral ones (i.e., trade integration instead of linkages). This is even more the case than for trade because of the difficulties in finding bilateral data of financial transactions. Among the aggregate measures, several authors have employed aggregate *de jure* indicators, namely a global index of capital account restrictions from the IMF Annual Report on Exchange Arrangements and Exchange Restrictions[5]. Imbs (2004b) uses the sum of these indices in two countries as a bilateral *de jure* measure of their financial linkages. Another *de jure* measure of aggregate financial integration is an index of stock market liberalization (Prasad et al (2003)). Among *de facto* measures, there are quantity and price measures, most of which are aggregate and not bilateral. The most comprehensive aggregate quantity measure is the sum of stocks of external assets and liabilities of foreign

[4] Edison et al (2002) and Prasad et al (2003) provide surveys of different measures of financial integration.

[5] Prasad et al. (2003), IMF (2001b) and IMF (2002).

direct investment and portfolio investment[6] (IMF WEO (2002), IMF WEO (2001b), Prasad et al. (2003)[7] and Heathcote and Perri (2003b)[8]).[9] Other aggregate measures are total capital flows as a share of GDP, but it suffers from large volatility (Prasad et al (2003)). Others are proxies of risk sharing obtained regressing GDP on disposable income (Kalemli-Ozcan et al (2003)) [10] A bilateral quantity measure (i.e., of financial linkages) is the sum of gross asset positions between two countries, but this is only readily available for the US against the rest of the world (Imbs, 2004b)). An alternative source of bilateral data are equity transaction flows (Portes and Rey (2003)) although it is only available for a few countries, and equity holdings from the Coordinated Portfolio Investment Survey conducted by the IMF in 1997 and 2001. The latter also has geographical limitations, as well as underreporting and a poor collection method (Lane and Milesi-Ferretti (2004)). There are also bilateral price measures, such as differences from covered interest rate parity, but with very limited data availability (Frankel, 1992), and asset price arbitrage (IMF, 2001) based on rolling correlations of stock and bond prices. The latter, though, suffers from potential reverse causality.

The methodology generally used in the literature to test for the relevance of trade and financial channels is the estimation of a single equation. The fact that there may be indirect effects going in opposite directions might account for the generally small impact found in studies using single equation regressions. To our knowledge, Imbs (2004b) is the only one who estimates a system of simultaneous equations to take into account direct and indirect effects on synchronization but there are a number of differences between his analysis and ours. First, he does not consider the possible two-way relationship between financial linkages and trade linkages (Aizenman and Noy (2001) or the incentives for financial linkages that might stem from a low correlation of business cycles Heathcote and Perri (2003b). Second, he works with a limited set of 24 countries, with a very high proportion of rich economies in the sample. Having mostly developed countries in the sample might induce a selection bias in the results, as developing countries are likely to be also very poorly linked commercially and financially. Third, his estimated coefficients might be picking up some other channels through which big economies affect other countries' business cycles. Finally, Imbs (2004b) includes output correlations from the 80s and 90s. However, the existence of a number global common shocks in the 80s (although less prevalent than in the 70s) makes it difficult to identify the source of output co-movements.

---

[6] Bank lending is not included.

[7] Prasad et al (2003) also separate financial flows into its main constituents: FDI, bank loans and portfolio flows.

[8] Heathcote and Perri (2003b) use, for assets, the sum of FDI plus the equity part of portfolio investment. They also test for separate measures (FDI on one side and equity holdings on the other).

[9] The original indices were also constructed by Lane and Milesi-Ferretti (2001) from the accumulation of financial flows and with some valuation adjustments.

[10] The idea is that with perfect risk sharing, disposable income should be unrelated to GDP, whereas in the absence of risk sharing, they should be closely related. Kalemli-Ozcan et al (2003) also use measures of consumption risk sharing. Imbs (2004b) uses pair wise sums of this estimate of risk sharing as measure of bilateral financial integration

3. Estimation

We assess empirically whether trade and financial linkages foster or hinder the synchronization of business cycles, while taking into account other potentially relevant determinants of synchronization. Both in the case of trade and financial linkages, there are arguments for and against their fostering synchronization.

Trade linkages should, in principle, lead to more synchronized business cycles as higher investment or consumption in one country implies an increase in imports from trade partners. However, depending on the patterns of trade, larger commercial linkages might increase or decrease synchronization. If both countries develop intra-industry trade, then output should be more synchronized even if shocks are mostly sector-specific. However, trade may also foster specialization in production, thereby reducing business cycle synchronization if shocks are mostly industry-specific.

Financial linkages could strengthen or weaken the co-movement of output, depending on its effect on specialization and the nature of shocks. On the one hand, there may be more synchronization if financial linkages allow for spillovers from demand shocks. On the other, there should be less synchronization if financial links lead to the reallocation of capital according to comparative advantage. This should contribute to specialization in production, fostering inter-industry instead of intra-industry trade.

The description of the way in which trade and financial linkages may affect synchronization is clearly multi-directional. This implies potential endogeneity problems. Moreover, the different directions of indirect effects might offset each other and lead to very small net effects if we just try to correct the endogeneity problem using instrumental variables in the estimation. We shall, thus, use a system of equations to deal with this issue.

We also consider other possible sources of synchronization, namely the convergence of economic policies, which we approximate with the volatility of exchange rates and the differences in inflation rates.

Finally, we use bilateral data to account for trade and financial linkages. Data on financial linkages is particularly difficult to find except for the US, which obliges us to focus on one aspect of financial integration for which bilateral data is available, namely FDI. We choose a small open economy as a benchmark country, Spain. This is unlikely to have other channels of influence on other countries, limiting the problem of omitted variables in previous studies with *de facto* bilateral data of financial linkages.

4. Estimation Strategy and Data Issues

The direct and indirect channels through which trade and financial linkages may affect business cycle synchronization can only be taken into account through a system of equations. We, therefore, estimate a system of four equations, in which we test for the determinants of business cycle synchronization (eq. 1), those of trade and financial linkages (eqs. 2 and 3, respectively) and those of the similarity in productive structure (eq. 4). As previously explained, the latter is a key variable both in the cases of trade linkages and also business cycle synchronization.

$$\rho_{i,t} = \alpha_0 + \alpha_1 T_{i,t} + \alpha_2 S_{i,t} + \alpha_3 F_{i,t} + \text{Controls}(\rho) + \varepsilon_\rho \quad \text{(Eq. 1)}$$

$$T_{i,t} = \beta_0 + \beta_1 S_{i,t} + \beta_2 F_{i,t} + \text{Controls}(T) + \varepsilon_T \quad \text{(Eq. 2)}$$

$$F_{i,t} = \delta_0 + \delta_1 \rho_{i,t} + \delta_2 T_{i,t} + \text{Controls}(F) + \varepsilon_F \quad \text{(Eq. 3)}$$

$$S_{i,t} = \gamma_0 + \gamma_1 T_{i,t} + \gamma_2 F_{i,t} + \text{Controls}(S) + \varepsilon_S \text{(Eq. 4)}$$

where:

$\rho_{i,t}$ is the correlation between Spain's business cycle and country i at time t.

$T_{i,t}$ is bilateral trade integration between Spain and country i at time t. In principle, the expected sign of its coefficient in Eq. 1 is positive but it could be dampened or even reversed if trade contributed to a high degree of specialization.

$S_{i,t}$ is an index of the similarity of economic structure between Spain and country i. This should be closely linked to the share of intra versus inter-industry trade. The more similar the economic structure (i.e., the lower the degree of specialization between two countries), a tighter business cycle synchronization is expected.

$F_{i,t}$ is bilateral financial integration with country i. As for trade, the expected sign of its coefficient in Eq. 1 is ambiguous for the reasons previously mentioned.

Although optimally one should conduct a panel data regression with the structure outlined above, given the poor quality of the geographical disaggregation of financial data prior to 1997, we choose to conduct a cross section regression using data for the period 1997-2003. We, therefore, drop the time subindex for all variables considered.

Among several possibilities in the literature, we choose to measure business cycle synchronization (ρ_I) as the Pearson correlation of the log difference of annual GDP.[11]

For trade linkages T_i between Spain and country i, we use the standard bilateral *de facto* measure, as in Frankel and Rose (1998) as a benchmark, namely the sum of bilateral imports and exports between Spain (*ESP*) and country i divided by the sum of their respective GDPs. Denoting this measure by $T^1_{ESP,i}$, we have:

$$T^1_{ESP,i} = \frac{1}{T}\sum_t \frac{X_{ESP,i,t} + M_{ESP,i,t}}{GDP_{ESP,t} + GDP_{i,t}}$$

where $X_{ESP,i,t}$ are exports from Spain to country i at time t, $M_{ESP,i,t}$ are imports to Spain from country i at time t, and $GDP_{i,t}$ is country i's GDP at time t.[12] Note that we are taking a time average (over the period under study) of this measure.

---

11 GDP is measured at purchasing power parity and was obtained from the IMF's World Economic Outlook database.

12 Data for exports and imports is obtained from the IMF's Direction of Trade Statistics. Data for GDP (at purchasing power parity) is obtained from the IMF's World Economic Outlook database. All data are annual.

As a robustness exercise, we also consider Clark and van Wincoop (2001)'s measure, which is independent of country size (and dependent only on trade barriers). Denoting this alternative measure $T^2_{ESP,i}$ we have:

$$T^2_{ESP,i} = \frac{\frac{1}{T}\sum_t \left(\frac{X_{ESP,i,t} + M_{ESP,i,t}}{GDP_{ESP,t} \times GDP_{i,t}} \right) GDP_{World,t}}{2}$$

Taking into account Deardorff (1998)'s, who shows that this measure is equal to one if preferences are homothetic and there are no trade barriers, we not that if we use $T^2_{ESP,i}$ in the regressions, we can drop $GDP_{World,t}$ from the computation of the index. This would just be a scaling factor which will multiply the coefficient of $T^2_{ESP,i}$ but will not change its sign or significance. All the results presented here are robust to measuring trade linkages in this alternative way.

In order to measure financial integration through a bilateral *de facto* measure, we initially used bilateral FDI flows from and to Spain from the OECD. Although data on stocks of FDI would have been a better indicator, it was not available for Spain. We measure financial integration by taking the sum of inward and outward FDI flows and computing a time average over the period of study:

$$F_{ESP,i} = \frac{1}{T}\sum_t I_{ESP,i,t} + I_{i,ESP,t}$$

where I_{ijt} represents financial flows from country i to country j (ESP denotes Spain) at time t.

The similarity in productive structure can be measured in several alternative ways. All of them are based on data of shares of each productive sector, and differ in the depth of disaggregation of economic activities and whether or not they concentrate on manufactures (at greater disaggregation[13]) or on all sectors (at lower disaggregation[14]). Let $s_{n,i,t}$ be the share of industry n in country i at time t. Then the first measure of economic similarity can be expressed as

$$S^1_{ESP,i} = -\frac{1}{T}\sum_t \sum_{n=1}^{N} \left| s_{n,ESP,t} - s_{n,i,t} \right|$$

where N is the number of sectors. Note that $S^1_{ESP,i}$ represents the time average of discrepancies in economic structures, as in Imbs (2004b).[15] $S^1_{ESP,i}$ might take values

[13] Typically, 2- or 3-digit ISIC classification groups.

[14] At 1-digit ISIC classification groups.

[15] We include a minus sign in front of the definition of structure similarity so that a higher value of S implies more similarity between the productive structures in both countries. This of course only changes the sign of its associated estimated parameter, but neither its size nor its significance.

between 0 for identical structures and –2 for disjoint productive structures. Therefore *higher* values for $S^1_{ESP,i}$ imply *more* similarity between the Spanish productive structure and that of country *i*. Clark and van Wincoop (2001) use a similar concept but taking time averages of structures before computing distances in shares.[16]

$$S^2_{ESP,i} = -\sum_{n=1}^{N} \frac{1}{T} \left| \sum_t s_{n,ESP,t} - \sum_t s_{n,i,t} \right|$$

Industry shares $s_{n,i,t}$ can be measured using a number of different indicators. The three main indicators are shares in total employment, shares of value added, or shares of production. All the results presented in the next section use the definition $S^1_{ESP,i}$ described above applied to shares of value added, although the results are robust to using other definitions or data on employment or production, as they are highly correlated. We use data for the industrial sector at the two-digit ISIC level from UNIDO.[17]

We also use a number of controls in the regressions as suggested by previous work on each subject. One potential source of business cycle synchronization is the similarity of macroeconomic policies and the similarity of productive structures. We therefore include a number of variables to approximate this effect, such as the volatility of the bilateral exchange rate, the average inflation differential and a dummy variable to account for use of the euro as official currency.

In the case of trade linkages, a number of studies have suggested that gravity variables play an important role in explaining the importance of trade between two countries. We therefore include distance, sum of land areas, product of populations, product of GDPs, and two dummy variables to account for sovereign access to the sea and a common main language.[18]

Recent studies[19] have suggested that gravity variables also explain bilateral financial linkages. We, thus, include distance, time difference between main financial centers, common language and the sum of per capita GDPs.[20] This last variable tries to capture the idea that richer countries tend to generate more financial flows (both inward and outward).

Surely the most difficult variable to control is the similarity of productive structure. Following on Imbs and Wacziarg (2003) we use the pair-wise difference of per capita GDPs, based on the idea that rich countries tend to be more diversified and thus possibly more similar, whereas poorer countries tend to be more specialized.

---

[16] Clark and van Wincoop (2001) use a similar concept but taking time averages of structures before computing distances in shares. Imbs (2001) uses the Pearson correlation coefficient between sectoral shares $s_{n,i,t}$.

[17] We could in principle use data at the three-digit ISIC level and increase the desegregations of activities. However, some countries in the sample do not report data at that level of desegregations, and therefore we opted for a lower level of desegregations in order to increase the sample size.

[18] Some studies include, instead of common language, a dummy variable capturing past colonial relationship. In the case of Spain both variables coincide.

[19] See, for example, Portes and Rey (2003).

[20] As the effect of distance on trade and financial integration might not be linear, but stronger for shorter distances (in other words, an increase in distance reduces trade and financial integration, but at a diminishing rate) we also try the log of distance and time differences, instead of its levels.

Results

As a preliminary step we show some stylized facts of the main variables of interest in this study: business cycle synchronization, trade and FDI linkages.

The degree of bilateral business cycle synchronization between Spain and EU countries increased substantially from 1960 to 1995 (figure 1). Since then, it has fallen somewhat and now hovers at 0.6 (in terms of Pearson correlation coefficient of annual growth rates). Bilateral synchronization between Spain and G7 countries also rose fast from 1970 to 1976 but then fell again. Since Spain's entry in EU in 1986, it has risen at a slower pace than synchronization with EU countries. Business cycles in Spain and in Latin American countries move in opposite directions since the late 1980s. All in all the period of closer synchronization between Spain and other countries was from 1975 to 1985.

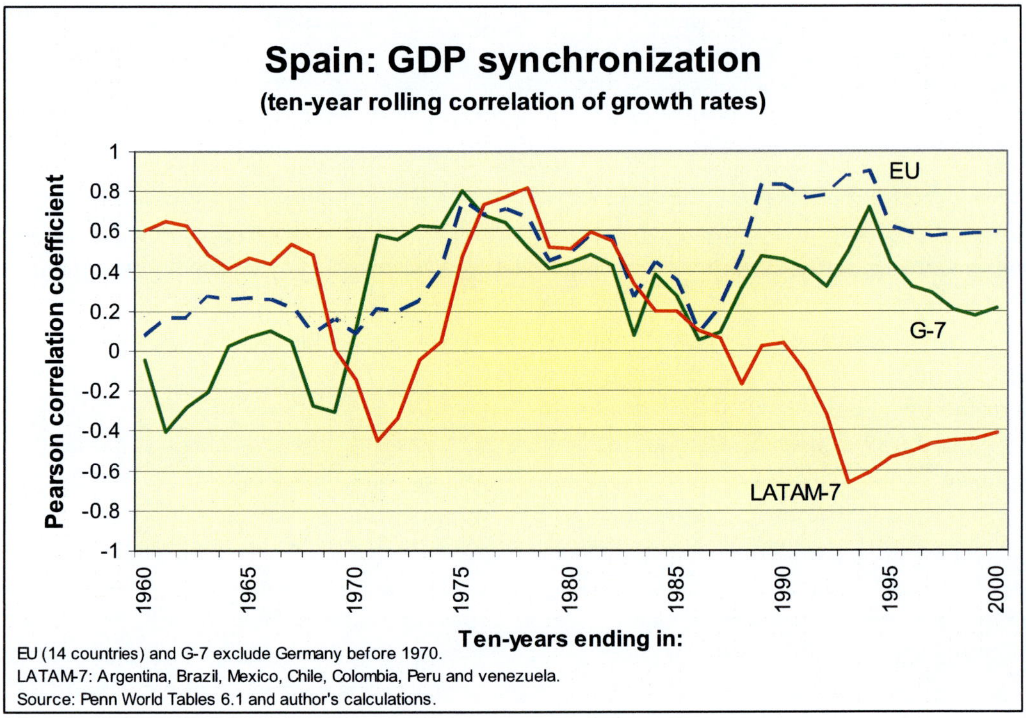

Figure 1. Evolution of GDP synchronization between Spain and selected regions.

Trade linkages between Spain and EU countries started to rise already ten years before Spain's entry into EU but since then the increase has been exponential (Figure 2). In fact the sum of imports from and exports to EU countries has reached 0.002% of those countries' combined GDP. Trade linkages with G7 countries began to grow later, in the mid 1980s and at a much lower pace, reaching about 0.0007% of their combined GDP as a sum of imports and exports. Trade linkages with Latin American countries haven remained relatively small throughout the period.

Spain started to have FDI linkages with EU and G7 countries in the mid-1980s, which increased enormously in the mid-1990s (Figure 3). FDI linkages with Latin American countries also rose then but at a lower pace. In 2000, there was a sharp fall of FDI linkages with all countries but it has recovered again with Latin American countries in the last few years. Still the size of these FDI linkages is smaller than that with EU and, to a lesser extent, G7 countries.

Turning to the estimation of the system of four equations, we first report the results of the estimation of each equation separately, using OLS. Since there are good reasons to suspect endogeneity problems, we complement the estimation of equation 1 (the main equation of interest to us) with the use of suitable instruments for trade and financial linkages (*T* and *F*) and similarity of structure *S*. In order to disentangle the direct and indirect effects of trade and financial linkages on business cycle synchronization, we finally turn to a joint estimation of the whole system of four equations, using three-stage least squares (3SLS).

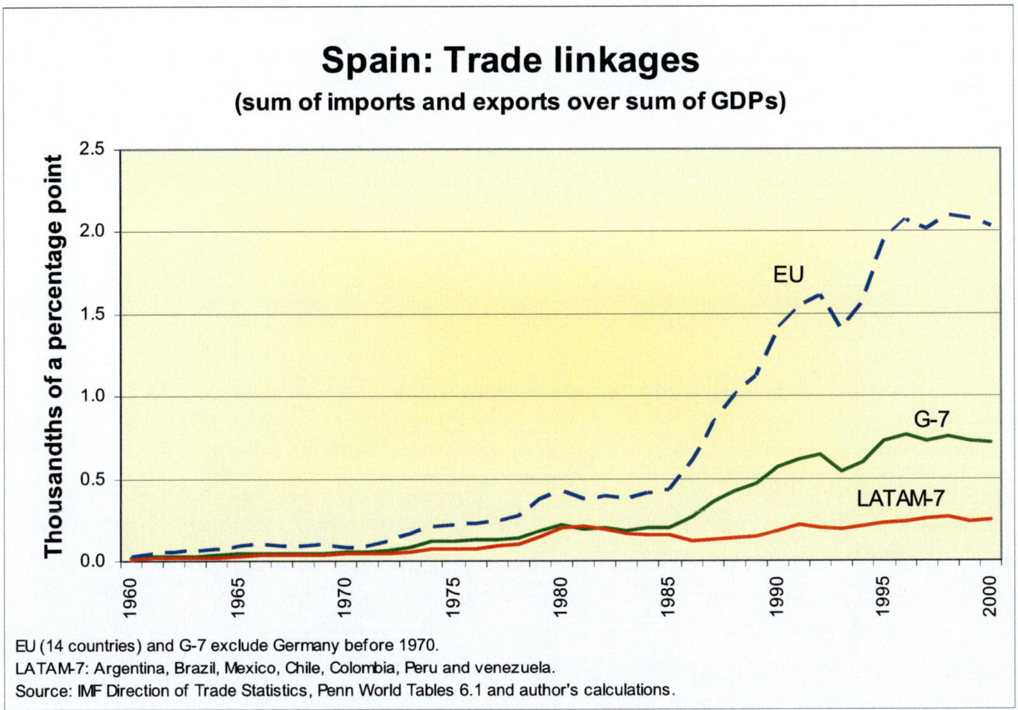

Figure 2. Evolution of trade linkages between Spain and selected regions.

As regards the determinants of business cycle synchronization, estimated by a single equation (equation 1), trade integration seems significant in explaining the correlation of business cycles (Table 1), although once we control for common policies (the volatility of exchange rates seems particularly significant), this effect vanishes. In these OLS estimations for equation 1, neither financial linkages nor the similarity of productive structure appear significant, However, the endogeneity of trade (*T*) and financial linkages (*F*) (measured with FDI only), and the similarity of the productive structure (*S*) might lead to highly biased coefficients. This problem is tackled later by the use of IV estimation as reported in the lower half of table 1. Before turning to the estimation of equation 1 using instrumental variables, we turn to the OLS estimation of equations 2 to 4.

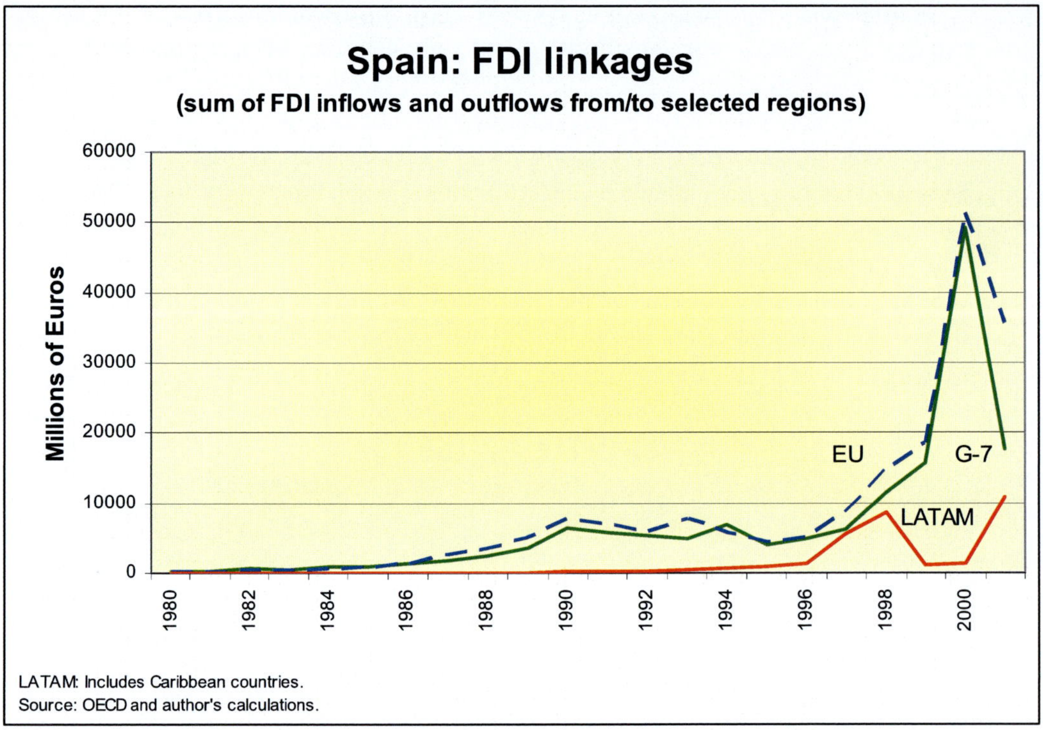

Figure 3. Evolution of FDI linkages between Spain and selected regions.

The estimation of trade linkages (Eq 2) shows that financial linkages, approximated by FDI, affect trade positively (β_2>0) and significantly (Table 2). Among the variables included to account for a gravity model, distance to the main city appears as highly significant and with the correct sign. The coefficient of the similarity in productive structure (β_1) is not significant. This could be due to endogeneity problems or because of conflicting effects, depending on whether intra or interindustry trade is more prevalent. The coefficient on the product of average GDPs should have a positive sign, although in specification V and VI it is significantly negative. Again this may point to a bias due to the endogeneity of FDI integration, as the problem only appears when *F* is included in the regression.

Financial linkages, estimated by OLS on equation 3 seem to be determined by trade linkages and distance. The only anomaly is in the sign of the time difference between financial centers, which might again point towards and endogeneity problem. The significance of lagged trade linkages might point out to a global effect of trade integration on financial integration, as described by Aizenman and Noy (2004). An alternative and simpler explanation could be the high correlation of trade integration in the 80s and 90s.

An OLS regression for the similarity in productive structure (Eq. 4) described in Table 4 points to the difference in percapita GDP as a good explanatory variable, as suggested by the theory. The similarity in productive structure seems to be positively influenced by trade linkages. In other words, trade linkages promote a similar economic structure. Again, all these coefficients might suffer from important biases stemming from the endogeneity of *T* and *F*.

Given the biases introduced in the estimation of equation 1 due to the endogeneity of *T*, *F*, and *S*, we proceed to estimate equation 1 using appropriate instruments for those variables.[21] We report estimates of instrumental-variable regressions with alternative specifications of equation 1 in the lower half of table 1. The last three regressions include our controls for common policies. Note that, because of the availability of instruments, the number of observations drop to 43. Although coefficients change slightly from the top half of table 1, overall we still see no significant contribution of trade or financial linkages to explain business cycle synchronization, once we control for our proxies for common policies.

Estimation of equation 1 by instrumental variables, however, still pools together the direct and indirect effects of trade and financial linkages over business cycles synchronization, for example through their effect over the convergence of productive structures between Spain and the other countries in the sample. If indirect effects through different channels point to opposite directions, the net effect might become small and thus contribute to its statistical insignificance. We therefore conduct a three-stage least-squares regression on the whole system of four equations.

Estimating the system of four equations, the results change to a large extent (Table 5a). The most relevant, for the purpose of our study, is that only the similarity in productive structure (S) is found significant in determining output synchronization, after controlling for the effect of common policies. In this regard, exchange rate volatility is found significant while differences in inflation are not. Trade linkages influence output synchronization only indirectly through their effect on the similarity of productive structure. The direct effect of trade on the similarity of productive structures is positive ($\gamma_1>0$): stronger trade links tend to make productive structures more similar, which might point to intra-industry trade. On the other hand, more trade promotes stronger financial links ($\delta_2>0$). The total effect of trade on business cycle synchronization is still positive ($\gamma_1\alpha_2>0$), in line with previous studies that do not separate the two effects.

The influence of financial linkages on output synchronization is also indirect, through its effect on trade. Since financial integration seems to foster trade integration ($\beta_2>0$), this means a positive indirect effect on the similarity of productive structures and thus on the synchronization of cycles. ($\alpha_2\,\gamma_1\,\beta_2>0$).

The important influence of a similar economic structure on business cycle synchronization is in line with Imbs (2004b) but the relevance of trade and financial linkages is smaller in our case, since he also finds direct effects. This difference might be related to the fact that we use a small open economy as a benchmark, and a wider set of countries, as opposed to Imbs (2004b). The latter may have biased upward the coefficients, as there are other channels of influence of the US economy which are not considered. Another reason, as regard financial linkages, might be the limitation of our data. FDI flows are only one type of financial linkages considered, albeit an important one.

There are also other findings from the system of equations, worth mentioning: (i) We did not find a reverse causality from business cycle synchronization to financial linkages, as argued by Heathcote and Perri (2003b); (ii) the model seems to confirm a double causality between trade and financial linkages; (iii) a similar productive structure, apart from contributing to higher output synchronization, also tends to foster trade. Such positive influence should be understood in terms of intra- more than inter-industry patterns of trade in line with the results by Kose and Yi (2001).

---

[21] In order to instrument T, F and S, we use the same independent variables as those in tables 2 to 4.

The relations that have been found significant in the system of equations can be summarized in the following diagram.

Another important question concerns the economic relevance of the statistically significant effects found in the previous exercise. As described before, the total effect of trade on the synchronization of business cycles is given indirectly through an increase in the similarity of productive structures. Specifically, in our benchmark 3SLS regression in table 5a, the effect of trade linkages on our measure of comovement of output is equal to $(\gamma_1 \alpha_2)$= 10727.62, whereas the total effect of financial linkages is given by $(\alpha_2\ \gamma_1\ \beta_2)$= 3.81 x 10^{-5}. This implies that increasing trade links by one standard deviation starting from its mean (see table 6), increases bilateral cross country correlation of GDP from 0.706 to 0.732. Increasing financial links by one standard deviation increases the correlation of output from 0.706 to 0.737.

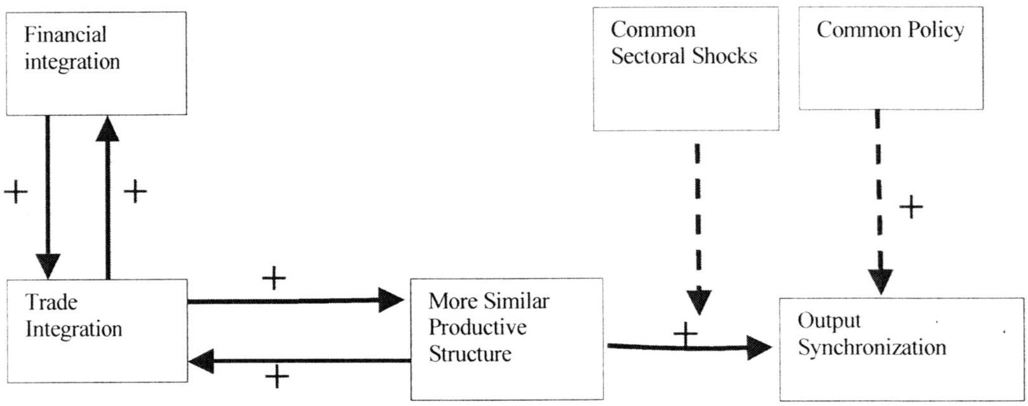

Figure 4. Channels leading to business cycle synchronization found in the empirical exercise.

This is hardly an economically meaningful change, and reflects that fact that business synchronization in the Spanish case for the last 15 years has been influenced more by common policies and presumably by common sectoral shocks. Performing the previous exercise with similarity of productive structure (S) and exchange rate volatility, we find that an increase in these variables by one standard deviation from its mean would imply a change in the degree of GDP correlation from 0.710 to 0.918 and 0.790, respectively, a much stronger effect than that of trade and financial links.

A number of additional tests are conducted to test for the robustness of our results.

First, we include an alternative hypothesis for the gravity models is that the effect of distance on trade and financial integration might not be linear, but stronger for shorter distances. In other words an increase in distance reduces trade and financial integration, but at a diminishing rate. This hypothesis is captured by including the log of distance and time differences, instead of its levels, and estimating with 3SLS as before. The gravity variables for trade and financial integration become more significant (Table 5b) than in the benchmark case. The significance of the variables of interest, and the channels of influence on business cycle synchronization does not change much. The exception is the bi-directional relationship between trade and the similarity of economic structure. This now becomes only one-way, with trade integration affecting the similarity of productive structure, but not vice-versa.

A second robustness exercise aims at tackling the problem of the low number of observations (43), in the system of equations. We extend the number of observations by imputing the value of zero to the observations where no data on FDI flows is available. The list of countries now included in the regression increases to 104.[22] As can be seen from Table 8 in the appendix,[23] this is a relatively safe assumption in many cases but not all[24]. The results are relatively similar to the extent that trade and financial linkages do not seem to affect business cycle synchronization directly but only indirectly through their effect on the similarity of productive structure (Table 5c). Still, there are a number of differences in the results worth mentioning. First, there is now a negative and significant effect from contemporaneous trade linkages to FDI linkages (Eq 3). However, the positive effect from previous trade integration is maintained. Second, the link from the similarity of productive structure to trade linkages also seems to be broken (Eq. 2). Third, FDI linkages appear significant in increasing the similarity of productive structure. This was not the case before, which implied an even more indirect impact of financial linkages on business cycle synchronization. The diagram in the appendix (figure 5) summarizes the relations that have been found significant in this case.

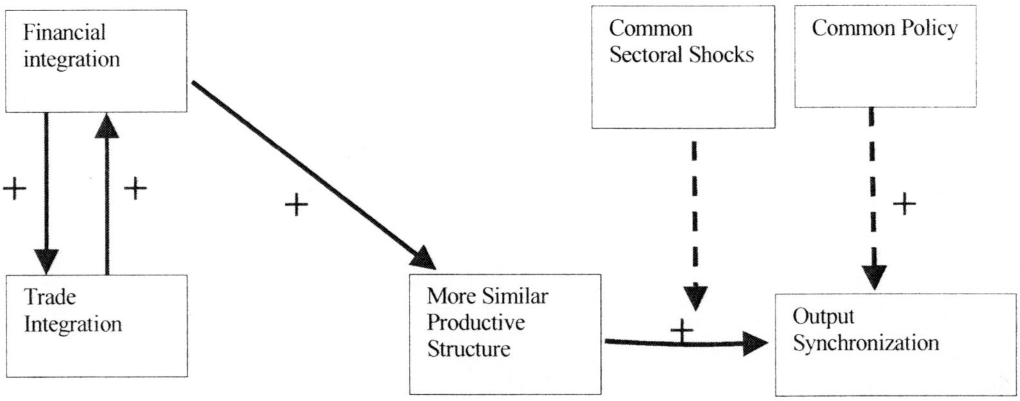

Figure 5. Channels of effects found in the empirical exercise with the extended set of countries (104).

Finally, in order to control for global shocks, we also introduced a variable to approximate the similarity in the exposure of both economies to oil shocks. For each country, we measure net imports of oil as a percentage of GDP and average that percentage for the period 1990-2002. We then multiply that measure with the equivalent one for Spain, which is positive[25]. In principle, countries that are more dependent of oil should have a high and positive dependency ratio, whereas oil exporting countries have a highly negative indicator. A

[22] Consistent with the inclusion of new observations in the estimation of the system of simultaneous equations, the table of cross correlations has been expanded (See Table 7b in Appendix). Correlation coefficients above 0.6 are highlighted.

[23] The table highlights the 44 countries included in the original regression.

[24] The main risk of introducing a bias lies in those countries in Latin America that are summarized in the OECD data, like Peru.

[25] Details of the construction and sources used for this oil dependency index can be found in Appendix B.

high and positive product of both indicators indicates countries that are affected by an oil shock in a similar way as Spain. A highly negative indicator represents countries that would benefit from an increase in the price of oil, as opposed to the Spanish economy.

We introduce this indicator as an explanatory variable for growth correlations. However, it turns out not to be statistically significant[26] in any of the specifications tried (OLS, IV or 3SLS estimations). This result could be interpreted as confirmation that in the period of study (1990-2003) oil shocks were not an important factor driving global economic fluctuations, as they were in the 70s or, to a lesser extent, in the 80s.

6. Conclusions

This paper assesses what is the role of trade and financial linkages in business cycle synchronization while considering a large number of interrelations between the relevant variables through a system of equations. This allows us to identify direct and indirect effects of trade and financial linkages on output co-movements. While there are number of possible endogeneity problems associated with trade and financial linkages as explanatory variables for output synchronization, in principle one could eliminate those biases by using suitable and readily available instruments. However, the reduced form IV estimates might appear small or not significant because, in theory, direct and indirect effects might run in opposite directions, cancelling each other. We, therefore, conducted the estimation of system of equations in order to separate direct and indirect effects of trade and financial linkages on output synchronization. This approach seems validated by our finding that only indirect effects (through their effect on the similarity of productive structure between the two countries) are significant.

The other contribution of the paper is to take a small, open economy as benchmark of the analysis and not the US or a group of rich countries accounting for a big share of world GDP. Business cycle synchronization between small open economies should depend more on trade and financial linkages than on other factors, many of which cannot be explicitly included in the analysis. These have probably biased upward the estimation of the trade and financial coefficients in previous studies. Our finding of no direct influence of trade or financial linkages on cycle synchronization is even more interesting for a small open economy, such as Spain. In addition, the significance of indirect influence justifies the use of a system of equations, instead of a reduced form.

Summarizing the results, we find that only the similarity in productive structure (*S*) is significant in determining output synchronization, after controlling for common policies (exchange rate volatility). Trade and financial linkages appear to increase output synchronization only indirectly, by fostering the specialization of productive structure. While trade and financial integration do lead to increased output synchronization, its indirect influence highlights that a precondition for this effect is the convergence of the productive structure of both countries. In particular, financial or trade liberalization without measures to allow the reallocation of productive resources inside a country might not lead to a correlation of business cycles. Another interesting policy conclusion is to weaken the idea that, with the

[26] P-values for a test of significance of this variable are never lower than 0.88 in all specifications.

increasing economic globalization, external demand both for goods and services, but also for financial assets, does not help boost the economy.

In any event, these results are only preliminary, mainly because of data limitations. In fact, financial integration is only measured through bilateral FDI flows and there is no account of portfolio or other capital flows.[27] This might lead to underestimating financial linkages and their effect on business cycle synchronization.

[27] New versions of this paper will make use of newly processed data for bilateral financial flows and stocks obtained from the Spanish Balance of Payments.

APPENDIX A: TABLES

Table 1. Dependent Variable: Growth correlations with Spain, 1990-2003 (ρ)

OLS Estimation

Specification	Ia	IIa	IIIa	IVa	Va	VIa	VIIa
Number of Observations	162	50	49	126	152	50	49
Trade Linkages 1990-1999[1] (T)	28270.24 **	17911.03	16519.16 *	21551.52 ***	14683.55	1282.891	2173.28
	(9326.31)	(11349.81)	(9885.22)	(8318.65)	(11181.21)	(11538.26)	(11045.42)
FDI Linkages 1991-2000[2] (F)		0.0000373	0.0000334			0.0000558	0.0000486
		(0.0000558)	(0.0000482)			(0.0000439)	(0.0000421)
Similarity in Productive Structure 1980-2000[3] (S)			-0.1234	0.0102476			-0.087102
			(0.2494)	(0.0783445)			(0.2140615)
Member of Euro Area (1=yes)					0.1048364	0.087204	0.0981344
					(0.1042206)	(0.0971558)	(0.0932183)
Average Inflation differencial 1990-2003					-0.000219 ***	0.0000239	0.0002579
					(0.00008)	(0.000305)	(0.0003062)
Exchange rate volatility 1990-2003[4]					-0.060645 **	-0.183092 ***	-0.169869 ***
					(0.0308499)	(0.0504493)	(0.0484815)
Adjusted R^2	0.05	0.08	0.07	0.05	0.21	0.46	0.41

Table 1. Continued

IV Estimation[5] (Two-Stage Least-Squares)

Specification	Ib	IIb	IIIb	IVb	Vb	VIb	VIIb
Number of Observations	43	43	43	43	43	43	43
Trade Linkages 1990-1999[1] (T)	15845.18 **	15396.28 *	13571.05	12904.9 *	11035.64	9515.291	8618.184
	(6123.641)	(7961.088)	(8346.635)	(6903.678)	(7568.933)	(9760.288)	(10202.96)
FDI Linkages 1991-2000[2] (F)		3.64E-06	-6.28E-06			9.45E-06	-5.29E-06
		(0.0000405)	(0.0000426)			(0.0000379)	(0.0000409)
Similarity in Productive Structure 1980-2000[3] (S)			0.3346314	0.3226887			0.4502342
			(0.3415994)	(0.3265886)			(0.3216657)
Member of Euro Area (1=yes)					0.0290518	0.034051	0.0136597
					(0.0726864)	(0.0758788)	(0.080493)
Average Inflation differencial 1990-2003					0.0000563	0.0000492	2.76E-06
					(0.0002409)	(0.0002442)	(0.0002569)
Exchange rate volatility 1990-2003[4]					-0.102627 **	-0.102297 **	-0.102971 **
					(0.0428706)	(0.0431826)	(0.0450546)
Adjusted R^2	0.89	0.07	0.03	0.06	0.25	0.24	0.18

Standard errors in parenthesis

[1] Measured as the average over the period of the sum of bilateral exports plus imports over the sum of the respective GDPs

[2] Measured as the average over the period of bilateral inflows and outflows of FDI to and from Spain

[3] Computed from value added from the industrial sector only. S may take values between -2 (disjoint structure) and 0 (identical structure)

[4] Coefficient of variation of the bilateral exchange rate with Spain (monthly average).

[5] Instruments used are the same as those used in the three-stage least-squares regression in tables 5a-c.

* Significant at 10%, ** Significant at 5%, *** Significant at 1%

Table 2

Dependent Variable: Trade Linkages with Spain 1990-19991 (T)

OLS Estimation

Specification	I	II	III	IV	V	VI
Number of Observations	164	50	49	165	50	49
FDI Linkages 1991-20002 (F)		2.49E-09 ***	2.35E-09 ***		3.90E-09 ***	3.71E-09 ***
		(5.81E-10)	(5.99E-10)		(7.98E-10)	(8.08E-10)
Similarity in Productive Structure 1980-2000[3] (S)			3.47E-06			4.87E-06
			(3.90E-06)		( )	(3.78E-06)
Distance to main city (km)	-2.33E-10 ***	-2.44E-10 **	-2.48E-10 **	-2.28E-10 ***	-1.57E-10	-1.52E-10
	(5.50E-11)	(1.04E-10)	(1.06E-10)	(5.38E-11)	(1.05E-10)	(1.06E-10)
Spanish spoken (1=yes)	1.02E-07	-4.21E-07	-1.61E-07	2.02E-07	-1.03E-06	-6.86E-07
	(5.85E-07)	(1.49E-06)	(1.54E-06)	(5.66E-07)	(1.44E-06)	(1.47E-06)
Access to seacoast (1=yes)	9.61E-07 **	1.61E-06	2.14E-06	7.94E-07	1.74E-06	2.49E-06
	(4.35E-07)	(1.52E-06)	(1.62E-06)	(4.19E-07)	(1.45E-06)	(1.54E-06)
Sum of Land Areas (in km^2)				-1.46E-13	-1.19E-13	-1.57E-13
				(1.03E-13)	(1.45E-13)	(1.47E-13)
Product of populations (in billions)				-3.38E-11	7.93E-11	7.08E-11
				(4.44E-11)	(6.41E-11)	(6.43E-11)
Product of average GDPs 1990-2003				1.86E-24 ***	-2.12E-24 **	-2.03E-24 **
				(5.00E-25)	(9.72E-25)	(9.73E-25)
Adjusted R^2	0.11	0.37	0.37	0.17	0.43	0.44

Standard errors in parenthesis

[1] Measured as the average over the period of the sum of bilateral exports plus imports over the sum of the respective GDPs

[2] Measured as the average over the period of bilateral inflows and outflows of FDI to and from Spain

[3] Computed from value added from the industrial sector only. S may take values between -2 (disjoint structure) and 0 (identical structure)

* Significant at 10%, ** Significant at 5%, *** Significant at 1%

Table 3

Dependent Variable: FDI Linkages with Spain 1991-20002 (F)

OLS Estimation

Specification	I	II	III	IV	V	VI	VI
Number of Observations	51	50	44	49	44	50	44
Trade Linkages 1990-19991 (T)		9.70E+07 ***	-5.73E+07	9.33E+07 ***		9.83E+07 ***	
		(2.73E+07)	(7.31E+07)	(2.85E+07)		(2.89E+07)	
Trade Linkages 1980-19891 (lagged T)			5.17E+08 **		3.42E+08 ***		3.68E+08 ***
			(2.27E+08)		(9.19E+07)		(9.30E+07)
Similarity in Productive Structure 1980-2000[3] (S)				551.822	436.485		
				(805.832)	(824.528)		
Growth correlations with Spain, 1990-2003 (ρ)						-66.499	-430.519
						(420.718)	(738.892)
Distance to main city (km)	-0.114 **	-0.088 *	-0.070	-0.089 *	-0.076	-0.088	-0.073
	(0.059)	(0.053)	(0.055)	(0.054)	(0.055)	(0.054)	(0.055)
Spanish spoken (1=yes)	275.891	198.125	16.674	243.758	106.274	195.286	16.831
	(346.251)	(312.821)	(330.851)	(325.407)	(332.493)	(316.938)	(337.539)
Access to seacoast (1=yes)	377.424	93.736	94.286	162.926	125.242	95.213	82.741
	(346.876)	(321.498)	(409.611)	(345.193)	(421.415)	(325.340)	(410.638)
Absolute time difference to main financial centre	113.809	128.538 *	110.780	130.867 *	119.524	129.090	120.118
	(86.830)	(78.352)	(80.699)	(79.876)	(80.685)	(79.333)	(80.654)
Sum of percapita GDPs (average 1990-2003)	0.042 ***	0.026 **	0.023 *	0.026 **	0.023 *	0.027 *	0.026 *
	(0.013)	(0.013)	(0.013)	(0.013)	(0.014)	(0.014)	(0.014)
Adjusted R^2	0.20	0.37	0.40	0.35	0.40	0.35	0.40

Standard errors in parenthesis

[1] Measured as the average over the period of the sum of bilateral exports plus imports over the sum of the respective GDPs

[2] Measured as the average over the period of bilateral inflows and outflows of FDI to and from Spain

[3] Computed from value added from the industrial sector only. S may take values between -2 (disjoint structure) and 0 (identical structure)

* Significant at 10%, ** Significant at 5%, *** Significant at 1%

Table 4

Dependent Variable: Similarity in Productive Structure 1980-2000³ (S)

OLS Estimation

Specification	I	II	III	IV	V	VI	VI
Number of Observations	128	50	49	128	50	49	128
Trade Linkages 1990-19991 (T)	42218.00 ***		5.47E+03	24043.81 *		2323.486	28199.85 ***
	(9.01E+03)		(5.79E+03)	(9293.399)		(6288.534)	(9079.603)
FDI Linkages 1991-20002 (F)		2.60E-05	0.0000113		0.0000275	0.0000208	
		(2.29E-05)	(2.84E-05)	( )	(0.0000255)	(0.0000318)	
Absolute difference of percapita GDPs				-0.000017	-9.24E-06	-8.10E-06	-2.45E-05 ***
(average 1990-2003)				(7.08E-06)	(5.83E-06)	(6.62E-06)	(5.77E-06)
Sum of percapita GDPs (average 1990-2003)				6.94E-06	-6.21E-07	-5.03E-07	
				(3.87E-06)	(2.88E-06)	(2.96E-06)	
Adjusted R^2	0.14	0.01	0.01	0.26	0.02	0.00	0.24

Standard errors in parenthesis

[1] Measured as the average over the period of the sum of bilateral exports plus imports over the sum of the respective GDPs

[2] Measured as the average over the period of bilateral inflows and outflows of FDI to and from Spain

[3] Computed from value added from the industrial sector only. S may take values between -2 (disjoint structure) and 0 (identical structure)

* Significant at 10%, ** Significant at 5%, *** Significant at 1%

Table 5a

Three-stage Least Square regression on the whole system of four equations

43 Observations

Dependent Variable	Output Synchron. (ρ) (Equation 1)	Trade Linkages (T) (Equation 2)	FDI Linkages (F) (Equation 3)	Similarity in Prod. Struct. (S) (Equation 4)
Trade Linkages 1990-1999[1] (T)	7553.61		-1.44E+08	15285.44 **
	(9082.60)		(1.31E+08)	(7190.144)
Trade Linkages 1980-1989[1] (lagged T)			8.34E+08 **	
			(3.61E+08)	
FDI Linkages 1991-2000[2] (F)	-2.27E-05	3.55E-09 ***		7.00E-05
	(3.69E-05)	(1.22E-09)		(5.64E-05)
FDI Linkages 1981-1990[2] (Lagged F)				-0.000374
				(0.0003418)
Growth correlations with Spain, 1990-2003 (ρ)			-607.2559	
			(1407.631)	
Similarity in Productive Structure 1980-2000[3] (S)	0.7018 ***	0.000032 ***		
	(0.2826)	(9.77E-06)		
Distance to main city (km)		-2.85E-11	-0.056278	
		(1.13E-10)	(0.0497338)	
Spanish spoken (1=yes)		6.03E-07	-144.9104	
		(1.63E-06)	(340.891)	
Access to seacoast (1=yes)		3.08E-06		
		(2.04E-06)		
Absolute time difference to main financial centre			99.70097	
			(72.85905)	
Member of Euro Area (1=yes)	0.0026			
	(0.0706)			
Average Inflation differencial 1990-2003	-0.0001			
	(0.0002)			
Exchange rate volatility 1990-2003[4]	-0.0970 ***			
	(0.0397)			
Sum of Land Areas (in km^2)		-5.21E-13 **		
		(2.52E-13)		
Product of populations (in billions)		8.55E-11		
		(8.55E-11)		
Product of average GDPs 1990-2003		-1.49E-24		
		(1.19E-24)		
Sum of percapita GDPs (average 1990-2003)			0.0250425 *	
			(0.0153059)	
Absolute difference of percapita GDPs (average 1990-2003)				-3.17E-07
				(5.73E-06)
Implicit R^2	0.16	0.00	0.48	-0.04

Standard errors in parenthesis

[1] Measured as the average over the period of the sum of bilateral exports plus imports over the sum of the respective GDPs

[2] Measured as the average over the period of bilateral inflows and outflows of FDI to and from Spain

[3] Computed from value added from the industrial sector only. S may take values between -2 (disjoint structure) and 0 (identical structure)

[4] Coefficient of variation of the bilateral exchange rate with Spain (monthly average).

* Significant at 10%, ** Significant at 5%, *** Significant at 1%

Table 5b

Three-stage Least Square regression on the whole system of four equations

43 Observations

Dependent Variable	Output Synchron. (ρ) (Equation 1)	Trade Linkages (T) (Equation 2)	FDI Linkages (F) (Equation 3)	Similarity in Prod. Struct. (S) (Equation 4)
Trade Linkages 1990-1999[1] (T)	2731.86		-1.04E+08	6725.705
	(9691.41)		(1.28E+08)	(7261.269)
Trade Linkages 1980-1989[1] (lagged T)			7.28E+08 **	
			(3.30E+08)	
FDI Linkages 1991-2000[2] (F)	0.000024	5.37E-09 ***		0.0000136
	(0.000040)	(1.44E-09)		(0.0000359)
FDI Linkages 1981-1990[2] (Lagged F)				
Growth correlations with Spain, 1990-2003 (ρ)			-359.0764	
			(1291.439)	
Similarity in Productive Structure 1980-2000[3] (S)	0.4816 **	0.0000198 ***		
	(0.2426)	(7.28E-06)		
Log of Distance to main city (km)		-3.98E-07	-119.8954	
		(7.91E-07)	(168.7232)	
Spanish spoken (1=yes)		4.87E-07	-73.63136	
		(1.72E-06)	(322.7569)	
Access to seacoast (1=yes)		2.45E-06		
		(1.94E-06)		
Log of absolute time difference to main financial centre			73.23183 **	
			(32.78706)	
Member of Euro Area (1=yes)	0.0347			
	(0.0707)			
Average Inflation differencial 1990-2003	0.0000			
	(0.0002)			
Exchange rate volatility 1990-2003[4]	-0.0987 ***			
	(0.0389)			
Sum of Land Areas (in km^2)		-4.33E-13 *		
		(2.41E-13)		
Product of populations (in billions)		1.28E-10 *		
		(7.21E-11)		
Product of average GDPs 1990-2003		-2.05E-24 *		
		(1.32E-24)		
Sum of percapita GDPs (average 1990-2003)			0.0300283 **	
			(0.0146192)	
Absolute difference of percapita GDPs (average 1990-2003)				-4.24E-06
				(6.06E-06)
Implicit R^2	0.31	0.27	0.52	0.09

Standard errors in parenthesis

[1] Measured as the average over the period of the sum of bilateral exports plus imports over the sum of the respective GDPs

[2] Measured as the average over the period of bilateral inflows and outflows of FDI to and from Spain

[3] Computed from value added from the industrial sector only. S may take values between -2 (disjoint structure) and 0 (identical structure)

[4] Coefficient of variation of the bilateral exchange rate with Spain (monthly average).

* Significant at 10%, ** Significant at 5%, *** Significant at 1%

Table 5c

Three-stage Least Square regression on the whole system of four equations

104 Observations

Dependent Variable	Output Synchron. (ρ) (Equation 1)	Trade Linkages (T) (Equation 2)	FDI Linkages (F) (Equation 3)	Similarity in Prod. Struct. (S) (Equation 4)
Trade Linkages 1990-19991 (T)	-6733.33		-1.82E+08 **	-4925.193
	(12268.77)		(9.33E+07	(12525.26)
Trade Linkages 1980-19891 (lagged T)			8.62E+08 ***	
			(2.51E+08)	
FDI Linkages 1991-20002 (F)	0.000062	7.55E-09 ***		0.0002277 ***
	(0.000054)	(1.16E-09)		(0.0000637)
FDI Linkages 1981-19902 (Lagged F)				
Growth correlations with Spain, 1990-2003 (ρ)			415.645	
			(589.1573)	
Similarity in Productive Structure 1980-2000[3] (S)	0.2075 **	1.45E-06		
	(0.1019)	(1.69E-06)		
Log of Distance to main city (km)		-1.92E-07	-32.50794	
		(4.43E-07)	(85.5454)	
Spanish spoken (1=yes)		-2.81E-07	-49.95582	
		(6.77E-07)	(115.1807)	
Access to seacoast (1=yes)		-7.38E-08		
		(6.60E-07)		
Log of absolute time difference to main financial centre			26.34079 *	
			(15.73312)	
Member of Euro Area (1=yes)	0.0738			
	(0.0827)			
Average Inflation differencial 1990-2003	0.0006 ***			
	(0.0002)			
Exchange rate volatility 1990-2003[4]	-0.1461 ***			
	(0.0378)			
Sum of Land Areas (in km^2)		-1.96E-13		
		(1.66E-13)		
Product of populations (in billions)		1.80E-10 ***		
		(5.98E-11)		
Product of average GDPs 1990-2003		-3.90E-24 ***		
		(1.08E-24)		
Sum of percapita GDPs (average 1990-2003)			0.0126983 *	
			(0.0073866)	
Absolute difference of percapita GDPs (average 1990-2003)				-2.85E-05 ***
				(5.97E-06)
Implicit R^2	0.19	0.34	0.43	0.30

Standard errors in parenthesis

[1] Measured as the average over the period of the sum of bilateral exports plus imports over the sum of the respective GDPs

[2] Measured as the average over the period of bilateral inflows and outflows of FDI to and from Spain

[3] Computed from value added from the industrial sector only. S may take values between -2 (disjoint structure) and 0 (identical structure)

[4] Coefficient of variation of the bilateral exchange rate with Spain (monthly average).

* Significant at 10%, ** Significant at 5%, *** Significant at 1%

Table 6

Summary Statistics

Variable	No. Observ.	Mean	Std. Dev.	Min	Max	Coeff. of Variation	Percentiles 5%	50%	95%
Growth correlations with Spain, 1990-2003 (ρ)	177	0.7063	0.2944	-0.3294	0.9890	0.42	0.0604	0.8339	0.9628
Trade Linkages 1990-1999[1] (T)	165	0.00000085	0.00000242	0.00000000	0.00001900	2.84	0.00000000	0.00000012	0.00000301
Trade Linkages 1980-1989[1] (lagged T)	122	0.00000045	0.00000092	0.00000000	0.00000612	2.07	0.00000000	0.00000012	0.00000194
FDI Linkages 1991-2000[2] (F)	52	397.66	815.66	0.17	3554.15	2.05	0.34	29.44	2333.90
Similarity in Productive Structure 1980-2000[3] (S)	142	-0.6636	0.2964	-1.4457	-0.1890	0.45	-1.1706	-0.6534	-0.2550
Member of Euro Area (1=yes)	199	0.080	0.273	0.000	1.000	3.39	0.000	0.000	1.000
Average Inflation differencial 1990-2003	163	85.357	336.407	0.533	3320.130	3.94	1.561	5.711	489.304
Exchange rate volatility 1990-2003[4]	183	0.568	0.887	0.003	5.303	1.56	0.075	0.200	2.442
Distance to main city (km)	199	6262	3923	494	19589	0.63	1282	6037	15374
Log of distance to main city	199	8.517	0.731	6.203	9.883	0.09	7.156	8.706	9.640
Spanish spoken (1=yes)	199	0.106	0.308	0	1	2.92	0	0	1
Access to seacoast (1=yes)	199	0.794	0.405	0	1	0.51	0	1	1
Absolute time difference to main financial center	199	3	3.177945	0	1.20E+01	0.95	0	2	10
Log of time difference to financial center	199	-0.49	3.31	-6.91	2.48	-6.73	-6.91	0.69	2.30
Sum of Land Areas (in km^2)	199	1182581	1898689	504784	17600000	1.61	505043	616872	3010592
Product of populations (in billions)	197	1145.52	4490.48	0.70	48145.25	3.92	2.56	222.89	4537.81
Product of average GDPs 1990-2003	167	1.E+17	5.E+17	1.E+14	5.E+18	3.42	5.E+14	1.E+16	7.E+17
Sum of percapita GDPs (average 1990-2003)	167	23414	7469	15554	50361	0.3189786	16493	20730	38921
Absolute difference of percapita GDPs	167	10192	4249	627	18802	0.4169212	2095	11072	14947

[1] Average over the period of the sum of bilateral exports plus imports over the sum of GDPs

[2] Average over the period of bilateral inflows and outflows of FDI to and from Spain

[3] Computed from value added from the industrial sector only. Higher values imply more similarity.

[4] Coefficient of variation of the bilateral exchange rate with Spain (monthly average).

Table 7a

Cross Correlations

(Based on common 44 observations. Boldface: correlations above 0.6)

	Growth correlations with Spain, 1990-2003 (ρ)	Trade Linkages 1990-1999[1] (T)	Trade Linkages 1980-1989[1] (lagged T)	FDI Linkages 1991-2000[2] (F)	Similarity in Productive Structure 1980-2000[3] (S	Member of Euro Area (1=yes)	Average Inflation differencial 1990-2003	Exchange rate volatility 1990-2003[4]	Distance to main city (km)	Log of distance to main city	Spanish spoken (1=yes)	Access to seacoast (1=yes)	Absolute time difference to main financial centre	Log of time difference to financial center	Sum of Land Areas (in km^2)	Product of populations (in billions)	Product of average GDPs 1990-2003	Sum of percapita GDPs (average 1990-2003)	Absolute difference of percapita GDPs
Growth correlations with Spain, 1990-2003 (ρ)	**1.000**																		
Trade Linkages 1990-1999[1] (T)	0.342	**1.000**																	
Trade Linkages 1980-1989[1] (lagged T)	0.345	**0.940**	**1.000**																
FDI Linkages 1991-2000[2] (F)	0.251	0.569	**0.642**	**1.000**															
Similarity in Productive Structure 1980-2000[3] (S)	0.199	0.256	0.244	0.210	**1.000**														
Member of Euro Area (1=yes)	0.359	**0.661**	0.567	0.253	0.231	**1.000**													
Average Inflation differencial 1990-2003	-0.329	-0.097	-0.105	0.058	0.101	-0.139	**1.000**												
Exchange rate volatility 1990-2003[4]	-0.496	-0.177	-0.121	-0.026	0.043	-0.214	**0.727**	**1.000**											
Distance to main city (km)	-0.099	-0.454	-0.456	-0.288	-0.178	-0.476	0.111	0.010	**1.000**										
Log of distance to main city	-0.168	-0.617	-0.573	-0.335	-0.195	-0.580	0.166	0.104	**0.931**	**1.000**									
Spanish spoken (1=yes)	-0.320	-0.132	-0.055	-0.052	-0.241	-0.182	0.208	0.023	0.223	0.293	**1.000**								
Access to seacoast (1=yes)	0.000	0.036	0.036	0.034	-0.233	-0.086	0.066	0.071	0.250	0.272	0.097	**1.000**							
Absolute time difference to main financial centre	-0.063	-0.418	-0.404	-0.180	-0.193	-0.457	0.019	-0.018	**0.924**	**0.875**	0.234	0.281	**1.000**						
Log of time difference to financial center	-0.201	-0.485	-0.482	-0.190	-0.344	-0.422	0.129	0.171	**0.665**	**0.690**	0.253	0.457	**0.755**	**1.000**					
Sum of Land Areas (in km^2)	0.073	-0.191	-0.155	0.202	0.282	-0.245	0.335	0.261	0.306	0.362	-0.008	0.145	0.385	0.342	**1.000**				
Product of populations (in billions)	0.101	-0.107	-0.116	0.008	0.142	-0.145	0.009	0.004	0.177	0.233	-0.082	0.100	0.247	0.214	0.510	**1.000**			
Product of average GDPs 1990-2003	0.190	0.083	0.135	**0.602**	0.196	-0.053	-0.007	-0.026	0.068	0.126	-0.108	0.115	0.233	0.141	0.588	0.512	**1.000**		
Sum of percapita GDPs (average 1990-2003)	0.482	0.321	0.317	0.407	0.179	0.314	-0.217	-0.367	-0.190	-0.259	-0.279	-0.157	-0.145	-0.388	0.003	-0.322	0.212	**1.000**	
Absolute difference of percapita GDPs	-0.256	-0.385	-0.271	-0.075	-0.204	-0.501	0.055	0.272	0.138	0.273	0.065	0.023	0.187	0.216	0.374	0.473	0.338	-0.476	**1.000**

[1] Average over the period of the sum of bilateral exports plus imports over the sum of GDPs

[2] Average over the period of bilateral inflows and outflows of FDI to and from Spain

[3] Computed from value added from the industrial sector only. Higher values imply more similarity.

[4] Coefficient of variation of the bilateral exchange rate with Spain (monthly average).

Table 7b

Table of Cross Correlations - extended set of observations

(Based on common 104* observations. Boldface: correlations above 0.6)

	Growth correlations with Spain, 1990-2003 (ρ)	Trade Linkages 1990-19991 (T)	Trade Linkages 1980-19891 (lagged T)	FDI Linkages 1991-20002 (F)	Similarity in Productive Structure 1980-2000[3] (S	Member of Euro Area (1=yes)	Average Inflation differencial 1990-2003	Exchange rate volatility 1990-2003[4]	Distance to main city (km)	Log of distance to main city	Spanish spoken (1=yes)	Access to seacoast (1=yes)	Absolute time difference to main financial centre	Log of time difference to financial center	Sum of Land Areas (in km^2)	Product of populations (in billions)	Product of average GDPs 1990-2003	Sum of percapita GDPs (average 1990-2003)	Absolute difference of percapita GDPs
Growth correlations with Spain, 1990-2003 (ρ)	**1.000**																		
Trade Linkages 1990-19991 (T)	0.246	**1.000**																	
Trade Linkages 1980-19891 (lagged T)	0.259	**0.944**	**1.000**																
FDI Linkages 1991-20002 (F)	0.184	**0.629**	**0.681**	**1.000**															
Similarity in Productive Structure 1980-2000[3] (S)	0.244	0.409	0.452	0.345	**1.000**														
Member of Euro Area (1=yes)	0.245	**0.660**	0.575	0.324	0.319	**1.000**													
Average Inflation differencial 1990-2003	-0.042	-0.051	-0.055	0.019	0.028	-0.073	**1.000**												
Exchange rate volatility 1990-2003[4]	-0.237	-0.112	-0.081	-0.037	0.034	-0.147	**0.838**	**1.000**											
Distance to main city (km)	-0.073	-0.381	-0.396	-0.242	-0.090	-0.391	0.110	0.075	**1.000**										
Log of distance to main city	-0.138	-0.577	-0.571	-0.336	-0.222	-0.514	0.133	0.125	**0.914**	**1.000**									
Spanish spoken (1=yes)	-0.029	-0.120	-0.096	-0.075	-0.044	-0.149	0.295	0.240	0.260	0.309	**1.000**								
Access to seacoast (1=yes)	0.185	0.130	0.159	0.100	0.300	0.063	0.076	0.017	0.076	0.013	0.075	**1.000**							
Absolute time difference to main financial centre	0.067	-0.269	-0.270	-0.105	0.037	-0.287	0.140	0.083	**0.860**	**0.767**	0.359	0.263	**1.000**						
Log of time difference to financial center	-0.088	-0.378	-0.409	-0.155	-0.138	-0.282	0.121	0.145	**0.630**	**0.661**	0.251	0.143	**0.719**	**1.000**					
Sum of Land Areas (in km^2)	0.096	-0.022	0.042	0.291	0.347	-0.109	0.153	0.149	0.190	0.173	-0.051	0.104	0.237	0.159	**1.000**				
Product of populations (in billions)	0.115	0.014	0.027	0.097	0.257	-0.049	-0.005	-0.015	0.118	0.125	-0.095	0.109	0.175	0.122	0.543	**1.000**			
Product of average GDPs 1990-2003	0.162	0.222	0.279	**0.654**	0.351	0.070	-0.009	-0.035	0.024	0.009	-0.104	0.140	0.168	0.061	**0.629**	0.551	**1.000**		
Sum of percapita GDPs (average 1990-2003)	0.323	0.470	0.490	0.497	0.598	0.397	-0.100	-0.211	-0.128	-0.281	-0.165	0.198	0.005	-0.208	0.201	-0.056	0.376	**1.000**	
Absolute difference of percapita GDPs	-0.233	-0.425	-0.390	-0.246	-0.550	-0.419	0.061	0.177	0.055	0.225	0.054	-0.297	-0.046	0.068	0.030	0.128	-0.038	-0.752	**1.000**

[1] Average over the period of the sum of bilateral exports plus imports over the sum of GDPs

[2] Average over the period of bilateral inflows and outflows of FDI to and from Spain

[3] Computed from value added from the industrial sector only. Higher values imply more similarity.

[4] Coefficient of variation of the bilateral exchange rate with Spain (monthly average).

* Includes 44 observations from previous table plus common observations included by setting FDI Linkages equal to zero for missing values.

Table 8

Countries included in the regressions (total=104)

ISO code	Country Name	ISO code	Country Name	ISO code	Country Name	ISO code	Country Name
ARG	**Argentina**	DZA	Algeria	JAM	Jamaica	**POL**	**Poland**
AUS	**Australia**	ECU	Ecuador	JOR	Jordan	**PRT**	**Portugal**
AUT	**Austria**	**EGY**	**Egypt**	**JPN**	**Japan**	PRY	Paraguay
BDI	Burundi	ETH	Ethiopia	KEN	Kenya	**ROU**	**Romania**
BEN	Benin	**FIN**	**Finland**	**KOR**	**Korea**	RWA	Rwanda
BFA	Burkina Faso	FJI	Fiji Is.	LCA	St. Lucia	SEN	Senegal
BGD	Bangladesh	**FRA**	**France**	LKA	Sri Lanka	**SGP**	**Singapore**
BLZ	Belize	GAB	Gabon	LSO	Lesotho	SLE	Sierra Leone
BOL	Bolivia	**GBR**	**UK**	**MAR**	**Morocco**	SLV	El Salvador
BRA	**Brazil**	**GER**	**Germany**	MDG	Madagascar	**SWE**	**Sweden**
BRB	Barbados	GHA	Ghana	**MEX**	**Mexico**	SYC	Seychelles
BWA	Bostwana	GMB	Gambia	MUS	Mauritius	SYR	Syria
CAF	Central African Republic	GNQ	Equatorial Guinea	MWI	Malawi	TGO	Togo
CAN	**Canada**	**GRC**	**Greece**	**MYS**	**Malaysia**	**THA**	**Thailand**
CHE	**Switzerland**	GTM	Guatemala	NER	Niger	TTO	Trinidad and Tobago
CHL	**Chile**	**HKG**	**Hong Kong**	NGA	Nigeria	TUN	Tunisia
CHN	**China**	HND	Honduras	NIC	Nicaragua	**TUR**	**Turkey**
CIV	Cote d'Ivoire	HTI	Haiti	**NLD**	**Netherlands**	TZA	Tanzania
CMR	Cameroon	**HUN**	**Hungary**	**NOR**	**Norway**	UGA	Uganda
COG	Congo Brazzaville	**IDN**	**Indonesia**	NPL	Nepal	URY	Uruguay
COL	**Colombia**	**IND**	**India**	**NZL**	**New Zealand**	**USA**	**USA**
CPV	Cape Verde	**IRL**	**Ireland**	PAK	Pakistan	**VEN**	**Venezuela**
CRI	Costa Rica	**IRN**	**Iran**	PAN	Panama	VNM	Vietnam
CYP	Cyprus	**ISL**	**Iceland**	PER	Peru	**ZAF**	**South Africa**
DNK	**Denmark**	**ISR**	**Israel**	**PHL**	**Phillipines**	ZMB	Zambia
DOM	Dominican Republic	**ITA**	**Italy**	PNG	Papua New Guinea	ZWE	Zimbabwe

In boldface: countries included in the original sample of 44 countries. The rest of countries (60) were added after setting Financial Integration (F) equal to zero for all missing observations of that variable.

APPENDIX B: DEFINITION OF VARIABLES AND SOURCES

Output Synchronization (ρ): Measured as the Pearson correlation between the log differences (growth rates) of annual GDP for Spain and those of a given country. Data for annual GDP at purchasing power parity was taken from the IMF's World Economic Outlook database.

Trade Linkages (T): Measured as the sum of imports and exports between Spain and a given country, over the sum of their respective GDPs. This measure is then averaged over the denoted period of time. That is,

$$T_{ESP,i} = \frac{1}{T}\sum_{t}\frac{X_{ESP,i,t} + M_{ESP,i,t}}{GDP_{ESP,t} + GDP_{i,t}}$$

Data for exports and imports was obtained from the IMF's Direction of Trade Statistics. GDP data was taken from the Penn World Tables version 6.1.

Financial Linkages (F): Measured as the sum of inflows and outflows of FDI between Spain and a given country. This measure is then averaged over the duration of the period. Data for FDI flows was obtained from the OECD's International Direct Investment Statistics.

Similarity in productive structure (S): Measured as the time average of discrepancies in economic structures. In particular, we take the shares $s_{n,i,t}$ of value added for industrial sector n in country i at time t and construct the following indicator of distance:

$$S^{1}_{ESP,i} = -\frac{1}{T}\sum_{t}\sum_{n=1}^{N}\left|s_{n,ESP,t} - s_{n,i,t}\right|$$

For value added, we take industrial sectors at 2-digit ISIC level. Data was obtained from the United Nations Industrial Development Organization (UNIDO).

Distance to main city: Computed at the great circle distance (in km) between Madrid (Spain), and the main city of a given country. In general, we take the capital city as the main city, except for the US (New York), Pakistan (Karachi), Brazil (Sao Paulo), China (Shanghai), Canada (Toronto), Switzerland (Zurich), Germany (Frankfurt), Turkey (Istambul), Israel (Tel Aviv), India (Mumbay), Australia (Sydney), Cote d'Ivoire (Abidjan), Kazakhstan (Almaty), Morocco (Casablanca), New Zealand (Auckland), Nigeria (Lagos), South Africa (Johannesburg) and Yemen (Aden). Data was obtained from http://www.indo.com/distance/index.html.

Spanish spoken: dummy variable which takes value 1 if a given country has Spanish as the main language. Data was elaborated by the authors.

Access to seacoast: dummy variable which takes value 1 if a country has sovereign access to the seacoast. Data elaborated by the authors.

Absolute time difference to main financial center: Absolute value of the standard time zone difference between the main city used for "distance" and mainland Spain. Source: http://www.timeanddate.com/worldclock/

Member of Euro Area: dummy variable which takes value 1 if a given country has joined the Euro. Data elaborated by the authors.

Average Inflation Differential: Computed as the time average over the period referred of the absolute difference of quarterly inflation rates between Spain and a given country. Annual inflation data was obtained from the IMF's International Financial Statistics.

Exchange Rate Volatility: Computed as the standard deviation (over the period referred) of the bilateral nominal exchange rate (monthly average) between Spain and a given country. Monthly exchange rate data was obtained from the IMF's International Financial Statistics using bilateral exchange rates for both countries vis-à-vis the US dollar.

Sum of land areas: Computed as the sum of land areas (in square km) of Spain and a given country. Data for land areas was obtained from http://www.infoplease.com/ipa/A0004379.html and the CIA World Factbook.

Product of Populations: Computed as the product of average populations in both countries for the period chosen (divided by 10^{12}). Data on countries' population was obtained from the World Bank.

Product of Average GDPs: obtained as the product of average annual GDPs measured at PPP. GDP data at PPP was obtained from the Penn World Tables 6.1.

Sum of per capita GDPs: time average of the sum of per capita GDP for Spain and a given country. Data was obtained from the Penn World Tables 6.1.

Absolute difference of per-capita GDPs: measured as the time average over the referred period. Data was obtained from the Penn World Tables 6.1.

Similarity of oil dependency: constructed as the product of average oil dependency in Spain and a given country i:

$$\left(\frac{1}{T}\sum_t \frac{Moil_{i,t} - Xoil_{i,t}}{GDP_{i,t}}\right) \times \left(\frac{1}{T}\sum_t \frac{Moil_{ESP,t} - Xoil_{ESP,t}}{GDP_{ESP,t}}\right)$$

where $Moil_{i,t}$ and $Xoil_{i,t}$ are imports and exports of oil in country i at time t and ESP represents Spain. Data for oil imports and exports as well as nominal GDP (all in current US dollars) was obtained from the World Bank.

REFERENCES

Aizenman, Joshua and Ilan Noy (2004): "On the Two Way Feedback Between Financial and Trade Openness," *NBER Working Paper* **10496**.

Baxter, Marianne and Robert King (1999): "Measuring Business Cycles: Approximate Band-Pass Filters for Economic Time Series," *Review of Economics and Statistics,* **81**, pp. 575-93.

Bordo, Michael and Thomas Helbling (2003): "Have National Business Cycles become More Synchronized?," *NBER Working Paper* **10130**.

Clark, Todd and Eric van Wincoop (2001): "Borders and Business Cycles," *Journal of International Economics,* vol. 55, pp. 59-85.

Deardorff, Alan (1998): "Determinant of Bilateral Trade: Does Gravity Work in a Neoclassical World?," in Frankel J. (ed.) *The Regionalization of the World Economy,* University of Chicago Press.

Edison, Hali, Michael Klein, Luca Ricci and Torsten Slok (2002): "Capital Account Liberalization and Economic Performance: Survey and Synthesis," *IMF Working Paper* **02/120**.

Forni, Mario, Marc Hallin, Marco Lippi and Lucrezia Reichlin (2000): "The Generalized Dynamic-Factor Model: Identification and Estimation," *The Review of Economics and Statistics*. **82**(4), pp. 540-554.

Frankel, Jeffrey (1992): "Measuring International Capital Mobility: A Review," *American Economic Review Papers and Proceedings*, **82**(2) pp. 197-202.

Frankel, Jeffrey and Andrew Rose (1998): "The Endogeneity of the Optimum Currency Area Criteria," *Economic Journal* **108**, pp. 1009-25.

Heathcote, Jonathan and Fabrizio Perri (2003a): "Why has the U.S. Economy Become Less Correlated with the Rest of the World?," *American Economic Review Papers and Procceedings*," vol 93, pp. 63-69

Heathcote, Jonathan and Fabrizio Perri (2003b): "Financial Globalization and Real Regionalization," *Working Paper*, Georgetown University.

Helbling, Thomas and Tamim Bayoumi (2003): "Are they all in the Same Boat? The 2000-01 Growth Slowdown and the G-7 Business Cycle Linkages," *IMF Working Paper* **03/46.**

Imbs, Jean (2003): "Co-Fluctuations," mimeo. (http://faculty.london.edu/jimbs/Research/Cofluct2001.pdf)

Imbs, Jean (2004a): "The Real Effects of Financial Integration," *Working Paper*, London Business School.

Imbs, Jean (2004b): "Trade, Finance, Specialization and Synchronization," *Review of Economics and Statistics*, forthcoming.

Imbs, Jean and Romain Wacziarg (2003): "Stages of Diversification," *American Economic Review*, **93**(1).

International Monetary Fund (1997): *World Economic Outlook*, May.

International Monetary Fund (2001a): "International Linkages: Three Perspectives," World Economic Outlook, Chapter II, October.

International Monetary Fund (2001b): "International Financial Integration and Developing Countries," *World Economic Outlook*, Chapter IV, October.

International Monetary Fund (2002): "Trade and Financial Integration," *World Economic Outlook*, Chapter III, April.

Kalemli-Ozcan, Sebnem, Bent Sorensen and Oved Yosha (2003): "Risk Sharing and Industrial Specialization: Regional and International Evidence," *American Economic Review*, vol 93, pp. 903-18.

Kose, Ayhan and Kei-MuYi (2001): "International Trade and Business Cycles: Is Vertical Specialization the Missing Link?," *American Economic Review Papers and Proceedings*, vol 91. pp 371-75.

Kose, Ayhan, Eswar Prasad and Marco Terrones (2003a): "Financial Integration and Macroeconomic Volatility," *IMF Staff Papers*, Vol 50, pp. 119-42.

Kose, Ayhan, Eswar Prasad and Marco Terrones (2003b): "How Does Globalization Affect the Synchronization of Business Cycles?," *IMF Working Paper* **03/27**

Lane, Philip and Gian Maria Milesi-Ferretti (2001): "The External Wealth of Nations: Measures of Foreign Assets and Liabilities for Industrial and Developing Countries," *Journal of International Economics* **55**, pp. 263-294.

Lane, Philip and Gian Maria Milesi Ferretti (2004): "International Investment Patterns," *IIIS Discussion Paper* **24**.

Loretan, M. and W. English (2000): "Evaluating 'correlation breakdowns' during periods of market volatility," *International Finance Discussion Paper* **658**, Board of Governors of the Federal Reserve System.

Lumsdaine Robin and Eswar Prasad (2003): "Identifying the Common Component of International Economic Fluctuations: A New Approach," *The Economic Journal*, **113** (484), pp. 101-127.

Nadal-de Simone, Francisco (2002): "Common and Idiosyncratic Components in Real Output: Further International Evidence," *IMF Working Paper* **02/229**.

Portes, Richard and Hélène Rey (2003): "The Determinants of Cross-Border Equity Flows," mimeo.

Prasad, Eswar, Kenneth Rogoff, Shang-Jin Wei and Ayhan Kose (2003): "Effects of Financial Globalization on Developing Countries: Some Empirical Evidence," mimeo, *IMF*.

Stock, James and Mark Watson (2003): "Understanding Changes in International Business Cycle Dynamics," *NBER Working Paper* **9859**.

In: Business Fluctuations and Cycles
Editor: T. Nagakawa, pp. 171-192
ISBN: 978-1-60021-503-2

Chapter 7

TESTING OF UNIT ROOT CYCLES IN U.S. MACROECONOMIC SERIES

Luis A. Gil-Alana*

University of Navarra, Department of Economics, Pamplona, Spain

ABSTRACT

We propose in this article the use of a procedure for testing unit root cycles in macroeconomic time series. Unlike most classic unit-root methods, which are embedded in autoregressive alternatives, the tests employed in this paper are nested in a fractional model and have standard null and local limit distributions. The tests are first applied to the real US GDP series, the results substantially varying depending on how we specify the I(0) disturbances and the inclusion or not of deterministic components in the model. A model selection criterion based on diagnostic tests on the residuals is used in order to determine which may be the best specification of this series. In the second application we analyse the monthly structure of the US interest rate (Federal Funds). The results here indicate that there is some kind of intra-year cyclical component in the data, with the number of periods per cycle oscillating between 6 and 12 periods. However, separating the series in two subsamples (1955m1-1981m2, and 1981m3-2001m3), the results show that the length of the cycles is longer during the second part of the sample.

Key words: Fractional integration, Unit root cycles

JEL classification: C22

---

* The author gratefully acknowledges financial support from the Ministerio de Ciencia y Tecnologia (SEJ2005-07657, Spain). The usual disclaimers apply.

1. INTRODUCTION

It is a stylised fact that many macroeconomic time series contain trends as well as seasonal and cyclical components. In relation to the trend, deterministic models based on linear functions of time were initially proposed. However, it was later observed that the trend component of many economic series changed or evolved over time. Then, following the work and ideas of Box and Jenkins (1970), Nelson and Plosser (1982) used tests of Fuller (1976) and Dickey and Fuller (1979), and found evidence of unit roots (also called stochastic trends) in many US macroeconomic series. Similarly, for the seasonal component, deterministic models based on seasonal dummy variables were discouraged in favour of stochastic approaches, and seasonal unit root models were proposed amongst others by Dickey, Hasza and Fuller (DHF, 1984) and Hylleberg, Engle, Granger and Yoo (HEGY, 1990). In this article, we concentrate on the cyclical part of the series, and look at the presence of cycles in macroeconomic time series.

There exist different approaches for modelling cycles. Traditionally, deterministic approaches based on trigonometric functions of time were proposed but they were shown to be inappropriate in many series. Stochastic models, based on stationary autoregressive processes were then considered (see, e.g.., Harvey, 1985). However, in many series, the cycles evolve or change over time, and nonstationary cycles have been studied by Ahtola and Tiao (1987). In that paper, they propose a test statistic for testing unit root cycles embedded in autoregressive (AR(2)) processes. Robinson (1994) also develops tests for unit root cycles, however, unlike Ahtola and Tiao (1987), they are not based on autoregressions but on fractional models of the form proposed by Gray et. al. (1989, 1994). Gil-Alana (2001a) shows that the tests of Robinson (1994) outperform Ahtola and Tiao (1986) in a number of cases, and that will be the approach employed in the present paper.

The outline of the article is as follows: Section 2 briefly describes the concept of unit root cycles. In Section 3 we present a version of the tests of Robinson (1994) that permits us to test this hypothesis. The tests are then applied in Section 4 to two US macroeconomic series, namely real GDP and interest rates (Federal Funds), while Section 5 contains some concluding comments and extensions.

2. UNIT ROOT CYCLES

Ahtola and Tiao (1987) proposed tests for unit root cycles which are embedded in an AR(2) model of form

$$x_t = \phi_1 x_{t-1} + \phi_2 x_{t-2} + u_t, \qquad t = 1, 2, \ldots$$

which, under the null hypothesis,

$$H_o : |\phi_1| < 2 \quad and \quad \phi_2 = 1$$

becomes the cyclical I(1) model specified below. Gray et. al (1989, 1994) extended the unit root model to allow for a fractional degree of integration. In particular, they considered processes like:

$$(1 - 2\mu L + L^2)^d x_t = u_t, \quad t = 1,2,... \tag{1}$$

where d can be any real number, L is the lag-opertor, and where u_t is an I(0) process, defined, in the context of the present paper, as a covariance stationary process with spectral density function which is bounded and bounded away from zero at any frequency. Gray et. al. (1989) showed that x_t in (1) is stationary if $|\mu| < 1$ and $d < 0.50$ or if $|\mu| = 1$ and $d < 0.25$. They also showed that the polynomial in (1) can be expressed in terms of the Gegenbauer polynomial $C_{j,d}(\mu)$ such that for all $d \neq 0$,

$$(1 - 2\mu L + L^2)^{-d} = \sum_{j=0}^{\infty} C_{j,d}(\mu) L^j, \tag{2}$$

where

$$C_{j,d}(\mu) = \sum_{k=0}^{[j/2]} \frac{(-1)^k (d)_{j-k} (2\mu)^{j-2k}}{k!(j-2k)!}; \qquad (d)_j = \frac{\Gamma(d+j)}{\Gamma(d)},$$

$\Gamma(x)$ means the Gamma function, and a truncation will be required below (2) to make (1) operational. Thus, the process in (1) becomes

$$x_t = \sum_{j=0}^{t-1} C_{j,d}(\mu)\, u_{t-j}, \qquad t = 1, 2, ...,$$

and when d = 1, we have

$$x_t = 2\mu\, x_{t-1} - x_{t-2} + u_t, \qquad t = 1, 2, ..., \tag{3}$$

which is a cyclic I(1) process with the periodicity determined by μ. We can take $\mu = \cos w_r$ with $w_r = 2\pi/r$ and r will indicate the number of periods required to complete the cycle. Figures 1 – 3 show different realizations of unit-root cyclical models with samples of sizes T = 40, 80 and 120 respectively. We generate models like (1) with d = 1; $\mu = \cos 2\pi/r$ and r = 20, 10, 4 and 2, and u_t generated as a Gaussian white noise process with zero mean and variance 1. The nonstationary nature of the series seems to assert itself in that the cycles evolve over time, though non-necessarily in an increasing way, (see, for example, Figures 2 and 3 with r = 4).

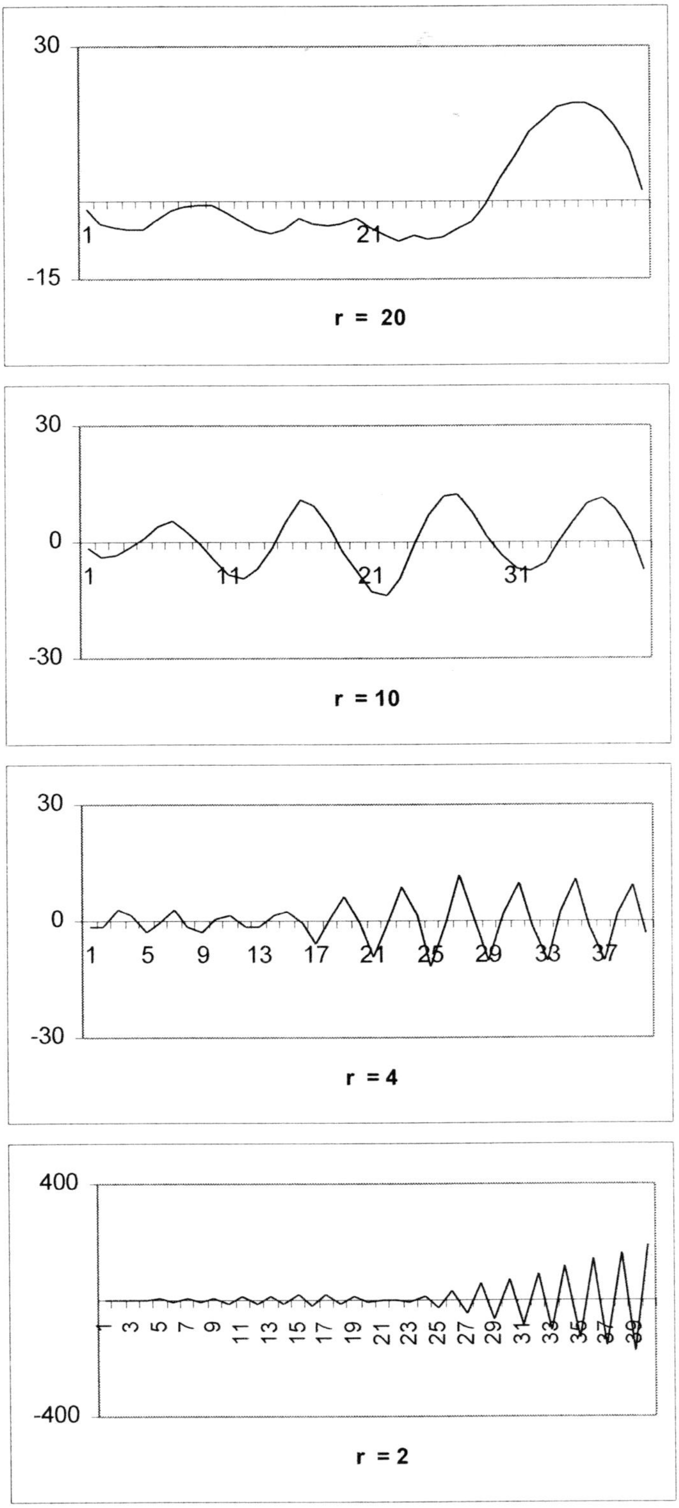

Figure 1. Simulated realizations of $(1 - 2\cos w_r L + L^2)\, x_t = \varepsilon_t;\ \varepsilon_t \sim N(0, 1)$ with $T = 40$

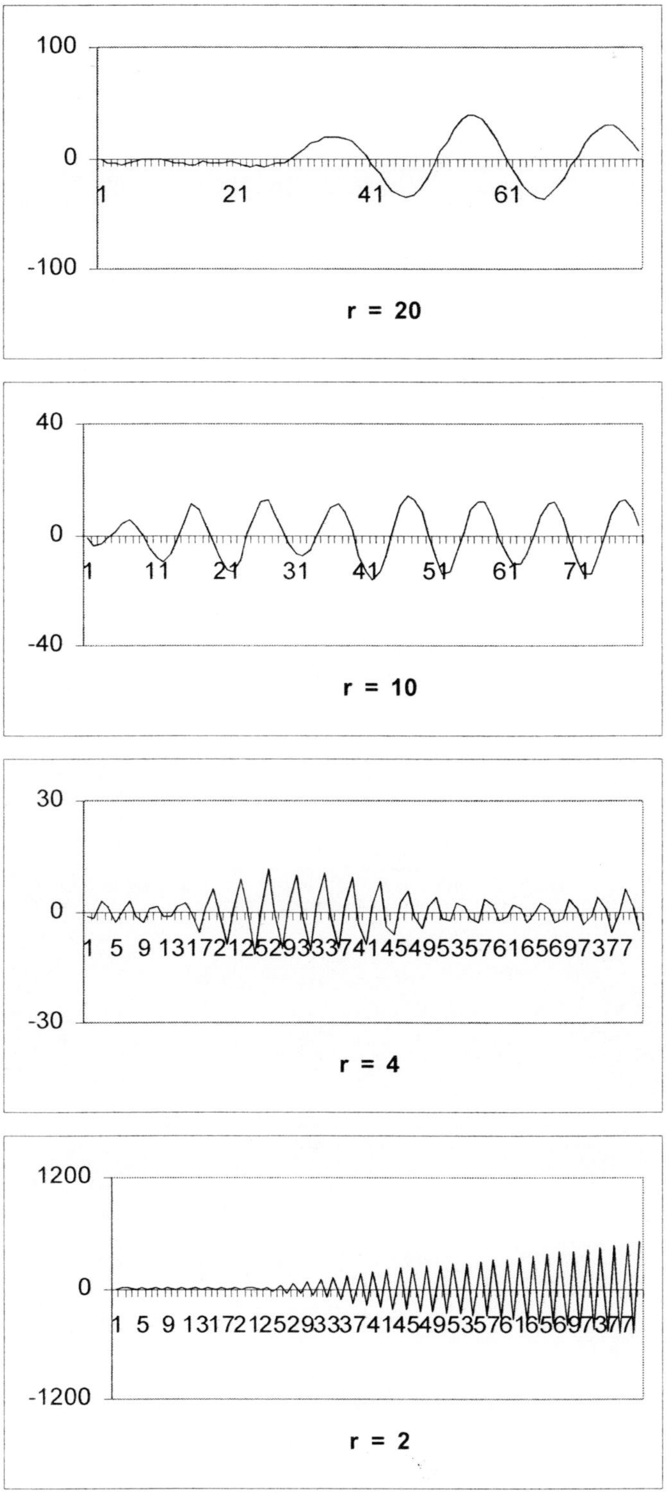

Figure 2. Simulated realizations of $(1 - 2 \cos w_r L + L^2) x_t = \varepsilon_t$; $\varepsilon_t \sim N(0, 1)$ with $T = 80$

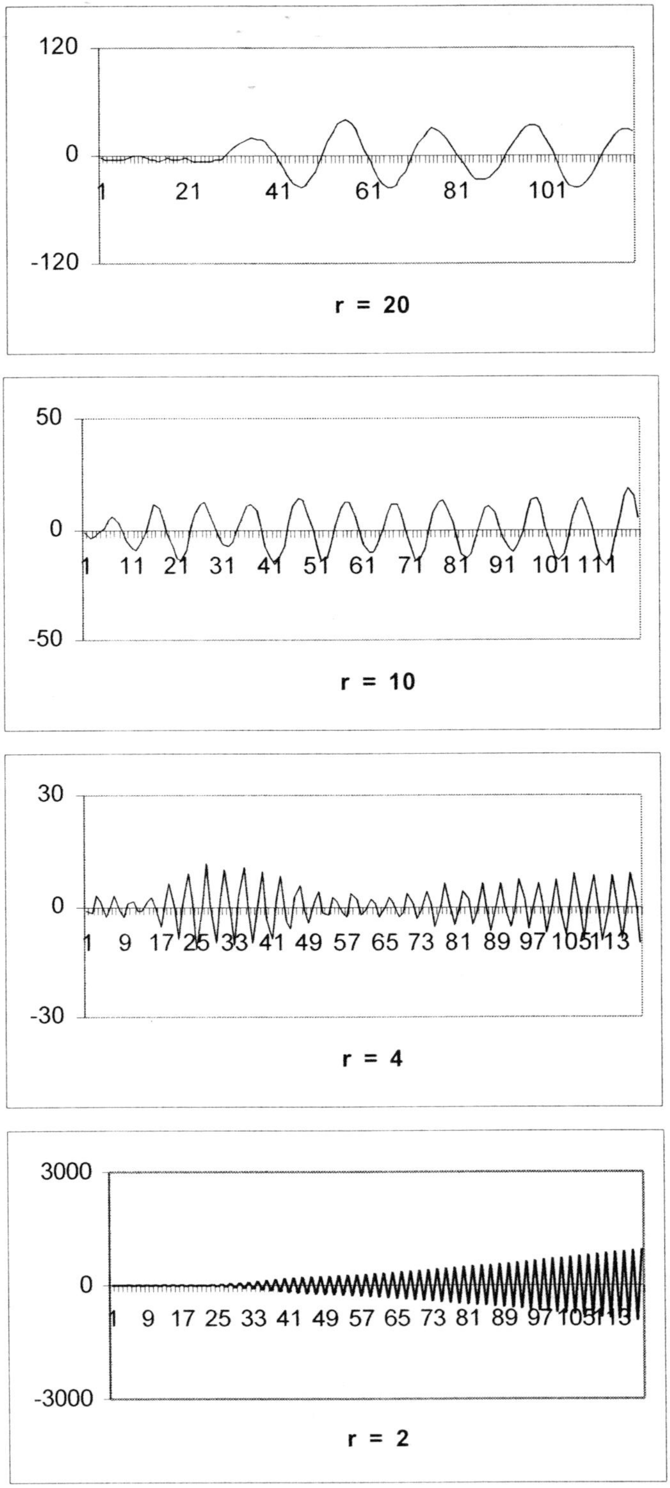

Figure 3. Simulated realizations of $(1 - 2\cos w_r L + L^2)\, x_t = \varepsilon_t$; $\varepsilon_t \sim N(0, 1)$ with $T = 120$

This is analogous to the seasonal unit-root models, where the seasonal (quarterly or monthly) components evolve or change over time. These figures also show the importance of the parameter r in determining the appropriate duration of the cycles. Thus, as r becomes smaller, the longitude of the cycle also becomes smaller and the series complete the cycles in shorter periods of time. The advantage of using this specification when modelling cycles in macroeconomic series is based on the fact that the cycles in economics do not occur at equal intervals of time and in fact, they seem to vary across time. In that respect, unit root cycles appear as alternative credible ways of modelling many series, including output and interest rates as is the case in this paper.

Robinson (1994) proposed a general testing procedure for testing unit root cycles embedded in fractional models like (1). The tests have several distinguishing features that make them particularly relevant in comparisons with other cyclical unit root tests based on AR alternatives. Thus, for example, they have standard null and local limit distributions, and this holds independently of the inclusion or not of deterministic regressors and autocorrelated disturbances. On the other hand, the tests of Robinson (1994) allow us to test not only unit but also fractional orders of integration and permit us to test that hypothesis for a different number of periods per cycle. Gil-Alana (2001) conducted several Monte Carlo experiments comparing Robinson's (1994) and Ahtola and Tiao's (1987) tests, and came to the conclusion that the tests of Robinson (1994) were more powerful when the alternatives were of a fractional type.

3. TESTING UNIT AND FRACTIONAL CYCLES WITH THE TESTS OF ROBINSON (1994)

Following discussions of Bhargava (1986), Schmidt and Phillips (1992) and others of parameterization of unit root models, Robinson (1994) considers the regression model,

$$y_t = \beta' z_t + x_t, \quad t = 1, 2, ..., \tag{4}$$

where y_t is the time series we observe; z_t is a (kx1) vector of deterministic regressors that may include, for instance, an intercept (if $z_t \equiv 1$) or an intercept and a linear trend ($z_t = (1,t)'$); β is a (kx1) vector of unknown parameters, and the regression errors, x_t, follow a cyclical model like (1) with $\mu = \cos 2\pi/r$, r as a given number indicating the number of periods per cycle. He proposes a Lagrange Multiplier (LM) test of the null hypothesis:

$$H_o : d = d_o, \tag{5}$$

for any real value d_o, and thus, also including the unit root in case of $d_o = 1$. Specifically, the test statistic is given by:

$$\hat{s} = \left(\frac{T}{\hat{A}}\right)^{1/2} \frac{\hat{a}}{\hat{\sigma}^2}, \tag{6}$$

$$\hat{a} = \frac{-2\pi}{T}\sum_{j=1}^{*}\psi(\lambda_j)g(\lambda_j;\hat{\tau})^{-1}I(\lambda_j); \qquad \hat{\sigma}^2 = \frac{2\pi}{T}\sum_{j=1}^{T-1}g(\lambda_j;\hat{\tau})^{-1}I(\lambda_j);$$

$$\hat{A} = \frac{2}{T}\left(\sum_{j=1}^{*}\psi(\lambda_j)^2 - \sum_{j=1}^{*}\psi(\lambda_j)\hat{\varepsilon}(\lambda_j)' \times \left(\sum_{j=1}^{*}\hat{\varepsilon}(\lambda_j)\hat{\varepsilon}(\lambda_j)'\right)^{-1} \times \sum_{j=1}^{*}\hat{\varepsilon}(\lambda_j)\psi(\lambda_j)\right)$$

$$\psi(\lambda_j) = \log\left|2\left(\cos\lambda_j - \cos w_r\right)\right|; \qquad \hat{\varepsilon}(\lambda_j) = \frac{\partial}{\partial\tau}\log g(\lambda_j;\hat{\tau}),$$

$I(\lambda_j)$ is the periodogram of $\hat{u}_t = (1 - 2\cos w_r L + L^2)^{d_o} y_t - \hat{\beta}'\bar{z}_t$, with

$$\hat{\beta} = \left(\sum_{t=1}^{T}\bar{z}_t\bar{z}_t'\right)^{-1}\sum_{t=1}^{T}\bar{z}_t(1 - 2\cos w_r L + L^2)^{d_o} y_t; \quad \bar{z}_t = (1 - 2\cos w_r L + L^2)^{d_o} z_t,$$

evaluated at $\lambda_j = 2\pi j/T$, and g is a known function coming from the spectral density function of $\hat{u}_t$: $f(\lambda;\tau) = \frac{\sigma^2}{2\pi}g(\lambda;\tau)$, with $\hat{\tau}$ obtained by minimising $\sigma^2(\tau)$. Finally, the summation on * in the above expressions are over $\lambda \in M$ where $M = \{\lambda: -\pi < \lambda < \pi, \lambda \notin (\rho_l - \lambda_1, \rho_l + \lambda_1), l = 1, 2, ..., s\}$, such that ρ_l, $l = 1, 2, ..., s < \infty$ are the distinct poles of $\psi(\lambda)$ on $(-\pi, \pi]$.

Based on H_o (5), Robinson (1994) established that under certain regularity conditions:

$$\hat{s} \to_d N(0,1) \qquad as \qquad T \to \infty, \tag{7}$$

and this standard limit distribution holds across the different types of regressors in z_t in (4) and also across the different types of disturbances u_t in (1). Thus, a one-sided $100\alpha\%$-level test of (5) against the alternative H_1: $d > d_o$ ($d < d_o$) is given by the rule: 'Reject H_o if $\hat{s} > z_\alpha$ ($\hat{s} < -z_\alpha$)', where the probability that a standard normal variate exceeds z_α is α. Furthermore, he shows that the above tests are efficient in the Pitman sense, i.e. that against local alternatives of form: H_a: $\theta = \delta T^{-1/2}$, for $\delta \neq 0$, the limit distribution is normal with variance 1 and mean which cannot (when u_t is Gaussian) be exceeded in absolute value by that of any rival regular statistic. Other versions of the tests of Robinson (1994), based on annual and seasonal (quarterly and monthly) data can be found respectively in Gil-Alana and Robinson (1997, 2001) and Gil-Alana (1999), and a small application of the present version of the tests is Gil-Alana (2004).

4. Empirical Applications

Two US macroeconomic series are examined in this section. The first one is the US real GDP and the second corresponds to the monthly structure of the US interest rates (Federal Funds).

4.1 US real GDP

The time series analysed in this section is the quarterly, seasonally adjusted, real GDP in the US from 1947.1 to 2000.2, obtained from the Reserve Federal Bank of St. Louis' database.

Figure 4 plots the original and first differenced series, with their corresponding correlograms and periodograms. We see that the original series increases over the sample period, though we also observe some apparent cyclical component in its behaviour. The correlogram and the periodogram clearly show the nonstationary nature of the series. Taking first differences, we still see a nonstationary component, especially through the correlogram, with significant autocorrelations even at lags relatively far away from zero.

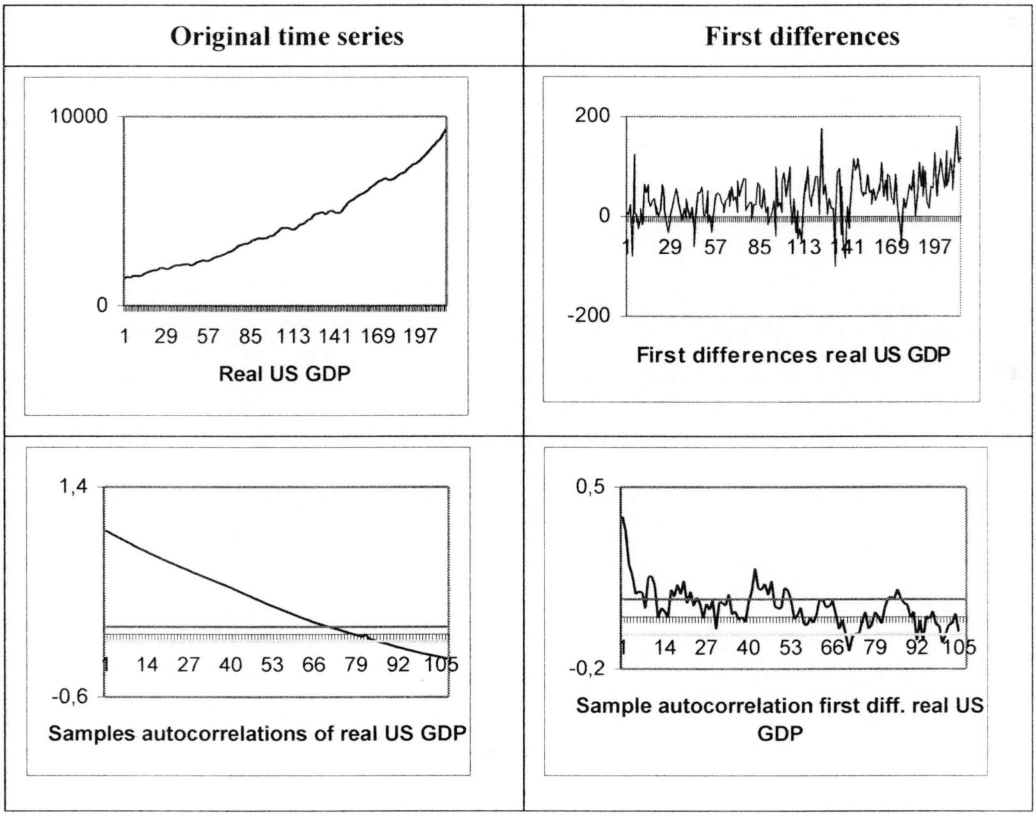

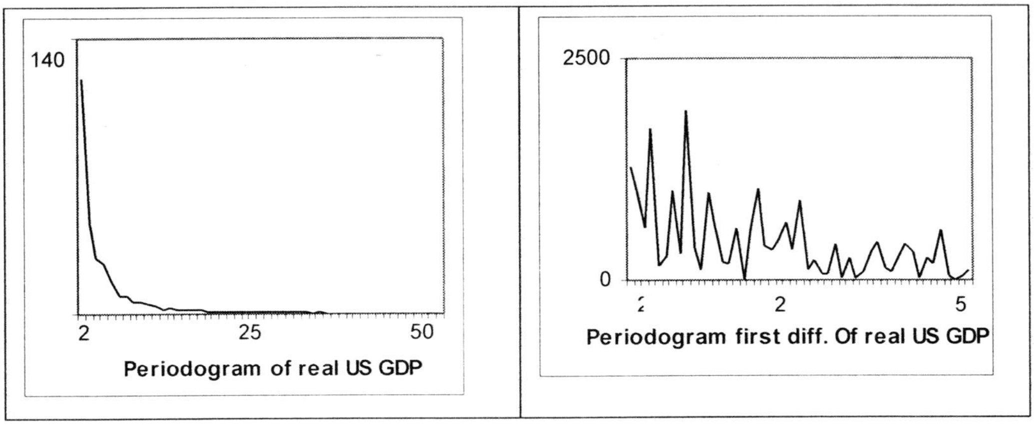

Figure 4. Plots for the US real GDP.

Denoting the GDP series y_t, we employ throughout the model in (4) and (1) with $z_t = (1,t)'$, $t \geq 1$, $(0,0)'$ otherwise, and $\mu = \cos 2\pi/r$, i.e., we consider the model,

$$y_t = \beta_0 + \beta_1 t + x_t, \qquad t = 1, 2, \ldots \tag{8}$$

$$(1 - 2\cos\frac{2\pi}{r}L + L^2)^d x_t = u_t, \quad t = 1, 2, \ldots, \tag{9}$$

testing the null hypothesis:

$$H_o: d = 1, \tag{10}$$

for values of r = 2, 3, …, T/2,[1] with white noise disturbances (in Table 1), and AR(1) and AR(2) u_t (in Tables 2 and 3). We treat separately the cases of $\beta_0 = \beta_1 = 0$ a priori, (i.e., including no regressors in (8)); β_0 unknown and $\beta_1 = 0$ a priori, (i.e., including an intercept); and β_0 and β_1 unknown, (i.e, with a linear time trend).

Across Tables 1 – 3 we report values of $\hat{s}$ given by (6). However, instead of presenting the results for the whole range of values of r, we only report in the tables the statistics for those cases where we found at least one non-rejection value across the different specifications in (8). Table 1 shows the results for white noise disturbances. Starting with the case of no regressors, we see that H_o (10) cannot be rejected when r ranges between 31 and 37, with the lowest statistic in absolute value occurring at r = 34, which corresponds to 8 complete years and two quarters. Including an intercept, the unit root null hypothesis always results in a rejection and, including a linear time trend, H_o (10) cannot be rejected if r ranges between 24 and 30, with the lowest value of $|\hat{s}|$ occurring at r = 27 (6 years and 3 quarters).

[1] Note that in case of r = 1 the model reduces to the I(d) model with the singularity or pole in the spectrum occuring at the zero frequency, since $(1 - 2\cos 2\pi L + L^2)^d = (1 - L)^{2d}$.

TABLE 1			
Testing $H_o(10)$ in (8) and (9) with white noise disturbances			
Periods per cycle	No regressors	An intercept	A linear time trend
24	6.558	8.552	**1.511'**
25	5.896	9.155	**0.921'**
26	5.065	9.454	**0.341'**
27	4.222	9.592	**-0.181'**
28	3.554	10.140	**-0.713'**
29	2.843	10.395	**-1.175'**
30	2.162	10.435	**-1.555'**
31	**1.542'**	10.498	-1.913
32	**0.962'**	10.745	-2.315
33	**0.420'**	10.767	-2.638
34	**-0.071'**	10.653	-2.902
35	**-0.494'**	10.373	-3.087
36	**-0.874'**	10.046	-3.248
37	**-1.319'**	10.008	-3.563

' and in bold: Non-rejection values of the null hypothesis at the 95% significance level.

Tables 2 and 3 extend the results to allow respectively AR(1) and AR(2) disturbances. Starting with AR(1) u_t, we see that if we do not include regressors, the only non-rejection values appear at r = 9 and 10. Including an intercept, the null is always rejected and, with a linear time trend, the non-rejection values occur when r is 19, 20 and 21, and when it ranges between 34 and 47. The lowest statistic appears in this case at r = 40, i.e., corresponding to cycles completed every ten years.

TABLE 2			
Testing $H_o(10)$ in (8) and (9) with AR(1) disturbances			
Periods per cycle	No regressors	An intercept	A linear time trend
9	**1.310'**	-7.796	-6.115
10	**-0.124'**	-8.007	-6.214
19	-7.476	-13.239	**-1.269'**
20	-8.034	-14.173	**0.114'**
21	-8.603	-14.342	**1.181'**
34	-14.182	-18.669	**1.569'**
35	-11.093	-18.373	**1.257'**
36	-9.054	-17.885	**0.960'**
37	-8.900	-22.115	**0.683'**
38	-8.077	-25.012	**0.403'**
39	-7.230	-27.317	**0.136'**
40	-6.449	-28.278	**-0.113'**
41	-5.733	-26.868	**-0.338'**
42	-5.015	-21.705	**-0.529'**
43	-4.260	-15.455	**-0.670'**
44	-4.416	-20.078	**-0.947'**
45	-4.267	-19.974	**-1.156'**
46	-4.090	-18.317	**-1.340'**
47	-3.922	-16.150	**-1.505'**

' and in bold: Non-rejection values of the null hypothesis at the 95% significance level.

TABLE 3

Testing $H_o(10)$ in (8) and (9) with AR(2) disturbances

Periods per cycle	No regressors	An intercept	A linear time trend
15	16.524	**1.388'**	6.873
16	15.024	**0.652'**	7.124
17	13.023	**0.192'**	7.248
18	10.220	**0.018'**	6.693
19	8.442	**0.072'**	7.095
20	6.298	**0.351'**	6.954
21	4.168	**0.817'**	6.650
22	2.323	**1.458'**	6.485
23	**0.605'**	2.234	6.253
24	**-0.840'**	2.964	5.726
36	-8.905	9.670	**1.617'**
37	-9.841	9.950	**1.191'**
38	-10.294	9.902	**0.681'**
39	-10.575	9.720	**0.164'**
40	-10.728	9.445	**-0.334'**
41	-10.735	9.084	**-0.786'**
42	-10.464	8.608	**-1.146'**
43	-9.787	7.975	**-1.359'**

' and in bold: Non-rejection values of the null hypothesis at the 95% significance level.

Imposing AR(2) disturbances, we see that the results also change depending on the inclusion or not of an intercept and/or a linear time trend. Thus, if there are no regressors, H_o (10) cannot be rejected with r = 23 and 24. Including an intercept, the non-rejection values appear when r is between 15 and 22 and finally, including a linear time trend, r oscillates between 36 and 43. The lowest statistics across r are obtained in these cases when r = 23 (with no regressors); 18 (with an intercept) and 42 (with a linear time trend).

We should mention here that the test statistic was also computed for the first differenced series, and the null hypothesis of a unit root cycle was rejected for all type of disturbances. The results in the preceding tables clearly show that the duration of the cycles is very sensitive to both, the inclusion of deterministic trends and model specification for the I(0) disturbances. In order to analyse now which may be the best model specification for this series, we proceed as follows: for each specification of z_t in (8) and for each type of disturbances in (9), we take the model with the value of r which produces the lowest statistic in absolute value across r. The intuition behind this is that the model with the lowest $|\hat{S}|$ will produce the residuals closest to white noise. Then, for each of the selected models, we perform several diagnostic tests to assure that they are white noise. In particular, we use tests for no serial correlation; functional form; normality and heterocedasticity, choosing as potential model specifications those which pass all the diagnostics. Results are given in Table 4.

TABLE 4

Best model specifications according to the lowest $|\hat{S}|$ across r

u_t	Model	z_t	r	$\hat{S}$	α	β	ϕ_1	ϕ_2	Diagnostics*
White noise	1	No	**34**	-0.071	-----	-----	-----	-----	A; D ;
	2	An intercept	---	------	-----	-----	-----	-----	----------
	3	A linear trend	**27**	-0.181	1407.58 (37.28)	28.96 (0.61)	-----	-----	A; B**; C; D;
AR (1)	4	No regressors	**10**	-0.124	-----	-----	0.998 (0.009)	-----	A; C; D;
	5	An intercept	---	------	-----	-----	-----	-----	----------
	6	A linear trend	**40**	-0.113	1451.39 (31.89)	28.77 (1.03)	-0.368 (0.06)	-----	A; C; D;
AR (2)	7	No regressors	**23**	0.605	-----	-----	0.556 (0.07)	-0.432 (0.07)	A; D;
	8	An intercept	**19**	0.072	3143.59 (70.20)	-----	0.542 (0.08)	-0.431 (0.08)	A; D;
	9	A linear trend	**39**	0.164	1450.13 (32.10)	28.77 (0.99)	-0.372 (0.06)	0.011 (0.06)	A; C; D ;

* : Non-rejection values at the 95% significance level of A): No serial correlation; B): Functional form; C): Normality and D): Homocedasticity. **: Non-rejection at the 99% significance level. Standard errors in parenthesis.

We see that the values of r substantially vary across the models. They range from r = 10 (in model 4) to r = 40 (in model 6). The coefficients of the intercept and of the linear time trend are all significant and only the second AR coefficient appears insignificantly different from zero. Looking at the diagnostics, we observe that only three models pass the tests of no serial correlation, normality and homocedasticity at the 95% significance level, (models 3, 4 and 9), and model 3 is the only one which also passes the diagnostics in relation to the functional form, though at the 99% level. In view of this, we can conclude by saying that the real US GDP may be well described in terms of the model,

$$(1 - 2\cos\frac{2\pi}{r}L + L^2)y_t = \varepsilon_t, \quad t = 1, 2, ...,$$

with white noise ε_t and r = 27, implying that the nonstationary cycles seems to repeat itself every 27 periods (i.e., six years and three quarters).

4.2. U.S. interest rates

Here we analyse the monthly structure of the US interest rates (Federal Funds) for the time period 1954m7 – 2001m3, obtained from the St. Louis Federal Reserve Bank database.

Figure 5 contains different plots of the original series. The first picture corresponds to the whole sample period and we observe that there is a clear cyclical component. This may be better seen across the other plots in the figure where the whole sample has been decomposed into 4 subsamples of 140 observations each. In Figure 6, we display plots of the first monthly differenced data and here we again observe a cyclical behaviour, especially when looking at the subsamples. We perfrom here the same procedure as in the previous case, testing for the existence of unit root cycles.

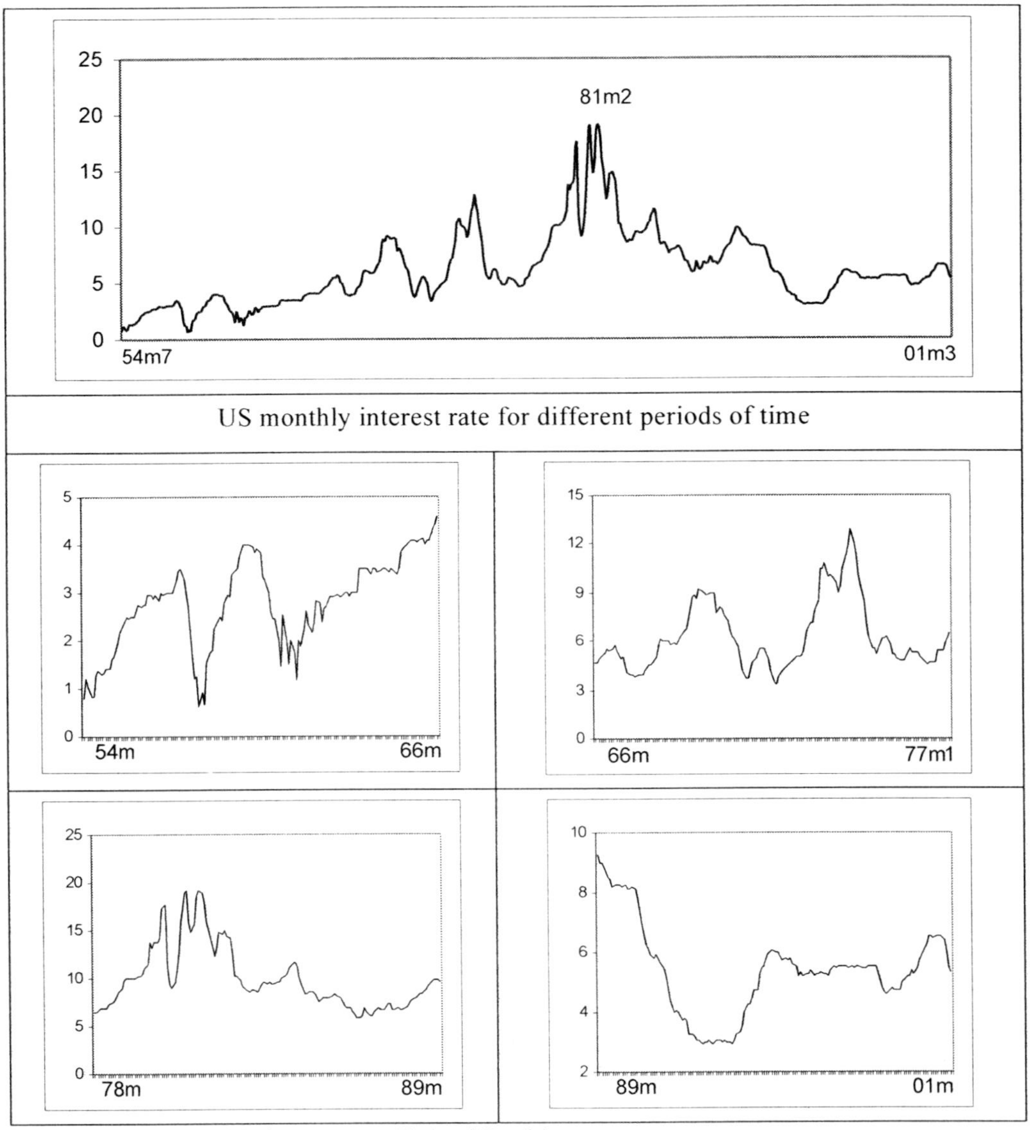

Figure 5. US monthly interest rate (Federal Funds)

Starting with the case of white noise disturbances, (in Table 5), we see that the unit root null hypothesis cannot be rejected when r is equal to 6 or when it is between 16 and 21. That means that if the time series truly contains unit root cycles, they seem to occur either every six periods (half a year) or approximately every one year and a half. However, the significance of these results may be due in large part to the un-accounted for I(0) autocorrelation in u_t. Thus, we also permit AR(1) and AR(2) disturbances. Modelling u_t in terms of AR(1) processes, the null was rejected in all cases, and allowing AR(2) u_t, the results are given in Table 6. We observe here less non-rejection values than in Table 5 and they occur when r = 6 and when it is between 15 and 19 periods, so that the same conclusion as in the previous table holds here.

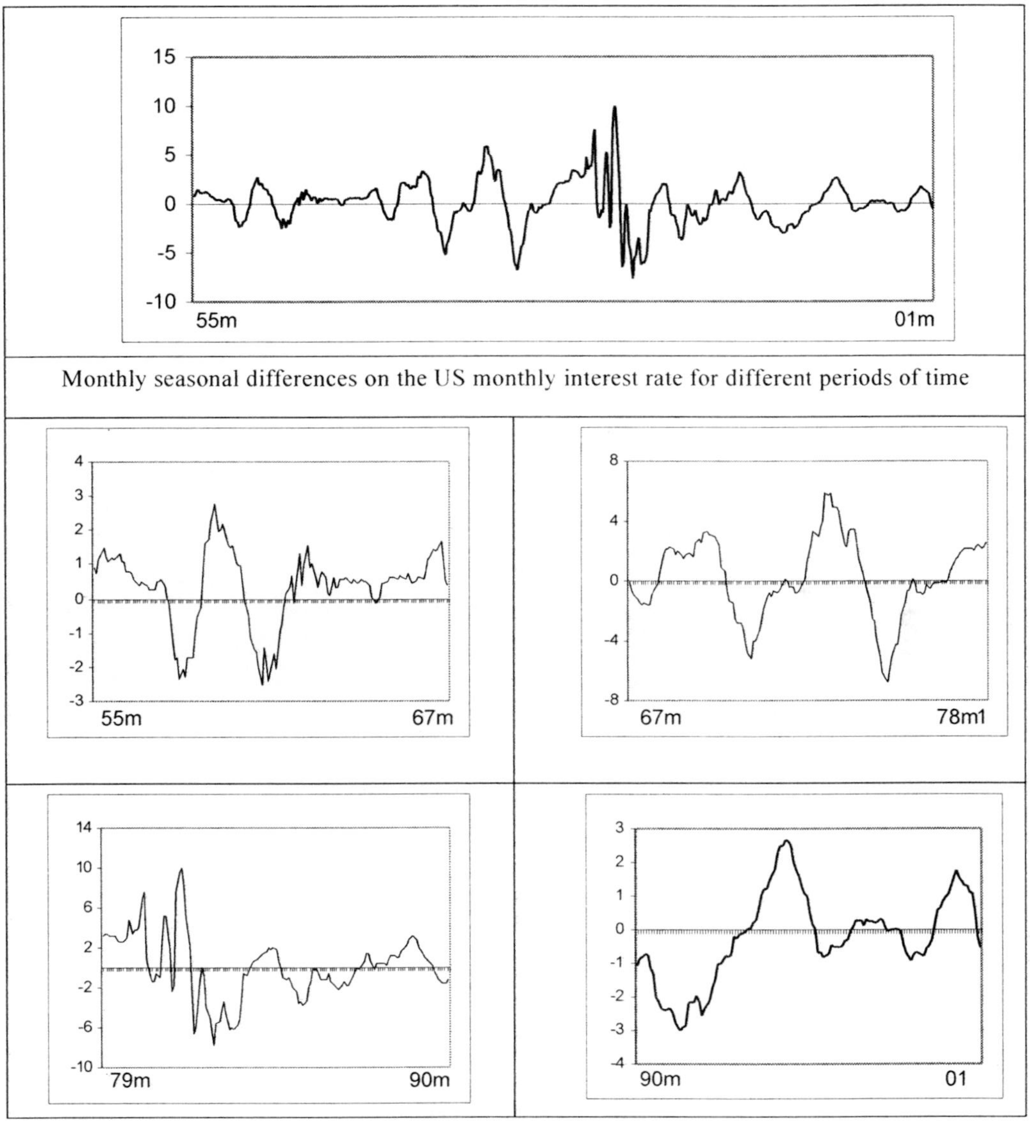

Figure 6. Monthly seasonal differences on the US monthly interest rate (Federal Funds)

TABLE 5

Testing of unit root cycles with the original time series and white noise disturbances

R	Type of regressors		
Number of periods per cycle	No regressors	An intercept	An intercept and a linear time trend
6	**0.055'**	**-0.031'**	**0.005'**
16	3.706	**1.783'**	2.384
17	2.176	**0.508'**	**1.115'**
18	**1.088'**	**-0.550'**	**0.138'**
19	**-0.043'**	**-1.508'**	**-0.807'**
20	**-1.015'**	-2.273	**-1.594'**
21	**-1885'**	-2.992	-2.327

' and in bold: Non-rejection values at the 99% significance level.

TABLE 6

Testing of unit root cycles with the original time series and AR(2) disturbances

R	Type of regressors		
Number of periods per cycle	No regressors	An intercept	An intercept and a linear time trend
6	**-1.679'**	-2.144	-1.997
15	**0.895'**	1.969	4.935
16	**-1.690'**	**0.256'**	3.129
17	-3.215	**-0.933'**	**1.187'**
18	-6.057	-2.885	**0.078'**
19	-7.925	-4.597	**-1.669'**

' and in bold: Non-rejection values at the 99% significance level.

Tables 7 and 8 are analogous to Tables 5 and 6 above but based on the monthly differenced series. In doing so, we try to eliminate a potential seasonal component in the series. Starting again with the case of white noise disturbances, (Table 7), we see that the non-rejection values take place when r = 6, 10, 11 and 12, and this is obtained independently of the inclusion or not of deterministic regressors in the regression model (4). If u_t follows an AR(1) process, the unit root null is rejected in all cases, and imposing AR(2) disturbances, the values of r where the null cannot be rejected are 6, 9, 10 and 11. The results in these two tables indicate that even removing the seasonal component throughout seasonal differences, there may still exist some kind of intra-year cyclical effect, with the unit root cycles occurring approximately every half-year or something slightly higher.

TABLE 7

Testing of unit root cycles with the monthly differenced series and white noise disturbances

R	Type of regressors		
Number of periods per cycle	No regressors	An intercept	An intercept and a linear time trend
6	**-0.017'**	**-0.016'**	**-0.014'**
10	**1.416'**	**1.424'**	**1.394'**
11	**-0.157'**	**-0.149'**	**-0.179'**
12	**-1.658'**	**-1.650'**	**-1.678'**

' and in bold: Non-rejection values at the 99% significance level.

Next, we are concerned with the potential effects that a structural break may have had in the above results, in particular, one due to the turbulent period at the beginning of 1981. (See again Figure 5). To analyse this, we divide the sample in two subsamples. One corresponding to the time period 1955m1-1981m2, and the other going from 1981m3 to 2001m3.

TABLE 8

Testing of unit root cycles with the monthly differenced series and AR(2) disturbances

R	Type of regressors		
Number of periods per cycle	No regressors	An intercept	An intercept and a linear time trend
6	**1.349'**	**1.359'**	**1.337'**
9	**1.143'**	**1.163'**	**1.137'**
10	**-0.058'**	**-0.026'**	**-0.057'**
11	**-1.664'**	**-1.628'**	**-1.657'**

' and in bold: Non-rejection values at the 99% significance level.

TABLE 9

Testing of unit root cycles with the original time series and white noise disturbances

	1955m1 – 1981m2			1981m3 - 2001m3		
R	Type of regressors			Type of regressors		
Number of periods per cycle	No regressors	An intercept	An intercept and a linear time trend	No regressors	An intercept	An intercept and a linear time trend
6	**0.576'**	**0.248'**	**0.327'**	**-0.374'**	**-0.068'**	**0.032'**
7	3.455	2.969	2.653	**1.214'**	2.277	2.344
8	4.560	3.941	3.040	**1.397'**	3.526	3.765
9	6.330	5.346	3.317	**0.703'**	4.120	4.482
10	5.819	4.703	2.082	**-0.458'**	3.944	4.485
11	6.207	4.746	2.075	**-1.685'**	3.436	4.190
12	5.606	3.990	-1.889	**-1.578'**	2.674	3.681
13	4.608	2.974	**-1.313'**	-3.817	**1.891'**	3.186
14	3.447	**1.915'**	-2.184	-4.500	**1.036'**	2.521
15	2.332	**0.948'**	-2.932	-4.923	**0.281'**	**1.847'**
16	**1.129'**	**0.080'**	-3.027	-5.321	**-0.339'**	**1.253'**
17	**0.284'**	**-0.681'**	-3.862	-5.754	**-0.872'**	**0.700'**
18	**-0.563'**	**-1.327'**	-4.190	-6.055	**-1.313'**	**0.151'**
19	**-1.273'**	**-1.852'**	-4.401	-6.211	**-1.655'**	**-0.367'**
20	**-1.612'**	-1.989	-3.983	-6.107	**-1.862'**	**-0.812'**

' and in bold: Non-rejection values at the 99% significance level.

Table 9 reports values of the same statistic as in Table 5 (i.e., $\hat{S}$ given by (6) with white noise disturbances) for the two subsamples. We see in this table that if r = 6, H_o (10) cannot be rejected for any type of disturbances in any of the two subsamples. If r is between 7 and 12, the null is rejected in the first subsample for all type of disturbances but it cannot be rejected in the second one in case of $z_t = 0$. Finally, if r is between 13 and 20, we observe several non-rejection values in both subsamples. Thus, the results across this table are not much conclusive. However, allowing AR(2) u_t, (in Table 10), we see that the non-rejection values take place when r is between 6 and 17 in case of the first subsample and when it ranges between 22 and 27 in the second one, suggesting that the unit root cycles are longer during the second part of the sample.

TABLE 10

Testing of unit root cycles with the original time series and AR(2) disturbances

	1955m1 – 1981m2			1981m3 - 2001m3		
R	Type of regressors			Type of regressors		
Number of periods per cycle	No regressors	An intercept	An intercept and a linear time trend	No regressors	An intercept	An intercept and a linear time trend
5	**-1.913'**	-4.352	-3.663	-7.664	-6.638	-5.885
6	**-1.789'**	-3.155	-4.277	-4.371	-2.185	-2.094
10	5.861	4.042	**1.675'**	-8.205	2.677	5.232
11	6.355	4.526	**1.261'**	-10.087	1.933	4.857
12	4.778	3.701	**0.137'**	-11.404	-1.936	4.438
13	2.681	2.657	**-1.223'**	-13.294	-2.324	4.396
14	**0.618'**	**1.651'**	-2.599	-13.603	-2.316	4.119
15	**-1.262'**	**0.829'**	-4.596	-13.222	-2.952	3.807
16	-1.997	**-0.006'**	-3.265	-13.465	-3.519	3.725
17	-4.218	**-0.990'**	-7.779	-14.405	-4.142	3.837
22	-8.713	-6.432	-14.493	-13.950	-4.879	**1.672'**
23	-8.472	-6.495	-12.729	-13.550	-5.398	**1.191'**
24	-9.608	-8.059	-15.490	-13.955	-5.037	**0.370'**
25	-9.751	-8.505	-16.150	-15.513	-5.576	**-0.339'**
26	-10.372	-9.444	-15.032	-15.370	-5.637	**-1.060'**
27	-10.232	-9.434	-16.953	-14.396	-5.456	**-1.575'**

' and in bold: Non-rejection values at the 99% significance level.

Finally, Tables 11 and 12 present the values of $\hat{S}$ for both subsamples in case of the first monthly differenced data. If u_t is white noise (Table 11), we see intra-year cycles in both subsamples, with r ranging between 6 and 11, however, and similarly to the previous table, we also observe several non-rejection values in the second sample if r is higher than 12, taking values between 13 and 28. Allowing AR(2) disturbances, the results are displayed in Table 12. We observe here less non-rejection values than in Table 11 and the results are much more conclusive. Thus, in the first subsample, the unit root cycles take place when r is between 7 and 10 while in the second one, they occur when r is between 18 and 21, implying once more that the length of the unit root cycles is longer during the second part of the sample.

TABLE 11

Testing of unit root cycles with the monthly differenced series and white noise disturbances

	1956m1 – 1981m2			1981m3 - 2001m3		
R	Type of regressors			Type of regressors		
Number of periods per cycle	No regressors	An intercept	An intercept and a linear time trend	No regressors	An intercept	An intercept and a linear time trend
6	**-0.240'**	**-0.262'**	**-0.281'**	**-0.766'**	**-0.837'**	**-1.185'**
7	**1.529'**	**1.512'**	**1.453'**	**0.138'**	**0.010'**	**-0.768'**
8	**1.835'**	**1.824'**	**1.704'**	**-0.214'**	**-0.365'**	**-1.291'**
9	**1.218'**	**1.213'**	**1.039'**	**-1.146'**	**-1.265'**	**-1.893'**
10	**0.096'**	**0.098'**	**-0.099'**	-2.207	-2.253	-2.257
11	**-1.124'**	**-1.116'**	**-1.308'**	-3.126	-3.080	-2.259
12	-2.145	-2.133	-2.297	-3.838	-3.687	-1.969
13	-2.996	-2.980	-3.115	-4.286	-4.056	**-1.492'**
14	-3.747	-3.726	-3.835	-4.645	-4.326	**-0.985'**
15	-4.185	-4.162	-4.244	-4.960	-4.547	**-0.524'**
16	-4.623	-4.596	-4.658	-5.133	-4.646	**-0.156'**
17	-4.890	-4.861	-4.905	-5.177	-4.581	**0.075'**
18	-5.084	-5.053	-5.084	-5.252	-4.556	**0.165'**
19	-5.233	-5.199	-5.221	-5.426	-4.609	**0.136'**
20	-5.328	-5.292	-5.305	-5.404	-4.489	**0.006'**
21	-5.301	-5.264	-5.273	-5.441	-4.418	**-0.191'**
22	-5.428	-5.389	-5.393	-5.464	-4.340	**-0.430'**
23	-5.498	-5.457	-5.458	-5.463	-4.249	**-0.688'**
24	-5.338	-5.297	-5.296	-5.419	-4.133	**-0.943'**
25	-5.546	-5.502	-5.500	-5.488	-4.115	**-1.212'**
26	-5.359	-5.513	-5.313	-5.320	-3.927	**-1.411'**
27	-5.560	-5.513	-5.511	-5.439	-3.963	**-1.669'**
28	-5.511	-5.464	-5.461	-5.459	-3.934	**-1.883'**

' and in bold: Non-rejection values at the 99% significance level.

TABLE 12

Testing of unit root cycles with the monthly differenced series and AR(2) disturbances

	1956m1 – 1981m2			1981m3 - 2001m3		
R	Type of regressors			Type of regressors		
Number of periods per cycle	No regressors	An intercept	An intercept and a linear time trend	No regressors	An intercept	An intercept and a linear time trend
7	**0.734'**	**0.726'**	**0.745'**	-4.038	-4.323	-6.404
8	**1.214'**	**1.246'**	**1.206'**	-5.495	-5.797	-7.795
9	**0.509'**	**0.621'**	**0.512'**	-7.217	-7.387	-8.554
10	**-0.770'**	**-0.564'**	**-0.742'**	-9.143	-9.181	-9.189
18	-13.942	-13.552	-13.658	-12.320	-12.948	**-1.546'**
19	-15.135	-14.714	-14.790	-13.935	-13.881	**-1.426'**
20	-15.925	-15.490	-15.541	-12.337	-13.191	**-1.382'**
21	-14.578	-14.207	-14.237	-13.597	-13.093	**-1.601'**

' and in bold: Non-rejection values at the 99% significance level.

5. Conclusions

We have presented in this article a new statistical way of modelling the cyclical component in macroeconomic time series. For this purpose, we have used a version of the tests of Robinson (1994) that permits us to test unit root cycles in a fractional context. The tests have standard null and local limit distributions and are easy to implement in raw time series. A diskette containing the FORTRAN code for the programs is available from the author upon request.

The tests were first applied to the US real GDP, the results substantially varying depending on the inclusion or not of deterministic trends and the way of modelling the I(0) disturbances. A model selection criterion, based on the lowest statistic across the number of periods per cycle along with several diagnostic tests carried out on the residuals seem to indicate that the cycles occur approximately every six or seven years. Similar conclusions were obtained in Gil-Alana (2001a) when applying the tests to an extended version of Nelson and Plosser's (1982) data set.

Then we examine the monthly structure of the US interest rate (Federal Funds) at each of the frequencies of the process. The results indicate that there is some kind of intra-year unit-root cyclical component in the data, with the cycles occurring when the number of periods per cycle is between 6 and 12. However, we have also study the possibility of a potential break in 1981. Separating the data in two subsamples (1995m1-1981m2 and 1981m3-2001m3), the results show that the length of the unit root cycles is longer during the second part of the sample.

This article can be extended in several directions. A natural following step would be to test for fractional cycles, i.e., allowing d_o in (5) to be a real number rather than 1. Of course, it would also be of interest in this context to estimate the order of integration of the series. There exist several procedures for estimating the fractional differencing parameter in seasonal and cyclical contexts, (e.g., Ooms, 1997; Arteche and Robinson, 1999, 2000; etc.), however, they are not only computationally more expensive, but it is then in any case confidence intervals rather than point estimates which should be stressed. Work in this direction is now under progress. Also, other forms of I(0) disturbances, for example, the Bloomfield (1973) exponential spectral model, (see, eg, Gil-Alana, 2001b), may be used in the specification of the u_t in (9). The latter model has several computational advantages when performing the tests of Robinson (1994). In particular, it does not require any matrix inversion in the estimation of the parameters and thus, enormously simplifies the computation of the test statistic. How these extensions may affect to the longitude and to the orders of integration of the cycles still remains to be investigated.

References

Ahtola, J. and Tiao, G.C., 1987, Distributions of least squares estimators of autoregressive parameters for a process with complex roots on the unit circle, *Journal of Time Series Analysis* 8, 1-14.

Arteche, J. and P.M. Robinson, Seasonal and cyclical long memory, in S. Ghosh ed., Asymptotics, *Nonparametrics and Time Series*, Marcel Dekker Inc., New York, 115-148.

Arteche, J. and P.M. Robinson, 2000, Semiparametric inference in seasonal and cyclical long memory processes, *Journal of Time Series Analysis* 21, 1-25.

Bhargava, A., 1986, On the theory of testing for unit roots in observed time series, Review of Economic Studies 53, 369-384.

Bloomfield, P.J., 1973, An exponential model for the spectrum of a scalar time series, *Biometrika* 60, 217-226.

Box, G.E.P. and G.M. Jenkins, 1970, *Time series analysis: Forecasting and control*, San Francisco, Holden Day.

Dickey, D.A., D. P. Hasza and W.A. Fuller, 1984, Testing for unit roots in seasonal time series, *Journal of the American Statistical Association* 79, 355-367.

Dickey, D.A. and W.A. Fuller, 1979, Distribution of the estimators for autoregressive time series with a unit root, *Journal of the American Statistical Association* 74, 427-431.

Fuller, W.A., 1976, Introduction to statistical time series, *Willey Series in Probability and Mathematical Statistics*, Willey, New York, NY.

Gil-Alana, L.A., 1999, Testing fractional integration with monthly data, *Economic Modelling* 16, 613-629.

Gil-Alana, L.A., 2001a, Testing stochastic cycles in macroeconomic time series, *Journal of Time Series Analysis* 22, 414-430.

Gil-Alana, L.A., 2001b, A fractionally integrated exponential model for the UK unemployment, *Journal of Forecasting* 20, 329-340.

Gil-Alana, L.A., 2004, Unit root cycles in the US unemployment rate, *Economics Bulletin* 3, 7, 1-10.

Gil-Alana, L.A. and Robinson, P.M., 1997, Testing of unit roots and other nonstationary hypothses in macroeconomic time series, *Journal of Econometrics* 80, 241-268.

Gil-Alana, L.A. and Robinson, P.M., 2001, Seasonal fractional integration in the UK and Japanese consumption and income, *Journal of Applied Econometrics* 16, 95-114.

Gray, H.L., Yhang, N. and Woodward, W.A., 1989, On generalized fractional processes, *Journal of Time Series Analysis* 10, 233-257.

Gray, H.L., Yhang, N. and Woodward, W.A., 1994, On generalized fractional processes. A correction, *Journal of Time Series Analysis* 15, 561-562.

Harvey, A., 1985, Trends and cycles in macroeconomic time series, *Journal of Business and Economics Statistics* 3, 216-227.

Hylleberg, S., R.F. Engle, C.W.J. Granger and B.S. Yoo, 1990, Seasonal integration and cointegration, *Journal of Econometrics* 44, 215-238.

Nelson, C.R. and C.I. Plosser, 1982, Trends and random walks in macroeconomic time series, *Journal of Monetary Economics* 10, 139-162.

Ooms, M., 1999, Flexible seasonal long memory and economic time series, *Preprint*.

Robinson, P.M., 1994, Efficient tests of nonstationary hypotheses, *Journal of the American Statistical Association* 89, 1420-1437.

Schmidt, P. and Phillips, P.C.B., 1992, LM tests for a unit root in the presence of deterministic trends, *Oxford Bulletin of Economics and Statistics* 54, 257-287.

In: Business Fluctuations and Cycles
Editor: T. Nagakawa, pp. 193-202
ISBN: 978-1-60021-503-2

Chapter 8

DO INTERNATIONAL STOCK PRICES REFLECT INTERNATIONAL BUSINESS CYCLES?

Shigeyuki Hamori
Faculty of Economics, Kobe University, Rokkodai, Nada-Ku, Kobe, Japan

ABSTRACT

This paper empirically analyzes the relationship between international stock prices and international business cycles, specifically focusing on the number of cointegration vectors of each variable. The empirical data were taken from statistics on Germany, Japan, the UK, and the USA tabulated from January 1980 to May 2001. No cointegrating vectors were identified in indices of international stock prices, whereas several were identified in indices of international industrial production. These empirical results suggest that international stock prices do not necessarily reflect international business cycles.

INTRODUCTION

Many studies have sought to identify and enumerate the common trends, or what are known as cointegrating relations, in international stock markets. Prominent examples include the studies by Kasa (1992), Corhay, Rad and Urbain (1993), Engsted and Lud (1997), and Ahlgren and Antell (2002).

Kasa (1992) identified a number of common stochastic trends among the equity markets of Canada, Germany, Japan, the UK, and the USA using monthly and quarterly data covering the period from January 1974 through August 1990. Cointegration tests to analyze the long-run co-movements in these five stock markets identified a single stochastic trend common to all of the markets, and estimates based on loading factors suggested that this trend was most important in the Japanese market and least important in the Canadian market.

Corhay, Rad and Urbain (1993) used bi-weekly data from France, Germany, Italy, the Netherlands, and the UK collected between March 1, 1975 and September 30, 1991 to investigate whether European stock markets displayed a common long-run trend in behavior.

In their cointegration test for empirical analysis, they identified several common stochastic trends among the five countries.

By showing cointegration in stock prices, these two earlier studies (Kasa, 1992; Corhay, Rad and Ubain, 1993) proved that world stock markets were at least partially driven by one or more common stochastic trends. The presence of a common trend can be interpreted as a natural consequence of well-functioning, well-integrated capital markets freely accessible to both domestic and foreign investors.

Several years later, Engsted and Lud (1997) performed a similar study using annual data from 1950 to 1988 from Denmark, Germany, Sweden, and the UK. According to empirical results derived from a vector error correction model (VECM), several common trends could be found in the dividends in these four countries.

In a more recent study, however, Ahlgren and Antell (2002) reexamined earlier findings using small sample corrections and found no evidence of cointegration among international stock prices. They applied the cointegration test to monthly and quarterly stock price data from Finland, France, Germany, Sweden, the UK, and the USA collected from January 1980 to February 1997. According to their findings, the cointegration test was sensitive to the lag length specification in the VAR model, and the previous empirical results such as those of Kasa (1992) and Corhay, Rad and Urbain (1993) could be explained by the small-sample bias and size-distortion of the cointegration test.

This paper takes a different tack in analyzing the issue of common trends in international stock markets by focusing on whether the number of common trends in international stock markets is equal to the number of common trends in international industrial production. If the international stock market is an integrated capital market freely accessible to both domestic and foreign investors, then the market should accurately reflect actual business cycles, i.e., investment, consumption, and other economic activities. If international stock prices contain abundant noise or bubbles, on the other hand, then the market would not reflect the actual economic activities. As the number of common trends in international stock markets can only equal the number of common trends in international industrial production if the former case holds true, we can rule out such an equivalence. This paper analyzes the problem for four major industrial countries, i.e., Germany, Japan, the UK, and the USA. This approach is an alternative to the usual method of empirically testing the efficiency of international stock markets.

DATA

The data consist of monthly observations of the aggregate stock price index and industrial production index for Germany, Japan, the UK, and the USA from January 1980 to May 2001, taken from the International Financial Statistics of the International Monetary Fund. Based on Fama (1990) and Schwert (1990), industrial production is used to both measure real economic activity and define the business cycle of each country. Real stock prices are obtained by dividing the nominal stock price index by the consumer price index during the study period.

Table 1 summarizes the statistics on the real growth of stock prices and industrial production. The real growth of each variable is calculated as: $\{\ln(y_t)-\ln(y_{t-1})\}\times 100$, where y_t is the real stock price index or the industrial production index.

Table 1. Summary Statistics

	Real Stock Price Index			
	Germany	**Japan**	**UK**	**USA**
Mean	0.564	0.300	0.527	0.642
Std. Dev.	5.335	4.363	3.894	3.605
Skewness	-0.858	-0.235	-1.278	-0.702
Kurtosis	5.822	3.727	9.713	5.778
Jarque-Bera	116.383	7.998	550.339	103.351
P-value	0.000	0.018	0.000	0.000
	Industrial Production Index			
	Germany	**Japan**	**UK**	**USA**
Mean	0.094	0.133	0.091	0.221
Std. Dev.	1.770	1.670	1.033	0.676
Skewness	0.246	-0.034	-0.382	-0.365
Kurtosis	11.723	3.269	3.965	4.203
Jarque-Bera	814.128	0.821	16.161	21.108
P-value	0.000	0.663	0.000	0.000

P-value is the probability value of Jarque-Bera test.

The average growth rates for stock prices are 0.564 for Germany, 0.300 for Japan, 0.527 for the UK, and 0.642 for the USA. The standard deviations are 5.335 for Germany, 4.363 for Japan, 3.894 for the UK, and 3.605 for the USA. The skewnesses are -0.858 for Germany, -0.235 for Japan, -1.278 for the UK, and -0.702 for the USA. The kurtoses are 5.822 for Germany, 3.727 for Japan, 9.713 for the UK, and 5.778 for the USA. The Jarque-Bera statistics (its associated *P*-value) are 116.383 (0.000) for Germany, 7.998 (0.018) for Japan, 550.339 (0.000) for the UK, and 103.351 (0.000) for the USA. Thus, the null hypothesis of normal distribution is rejected for every country at the 5 percent significance level.

The average growth rates of industrial production are 0.094 for Germany, 0.133 for Japan, 0.091 for the UK, and 0.221 for the USA. The standard deviations are 1.770 for Germany, 1.670 for Japan, 1.033 for the UK, and 0.676 for the USA. The skewnesses are 0.246 for Germany, -0.034 for Japan, -0.382 for the UK, and -0.365 for the USA. The kurtoses are 11.723 for Germany, 3.269 for Japan, 3.965 for the UK, and 4.203 for the USA. The Jarque-Bera statistics (its associated *P*-value) are 814.128 (0.000) for Germany, 0.821 (0.663) for Japan, 16.161 (0.000) for the UK, and 21.108 (0.000) for the USA. Thus, the null hypothesis of normal distribution is rejected for every country except Japan at the 5 percent significance level.

EMPIRICAL RESULTS

The unit root test developed by Phillips and Perron (1988) is used to test whether each variable has a unit root. The unit root test statistic is the t-value of γ obtained from the following regressions:

$$\Delta y_t = \mu + \delta t + \gamma y_{t-1} + u_t, \quad \text{(CT)} \tag{1}$$

$$\Delta y_t = \mu + \gamma y_{t-1} + u_t, \quad \text{(C)} \qquad (2)$$

$$\Delta y_t = \gamma y_{t-1} + u_t, \quad \text{(None)} \qquad (3)$$

where Δ is a difference operator, i.e., $\Delta y_t = y_t - y_{t-1}$, t is the time trend, and u_t is a disturbance term. The first equation (CT) includes a constant term and a time trend, the second equation (C) includes a constant term, and the third equation (None) includes no deterministic term. The null hypothesis (H_0) and the alternative hypothesis (H_A) are shown as follows:

$$H_0 : \gamma = 0,$$
$$H_A : \gamma < 0.$$

Table 2. Unit Root Test

Variable	Country	Test Statistics		
		CT	C	None
Real Stock Price Index		**Level**		
	Germany	-2.301	-1.011	-1.173
	Japan	-1.336	-1.843	-1.887
	UK	-2.299	-1.510	-2.247
	USA	-2.520	-0.009	-1.091
		First Difference		
	Germany	-14.782†	-14.810†	-14.708†
	Japan	-11.237†	-11.232†	-11.222†
	UK	-12.682†	-12.691†	-12.597†
	USA	-11.530†	-11.539†	-11.398†
Industrial Production Index		**Level**		
	Germany	-3.183	-0.391	1.331
	Japan	-1.027	-1.814	1.568
	UK	-3.253	-0.341	1.582
	USA	-2.557	0.799	3.467
		First Difference		
	Germany	-24.997†	-25.364†	-25.916†
	Japan	-22.971†	-22.692†	-22.441†
	UK	-19.526†	-19.562†	-19.288†
	USA	-12.526†	-12.417†	-12.068†

* shows that the null hypothesis of a unit root is rejected at the 5 percent significance level.

† shows that the null hypothesis of a unit root is rejected at the 1 percent significance level.

CT corresponds to the following regression: $\Delta y_t = \mu + \delta t + \gamma y_{t-1} + u_t$.

C corresponds to the following regression: $\Delta y_t = \mu + \gamma y_{t-1} + u_t$.

None corresponds to the following regression: $\Delta y_t = \gamma y_{t-1} + u_t$.

Thus, the null hypothesis shows that a unit root is included and the alternative hypothesis shows that a unit root is not included. Each equation is applied to both the level and the first difference of the log of the real stock price index and the log of the industrial production index. The empirical results are shown in Table 2. Taking Japan as an example, we find that the test statistics for the level and first difference of the real stock price index are -1.336 and -11.237 for CT, -1.843. and -11.232 for C, and -1.887 and -11.222 for None, respectively, while the test statistics for the level and first difference of the industrial production index are -1.027 and -22.971 for CT, -1.814 and -22.692 for C, and 1.568 and -22.441 for None. Thus, the null hypothesis of a unit root is not rejected for any of the specifications on the levels of the real stock price index and industrial production index, whereas it is rejected for all specifications on the first difference of the real stock price index and the industrial production index. As these results are robust to all countries, the real stock price index and industrial production are found to be a I(1) process for all countries.

The theory of non-stationary time series was developed soon after researchers discovered that multiple macro time series may obtain a unit root. Engle and Granger (1987) pointed out that a linear combination of non-stationary series may be stationary. When such a stationary linear combination exists, the non-stationary variables are said to be cointegrated. The stationary linear combination is called the cointegrating equation and is interpreted as a long-run equilibrium relationship among the variables. Given that the variables in an equilibrium relationship cannot move independently of each other, any equilibrium relationship among a set of non-stationary variables implies that the stochastic trends of the variables must be linked. This linkage among the stochastic trends necessitates that the variables be cointegrated. Since the trends of cointegrated variables are linked, the dynamic paths of such variables must bear some relation to the current deviation from the equilibrium relationship.

The cointegration test is applied to determine whether a group of non-stationary series are cointegrated or not. The presence of a cointegrating relation forms the basis of the vector error correction (VEC) specification. Consider a VAR of order p

$$y_t = A_1 y_{t-1} + \cdots A_p y_{t-p} + Bx_t + u_t \tag{4}$$

where y_t is a k-vector of non-stationary I(1) variables, x_t is a vector of deterministic variables, and u_t is a vector of innovations. We can rewrite this VAR as

$$\Delta y_t = \Pi y_{t-1} + \sum_{i=1}^{p-1} \Gamma_i \Delta y_{t-i} + Bx_t + u_t \tag{5}$$

where

$$\Pi = \sum_{i=1}^{p} A_i - I \, , \; \Gamma_i = -\sum_{j=i+1}^{p} A_j \, .$$

Granger's representation theorem asserts that if the coefficient matrix Π has reduced rank $r < k$, we come up with $k \times r$ matrices α and β , each with rank r such that

$\Pi = \alpha\beta'$ and $\beta' y_t$ is I(0). r is the number of cointegrating relations, and each column of β is the cointegrating vector. Johansen's method is used to estimate the Π matrix from an unrestricted VAR and to test whether we can reject the restrictions implied by the reduced rank of Π (Johansen, 1988, and Johansen and Juselius, 1990).

Johansen (1988) considers the following five cases for the deterministic trend:[1]

(case 1) $\Pi y_{t-1} + Bx_t = \alpha\beta' y_{t-1}$

(case 2) $\Pi y_{t-1} + Bx_t = \alpha(\beta' y_{t-1} + \rho_0)$

(case 3) $\Pi y_{t-1} + Bx_t = \alpha(\beta' y_{t-1} + \rho_0) + \alpha \perp \gamma_0$

(case 4) $\Pi y_{t-1} + Bx_t = \alpha(\beta' y_{t-1} + \rho_0 + \rho_1 t) + \alpha \perp \gamma_0$

(case 5) $\Pi y_{t-1} + Bx_t = \alpha(\beta' y_{t-1} + \rho_0 + \rho_1 t) + \alpha \perp (\gamma_0 + \gamma_1 t)$

where the term associated with $\alpha \perp$ is the deterministic term outside the cointegrating relations.[2] In case 1, the level data y_t have no deterministic trends and the cointegrating equations have no intercepts. In case 2, the level data y_t have no deterministic trends and the cointegrating equations have intercepts. In case 3, the level data y_t have linear trends but the cointegrating equations have only intercepts. In case 4, both the level data y_t and cointegrating equations have linear trends. In case 5, the level data y_t have quadratic trends and the cointegrating equations have linear trends.

Thus, the cointegration test developed by Johansen (1988) and Johansen and Juselius (1990) is applied to two data sets, i.e., a log of the stock price indices and a log of the industrial price indices of the four countries. This necessitates estimations of four-variable VAR models for the stock price and industrial production indices. Care must be taken in selecting the model, as the test results can be sensitive to the lag length of VAR. The common procedure is to estimate a VAR using the undifferenced data and then to select the lag length using the Akaike information criterion (AIC), a criterion often used to select the appropriate model. As clearly shown in Table 3, a lag length (p) of two is selected for the stock price indices and a lag length of three is selected for the industrial production indices.

---

1 See EViews 4 User's Guide.

2 When a deterministic term appears both inside and outside the cointegrating relation, the decomposition is not uniquely identified. Johansen (1995) identifies the part that belongs inside the error correction term by orthogonally projecting the exogenous terms onto the α space so that $\alpha \perp$ is the null space of α such that $\alpha' \alpha \perp = 0$

Table 3. AIC

Number of Lag	Real Stock Price Index	Industrial Production Index
1	-14.816	-24.202
2	-14.920*	-24.571
3	-14.852	-24.576*
4	-14.718	-24.561
5	-14.619	-24.480
6	-14.492	-24.389

* shows the smallest value of AIC.

Table 4 shows the results of the cointegration test for the aggregate index of real stock prices in the four countries. Two test statistics are reported, i.e., the trace test statistic and the maximum eigenvalue test statistic. The critical values for these tests were tabulated by Osterwald-Lenum (1992). The specification (Case 5) is used for empirical analysis. For the null hypothesis of no cointegration, the test statistics are 43.635 for the trace test and 24.450 for the maximum eigenvalue test. As both these values fall below the corresponding 5 percent critical value (54.64 for the trace test and 30.33 for the maximum eigenvalue test), the null hypothesis of no cointegration is statistically accepted at the 5 percent significance level.

Table 4a. Trace Test for Cointegration: Real Stock Price Index

Hypothesized No. of CE(s)	Eigenvalue	Trace Statistic	5 Percent Critical Value	1 Percent Critical Value
None	0.091	43.635	54.64	61.24
At most 1	0.040	19.185	34.55	40.49
At most 2	0.022	8.739	18.17	23.46
At most 3	0.012	3.048	3.74	6.40

*(†) shows the rejection of the null hypothesis at the 5%(1%) level.

Table 4b. Maximum Eigenvalue Test for Cointegration: Real Stock Price Index

Hypothesized No. of CE(s)	Eigenvalue	Trace Statistic	5 Percent Critical Value	1 Percent Critical Value
None	0.091	24.450	30.33	35.68
At most 1	0.040	10.446	23.78	28.83
At most 2	0.022	5.691	16.87	21.47
At most 3	0.012	3.048	3.74	6.40

*(†) shows the rejection of the null hypothesis at the 5%(1%) level.

Table 5 shows the results of the cointegration test for the aggregate index of industrial production in the four countries. For the null hypothesis of no cointegration, the test statistics are 80.300 for the trace test and 41.242 for the maximum eigenvalue test. As both these values are larger than the corresponding 5 percent critical value (54.64 for the trace test and 30.33 for the maximum eigenvalue test), the null hypothesis of no cointegration is statistically rejected at the 5 percent significance level. For the null hypothesis of at most one cointegration relation, the test statistics are 39.058 for the trace test and 25.355 for the maximum eigenvalue test. As both values are larger than the corresponding 5 percent critical value (34.55 for the trace test and 23.78 for the maximum eigenvalue test), the null hypothesis of at most one cointegration relation is statistically rejected at the 5 percent significance level. For the null hypothesis of at most two cointegration relations, the test statistics are 13.703 for the trace test and 13.312 for the maximum eigenvalue test. As both values are smaller than the corresponding 5 percent critical value (18.17 for the trace test and 16.87 for the maximum eigenvalue test), the null hypothesis of at most two cointegration relations is statistically accepted at the 5 percent significance level.

Table 5a. Trace Test for Cointegration: Industrial Production Index

Hypothesized No. of CE(s)	Eigenvalue	Trace Statistic	5 Percent Critical Value	1 Percent Critical Value
None †	0.150	80.300	54.64	61.24
At most 1 *	0.095	39.058	34.55	40.49
At most 2	0.051	13.703	18.17	23.46
At most 3	0.002	0.391	3.74	6.40

*(†) shows the rejection of the null hypothesis at the 5%(1%) level.

Table 5b. Maximum Eigenvalue Test for Cointegration: Industrial Production Index

Hypothesized No. of CE(s)	Eigenvalue	Trace Statistic	5 Percent Critical Value	1 Percent Critical Value
None †	0.150	41.242	30.33	35.68
At most 1 *	0.095	25.355	23.78	28.83
At most 2	0.051	13.312	16.87	21.47
At most 3	0.002	0.391	3.74	6.40

*(†) shows the rejection of the null hypothesis at the 5%(1%) level.

According to these results, the number of cointegration relations is zero for the stock price index and two for the industrial production index. Thus, the number of common trends for the real stock price index is not equal to the number of common trends for the industrial production index.

Given that the results of the cointegration test depend on the model specification, this paper carries out the cointegration test for various specification to check the robustness of the empirical results. Table 6 and Table 7 show the number of cointegrations for five types of specification. As the table clearly illustrates, the number of cointegrating relations is zero in every case for stock prices, versus one or two in most cases for industrial production. These values are not equal in most cases, hence the number of common trends for the real stock price index does not equal the number of common trends for the industrial production index.

Table 6. Selected (5% level) Number of Cointegrating Relations by Model: Real Stock Price Index

	(Case 1)	(Case 2)	(Case 3)	(Case 4)	(Case 5)
Trace	0	0	0	0	0
Max-Eig	0	0	0	0	0

Trace is the trace test.
Max-Eig is the maximum eigenvalue test.

Table 7. Selected (5% level) Number of Cointegrating Relations by Model: Industrial Production Index

	(Case 1)	(Case 2)	(Case 3)	(Case 4)	(Case 5)
Trace	1	1	1	2	2
Max-Eig	1	1	0	1	2

Trace is the trace test.
Max-Eig is the maximum eigenvalue test.

Some Concluding Remarks

This paper empirically analyzes the relationship between international stock prices and international industrial production, specifically focusing on the number of cointegration vectors of each variable. The empirical data were taken from statistics on Germany, Japan, the UK, and the USA covering the period from January 1980 to May 2001.

The indices of international industrial production were found to have several cointegrating vectors, whereas the international stock price indices had none. If international stock prices contain abundant noise or bubbles, the market will not reflect actual economic activities; hence the number of common trends in international stock markets cannot be equal to the number of common trends in international industrial production. These empirical results suggest that international stock prices do not necessarily reflect international business cycles.

References

Ahlgren, N. and Antell, J., (2002), Testing for cointegration between international stock prices, *Applied Financial Economics,* Vol. 12, pp. 851-861.

Corhay, A., Rad, A. T., and Urbain, J. P., (1993), Common stochastic trends in European stock markets, *Economics Letters*, Vol. 42, pp. 385-390.

Engle, R. F. and Granger, C. W. J., (1987), Cointegration and error correction: representation, estimation and testing, *Econometrica*, Vo. 55, pp. 251-276.

Engsted, T. and Lund, J., (1997), Common stochastic trends in international stock prices and dividends: an example of testing overidentifying restrictions on multiple cointegration vectors, *Applied Financial Economics*, Vol. 7, pp. 659-665.

Fama, E. F., (1990), Stock returns, expected returns, and real activity, *Journal of Finance*, Vol. 45, pp. 1089-1108.

Johansen, S., (1988), Statistical analysis of cointegration vectors, *Journal of Economic Dynamics and Control,* Vol. 12, pp. 231-254.

Johansen, S., (1995), *Likelihood-based Inference in Cointegrated Vector Autoregressive Models,* Oxford University Press, Oxford.

Johansen, S. and Juselius, K., (1990), Maximum likelihood estimation and inference on cointegration with application to the demand for money, *Oxford Bulletin of Economic and Statistics*, Vol. 52, pp. 169-209.

Kasa, K., (1992), Common stochastic trends in international stock markets, *Journal of Monetary Economics,* Vol. 29, pp. 95-124.

Osterwald-Lenum M., (1992), A note with quantiles of the asymptotic distribution of the maximum likelihood cointegration rank test statistics, *Oxford Bulletin of Economic and Statistics*, Vol. 54, pp. 461-472.

Phillips, P. C. B. and Perron, P., (1988), Testing for a unit root in time series regression, *Biometrika*, Vol. 75, pp. 335-346.

Quantitative Micro Software, (2000), *EViews 4 User's Guide.*

Schwert, G. W., (1990), Stock returns and real activity: a century of evidence, *Journal of Finance,* Vol. 45, pp. 1237-1257.

In: Business Fluctuations and Cycles
Editor: T. Nagakawa, pp. 203-264
ISBN 978-1-60021-503-3

Chapter 9

BUSINESS FLUCTUATIONS AND LONG-PHASED CYCLES IN HIGH ORDER MACROSYSTEMS

***Carl Chiarella*[1]*, Peter Flaschel*[2]*, Willi Semmler*[3] *and Peiyuan Zhu*[1]**
[1]School of Finance and Economics, University of Technology, Sydney
Sydney, Australia
[2]Faculty of Economics, University of Bielefeld
Bielefeld, Germany
[3]Department of Economics, New School University
New York, USA

Abstract

In this paper we investigate, from the numerical perspective, the 18D core dynamics of a theoretical 39D representation of an applied Keynesian disequilibrium model of monetary growth of a small open economy. After considering the model from the viewpoint of national accounting, we provide a compact description of the intensive form of the model, its laws of motion and accompanying algebraic expressions and its unique interior steady state solution. We then give a survey of various types of subsystems that can be isolated from the integrated 18D dynamics by means of suitable assumptions. These subsystems and the full 18D dynamics are investigated and compared in the remainder of the paper from the perspective of bifurcation diagrams that separate situations of asymptotic stability from stable cyclical behavior as well as pure explosiveness. In this way we lay the foundations for an analysis of business cycle fluctuations in applicable high order macrosystems, which will show, in contrast to what is generally believed to characterize such structural macroeconometric models, that applied integrated macrodynamical systems can have a variety of interesting more or less complex attractors which are surrounded by more or less long-phase transient behavior. Such attractors are obtained in particular when locally explosive situations are turned into bounded dynamics by the addition of specifically tailored extrinsic behavioral nonlinearities. In this way we establish a Keynesian theory of endogenously generated business cycles where turning points are caused by globally nonlinear behavior, rather than by complex eigenvalues, around the steady state position of the economy.

1. Introduction

Structural macroeconometric model building, viewed from today's perspective now looks back onto a long gestation period with considerable ups and downs and a variety of alternative procedures, ranging from the early attempts after World War II to the huge models that were build when this type of applied economic theory as ruling the roost to micro-founded contemporary approaches which stress optimizing and forward-looking behavior and the rational expectations methodology to deal with the forward looking parts of the model. The history of such model building is presented in Bodkin et al. (1991), while more recent views on this subject are discussed in Whitley (1994). Recent approaches to structural model building have often the market-clearing approaches to macrodynamics, as for example McKibbin and Sachs (1991), but there are also approaches that allow for disequilibrium in the goods market and within firms, see Powell and Murphy (1997), Fair (1994), Barnett et al. (1996) and Bergstrom et al. (1994) in this regard.

There is however also the well-established view, see Whitley (1994), that short-run restrictions on the formulation of macroeconometric models are too arbitrary in nature in order to be of real help and that at best long-run restrictions as they are discussed in Garratt et al. (1998) and Deleau et al. (1990) can be justified by economic theory, and if short-run behavioral equations are used than only of the basis of equilibrium relationships, since disequilibrium is not at all properly understood by economic theory and often specified in very arbitrary terms.

This paper takes the following positions in these matters. We believe that real markets (as opposed to financial markets) are generally in equilibrium and subject to sluggish disequilibrium adjustment processes for the specifications of which there is a long tradition in economic theorizing with a common core, but often with a fairly partial perspective. This paper indeed provides a long list of partial feedback channels which are well known since long, but have never been analyzed from an integrated point of view. Would that have been done as in the present paper the outcome that balanced growth paths are likely to be surrounded by (moderate) centrifugal forces would not look so strange as it looks from the perspective of for example the McKibbin and Sachs (1991) model that is of shock-absorber type by its very construction (based on the rational expectations methodology). Unstable steady states are indeed observed when estimating structural macrodynamic models, explicitly in the Bergstrom model, see Barnett and He (1998, 199a,b), or implicitly present in the Murphy model for the Australian, see Powell and Murphy (1997), as simulations of the model seem to imply. We therefore suggest that the findings on partial feedback chains, when taken together, suggest that instability of balanced growth is more likely than the opposite and suggest in this paper a variety of aspects that allow make this conclusion more certain.

In sum this paper therefore attempts to demonstrate that structural macroeconometric model building should use small, but complete models at least as theoretical reference point, should allow for disequilibrium in the real markets and within firms, should decompose and re-integrate their theoretical reference point in various ways to analyze the interaction of the important feedback structures that are summarized in this paper and in the other works of Chiarella et al., quoted in this paper, which in our view imply that progress can now be made in this area of research.

In this paper we will investigate the dynamical model of disequilibrium growth, with applied orientation, introduced in Chiarella and Flaschel (2000,1999b). This model is discussed in Chiarella and Flaschel (1999c) with respect to the various feedback loops it contains, from the analytical and the numerical point of view on various levels of generality, but always as subdynamics of the simplified 18D core dynamics we have derived in Chiarella and Flaschel (1999b) from the general 35D case. The first thing we do, in this introductory section, is to repeat briefly the economic framework within which these dynamics have been formulated. This will be done immediately on the intensive form level needed for steady state analysis and for the final presentation of the laws of motion of the state variables to be employed. We thereby also supply an introduction to the concepts (and their notation) we employ in this paper.

Section 2 then provides a short description of the interior steady state of the model, its laws of motion and of various algebraic equations that supplement these dynamical laws. We do this in a way which removes the cross-references still present between some of the 18 laws of motion we derived in Chiarella and Flaschel (1999b). We also reformulate the intensive form model in an order that is close to a representation for programming purposes. Section 3 will then isolate the 9D real dynamics of these 18D dynamics by suppressing in an appropriate way the feedbacks from financial markets and from government policy rules.

It is then the task of sections 4 and 5, respectively, to add again, on the one hand, the dynamics obtained from the fiscal and monetary policy rules and, on the other hand, the interaction with financial market dynamics employed in the general 18D dynamics. The numerical investigation of the full 18D dynamics, finally, is started in section 6. We there find that these applied disequilibrium dynamics do not often support the view of related structural macroeconometric modeling that the steady state of such models will be surrounded by centripetal forces, locally or even globally. Rather we find instead that locally centrifugal forces are a typical outcome of such disequilibrium growth models and these can lead to persistent fluctuations or more complex dynamics around its steady state or even to purely explosive movements. In this latter case the obtained dynamics must be regarded as incompletely specified and must be supplemented by forces that keep them bounded in an economically meaningful way. This additional task, up to one exception, will not be tackled in the present paper however, but is left for future reformulations and investigations of our modeling framework, see Chiarella, Flaschel and Zhu (1999a). Section 7 will summarize and put into perspective what has been achieved in this paper with respect to the numerical properties of the 18D core dynamics of the disequilibrium model of monetary growth of a small open economy as introduced in Chiarella and Flaschel (2000).

In summary, this paper continues the investigation of applied integrated disequilibrium models of monetary growth begun in Chiarella, Flaschel, Groh and Semmler (2000). It deepens the insights of that book, that such high order dynamical systems are already well represented in their fundamental dynamical features by its prototype 6D KMG dynamics and thus basically add numerous interesting details to this working model of integrated disequilibrium growth. Adding descriptive detail to this model type therefore puts it into a broader perspective without losing sight of the theoretical core that has been the starting point of this work, namely that of Chiarella and Flaschel (2000).

1.1. The structure of the economy

In order to give an overview of the type of economic modeling made use of in the following intensive form presentations and their numerical investigation we first of all consider the economy's structure by separating it in two parts: The real and the financial sector (which of course interact in the following modeling of them). We begin with the real part of the economy. Note that all magnitudes considered in the following are already expressed in intensive form (denoted by lower case letters in the place of formerly capital ones), by representing their analogs per unit of real or nominal capital (depending on whether we consider real or nominal extensive expressions) and by using efficiency units in the case of labor (due to the assumption of Harrod neutral technical progress in the fixed proportions technology employed in the sector of firms).

Table 1: *The real part of the economy*

	Labor	Non traded Goods	Exports	Imports	Dwellings
Workers	$l^e = \alpha_l l_1^e$	c_g^o	-	-	c_h^o
Asset holders	-	g_h^d	-	-	c_h^s, g_h^d
Firms	l_f^{de}, l_f^{we}	$y^p, y, g_k^d, \mathcal{I}/K$	x	j^d	-
Government	$l_g^{de} = l_g^{dw}$	g	-	-	-
Prices	$w^e, w^{re}, w^{be}, w^{ue}$	$p_v = (1+\tau_v)p_y$	$p_x = ep_x^*$	$p_m = (1+\tau_m)ep_m^*$	$p_h; p_y$
Expectations	$\pi = \hat{p}_v^e$	$\pi = \hat{p}_v^e$	-	-	$\pi = \hat{p}_v^e$
Stocks	l_1^e	$K/K = 1$, ν=N/K	-	-	k_h
Growth	n	$\hat{K} = g_k^d - \delta$ $\hat{N} = (y - y^d)/\nu$	-	-	$\hat{K}_h = g_h^d - \delta_h$

The columns of the table refer to the different goods in our model: labor, non traded good, exports, imports and dwellings. The first four rows refer to the considered sectors: private households, firms, and the government (fiscal and monetary authority), with the private sector split into asset holders and workers in addition. We distinguish between workers and asset holders to allow for a simple treatment of income distribution and its implications. Other important items of this table are the goods' prices and their expected rate of change as well as the stocks of labor force, capital and houses and their growth rates. Note that the foreign countries do not appear explicitly in the table. But by allowing for exports and imports it is clear that imports for the home country implies that this goods are exports for the foreign countries and vice versa. So we have to introduce prices for those goods that must be sold or bought abroad: p_x^* denotes the price for the export good of the domestic economy, while p_m^* denotes the price that firms pay for the imported good. Note that these prices are considered as fixed in the following model economy.

Only the workers of the sector of private households supply labor. The amount of this supply l^e depends on the number of workers in working age l_1^e and the given participation rate α_l. Therefore the dimension of the supplied labor l^e is a number of persons (representing the normal working day and per unit of capital and measured in efficiency units). In contrast to this the dimension of l_f^{de}, the labor demand, is hours actually worked. This distinction is used for modeling over– and under–utilization of labor in the firms' sector. Intermediate between hours worked and labor supply is the workforce employed by firms l_f^{we}, that is the number of persons who work within firms. The column representing the labor market lacks an entry in the row of asset holders because asset holder do not supply labor nor do they demand it. The government needs labor l_g^{de} for providing public goods. But in contrast to firms we assume that there is no need for over– or under–utilization of this part of the labor force which by assumption gives $l_g^{de} = l_g^{we}$.

There is a set of price expressions for labor effort: w^e is the nominal wage rate (before taxes and in efficiency units) that workers get for a time unit of labor. In contrast to this w^{be} represents the amount that firms or the public sector have to pay for one unit of labor, because they have to pay payroll taxes in addition. The income of unemployed and workers beyond working age is also considered as a kind of wage rate and thus represented in the labor market column. They are denoted by w^{ue} and w^{re} (where e stands again for efficiency unit). Expectations about price and wage inflation are here simply based on expected price inflation throughout. They will appear as medium run expectations π^l solely in the following. The growth rate of the stock of workers in working age (as well as the one of retired persons) is assumed to be a constant: n.

The non traded good serves for workers, but not for asset holders (due to our simplified 18D dynamics), as consumption good in the amount c_g^o. For the latter group it serves as investment good for the supply of dwelling services. The firms' sector produces the quantity of the non–traded good y restricted by a full capacity production of y^p. Secondly the firms use the domestic good for intended inventory investments $\mathcal{I}/K$ as well as for business fixed capital investments g_k^d. The government uses the domestic good as public consumption good. The prices for the non–traded good can be denoted inclusive or exclusive of a given value added tax, by p_v and p_y respectively, and expectations refer to the expected growth rate of both p_v, p_y. Stocks of the domestic good are held only by the firms' sector. The business fixed capital stock is K and the actual inventories per unit of capital are denoted by ν.

The export good is the second output good of the firms. It cannot be sold in the domestic economy. We assume, that every amount x of this good that is produced can be sold on the world market at a price p_x that depends on the given price abroad p_x^* and the exchange rate e. The import good is only for use in the sector of firms. They need it as an input factor for production. Its price depends on the exchange rate e and the given foreign price p_m^* augmented by the rate of import taxation τ_m.

The asset holders supply the dwelling services c_h^s. For simplicity we assume that only workers have demand for dwelling services c_h^o. The domestic good serves for gross investments into dwelling services g_h^d. We thus have to consider two prices in this sector of the economy: p_h, the rent for dwelling services, and p_y, the price per unit of investment into dwellings. There are no value added taxes on investment good purchases. The capital stock in the housing sector is k_h and its growth rate depends on gross investment in dwellings minus depreciation.

Next we have to consider the financial part of the economy. The rows of table 2 describe all financial assets of our model. They consist of short–term bonds, long–term bonds, equities and foreign (long-term) bonds. Note that money is not considered as a store of value in

Table 2: *The financial part of the economy*

	Short-term Bonds	Long-term Bonds	Equities	Foreign Bonds	
Workers	$\dot{B}_w/(p_v K) = \hat{B}_w b_w$	–	–	–	
Asset holders	$\dot{B}_c/(p_v K) = \hat{B}_c b_c$	$\dot{B}_1^l/(p_v K)$	$\dot{E}/(p_v K)$	$\dot{B}_2^l/(p_v K)$	
Firms	–	–	–	$\dot{E}/(p_v K)$	–
Government	$\dot{B}/(p_v K) = \hat{B} b$	$\dot{B}^l/(p_v K)$	–	–	
Prices	1 $[r]$	$p_b = 1/r_l$	p_e	$ep_b^* = e \cdot 1/r_l^*$	
Expectations	–	$\pi_b = \hat{p}_b^e$	$\pi_e = \hat{p}_e^e$	$\epsilon = \hat{e}^e$	
Stocks	$b = B/(p_v K)$	$b^l = B^l/(p_v K), b_1^l = B_1^l/(p_v K)$	$\varepsilon = E/(p_v K)$	$b_2^l = B_2^l/(p_v K)$	
Growth	$\hat{B}$	$\hat{B}^l, \hat{B}_1^l$	$\hat{E}$	$\hat{B}_2^l$	

the present model, see Chiarella and Flaschel (2000) for the details and justifications. The first four rows show, how the sectors interact on all the asset markets. Note that only flows are considered in the first part of this table.

The first row has only one entry. We assume that the only way workers do participate in the asset markets is by holding short-term bonds (saving deposits). In contrast to this the pure asset holders do spread their savings to all kinds of financial assets: bonds (domestic short and long term bonds as well as foreign long term bonds), and equities. The latter are issued by the firms' sector and represent the only way of financing the deficits of firms in the present model, i.e., bonds are issued only by the domestic and the foreign government. Short term bonds have a fixed price equal to unity and the flexible interest rate they offer is r. The long term bonds' price is $1/r$ and the interest consists of the annual payment of one dollar (so-called consols or perpetuities).

The above represents only a short description of the structure of the economy underlying its laws of motion to be considered in the following section. The reader is referred to Chiarella and Flaschel (2000) for more details, also with respect to the following brief representation of the national accounts of the sectors allowed for in this approach to disequilibrium growth theory.

1.2. National Accounting (in intensive form)

The structure of the considered economy from the viewpoint of national accounting is the following (everything being measured in nominal domestic currency units per gross value of the capital stock):

1.2.1. The sector of firms (Table 3)

The firms produce two kinds of output, the pure export good which is tradeable only on the world market and the domestic good which can solely be sold in the domestic economy. The domestic good serves as the consumption good for the workforce and the government (in our simplified 18D dynamical version of the model). It can also be used for investments in inventories, in business fixed capital and in housing. Firms use three kinds of inputs for their production: imports, capital, and labor. The capital stock in the firms' sector depreciates by a given rate δ. Value added taxes (on consumption goods solely) appear on the left side of the production account and have to be paid to the government. The balance of this account is the profit of the firms' sector. Note again that all expressions are in intensive form as already discussed in the preceding subsection (they have all been measured in domestic currency units in Chiarella and Flaschel (2000) and are divided here uniformly by $p_v K$, the value of the capital stock (including value added taxation by assumption). [1] We stress that the profits are not subject to any direct tax. By assumption profits are only used to be paid as dividends to asset holders (and then taxed) or to be used for planned inventory investments. One can clearly see this in the income account. The accumulation account displays again that investments in business fixed capital and in inventories are the only stocks which can be accumulated by firms. There is no possibility to accumulate financial stocks, i.e., no holding of bonds by firms in the present context. The financial deficit of firms must be financed in our present model by selling new equities. This assumption is of course not very realistic, and thus should be modified in future reconsiderations of the model to allow in particular for bond financing and loans of firms in addition.

1.2.2. Asset holders (Table 4a)

While firms produce and sell two types of goods, the sector of the private asset holders sells dwelling services. Hence there is a production account for this sector. The income of this sector consists of interest payments (long and short term bonds, the former also from abroad), dividend payments from the sector of firms, and the profits from selling dwelling services. This income is reduced through profit income taxation. The remaining amount is the saving of this sector (since asset holders do not consume in the 18D core dynamics of our general model to be considered in this paper). Savings plus depreciation is split into gross investment in housing and the financial surplus in the following account. The financial surplus is distributed by asset owners to all kinds of financial assets that exist in our model.

1.2.3. Households (Workers) (Table 4b)

This sector does not take part in private ownership production, but only provides the labor input for firms. Therefore the production account remains empty. The income account includes wages, unemployment benefits, and pensions. Worker's income is allocated to income taxes and consumption and savings. All savings is allocated to short-term bonds.

[1]Note that all investment and thus also the value of the capital stock and the measure of the rate of profit based on it are in prices p_y net of value added tax, since these taxes are only applied to consumption purchases and not to investment purchases in the present model. Note also that the following uniform intensive form representation of the model does not immediately apply to the structural form of the model in intensive form, since we do not need accounting homogeneity in this structural form as is necessary in the present subsection.

Table 3: *Accounts of Firms*

Production Account of Firms:

Uses	Resources
Imports $ep_m^* j^d / p_v$	Consumption c_g^o
Depreciation $\delta p_y / p_v$	–
Value Added Taxes $\tau_v (c_g^o + g) p_y / p_v$	Consumption g
Taxes on imports $\tau_m e p_m^* j^d / p_v$	Exports $e p_x^* x / p_v$
Wages (excluding payroll taxes) $w^e / p_v l_f^{de}$	Gross Investment $g_k^d p_y / p_v$
Payroll Taxes $\tau_p w^e / p_v l_f^{de}$	Durables (Dwellings) $g_h^d p_y / p_v$
Profits $(\rho^e + \mathcal{I}/K) p_y / p_v$	Inventory Investment $p_y \dot{N} / (p_v K) = p_y (y - y^d) / p_v$

Income Account of Firms:

Uses	Resources
Dividends $\rho^e p_y / p_v$	Profits $(\rho^e + \mathcal{I}/K) p_y / p_v$
Savings $\mathcal{I}/K\, p_y / p_v$	

Accumulation Account of Firms:

Uses	Resources
Gross Investment $g_k^d p_y / p_v$	Depreciation $\delta p_y / p_v$
Inventory Investment $\dot{N}/K\, p_y / p_v$	Savings $S_f^n / (p_v K)$
	Financial Deficit $FD / (p_v K)$

Financial Account of Firms:

Uses	Resources
Financial Deficit $FD / (p_v K)$	Equity Financing $p_e \dot{E} / (p_v K)$

Table 4a: *Accounts of Households (Asset Owners)*[2]

Production Account of Households (Asset Owners/Housing Investment):

Uses	Resources
Depreciation $\delta_h k_h p_y / p_v$	Rent $p_h c_h^o / p_v$
Earnings $\Pi_h / (p_v K)$	

Income Account of Households (Asset Owners):

Uses	Resources
Tax payment $\tau_c r b$	Interest payment $r b$
Tax payment $\tau_c b_1^l$	Interest payment b_1^l
Taxes $\tau_c (p_h c_h^o / p_v - \delta_h k_h p_y / p_v)$	Interest payment $e(1 - \tau_c^*) b_2^l$
Tax payment $\tau_c \rho^e p_y / p_v$	Dividend payment $\rho^e p_y / p_v$
Savings $S_c^n / (p_v K)$	Earnings $\Pi_h / (p_v K)$

[2]Expressions such as $\hat{B}b (= \dot{B}/(p_v K))$ are used to indicate the way the law of motion, of here $b = B/(p_v K)$, has to be derived.

Accumulation Account of Households (Asset Owners):

Uses	Resources
Gross Investment $g_h^d p_y / p_v$	Depreciation $\delta_h k_h p_y / p_v$
Financial Surplus $FS/(p_v K)$	Savings $S_c^n / (p_v K)$

Financial Account of Households (Asset Owners):

Uses	Resources
Short-term bonds $\hat{B} b$	Financial Surplus $FS/(p_v K)$
Long-term bonds $p_b \hat{B}_1^l b_1^l$	
Foreign Bonds $e \hat{B}_2^l b_2^l / r_l^*$	
Equities $p_e \hat{E} \varepsilon$	

Table 4b: *Accounts of Households (Workers)*

Production Account of Households (Workers):

Uses	Resources
–	–

Income Account of Households (Workers):

Uses	Resources
Taxes $\tau_w [w^e l^{de} + w^{ue}(l^e - l^{we}) + w^{re} l_2^e] / p_v$	Wages $w^e l^{de} / p_v = (w^e l_f^{de} + w^e l_g^{de}) / p_v$
Consumption $c_g^o + p_h c_h^o / p_v$	Unemployment benefits $w^{ue}(l^e - l^{we}) / p_v$
Savings $S_w^n / (p_v K)$	Pensions $w^{re} l_2^e / p_v$

Accumulation Account of Households (Workers):

Uses	Resources
Financial Surplus $FS/(p_v K)$	Savings $S_w^n / (p_v K)$

Financial Account of Households (Workers):

Uses	Resources
Short-term bond accumulation $\hat{B}_w b_w$	Financial Surplus $FS/(p_v K)$

1.2.4. Fiscal and Monetary Authorities

The government sector's production account takes up the costless provision of public goods which is defined to be identical to self consumption of the government. To provide the economy with those provisions the government has to buy goods and pay wages to the workers it employs.

The only sources of income for the government are the various taxes. They are used for interest payments, pensions, unemployment benefits and salaries. The balance of this account are the savings of the government. Generally these savings are negative hence there is a financial deficit in the accumulation account, rather than an financial surplus in general.

In financial accounting of the government one can see the sources from which the deficit is financed: issuing short- and long-term bonds.

Table 5: *Accounts of the Fiscal and Monetary Authorities*

Production Account of Fiscal and Monetary Authorities:

Uses	Resources
Government expenditure for goods g	Costless Provision of
Salaries $w^{be}l_g^{de}/p_v = (w^e l_g^{de} + \tau_p w^e l_g^{de})/p_v$	public goods = self consumption

Income Account of Fiscal and Monetary Authorities:

Uses	Resources
Interest payment rb	Wage income taxation $\tau_w[w^e l^{de} + w^{ue}(l^e - l^{we}) + w^{re}l_2^e]/p_v$
Interest payment $b_1^l + b_1^{l*}$	Profit and interest taxation $\tau_c \rho^e p_y/p_v + \tau_c rb + \tau_c b_1^l + \tau_c b_1^{l*}$
Pensions $w^{re}l_2^e/p_v$	Rent income taxation $\tau_c(p_h c_h^o/p_v - \delta_h k_h p_y/p_v)$
Unemployment benefits $w^{ue}(l^e - l^{we})/p_v$	Payroll taxes $(\tau_p w^e l_f^{de} + \tau_p w^e l_g^{de})/p_v$
self consumption g	Value added tax $\tau_v(c_g^o + g)p_y/p_v$
Savings $S_g^n/(p_v K)$	Import taxes $\tau_m e p_m^* j^d/p_v$

Accumulation Account of the Fiscal Authority:

Uses	Resources
	Savings $S_g^n/(p_v K)$
	Financial Deficit $FD/(p_v K)$

Financial Account of Fiscal and Monetary Authorities:

Uses	Resources
Financial deficit $FD/(p_v K)$	Short-term debt $\hat{B}b$
	Long-term debt $\hat{B}^l b^l/r_l$

1.2.5. International relationships

The external account contains all transactions with the foreign countries. It exhibits the amounts of goods, capital, and interest payments that cross the borders.

Table 6: International Relationships

External Account:

Uses	Resources
Exports $ep_x^* x/p_v$	Imports $ep_m^* j^d/p_v$
Factor Income from Abroad $e(1-\tau_c^*)b_2^l$	Factor Income to Abroad $(1-\tau_c)b_1^{l*}$
Capital Imports $\hat{B}_1^{l*} b_1^{l*}/r_l$	Capital Exports $e\hat{B}_2^l b_2^l/r_l^*$

This closes this section on the national accounts of the model to be investigated numerically in the following sections.

2. Explicit representation and feedback structure of the core 18D dynamical system

We will base our subsequent numerical investigation of the 18D core model of the general model, see Chiarella and Flaschel (1999b), in this paper on the following condensed form of its 18 laws of motion (adjusted to and to be used for programming purposes in the following) and the unique interior steady state (up to the level of nominal magnitudes) that this dynamical model exhibits. In order to simplify the notation to some degree we assume in the following, in addition to what is assumed in Chiarella and Flaschel (1999c), that the risk and liquidity premium $\xi = 0$ and thus will have $r = r^l = r^{l*} = \rho^e$ for interest and profit in the steady state. For the same reason we also assume for the normal employment rate $\bar{V}_f^w = 1$, and also $C_c = 0, i.e.$, there is no consumption goods demand of asset holders who thus save all of their income. All these assumptions have only slight influences on the steady state position of the economy, and do not alter at all the dynamics around the steady state.

We consider the 18 steady state values of the model first. All these values have an index 'o' (denoting their steady state character) when used for programming purposes. To not overload the notation here we do not add this index to the following list of steady state values. Note again that all steady state values are expressed in per unit of capital form and if necessary in efficiency units.

$$y_o^e = \frac{y^p\bar{U}}{1+\gamma\beta_{n^d}}, \quad [y_o = y^p\bar{U}] \tag{1}$$

$$\nu_o = \beta_{n^d} y_o^e \tag{2}$$

$$l_{f,o}^{we} = l_{fo}^{de} = l_y y^p \bar{U} \quad [\text{total employment: } l_o^{we} = l_{fo}^{we} + l_{go}^{we}, l_{go}^{we} = \alpha_g g y_o^e] \tag{3}$$

$$l_o^e = (l_{fo}^{we} + \alpha_g g y_o^e)/\bar{V} \tag{4}$$

$$p_y^o = \frac{p_v}{1+\tau_v}, \quad [p_v \quad \text{arbitrarily given}] \tag{5}$$

$$w_o^e = \frac{\omega_o^{be} p_y^o}{1+\tau_p}, \quad [\omega_o^{be} = (1+\tau_p)\frac{w_o^e}{p_y^o} = \frac{y_o^e - \delta - r_l^*}{l_{fo}^{we}}] \tag{6}$$

$$\pi_o^l = 0 \tag{7}$$

$$p_h^o = p_y^o(r_l^* + \delta_h)/\bar{U}_h \tag{8}$$

$$k_h^o = \frac{c_2(y_o^e(1-g) - (\gamma+\delta))}{c_1(r_l^* + \delta_h)/(1+\tau_v) + c_2(\gamma + \delta_h)} \tag{9}$$

$$b^o = \alpha_b^g \bar{d} y_o^e \tag{10}$$

$$b_l^o = r_l^*(1-\alpha_b^g)\bar{d} y_o^e \tag{11}$$

$$p_b^o = 1/r_l^* \tag{12}$$

$$\pi_{bs}^o = 0 \tag{13}$$

$$\epsilon_s^o = 0 \tag{14}$$

$$r^o = r_l^* \quad [= \rho_o^e] \tag{15}$$

$$\tau_m^o = \frac{p_x^* x_y - p_m^* j_y}{p_m^* j_y} \tag{16}$$

$$\tau_w^o = 1 - \frac{p_h^o \bar{U}_h k_h^o}{c_2(1+\tau_v)p_y^o y_{w1}^o} \tag{17}$$

$$e^o = \frac{s_o - [\tau_w y_{w1}^o + \frac{\tau_p}{1+\tau_v}\frac{w_o^e}{p_y^o} l_o^{we} + \frac{\tau_v}{1+\tau_v}(y_o^e - (\gamma+\delta) - (\gamma+\delta_h)k_h^o)]}{\tau_m p_m^* j_y y_o/((1+\tau_v)p_y^o)} \tag{18}$$

With respect to the last two of the above equations, for the taxation rate τ_w and for the rate of exchange e of the model, we have to apply (besides the above definitions of y_o, l_o^{we}, and ω_o^{be}, see the above) the further defining expressions:

$$
\begin{aligned}
c_h^o &= \bar{U}_h k_h^o \\
t_o^c &= \tau_c[r_l^*/(1+\tau_v) + r_o b_o + b_o^l + (p_h^o/p_y^o)c_h^o/(1+\tau_v) - \delta_h k_h^o/(1+\tau_v)] \\
s_o &= g y_o^e + r_o b_o + b_o^l - t_o^c + \frac{w_o^e}{(1+\tau_v)p_y^o}[\alpha^u(l_o^e - l_o^{we}) + \alpha^r L_2(0)/L_1(0) l_o^e] \\
&+ (1+\tau_p)\frac{w_o^e}{(1+\tau_v)p_y^o}\alpha_g g y_o^e - \frac{\gamma b_o}{\alpha_b^g} \\
y_{w1}^o &= w_o^e[l_o^{we} + \alpha^u(l_o^e - l_o^{we}) + \alpha^r L_2(0)/L_1(0) l_o^e]/((1+\tau_v)p_y^o)
\end{aligned}
$$

in order to have a determination of the steady state that is complete.

Note that the value of the exchange rate e_o will be indeterminate when we have $\tau_m = 0$ in the steady state in which case the above formula for e_o cannot be applied. Note furthermore that the parameters of the model have to be chosen such that $k_{ho}, \tau_{wo}(\tau_{mo}), e_o$ are all positive in the steady state.[3] Note finally that the parameter α_s must always be larger than

[3]There are further simple restrictions on the parameters of the model due to the economic meaning of the variables employed. Note also that the steady state rate of wage taxation must be defined in a different way when the housing sector is removed from the model.

$1 - 1/\beta_x$ for $x = p_b, e, p^e$ in order to satisfy the restrictions established in Chiarella and Flaschel (1999b).

Equation 1 gives (the steady state solution of) expected sales per unit of capital K (and also output per K) and eq. 2 provides on this basis the steady inventory-capital ratio N/K. Eq. 3 provides the amount of workforce per K employed by the firms which in the steady state is equal to the hours worked by this workforce (assuming that the normal working day or week is represented by 1). It also shows total employment per K where account is taken of the employment in the government sector in addition. Eq. 4 is the full employment labor intensity (in the steady state). Eq. 5 provides the price level (net of value added tax) and eq. 6 gives the wage level (net of payroll taxes) on the basis of the steady state value for the real wage ω^{be}. The steady state value of the inflation rate expected to hold over the medium run is zero, since the inflationary target of the central bank is zero in the present formulation of the model.

Next we have the price level for housing rents (in eq. 8) and the stock of houses per unit of the capital stock K (in eq. 9). There follows the steady state value of $b = B/(p_v K)$ as well as the one for long-term domestic bonds. The price of these bonds is given by the given price $1/r_l^*$ of foreign long-term bonds in the steady state, see eq. 12. Since there is no steady state inflation there is no change in the expected exchange rate and there is also (always) no change in the price of long term bonds, i.e., both markets exhibit rational expectations in the long-run. The steady state value of the short term rate of interest settles at its long-run equivalent as there is no risk or liquidity premium allowed for in the 18D version of the general model. Import taxes τ_m just balance the trade balance in the steady state, see eq. 16, while the wage tax rate τ_w must be calculated by means of gross steady wage income y_{w1} and the marginal propensity to spend this income for housing services, see eq. 17. Eq. 18, finally, is the most complicated one and it provides the steady state value of the rate of exchange which depends on nearly all of the parameters of the model, due to the definitional terms shown that have still be inserted into the expression for e shown in eq. 18.

This closes the description of the interior steady state solution of our dynamical model. Next we present the 18 laws of motion which have been derived in Chiarella and Flaschel (1999b) and which of course also employ the state variables we have just discussed.

Making use of the formula:

$$\Delta\hat{p}_y = \hat{p}_y - \pi^l = \kappa[\kappa_p(\beta_{w_1}(V - \bar{V}) + \beta_{w_2}(l_f^{de}/l_f^{we} - 1)) + \beta_p(y/y^p - \bar{U})],$$

with $\kappa = 1/(1 - \kappa_w \kappa_p)$, for the deviation of the actual inflation rate from the one expected over the medium run, the laws of motion around the above steady state solutions of the dynamics read as follows:[4]

$$\dot{y}^e = \beta_{y^e}(y^d - y^e) + (\gamma - (g_k^d - \delta))y^e, \tag{19}$$

[4]Note here that we assume $\bar{\pi} = 0$ for the target rate of inflation of the central bank which implies that there is no inflation in the steady state. We therefore can use price levels (for goods and housing services) as state variables of the model. Furthermore, since money supply is driven by money demand in the case of a Taylor interest rate policy rule we (implicitly) get that money supply will grow with the same rate as the real economy in the steady state. Note also that the Tobin's q is a further state variable of the model (representing the dynamics of share prices in particular) which however does not feed back into the 18D core dynamics since neither investment nor consumption depends here on the evolution of share prices by assumption.

$$
\begin{aligned}
\dot{\nu} &= y - y^d - (g_k^d - \delta)\nu, && (20)\\
\hat{l}_f^{we} &= \beta_l(l_f^{de} - l_f^{we}) + [\gamma - (g_k^d - \delta)]l_f^{we}, && (21)\\
\hat{l}^e &= \gamma - (g_k^d - \delta), && (22)\\
\hat{w}^e &= \pi^l + \kappa[\beta_{w_1}(l^{we}/l^e - \bar{V}) + \beta_{w_2}(l_f^{de}/l_f^{we} - 1) + \kappa_w\beta_p(y/y^p - \bar{U})], && (23)\\
\hat{p}_y &= \pi^l + \kappa[\kappa_p(\beta_{w_1}(l^{we}/l^e - \bar{V}) + \beta_{w_2}(l_f^{de}/l_f^{we} - 1)) + \beta_p(y/y^p - \bar{U})], && (24)\\
\dot{\pi}^l &= \beta_{\pi^l}(\alpha_{\pi^l}\Delta\hat{p}_y + (1 - \alpha_{\pi^l})(0 - \pi^l)), && (25)\\
\hat{p}_h &= \beta_h(\frac{c_h^o}{k_h} - \bar{U}_h) + \kappa_h\Delta\hat{p}_y + \pi^l, && (26)\\
\hat{k}_h &= g_h^d - \delta_h - (g_k^d - \delta), && (27)\\
\dot{b} &= \alpha_b^g[gy^e + rb + b^l - t^a - t^c + g^a] - (\Delta\hat{p}_y + \pi^l + g_k^d - \delta)b, && (28)\\
\dot{b}^l &= (1 - \alpha_b^g)/p_b[gy^e + rb + b^l - t^a - t^c + g^a] - (\Delta\hat{p}_y + \pi^l + g_k^d - \delta)b^l, && (29)\\
\hat{\tau}_w &= \alpha_{\tau_{w1}}(\frac{d}{\bar{d}} - 1), \quad d = \frac{b + p_b b^l}{y^e}, && (30)\\
\dot{r} &= -\beta_{r_1}(r - r_l^*) + \beta_{r_2}(\Delta\hat{p}_y + \pi^l) + \beta_{r_3}(y/y^p - \bar{U}), && (31)\\
\hat{p}_b &= \frac{\beta_{p_b}}{1 - \beta_{p_b}(1 - \alpha_s)}[(1 - \tau_c)r_l + \alpha_s\pi_{bs} - (1 - \tau_c)r], \quad r_l = 1/p_b, && (32)\\
\dot{\pi}_{bs} &= \beta_{\pi_{bs}}(\hat{p}_b - \pi_{bs}), && (33)\\
\hat{\tau}_m &= \alpha_{\tau_m}\frac{p_x^* x - (1 + \tau_m)p_m^* j^d}{p_x^* x}, \quad x = x_y y, j^d = j_y y, && (34)\\
\hat{e} &= \frac{\beta_e}{1 - \beta_e(1 - \alpha_s)}[(1 - \tau_c)r_l^* + \alpha_s\epsilon_s - ((1 - \tau_c)r_l + \pi_b)], \quad r_l = 1/p_b, && (35)\\
\dot{\epsilon}_s &= \beta_{\epsilon_s}(\hat{e} - \epsilon_s). && (36)
\end{aligned}
$$

These laws of motion make use of the following supplementary definitions and abbreviations, which provide the algebraic equations of the model:

$$
\begin{aligned}
y &= y^e + \beta_n(\beta_{n^d}y^e - \nu) + \gamma\beta_{n^d}y^e,\\
l_f^{de} &= l_y y,\\
l_g^{de} &= l_g^{we} = \alpha_g g y^e,\\
l^{de} &= l_f^{de} + l_g^{de},\\
l^{we} &= l_f^{we} + l_g^{we},\\
y_{w1} &= w^e[l^{de} + \alpha^u(l^e - l^{we}) + \alpha^r\frac{L_2(0)}{L_1(0)}l^e]/[(1 + \tau_v)p_y],\\
c_g^o &= c_1(1 - \tau_w)y_{w1},\\
c_h^o &= (1 + \tau_v)p_y c_2(1 - \tau_w)y_{w1}/p_h,\\
\rho^e &= y^e - \delta + (ep_x^*/p_y)x_y y - ((1 + \tau_p)w^e/p_y)l_f^{de} - ((1 + \tau_m)ep_m^*/p_y)j_y y,\\
g_k^d &= \alpha_1^k((1 - \tau_c)\rho^e - ((1 - \tau_c)r_l - \pi^l)) + \alpha_2^k(r_l - r),\\
&+ \alpha_3^k(y/y^p - \bar{U}) + \gamma + \delta, \quad r_l = 1/p_b,\\
g_h^d &= \alpha_1^h((1 - \tau_c)((p_h/p_y)c_h^o/k_h - \delta_h) - ((1 - \tau_c)r_l - \pi^l)) + \alpha_2^h(r_l - r),
\end{aligned}
$$

$$
\begin{aligned}
& + \quad \alpha_3^h(\frac{c_h^o}{k_h} - \bar{U}_h) + \gamma + \delta_h, \quad r_l = 1/p_b, \\
y^d &= c_g^o + g_k^d + g_h^d k_h + g y^e, \\
\pi_b &= \alpha_s \pi_{bs} + (1-\alpha_s)\hat{p}_b, \\
g^a &= w^e[\alpha^u(l^e - l^{we}) + \alpha^r \frac{L_2(0)}{L_1(0)} l^e + (1+\tau_p) l_g^{de}]/(1+\tau_v)p_y, \\
t^a &= \tau_w w^e[l^{de} + \alpha^u(l^e - l^{we}) + \alpha^r \frac{L_2(0)}{L_1(0)} l^e]/((1+\tau_v)p_y) \\
& + \quad \tau_p w^e l^{de}/((1+\tau_v)p_y) \\
& + \quad \frac{\tau_v}{1+\tau_v}(y^d - g_k^d - g_h^d k_h) + \tau_m e p_m^* j_y y/((1+\tau_v)p_y), \\
t^c &= \tau_c[\rho^e/(1+\tau_v) + rb + b^l + (p_h/p_y)c_h^o/(1+\tau_v) - \delta_h k_h/(1+\tau_v)].
\end{aligned}
$$

Inserting these equations into the above 18 laws of motion gives an explicit system of eighteen autonomous nonlinear differential equations in the 18 state variables (19) - (36) shown above. Note that we have to supply as initial conditions the relative magnitude $\frac{L_2(0)}{L_1(0)}$ in order to get a complete characterization of the dynamics and that the evolution of price levels is subject to hysteresis, since it depends on historical conditions due to our assumptions on costless transaction balances for the behavior of the four agents of the model.

In table 7 we break down the state vector X of the 18D dynamics into subsectors corresponding to the subsectors and their subdynamics that we investigate in sections 3,4 and 5 below. These subsectors are: $X_r = (y^e, l_f^{we}, l^e, w^e, p_y)$, for the real core subsector (with separate equations for wage and price inflation); $X_{mund} = (\pi^l)$, for the subsector engendering the Mundell effect; $X_h = (p_h, k_h)$, for the housing subsector; $X_{fi} = (b, b^l, \tau_w)$, for the fiscal policy subsector; $X_{mo} = (r)$, for the monetary policy subsector; $X_d = (p^b, \pi^b)$, for the domestic assets subsector; $X_f = (\tau_m, e, \epsilon_s)$, for the foreign assets subsector (including import taxation). All of the statically endogenous variables are gathered in the vector Z. With these definitions the full 18D dynamics that contains all the complex feedbacks between the various sectors identified above is succinctly represented by $\dot{X} = F_{18}(X, Z)$.

The methodology we use to analyze such a high dimensional dynamical system is to switch off most of these feedback mechanisms so as to focus on the core real part of the model. After analyzing these subdynamics we gradually switch back on the other feedback mechanisms. Table 8 lays out what we call the on/off switches. These are the amendments that need to be made to the 18D system in equations (19)-(36) to suppress the feedbacks from the various subsectors (by way of assumptions shown below).

We investigate the dynamics via numerical simulations that attempt to give the reader global information. In particular we display (i) bifurcation diagrams of output with respect to key parameters such as speed of adjustment of wages, prices, expectations on inflation and sales and inventories, (ii) eigenvalue diagrams, (iii) stability basins with respect to the same key parameters, and (iv) some typical time series patterns of the key economic variables. We display in table 9 the common parameter set used in the simulations.

The stability basins indicate parameter combinations for which the system dynamics:-

1. are converging to the interior steady state,
2. exhibit sustained oscillations around the steady state, or
3. are totally explosive.

the initial values for all basin calculations were obtained by perturbing the steady state value of sales expectations by five percent. It should be borne in mind that a different shock (and hence different initial conditions) could produce different looking basins.

We stress that the above dynamical system is intrinsically nonlinear due to:

- the growth rate formulations employed in the model, and
- due to various unavoidable products and fractions of the state variables of the model.

Table 7: *The Structure of the 18D Dynamics*

The state vector X:

$X =$

State variables	Sector	Block
y^e, ν, l_f^{we}, l^e, w^e, p_y	real core	X_r
π^l	Mundell	X_{mund}
p_h, k_h	housing sector	X_h
b, b^l, τ_w	fiscal policy	X_{fi}
r	monetary policy	X_{mo}
p^b, π^{b_s}	domestic assets	X_d
τ_m, e, ϵ_s	foreign assets	X_f

The vector Z of statically endogenous variables:

$$Z = (y, l_f^{de}, l_g^{de}, l_g^{we}, l^{de}, l^{we}, y_{w_1}, c_g^o, c_h^o, \rho^e, g_k^d, g_h^d, y^d, \pi_b, g^a, t^a, t^c)$$

The dynamical system:

$$\dot{X} = F_{18}(X, Z(X))$$

Table 8: *The On/Off Switches for the Analysis of the Subdynamics*

$\beta_{\pi_l} = 0,\ \pi_l = \pi_l^0$	$\Rightarrow$	Mundell effect off
$c_2 = 0,\ g_h^d = 0, \beta_h = 0, k_h(0) = 0$	$\Rightarrow$	housing off (except irrelevant movements of p_h via π^e)
$\tau_m = \dfrac{p_x^* x - p_m^* j^d}{p_m^* j^d} = \dfrac{p^* x_y - p_m^* j_y}{p_m^* j_y}$ $\beta_e = \beta_{\epsilon_s} = 0;\ e = e^0$	$\Rightarrow$	foreign assets off
$\beta_{p_b} = \beta_{\pi_{b_s}} = 0;\ p_b = p_b^0$	$\Rightarrow$	domestic assets off
$\alpha_{\tau_{w_1}} = 0,\ \tau_w = \tau_w^0$ $b = b_0,\ b^l = b_0^l$	$\Rightarrow$	fiscal policy off (except irrelevant movements of b, b^l)
$\beta_{r_1} = \beta_{r_2} = \beta_{r_3} = 0;\ r = r^0$	$\Rightarrow$	monetary policy off
$\kappa_w = 1$	$\Rightarrow$	Rose real wage effect off

In order to put the above into perspective and to show the relationship of the above 18D dynamics to the general structure that can be associated with integrated models of disequilibrium growth we close this section with a general survey and a brief discussion of the partial feedback chains that can be part of models of disequilibrium growth. Table 8a shows in this respect the feedback mechanisms that may be part of the dynamics of the real part of the economy (concerning goods and labor markets dynamics). This table shows the Keynes and the Mundell effects and the two types of Rose effects (all present in our 18D dynamics) and furthermore the Pigou and the Fisher debt effect (not present in the 18D dynamics due to the neglect of wealth effects in consumption and the neglect of debt in consumption and investment behavior). We also consider in table 8a certain real accelerator mechanisms of which only the Metzlerian inventory accelerator is present in our model (as an improvement of Kaldor's dynamic multiplier trade cycle component). Harrod's investment accelerating mechanism is however partly present in the 18D dynamics, since the rate of capacity utilization of firms influences their investment behavior in a proportional, but not yet in a derivative way. We thus see that our 18D dynamics already contains a variety of mechanisms (but not all) that are typical for the Keynesian analysis of disequilibrium growth.

Table 8a: Partial Feedback Mechanisms in the Real Part of the Economy: Summary.

Feedback Mechanisms in Models of AS-AD Growth
in the Real Part of the Economy

Type (cet. par.)	Name (in part.)	Feedback Chain	Extr. Bounds Policy Rules
Wage -Price Adjustment Mechanisms and the Stability of the Full Employment Position	**Keynes Effect**	$w\uparrow \Rightarrow p\uparrow \Rightarrow r\uparrow \Rightarrow I\downarrow C\downarrow$ $\Rightarrow Y\downarrow \Rightarrow L\downarrow \Rightarrow w\downarrow$	known to be stabilizing
	Pigou Effect	$w\uparrow \Rightarrow p\uparrow \Rightarrow M/p\downarrow \Rightarrow C\downarrow$ $\Rightarrow Y\downarrow \Rightarrow L\downarrow \Rightarrow w\downarrow$	known to be stabilizing
	Normal Rose Effects	$w/p\uparrow \Rightarrow I\Downarrow C\uparrow \Rightarrow Y\downarrow L\downarrow$ $w\Downarrow p\downarrow \Rightarrow w/p\downarrow$ or $I\downarrow C\Uparrow$ and $Y,L\uparrow w\uparrow p\Uparrow w/p\downarrow$	can be stabilizing, depending on C,I and adjustment speeds
	Adverse Rose Effects	$w/p\uparrow \Rightarrow I\Downarrow C\uparrow \Rightarrow Y\downarrow L\downarrow$ $\Rightarrow w\downarrow p\Downarrow \Rightarrow w/p\uparrow$ or $I\downarrow C\Uparrow$ and $Y,L\uparrow w\Uparrow p\uparrow w/p\uparrow$	2 unstable cases. remedy: sluggish wage and price adjustments
	Mundell Effect	$w\uparrow \Rightarrow \pi\uparrow \Rightarrow \pi^e\uparrow r-\pi^e\downarrow$ $\Rightarrow I\uparrow C\uparrow \Rightarrow Y,L\uparrow \Rightarrow \pi\uparrow w\uparrow$	real interest rate rule, kinked Phillips curve
	Fisher Debt Effect	$w\downarrow \Rightarrow p\downarrow \Rightarrow D/p\uparrow$ $\Rightarrow I\downarrow C\downarrow \Rightarrow Y,L\downarrow \Rightarrow w,p\downarrow$	downward rigid wages and prices + ...?
Real Accelerator Mechanisms	**Harrod Type Investment Accelerators**	$Y\uparrow \Rightarrow I\uparrow\uparrow \Rightarrow Y^d\uparrow Y^e\uparrow Y\uparrow$	fiscal policies of PID controller type
	Kaldor Type Dynamic Multiplier Instability	$Y\uparrow \Rightarrow Y^d\uparrow\uparrow \Rightarrow Y^e\uparrow Y\uparrow$	nonlinear investment function
	Metzler Type Inventory Accelerator	$Expected.Sales.Y^e\uparrow$ $Planned.Inventories.\Im\uparrow$ $Y=Y^e+\Im\uparrow C\uparrow I\uparrow Y^d\uparrow$ $Actual.Inventories\downarrow Y^e,\Im\uparrow$	cautious inventory adjustment far off the steady state

Table 8b: Partial Feedback Mechanisms in the Financial Part of the Economy: Summary.

Feedback Mechanisms in Models of AS-AD Growth
in the Financial Part of the Economy

Type (cet. par.)	Name (in part.)	Feedback Chain	Extr. Bounds Policy Rule
Financial Accelerator Mechanisms	**Capital Gain Accelerator: Long-term Bonds**	$p_b^e \uparrow Expected.Return \uparrow$ $B_l^d \uparrow p_b \uparrow p_b^e \uparrow$	cautious adjustment for large discrepancies in returns
	Capital Gain Accelelerator: Equities	$p_e^e \uparrow Expected.Return \uparrow$ $E^d \uparrow p_e \uparrow p_e^e \uparrow$	cautious adjustment for large discrepancies in returns
	Capital Gain Accelerator: Foreign Exchange	$e^e \uparrow Expected.Return \uparrow$ $B^{*d} \uparrow e \uparrow e^e \uparrow$	Cautious adjustment for large discrepancies in returns
Real-Financial Accelerator Mechanisms	**E.g.: Anti-Cyclical Behavior of Interest on Loans**	$Y \uparrow Screening - costs \downarrow r \downarrow$ $I, C \uparrow Y^d, Y^e \uparrow Y \uparrow$	Taylor type interest rate policy rule?
Portfolio Effects	**E.g.: Wealth Effects in Money Demand**	$W/p \uparrow M^d/p \uparrow r \uparrow C, I \downarrow$ $Y^d, Y^e, Y \downarrow p \downarrow W/p \uparrow$	Pure money financing of government debt?
Disposable Income Measurements	**Changes in Disposable Income, Aggregate Demand and Economic Activity**	$p \uparrow \pi^e \uparrow$ $Y^D = Y - T - \pi^e W/p \downarrow$ $C \downarrow Y^d, Y^e \downarrow Y \downarrow p \downarrow$	is stabilizing, since inflation decreases disposable income and thus economic activity

Let us consider next the partial feedback mechanisms shown in table 8b which basically concern the financial sector of our economy. The financial accelerator mechanisms of this table are all present in our model underlying the 18D dynamics, though the one concerning equity markets does not feed back into these dynamics. They all state that expected returns exercise a positive feedback on actual returns and are thus destabilizing to a certain degree. The real financial accelerator mechanism is however not part of the model underlying the 18D dynamics, since it concerns loans to firms which may become cheaper in the boom and more expensive in the depression which strengthens booms and deepens depressions. Also not included in the dynamics are wealth effects in asset and in particular money demand, due to our neglect of money transactions on the one hand and the neglect of portfolio considerations on the other hand. Finally, the concept of disposable income we employ is still of the simple Keynesian type that does not yet consider the influence of inflation on the wealth of economic agents and thus on their concept of disposable income. This brief characterization of the financial elements contained or not contained in the 18D dynamics shows that its formulation of the dynamics of the financial part is still of a fairly preliminary nature.

Tables 8a,b therefore also indicate what remains to be done in order to arrive at a fully developed descriptively oriented macrodynamics that incorporates all important feedback chains of a modern market economy. Our development of theoretical representations of structural macroeconometric model buildings will continue to approach structures as surveyed in tables 8a,b, see for example Chiarella, Flaschel, Groh, Köper and Semmler (1999a,b) for intermediate steps in this direction. In the next section we now begin with the numerical analysis of the considered structural model. The reader interested in theoretical results on the stability and the loss of stability in models of this type is referred to Chiarella, Flaschel and Franke (2003) and Asada, Chiarella, Flaschel and Franke (2003), in particular with respect to a typical methodology that allows to establish asymptotic stability theorems in high order dynamical systems.

3. Numerical simulations of the real part of 18D dynamics

In this section we consider the dynamics of the real part of the economy on various levels of generality,by switching off the feedbacks from the financial markets as well as from fiscal and monetary policy. These aspects of the full 18D dynamics will be added back successively in subsequent sections. Table 10 lays out the way we develop the various real subdynamics by use of the on/off switches.

Due to the fact that the laws of motion contain the housing capital stock in the denominator in some places we have set adjustment speeds in this section only to very small magnitudes, but not to zero in order to avoid division by zero during the simulations. Note finally that the external rate of growth γ has been chosen very high. In the current low dimensional real dynamics there exist stability problems when both the rate g, determining government expenditures, and γ are chosen reasonably low. It appears as if the dynamics is more rigid and explosive in such low dimensions than it is in a full 18D setup (as we shall see later on).

We start with the full 9D version of these real dynamics (which includes the nominal dynamics of wages and prices and expectations about their rate of change).

3.1. The 9D real part of the economy

We separate the real part of the dynamics, i.e., labor and goods markets, from the rest of model by switching off foreign assets, domestic assets, fiscal policy and monetary policy.

The condition for switching off foreign assets must be guaranteed via an appropriate choice of the four parameters that govern the equation underlying it. This condition freezes the nominal exchange rate at its steady state value. The condition for switching off fiscal policy says that government does not care about the evolution of its debt position and keeps the rate of wage taxation (and import taxation) fixed at its steady state value. The condition for switching off domestic assets freezes domestic asset prices at their steady state position. Finally, the condition for switching off monetary policy does the same for the short-term nominal rate of interest.

Table 9: *The Parameter Set*

β_{w1}	0.40	β_{w2}	0.50	β_p	0.70
β_{pi^l}	0.50	β_{p_b}	0.10	$\beta_{\pi_{bs}}$	0.10
β_e	0.10	β_ϵ	0.10	β_n	0.20
β_{nd}	0.10	β_h	0.80	β_l	0.50
β_{r1}	0.10	β_{r2}	0.50	β_{y^e}	1.00
β_{r3}	0.10	α_g	0.20	α_l	0.50
α_b^g	0.50	α_{π^l}	0.10	α_{h1}	0.10
α^u	0.50	α_{h2}	0.50	α^r	0.50
α_{h3}	0.10	α_{τ_w}	0.50	α_{k1}	0.10
α_{τ_m}	0.50	α_{k2}	0.50	α_s	0.50
α_{k3}	0.10	$L_1(0)$	20.00	$L_2(0)$	5.00
κ_p	0.50	κ_w	0.50	$\bar{U}$	0.90
$\bar{U}_h$	0.90	$\bar{V}$	0.90	$\bar{d}$	0.60
l_y	2.00	α_p	0.00	shock	1.05
p_m^*	1.00	p_x^*	1.00	c_1	0.50
δ	0.10	δ_h	0.10	g	0.33
γ	0.06	r_l^*	0.08	τ_c	0.50
τ_p	0.30	τ_v	0.15	c_2	0.33
j_y	0.10	κ_h	0.50	x_y	0.20
y^p	1.00	p_v	1.00		

Using again as abbreviation:

$$\Delta\hat{p}_y = \hat{p}_y - \pi^l = \kappa[\kappa_p(\beta_{w_1}(l^{we}/l^e - \bar{V}) + \beta_{w_2}(l_f^{de}/l_f^{we} - 1)) + \beta_p(y/y^p - \bar{U})],$$

with $\kappa = 1/(1-\kappa_w\kappa_p)$, the 18 laws of motion of the economic dynamics around the steady state solution are then reduced to the 9D real dynamics:

$$\dot{y}^e = \beta_{y^e}(y^d - y^e) + (\gamma - (g_k^d - \delta))y^e, \tag{37}$$

$$\dot{\nu} = y - y^d - (g_k^d - \delta)\nu, \tag{38}$$

$$\dot{l}_f^{we} = \beta_l(l_f^{de} - l_f^{we}) + [\gamma - (g_k^d - \delta)]l_f^{we}, \tag{39}$$

$$\hat{l}^e = \gamma - (g_k^d - \delta), \tag{40}$$

$$\hat{w}^e = \pi^l + \kappa[\beta_{w_1}(l^{we}/l^e - \bar{V}) + \beta_{w_2}(l_f^{de}/l_f^{we} - 1) + \kappa_w\beta_p(y/y^p - \bar{U})], \tag{41}$$

$$\begin{aligned}
\hat{p}_y &= \pi^l + \Delta\hat{p}_y, &(42)\\
\dot{\pi}^l &= \beta_{\pi^l}(\alpha_{\pi^l}\Delta\hat{p}_y + (1-\alpha_{\pi^l})(0-\pi^l)), &(43)\\
\hat{p}_h &= \beta_h(\frac{c_h^o}{k_h} - \bar{U}_h) + \kappa_h\Delta\hat{p}_y + \pi^l, &(44)\\
\hat{k}_h &= g_h^d - \delta_h - (g_k^d - \delta), &(45)
\end{aligned}$$

with the following supplementary definitions, abbreviations and statically endogenous variables:

$$\begin{aligned}
y^d &= c_g^o + g_k^d + g_h^d k_h + g y^e,\\
y &= y^e + \beta_n(\beta_{n^d} y^e - \nu) + \gamma\beta_{n^d} y^e,\\
l_f^{de} &= l_y y,\\
l_g^{de} &= l_g^{we} = \alpha_g g y^e,\\
l^{de} &= l_f^{de} + l_g^{de},\\
l^{we} &= l_f^{we} + l_g^{we},\\
c_g^o &= c_1(1-\tau_w^o)y_{w1}, &(46)\\
c_h^o &= (1+\tau_v)p_y c_2(1-\tau_w^o)y_{w1}/p_h,\\
y_{w1} &= w^e[l^{de} + \alpha^u(l^e - l^{we}) + \alpha^r\frac{L_2(0)}{L_1(0)}l^e]/[(1+\tau_v)p_y],\\
g_k^d &= \alpha_1^k((1-\tau_c)\rho^e - ((1-\tau_c)r_l^* - \pi^l)) + \alpha_3^k(y/y^p - \bar{U}) + \gamma + \delta,\\
\rho^e &= y^e - \delta - ((1+\tau_p)w^e/p_y)l_f^{de},\\
g_h^d &= \alpha_1^h((1-\tau_c)\frac{(p_h/p_y)c_h^o}{k_h} - \delta_h - ((1-\tau_c)r_l^* - \pi^l))\\
&+ \alpha_3^h(\frac{c_h^o}{k_h} - \bar{U}_h) + \gamma + \delta_h.
\end{aligned}$$

Inserting these equations into the above laws of motion gives a system of nine autonomous differential equations in the 9 state variables shown above. Note that we have to supply again as initial conditions the relative magnitudes $\frac{L_2(0)}{L_1(0)}$ in order to get a complete characterization of these 9D dynamics.

As shown in Chiarella and Flaschel (1999b,c) the law of motion for real wages (in reduced form) reads:

$$\hat{\omega}^e = \kappa[(1-\kappa_p)(\beta_{w_1}(l^{we}/l^e - \bar{V}) + \beta_{w_2}(l_f^{de}/l_f^{we} - 1)) - (1-\kappa_w)\beta_p(y/y^p - \bar{U})] \quad (47)$$

Inspecting the above statically endogenous relationship then shows that – ignoring the housing sector[5] – it is only the expected inflation rate that brings about an influence of the nominal magnitudes on the real magnitudes of this real part of the economy. Therefore, if inflationary expectations are stationary, we can decouple the real dynamics of the real part of the economy from the nominal dynamics in this subsystem as will be shown in more detail below.

[5]which however can also be reformulated in terms of real magnitudes

The solution for the interior steady state or point of rest of these dynamics is obtained in the following way. Equations (40), (45) imply that $g_k^d = \gamma + \delta, g_h^d = \gamma + \delta_h$ must hold in the steady state. The remaining adjustment equations for quantities then imply: $y_o^d = y_o^e, y_o = y_o^d + \gamma\nu_o, l_{fo}^{de} = l_{fo}^{we}$. Setting equation (43) equal to zero implies furthermore: $\Delta\hat{p}_y^o = \frac{1-\alpha_{\pi_o^l}}{\alpha_{\pi^l}}\pi_o^l$ which when inserted into (42), set equal to zero, implies that π_o^l must be zero. Equations (41), (42), set equal to zero, then imply two equations in the unknowns $l_o^{we}/l_o^e - \bar{V}, y_o/y^p - \bar{U}$, which are linearly independent of each other and which therefore imply $l_o^{we}/l_o^e = \bar{V}, y_o = y^p\bar{U}$. This provides us with the steady state value of y_o and therefore also with the ones for $l_{fo}^{we}, l_{go}^{we}, l_o^{we}$, since we have according to the above $y_o = y_o^e + \gamma\nu_o, y_o = y_o^e + \beta_n(\beta_{n^d}y_o^e - \nu_o) + \gamma\beta_{n^d}y_o^e$ and thus $y_o^e = \frac{y^p\bar{U}}{1+\gamma\beta_{n^d}}, \nu_o = \beta_{n^d}y_o^e$. The equation $l_o^{we}/l_o^e = \bar{V}$ then provides us with the steady state value of l_o^e.

Table 10: *Structure of the Real Part of the 18D Dynamics*[6]

18D

↓

foreign assets off
domestic assets off
fiscal policy off
monetary policy off
$X = (X_r, X_{mund}, X_h)$

↓

9D
$\dot{X} = F_9(X, Z(X))$
Sections 3.1 and 3.5

↓

Mundell off
$\omega^e = w^e/p_y, \phi_h = p_h/p_y$
$X_r \to \tilde{X}_r = (y^e, \nu, l_f^{we}, l^e, \omega^e) \to \tilde{X}_h = (\phi_h, k_h)$
$X = (\tilde{X}_r, \tilde{X}_h)$

↓

7D
$\dot{X} = F_7(X, Z(X))$
Section 3.3

↓

housing off; $X \to \tilde{X}_r$

↓

5D
$\dot{X} = F_5(X, Z(X))$ Section 3.2

Due to what has been shown for y_o we get from the equation for g_k^d the equality $\rho_o^e = r_l^*$ and thus as real wage $\omega_o^e = w_o^e/p_y^o$ since all other expressions that define the rate of profit ρ_o^e have already been determined. Inserting this real wage into the definition of y_{w1o} then provides us with the steady state value of this part of workers' income, since again all other steady state expressions that form this expression have already been determined. From this income value we immediately get c_g^o and thus from goods market equilibrium

$$y_o^d = y_o^e = c_g^o + \gamma + \delta + (\gamma + \delta_h)k_{ho} + gy_o^e, \tag{48}$$

[6]We add here that turning housing off before Mundell is turned of gives rise to another 7D subdynamics where however the price level does not feed back into the remaining 6D system, see also our discussion of this type of subdynamics below.

the steady state value of k_{ho}. Equation (44), set equal to zero, next implies that $c^o = k_{ho}\bar{U}_h$ must hold true, which finally implies via the investment function in the housing sector:

$$(p_h^o/p_y^o)c_h^o/k_{ho} - \delta_h - r_l^* = 0,$$

and provides us with the steady state value of p_h^o/p_y^o.

This is however all that can be deduced for the steady state positions of this economy, since the above system of differential equations and its static definitional equations all depend only on the relative prices $\omega^e = w^e/p_y, \phi_h = p_h/p_y$ and thus do not imply anything for the absolute levels of the prices shown in these expressions. The laws of motion for $\omega^e = w^e/p_y, \phi_h = p_h/p_y$ are given by

$$\hat{\omega}^e = \hat{w}^e - \hat{p}_y, \quad \hat{\phi}_h = \hat{p}_h - \hat{p}_y.$$

By inserting the above nominal laws of motion into these dynamical equations would indeed reduce the above dynamical system to a system with dimension 8, with the law of motion for $\hat{p}_y$ as an appended dynamics that does not feed back into the now truly real part of the economy.

The interior steady state of the dynamics of this section is therefore only uniquely determined up to the level of p_y^o which can be preset to any positive value. From the above we also conclude that the determinant of the Jacobian J of the dynamics at the steady state must be zero (the matrix J has rank 8), which in addition implies that the system is subject to hysteresis in that all of its nominal price magnitudes depend on historical conditions and the shocks to which the system is subjected. The actual steady state values are the ones determined in the preceding section if one neglects those of the state variables not involved in the 9D dynamics here under consideration. Finally, we conjecture, on the basis of the knowledge on the dynamics of related, but smaller dynamical models considered in Chiarella and Flaschel (2000) that the steady state of the dynamics will be asymptotically stable for low adjustment speeds of prices, low adjustment speeds of inventories and a fast sales expectations mechanism, but that such stability will get lost (via Hopf-bifurcations, implying the birth or death of periodic orbits at the Hopf bifurcation point) as the speed of adjustment of the slow variables is increased. However, these are all issues which shall be investigated in the simulations reported in the rest of the paper.

3.2. The Keynes-Metzler-Goodwin core 5D dynamics

The 9D dynamics[7] can be reduced to a 7D dynamical system by switching off the Mundell effect (i.e. by setting $\beta_{\pi_l} = 0$ and π_l set to its steady state value) and formulating the model in real terms by introducing the real wage $\omega^e (= \omega^e/p_y)$ and real rental prices $\phi_h (= p_h/p_y)$. The resulting 7D dynamical system is

$$\hat{\omega}^e = \kappa[(1-\kappa_p)(\beta_{w_1}(l^{we}/l^e - \bar{V}) + \beta_{w_2}(l_f^{de}/l_f^{we} - 1))$$

[7]The Keynes-Metzler-Goodwin core dynamics to which we refer in this section is a special case of the Keynes-Metzler model of Chiarella and Flaschel (2000) and the Keynes-Metzler-Goodwin model of Chiarella, Flaschel, Groh and Semmler (2000) in that inflation is frozen at its steady state value. Also real balances are treated differently here because of use of the Taylor interest rate rule

$$-(1-\kappa_w)\beta_p(y/y^p-\bar{U})], \tag{49}$$

$$\hat{l}^e = -[\alpha_1^k(1-\tau_c)(y^e-\delta-(1+\tau_p)\omega^e l_f^{de}-r_l^*)+\alpha_3^k(y/y^p-\bar{U})], \tag{50}$$

$$\dot{l}_f^{we} = \beta_l(l_f^{de}-l_f^{we})-[\alpha_1^k(1-\tau_c)(y^e-\delta-(1+\tau_p)\omega^e l_f^{de}-r_l^*) +\alpha_3^k(y/y^p-\bar{U})]l_f^{we}, \tag{51}$$

$$\dot{y}^e = \beta_{y^e}(y^d-y^e)-[\alpha_1^k(1-\tau_c)(y^e-\delta-(1+\tau_p)\omega^e l_f^{de}-r_l^*) +\alpha_3^k(y/y^p-\bar{U})]y^e, \tag{52}$$

$$\dot{\nu} = y-y^d-[\alpha_1^k(1-\tau_c)(y^e-\delta-(1+\tau_p)\omega^e l_f^{de}-r_l^*) +\alpha_3^k(y/y^p-\bar{U})+\gamma]\nu, \tag{53}$$

$$\hat{\phi}_h = \beta_h(\frac{c_h^o}{k_h}-\bar{U}_h)+(\kappa_h-1)\delta\hat{p}_y, \tag{54}$$

$$\hat{k}_h = g_h^d-\delta_h-(g_k^d-\delta), \tag{55}$$

where

$$\begin{aligned}
y^d &= c_g^o+g_k^d+g_h^d k_h+gy^e,\\
y &= y^e+\beta_n(\beta_{n^d}y^e-\nu)+\gamma\beta_{n^d}y^e,\\
l_f^{de} &= l_y y,\\
l_g^{de} &= l_g^{we}=\alpha_g g y^e,\\
l^{de} &= l_f^{de}+l_g^{de},\\
l^{we} &= l_f^{we}+l_g^{we},\\
y_{w1} &= \omega^e[l^{de}+\alpha^u(l^e-l^{we})+\alpha^r\frac{L_2(0)}{L_1(0)}l^e]/(1+\tau_v),\\
c_g^o &= c_1(1-\tau_w^o)y_{w1},\\
c_h^o &= (1+\tau_v)\frac{c_2}{c_1}\frac{c_g^o}{\phi_h},\\
g_k^d &= \alpha_1^k((1-\tau_c)(y^e-\delta-(1+\tau_p)\omega^e l_f^{de}-r_l^*))+\alpha_3^k(y/y^p-\bar{U})+\gamma+\delta,\\
g_h^d &= \alpha_1^h((1-\tau_c)\frac{\phi_h c_h^o}{k_h}-\delta_h-(1-\tau_c)r_l^*)+\alpha_3^h(\frac{c_h^o}{k_h}-\bar{U}_h)+\gamma+\delta_h
\end{aligned}$$

with steady state solution as in the case of the 9D system (given by the subsystem of steady state values of the preceding section that corresponds to the state variables here considered). Note that c_g^o, c_h^o do not represent steady state values in this set of algebraic equations, but denote concepts of desired consumption of goods and housing services which are no longer subject to an error correction process.

This 7D system is reduced to the Keynes-Metzler-Goodwin (or KMG) core 5D dynamics by switching off the housing sector by setting $c_2=0, g_h^d=0, \beta_h=0, k_h(0)=0$. These imply that the ratio k_h stays at zero, that equations where divisions through k_h occur are suppressed and that the then still given, but purely formal evolution of the price level p_h does not matter for the rest of the dynamics. Due to $c_2=0$ there is then of course also no demand for housing services. It is likely for the present formulation of the dynamics that the housing sector is not of central importance for the overall dynamical features of the full

18D or real 9D dynamics as far as interesting feedback mechanisms are concerned. This however is in part due to the approach chosen to model it in the present series of papers and may be different if other formulations of housing investment and housing services are attempted.

This 5D system with which we are dealing becomes

$$\begin{aligned}
\hat{\omega}^e &= \kappa[(1-\kappa_p)(\beta_{w_1}(l^{we}/l^e - \bar{V}) \\
&\quad + \beta_{w_2}(l_f^{de}/l_f^{we} - 1)) - (1-\kappa_w)\beta_p(y/y^p - \bar{U})], && (56) \\
\hat{l}^e &= -[\alpha_1^k(1-\tau_c)(y^e - \delta - (1+\tau_p)\omega^e l_f^{de} - r_l^*) + \alpha_3^k(y/y^p - \bar{U})] && (57) \\
\dot{l}_f^{we} &= \beta_l(l_f^{de} - l_f^{we}) - [\alpha_1^k(1-\tau_c) && (58) \\
&\quad (y^e - \delta - (1+\tau_p)\omega^e l_f^{de} - r_l^*) + \alpha_3^k(y/y^p - \bar{U})]l_f^{we} \\
\dot{y}^e &= \beta_{y^e}(y^d - y^e) - [\alpha_1^k(1-\tau_c) && (59) \\
&\quad (y^e - \delta - (1+\tau_p)\omega^e l_f^{de} - r_l^*) + \alpha_3^k(y/y^p - \bar{U})]y^e \\
\dot{\nu} &= y - y^d - [\alpha_1^k(1-\tau_c)(y^e - \delta - (1+\tau_p)\omega^e l_f^{de} - r_l^*) && (60) \\
&\quad + \alpha_3^k(y/y^p - \bar{U}) + \gamma]\nu
\end{aligned}$$

with the following supplementary definitions for the statistically endogenous variables

$$\begin{aligned}
y^d &= c_g^o + \alpha_1^k(1-\tau_c)(y^e - \delta - (1+\tau_p)\omega^e l_f^{de} - r_l^*) \\
&\quad + \alpha_3^k(y/y^p - \bar{U}) + \delta + \gamma + gy^e, \\
y &= y^e + \beta_n(\beta_{n^d} y^e - \nu) + \gamma\beta_{n^d} y^e, \\
l_f^{de} &= l_y y, \\
l_g^{de} &= l_g^{we} = \alpha_g g y^e, \\
l^{de} &= l_f^{de} + l_g^{de}, \\
l^{we} &= l_f^{we} + l_g^{we}, \\
c_g^o &= c_1(1-\tau_w^o)y_{w_1}, \\
y_{w1} &= \omega^e[l^{de} + \alpha^u(l^e - l^{we}) + \alpha^r \frac{L_2(0)}{L_1(0)} l^e]/(1+\tau_v)
\end{aligned}$$

Note that the foregoing expression for c_g^o, which is not restricted to the state value of this magnitude, makes again use of the steady state value of the rate of wage taxation which however can no longer be given by eq. (17) in the preceding section, since we now have not only $k_h = 0$, but also $c_2 = 0$. Instead, we now take from eq. (48) in the steady state the expression $c_g^o = (1-g)y_o^e - (\gamma+\delta)$ and determine the steady state value of τ_w by:

$$\tau_w^o = 1 - c_g^o/(c_1 y_{w1}^o)$$

with y_{w1}^o the steady state value of wage income (as determined in section 2).

In the special case $\kappa_w = 1$ this core model consists of a Goodwin (1967) type accumulation and income distribution mechanism, coupled with a Keynesian goods market demand block that is here based on sluggish quantity adjustment as in Metzler (1941). This version of the KMG model therefore represents a very basic way of marrying the Goodwin growth

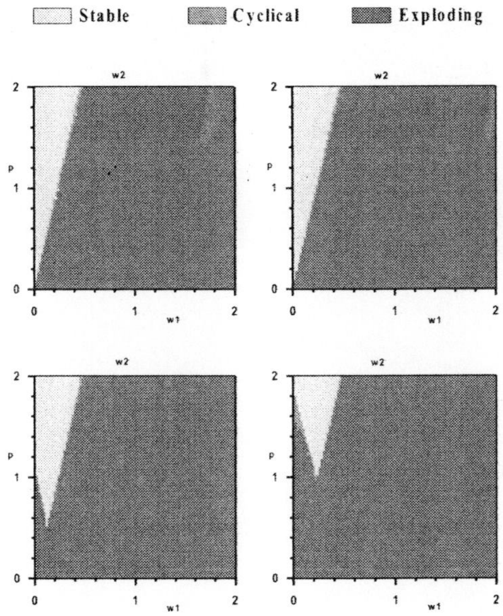

Figure 1. *Stability regions for the KMG core 5D dynamics;* β_p *vs.* β_w

cycle idea (also with inside labor) with the Keynesian problem of deficient aggregate demand on the market for goods and a sluggish quantity adjustment of Metzlerian type. This special case we label the KMG core 5D dynamics of our general 18D dynamics.

In the more general case $\kappa_w < 1$ the KMG core 5D dynamics are augmented by the Rose real wage effect as formulated in Chiarella and Flaschel (2000) which integrates goods market dynamics into the subdynamics of income distribution and growth (but not yet the Mundell effect of inflationary expectations which would add their law of motion to the 5D dynamics and also the dynamics of the price level p_y).

The steady state values of the state variables of the dynamical system (56) - (60) are given by:

$$
\begin{aligned}
y_o^e &= \frac{y^p \bar{U}}{1+\gamma\beta_{n^d}}, \\
\nu_o &= \beta_{n^d} y_o^e, \\
l_{fo}^{we} &= l_y y^p \bar{U} \quad [l_o^{we} = l_{fo}^{we} + \alpha_g g y_o^e], \\
l_o^e &= (l_{fo}^{we} + \alpha_g g y_o^e)/\bar{V}, \\
\omega_o^e &= \frac{y_o^e - \delta - r_l^*}{l_{fo}^{we}(1+\tau_p)}.
\end{aligned}
$$

Next we analyze the KMG 5D dynamics augmented with Rose goods market effects.

Figure 1 shows the (β_p, β_w) stability basin at various values of β_{w_2} for the 5D core with the Rose effect turned on ($\kappa_w < 1$). We see a stable region at low β_{w_1}; in the stable region at a given level of wage flexibility, increasing price flexibility leads to greater stability. The effect of increasing β_{w_2} is to reduce (and slightly distort) the stable region.

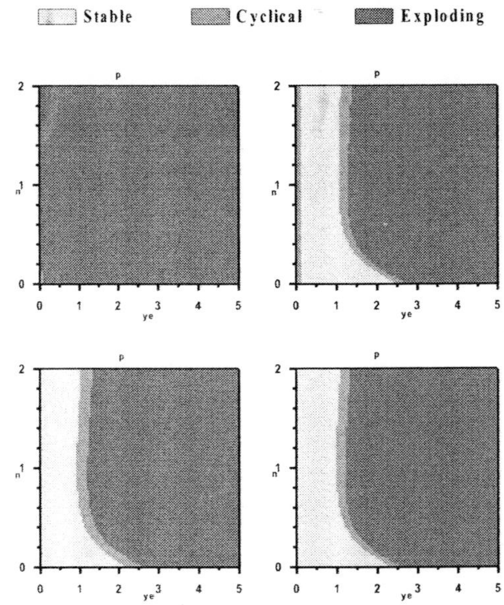

Figure 2. *The stability regions for the KMG core 5D dynamics;* β_n *vs.* β_{y_e}

Figure 2 shows the (β_{y_e}, β_n) stability basin at various values of β_p. A relatively high value of β_p is required before a stable region emerges. In the stable region, at a fixed β_n an increase in β_{y_e} is destabilizing, indicating that a strong Metzlerian quantity adjustment process is destabilizing for such values of β_n.

It appears that the nonlinearities of the 5D dynamics, which are all intrinsic in nature, are still too weak to bound the dynamics globally once the steady state has become a repeller.

We have also computed figures 1 and 2 for the case when $\kappa_w = 1$, the corresponding Goodwinian type of dynamics. However the stability regions are totally explosive in this case and so we have not bothered to reproduce them here.

3.3. The KMG core dynamics with a housing sector

Next we augment the 5D dynamics by switching on the housing sector and consider the 7D dynamics that are generated thereby. The relevant differential equations are equations (49) - (55).

Figure 3 displays the (β_p, β_{w_1}) stability regions for various values of β_h, the speed of response of housing prices to excess capacity. Compared to the corresponding (at $\beta_{w_2} = 0.5$) 5D case in figure 1 we see that an increase in β_h has very little effect on stability.

Figure 4 displays the stability trade-off between β_h and α_{h_3} (the relative strength of excess capacity on housing investment) at various values of β_{w_1} and β_p, with the stable region seeming almost invariant to these latter parameters. We see from these figures that at a given β_h, increasing α_{h_3} tends to be destabilizing.

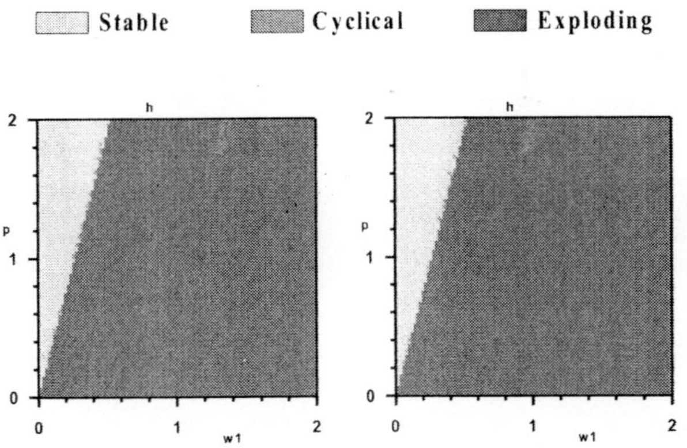

Figure 3. *Stability region (β_{w_1} vs. β_p) for the KMG (core and housing) 7D dynamics*

3.4. The KMG 5D dynamics and the Mundell effect

If we now add to the KMG 5D dynamics (with the housing sector switched off in the same way as in section 3.2 and the same steady state formula for the wage taxation rate) the dynamic equation for inflationary expectations (i.e. the Mundell effect is switched on) then we are considering the 7D dynamical system (37) – (43).[8]

At the present stage of the investigation we might expect that the addition of the Mundell effect ($\beta_{\pi^l} > 0$) is generally destabilizing. This is so since from a local point of view – which only involves intrinsic nonlinearities – the Mundell inflationary positive feedback mechanism seems to imply not only additional cyclical explosiveness to the plots so far shown, but also leads to saddlepoint effects in the sense of a superimposed positive or negative trend around which the cycles occur (and this also in real magnitudes which therefore fluctuate around a path that is diverging from the steady state). Adding the Mundell effect of inflationary expectations as a sixth law of motion (and price inflation as an appended seventh law) to the real 5D dynamics in fact means that one adds a positive nominal feedback mechanism without any other nominal feedback mechanism that can keep this mechanism bounded, since nominal interest rates are still fixed at their steady state values.

We have computed the stability regions corresponding to figure 1 and 2 with the Mundell effect switched on. There is very little change to the stability regions displayed in figures 2 and 3, since β_{π^l} is still chosen relatively small, so we have not bothered to reproduce them here. We also note that a sufficiently large increase in this parameter value will make the dynamics purely explosive.

[8]We stress here again that the evolution of p_y does not influence any of the other laws of motion if nominal wage dynamics are reformulated as real wage dynamics as in Chiarella and Flaschel (2000):

$$\hat{\omega}^e = \kappa[(1-\kappa_p)(\beta_{w_1}(l^{we}/l^e - \bar{V}) + \beta_{w_2}(l_f^{de}/l_f^{we} - 1) - (1-\kappa_w)\beta_p(y/y^p - \bar{U})].$$

The 5D real part of the economy (and the evolution of inflationary expectations) then depend on the evolution of this real wage, but nowhere on the evolution of the price level itself, which in particular means that the dynamical system based on the state variables $y^e, \nu, l_f^{we}, l^e, \omega^e, p_y, \pi_l$ has a vanishing sixth column in its Jacobian at the steady state.

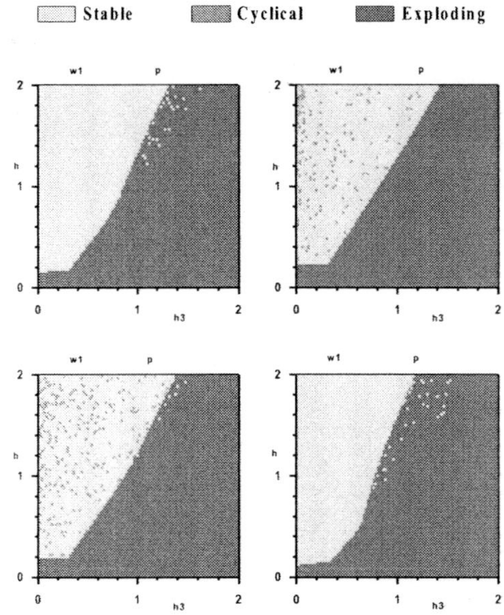

Figure 4. *Stability region (β_h vs. α_3^h) for the KMG (core and housing) 7D dynamics*

3.5. The integrated dynamics of the real part of the economy

We turn now to the full 9D dynamics of the real sector of the economy expressed in real and nominal terms in equations (37) – (45). This essentially considers the interaction of all the feedback mechanisms of the real sector; the 5D core (Rose effect), the Mundell effect and the housing sector.

Figure 5 displays the β_p, β_{w_1} stability region for $\beta_{w_2} = 0.5$. We see that the stability region is quite small. A very similar picture is obtained for a wide range of β_{w_2}. Figure 5 also displays the β_n, β_{y_e} stability region for $\beta_{w_1} = 0.05, \beta_{w_2} = 0.5$ and $\beta_p = 1.0$. Overall these stability regions indicate that the interaction of all the mechanisms of the real sector

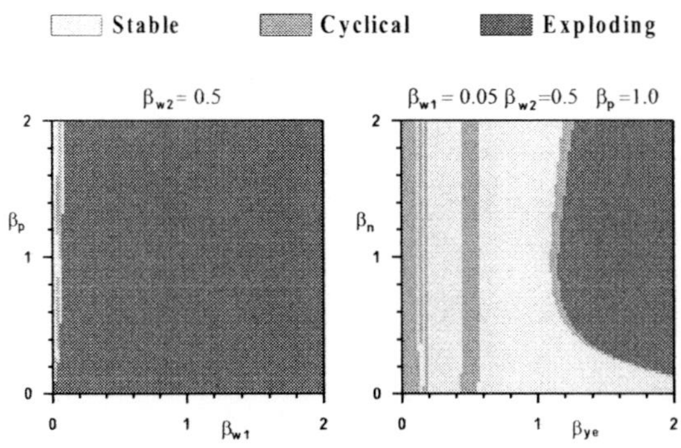

Figure 5. *Stability region (β_{w_1} vs. β_p) and (β_n vs. β_{y_e}) for the KMG (real) 9D dynamics*

is destabilizing.

4. Adding policy issues to the real dynamics

In this section we consider the impact of fiscal and monetary policy on the stability basins of the 9D real dynamics studied in section 3.5. Tables 11,12 and 13 summarize the various submodels we consider in this regard and how they are obtained from the full 18D model. Thus in table 11 we see that by turning off foreign assets, domestic assets and fiscal policy, the 18D model is reduced to a 10D system which consists of the 9D real dynamics together with the Taylor interest rate rule (equation 31). Table 12 shows that when foreign assets, domestic assets and monetary policy are switched off, the 18D model reduces to a 12D system consisting of the 9D real dynamics plus the 3D fiscal policy dynamics (equations 28,29 and 30). Finally table 13 shows how the 9D real dynamics with both the Taylor interest rate policy rule and fiscal policy dynamics (resulting in a 15D system consisting of equations (19)-(33)) is obtained from the 18D dynamics by switching off foreign assets and domestic assets. In the following subsections we investigate in turn each of the foregoing subdynamics.

Table 11: *Reducing the 18D model to the 9D real dynamics with the Taylor interest rate rule*

18D

↓

foreign assets off
domestic assets off
fiscal policy off

$$X = (X_r, X_{mund}, X_h, X_{mo})$$

$$Z = (y, l_f^{de}, l_g^{de}, l_g^{we}, l^{de}, l^{we}, y_w, c_g^o, c_h^o, \rho^e, g_k^d, g_h^d, y^d, \pi_b, g^a, t^a, t^c)$$

↓

$$\dot{X} = F_{10}(X, Z(X))$$

↓

real dynamics (9D) + Taylor interest rate rule (10)
Section 4.1

Table 12: *Reducing the 18D model to the 9D real dynamics with fiscal policy dynamics*

18D
↓
foreign assets off domestic assets off $X = (X_r, X_{mund}, X_h, X_{mo}, X_{fi})$ $Z = (y, l_f^{de}, l_g^{de}, l_g^{we}, l^{de}, l^{we}, y_w, c_g^o, c_h^o, \rho^e, g_k^d, g_h^d, y^d, \pi_b, g^a, t^a, t^c)$
↓
$\dot{X} = F_{15}(X, Z(X))$
↓
real dynamics (9D) + Taylor interest rate rule + fiscal policy Section 4.3

Table 13: *Reducing the 18D dynamical model to the 9D real dynamics with both the Taylor interest rate policy rule and fiscal policy dynamics*

18D
↓
foreign assets off domestic assets off monetary policy off $X = (X_r, X_{mund}, X_h, X_{fi})$ $Z = (y, l_f^{de}, l_g^{de}, l_g^{we}, l^{de}, l^{we}, y_w, c_g^o, c_h^o, \rho^e, g_k^d, g_h^d, y^d, \pi_b, g^a, t^a, t^c)$
↓
$\dot{X} = F_{12}(X, Z(X))$
↓
real dynamics (9D) + fiscal policy dynamics Section 4.2

4.1. Interest rate policy rules

The subdynamics of this subsection consist of the 9D real dynamics of section 3 plus the interest policy rule of the central bank, viz.

$$\dot{r} = -\beta_{r_1}(r - r_l^*) + \beta_{r_2}(\Delta\hat{p}_y + \pi^l) + \beta_{r_3}(y/y^p - \bar{U}) \tag{61}$$

This brings back the negative feedback effects of the short-term rate of interest on fixed business and housing investment, at present only compared with a given rate of interest on long-term bonds r_l^* through the α_2 terms in the two investment functions. We now consider here a situation where the Mundell effect is at work (i.e., at least a 7D dynamical system) and where the system would experience breakdown if the interest rate policy would be switched off (even for very sluggish adjustments of inflationary expectations). By having this policy rule present, we would expect that a positive and increasing rate of inflation is counteracted, since the rule will work against economic expansion and further increases in the rate of inflation and expectations about it in such cases. This policy – as we know already from Chiarella, Flaschel and Zhu (1999a) – should reduce, and indeed does significantly reduce, the extent of nominal instability inherent in the real part of private sector of the economy, since it works against the Mundell-effect of a positive feedback structure between the expected and the actual rate of inflation, which we found to be very destabilizing and problematic in the observations made in the last subsection.

Figure 6 displays the β_p vs. β_{w_1} and β_{n^1} vs. β_{y_e} stability regions. Both stability regions indicate that, compared to the 9D real dynamics (see figure 5) without the interest rate policy rule, the Taylor interest rate policy rule is stabilizing.

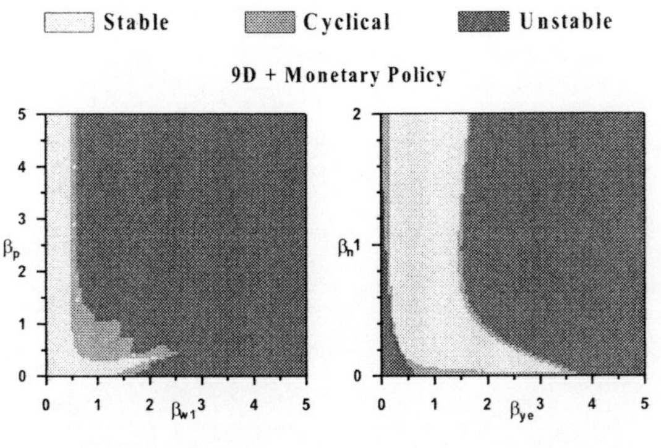

Figure 6. *The 9D real dynamics with the Taylor rule switched on*

We stress, but do not prove this here that a Taylor rule of the type:

$$r = \pi^e + \beta_{r_1}(\pi^e - \bar{\pi}) + \beta_{r_2}(l^{we}/l^e - \bar{V}), \qquad \beta_{r_1}, \beta_{r_2} > 0.$$

would be even more successful in fighting the explosiveness caused by the Mundell effect. This rule states that the central bank sets the expected real rate of interest according to the discrepancy that exists between the expected rate of inflation π^e and the target rate $\bar{\pi}$ of the central bank and the deviation of the actual rate of employment from the NAIRE-rate [9] and this in such a way that interest rates counteract what is observed at high or low economic

[9]The Non-Accelerating-Inflation Rate of Employment.

activity and inflation.[10] This rule is not based on a dynamic law, but concerns levels and thus reduces the dimension of the system of differential equations considered by one. In addition it directly attempts to steer the expected real rate of interest and thus appears to be more powerful as it immediately attacks the source of the Mundell effect, and is not only counteracting it via the Keynes-effect.

4.2. Fiscal policy rules

We have so far ignored the role of the government budget constraint, since it did not exercise any influence on the real dynamics of the model as considered in the preceding section 3. This is however problematic, since the accumulation of government debt may follow an explosive path in the background of the dynamics that has been explicitly considered so far. Furthermore it may be of a kind which would not be tolerated by the present or a subsequent government. We therefore have to consider the evolution of government debt explicitly and will do this of course subject to the hopefully stabilizing influence that may come from the assumed adjustment in the wage taxation rate in the pursuit of a given target ratio of government debt per unit of an appropriate index for the social product, of the type shown in equation (30). The dynamics now consist of equations (19)-(30). Thus bond dynamics have thereby been integrated again into the dynamics of the real part of the economy as shown in section 2.

This is a decisive extension of the dynamics of the model, since it brings back into the considered dynamics the complicated evolution of short and long term bonds per unit of capital, b, b^l, together with the law of motion of the taxation rate τ_w. Figure 7 shows the β_p vs. β_{w_1} and β_{n^1} vs. β_{y_e} stability regions. Compared to the 9D stability regions with no fiscal policy dynamics we see that if anything instability has increased. The previous stable regions in figure 5 have disappeared. The intuition that the bond dynamics are highly destabilizing seems to be borne out by these stability regions.

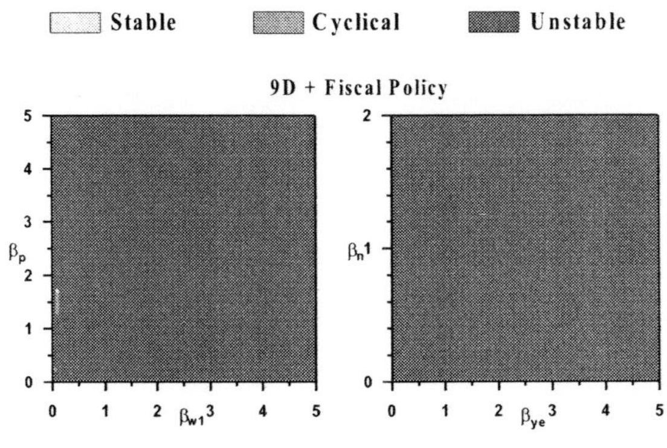

Figure 7. *The 9D real dynamics with the fiscal policy dynamics switched on:*

Employing the wage income taxation rule in the place of the interest rate policy rule is thus not stabilizing in the 9D real dynamics in contrast to what might be expected from

[10] See Flaschel and Groh (1998) for a further discussion of the properties of this monetary policy rule.

such a rule according to the comments made in Powell and Murphy (1997). This seems to be due to the cumulative effect that the evolution of government debt has on the change in the wage taxation rate (which makes things worse instead of better).

Quite the contrary to what we expect on the basis of Chiarella, Flaschel and Zhu (1999a) and its treatment of the GBR even small positive parameters α_{τ_w} contribute significantly to the instability of the steady state and are therefore problematic. This may also be due to the complicated government bond feedback mechanism which so far did not influence the dynamics shown and which may not have the properties found to hold (Chiarella, Flaschel and Zhu (1999a)) where it worked in isolation. The evolution of the government debt based on our complicated formulation of the GBR is however always there and must be integrated into the full dynamics at some stage of the investigation. The question can then only be whether its evolution is less or more problematic in its consequences for the whole system when the taxation rule is switched on with the aim of stabilizing government debt at a certain target ratio.

4.3. Fiscal and monetary policy rules in interaction

The next and final figures of this section show the joint working of the tax policy rule and the interest rate policy rule. The dynamical system now consists of equations (19)-(33). Figure 8 displays the stability regions for this case. We see that they are very similar to the corresponding regions for the 9D plus Taylor interest policy rule in figure 6. So the monetary policy is also able to stabilize the explosiveness of the fiscal policy dynamics. There are of course many further possibilities for feedback policy rules that have not yet been included into the general model of this paper, but which merit further research.

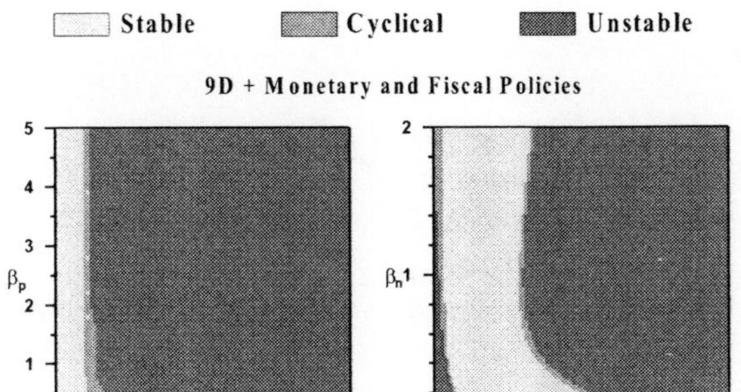

Figure 8. *The 9D real dynamics with monetary and fiscal policy rules*

5. Adding asset price dynamics to the real dynamics

In this section we consider the interaction of the 5D real case and the asset sets, both domestic and foreign.

This extension of the real dynamics adds first of all and most importantly long-term interest rate movements (expected and actual long term bond price dynamics) through their influence on the investment in fixed capital and housing and thus on aggregate demand and the output of firms. We therefore now integrate into the real dynamics the two dynamic equations (32) and (33) namely:[11]

$$\begin{aligned} \hat{p}_b &= \frac{\beta_{p_b}}{1-\beta_{p_b}(1-\alpha_s)}[(1-\tau_c)\frac{1}{p_b} + \alpha_s \pi_{bs} - (1-\tau_c)r] \\ \dot{\pi}_{bs} &= \beta_{\pi_{bs}}(\hat{p}_b - \pi_{bs}) \end{aligned}$$

and their two (opposing) effects on the two types of investment just considered, via profitability differentials, here shown for fixed business investment $(1-\tau_c)\rho^e - ((1-\tau_c)r_l - \pi^l)$, $r_l = 1/p_b$, and via the interest rate spread $r_l - r$. This extension would generally be expected to add instability to the real dynamics, since it represents a positive feedback loop between the expected and the actual increase in the growth rate of long-term bond prices, if the adaptive component in the expectations mechanism works with sufficient strength. We stress that these asset market dynamics are independent of the movements in the real part of the economy as long as the central bank keeps the short-term rate of interest fixed to its steady state value, in which case there is only a one way route leading from the market for long-term bonds to the real part of the economy.

A similar observation does not so obviously hold, if we allow the exchange rate e to influence the evolution of the real part of the dynamics, by removing the assumption that the rate of import taxation is always set such that the trade account of firms is balanced (when measured in domestic prices). In this latter case, the expected rate of profit of firms does not depend on their exports and imports levels and thus on exchange rate changes. As long as there are no wealth effects in the model and as long as the individual allocation of bonds on the various sectors does not matter, there is indeed only this one channel through which the nominal exchange rate can influence the real economy (besides of course through the GBR which includes the tax income of the government deriving from import taxation, but which does not play a role for the real part of the model unless wage taxation is responsive to the evolution of government debt as we have seen in the preceding section). To have this influence of the exchange rate we thus have to extend the 9D real dynamics by the following three laws of motion (34)-(36) namely[12]

$$\begin{aligned} \hat{\tau}_m &= \alpha_{\tau_m} \frac{p_x^* x - (1+\tau_m)p_m^* j^d}{p_x^* x}, \\ \hat{e} &= \frac{\beta_e}{1-\beta_e(1-\alpha_s)}[(1-\tau_c)r_l^* + \alpha_s \epsilon_s - ((1-\tau_c)\frac{1}{p_b} + \pi_b)], \\ \dot{\epsilon}_s &= \beta_{\epsilon_s}(\hat{e} - \epsilon_s). \end{aligned}$$

The exchange rate dynamics is more difficult to analyze, since their two laws of motion need the influence of the bond dynamics in order to be meaningful. Otherwise these

[11] Note that α_s has been assumed to be larger than $(1 - 1/\beta_{p_b})$ in the presentation of the structural form of the model in Chiarella and Flaschel (2000) which makes the parametric expression in front of the first law of motion positive. Note also that the parameter τ_c can be neglected in the numerical simulations that follow.

[12] Where the first one is independent of the changes of the exchange rate.

two laws of motion would imply monotonic implosion or explosion of exchange rate expectations and the actual exchange rate depending on whether the adjustment speed of the exchange rate is smaller or larger than one (for $\alpha_s = 1$). The financial dynamics is therefore in this respect immediately of dimension 5 and it also needs input from the real dynamics to get the effects from the exchange rate e on bond prices p_b and thus an interdependent dynamics and not one of the appended monotonic form just discussed. Yet, the effect of changes in e via the rate of profit ρ^e of firms and the investment decisions that are based on it, needs to extend a long way in order to reach the market for long term bonds. Changes in investment lead to changes in aggregate goods demand and thus to changes in sales expectations and actual output. This leads to changes in capacity utilization of firms and domestic price inflation which – if and only if monetary policy responds to them – are transferred to changes in the short-term rate of interest and thus to changes in the long-term rate of interest. In this way there is a feedback of a change in the exchange rate on its rate of change which has to be analyzed if the full dynamics are investigated.

Taken together the above two extensions which integrate the financial dynamics with the real dynamics will lead us to a 14D dynamics of the real financial interaction, but with no feedbacks from government policy and the GBR yet. This system will be investigated numerically on various levels of generality, i.e., by means of appropriate subcases, in this section.

Clearly the bond dynamics is the more important one from among these two possibilities of making the real dynamics dependent on what happens in the financial part of the economy.[13] We will therefore investigate next how independent monotonic or cyclical movements in long-term bond prices act by themselves (with no coupling with the exchange rate dynamics) on the real part of the dynamics and how they can be bounded in an economically sensible way in the case where their steady state solution is surrounded by centrifugal forces. We shall assume here, as discussed in Chiarella, Flaschel and Zhu (1999a), that locally explosive asset market dynamics can give rise to limit or even limit limit cycle behavior (relaxation oscillations) in the bond market and thus to more or less fast, persistent fluctuations in the long-term rate of interest and expectations about its rate of change. This result is of interest in its own right, but of course also important when studying its consequences for the economy as a whole, without (or with) feedback from the real side to the financial markets.

Arriving at such a situation thus provides an interesting intermediate step in the analysis of the full 18D dynamics, since we can study here the role of fluctuations in long-term interest rates (and the exchange rate) on the real dynamics in isolation before coming to a real-financial interaction of these two fundamental modules of our model. The obtained result can be usefully contrasted with the one way investigation of the real-financial interaction of Franke and Semmler (2000), who study the behavior of a fully specified set of asset markets in its dependence on a given wave form of the business cycle in the real sector, whereas this section considers how the opposite situation can be investigated as a natural subcase of our general model of the real-financial interaction, where asset market fluctuations only work on the functioning of the goods and the labor markets of the economy.

[13]The third asset, equities, does not have any impact on the dynamics of the model of this paper, since neither consumption nor investment depends on share prices here, see Chiarella and Flaschel (1999b,c) for details.

Table 14: *The 5D Real Core plus Domestic Asset Market*

18D

↓

foreign assets off
fiscal policy off
monetary policy off

$$X = (X_r, X_{mund}, X_h, X_d)$$

$$Z = (y, l_f^{de}, l_g^{de}, l_g^{we}, l^{de}, l^{we}, y_w, c_g^o, c_h^o, \varphi^e, g_k^d, g_h^d, y^d, \pi_b, g^a, t^a, t^c)$$

↓

$$\dot{X} = F_{11}(X, Z(X))$$

↓

Mundell off
housing off

$$X_r \to \tilde{X}_r$$

$$X = (\tilde{X}_r, X_d)$$

↓

$$\dot{X} = F_7(X, Z(X))$$

↓

Core real dynamics (5D)
+ domestic asset market dynamics (2D)

Table 15: *The 5D real core plus domestic and foreign assets*

18D

↓

fiscal policy off
monetary policy off
Mundell off
housing off
$X_r \to \tilde{X}_r$
$X = (\tilde{X}_r, X_d, X_f)$

↓

$\dot{X} = F_{10}(X, Z(X))$

↓

Core real dynamics (5D)
+ domestic asset market dynamics (2D)
+ foreign asset market dynamics (3D)

We first apply these observations to the numerical investigation of the 5D real dynamics (the core dynamics of this paper) augmented by the 2D dynamics in long-term bond prices and interest rates and their impact on the real part of the economy. Table 14 shows how the 7D system consisting of the 5D real core plus the domestic asset dynamics is obtained from the full 18D dynamics. This is done by switching off foreign assets, fiscal policy, monetary policy, the Mundell effect and the housing sector.

Figure 9 shows the β_p vs. β_{w_1} and β_n vs. β_{y_e} stability regions for these situations at $\beta_{w_2} = 0.5$ and 1.0. We observe that there is very little change compared to the corresponding 5D real core situation of figures 1 and 2. In the β_p vs. β_{w_1} region a cyclical region appears before the onset of instability. In the β_{n^1} vs. β_{y_e} region there is some contraction of the stable region for $\beta_{w_2} = 1.5$.

We stress with respect to the simulations shown in figure 9 that they are based on the 5D dynamics with which we began the numerical investigations of the 18D dynamics in this paper. There are thus no housing activities involved, no Rose or Mundell effects at work and no policy rules implemented in the dynamics shown. This closes our considerations of the basic case of a one-sided analysis of the real-financial interaction of lowest dimension 7D.

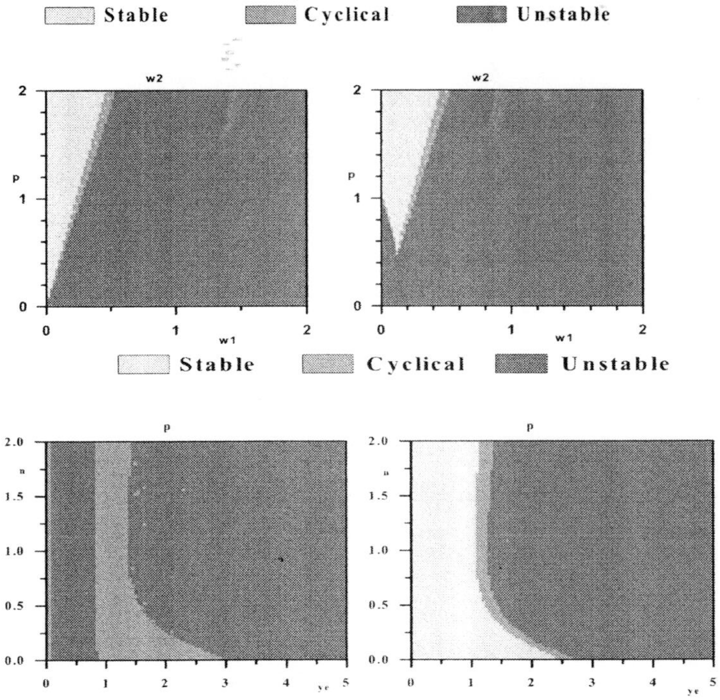

Figure 9. *The 5D core real dynamics with domestic assets.*

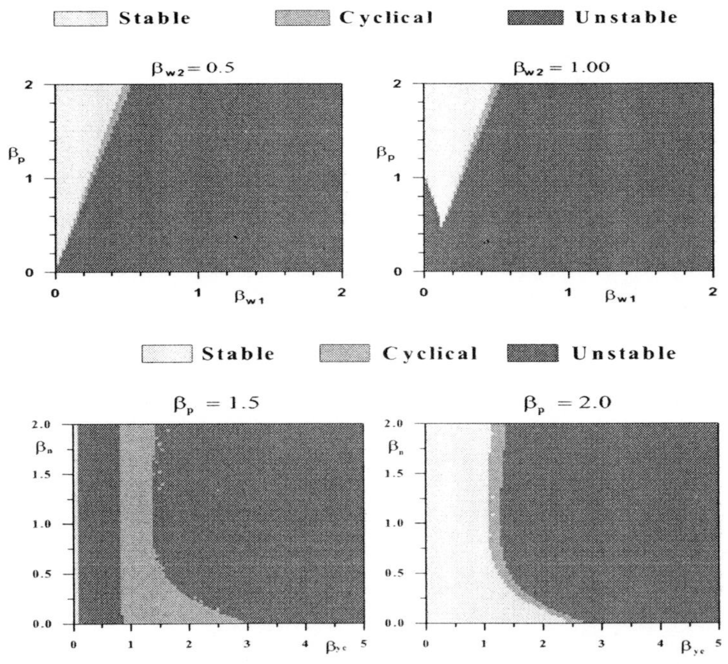

Figure 10. *The 5D core real dynamics with domestic and foreign asset markets.*

We consider next the integrated financial market interaction (between domestic and foreign bonds and their expected rates of return) which are of the following final form:

$$\begin{aligned}
\hat{p}_b &= \beta_{p_b}[(1-\tau_c)\frac{1}{p_b} + \pi_{bs} - (1-\tau_c)r_l^* - \beta_r(e-e_o)], \\
\dot{\pi}_{bs} &= \beta_{\pi_{bs}}(\hat{p}_b - \pi_{bs}), \\
\hat{e} &= \beta_e[(1-\tau_c)r_l^* + \epsilon_s - ((1-\tau_c)\frac{1}{p_b} + \pi_{bs})], \\
\dot{\epsilon}_s &= \beta_{\epsilon_s}(\hat{e} - \epsilon_s), \\
\hat{\tau}_m &= \alpha_{\tau_m}\frac{p_x^* x - (1+\tau_m)p_m^* j^d}{p_x^* x}, \quad x = x_y y, j^d = j_y y,
\end{aligned}$$

Table 15 shows the derivation of the 10D dynamics consisting of the 5D core real dynamics together with domestic and foreign asset market dynamics from the 18D dynamics by switching off both policy rules, the Mundell effect and the housing sector. The system consists of equations (56)-(60) and equations (32)-(36). Figure 10 displays the stability regions. We observe that these are very little changed from figure 9 which involved only the domestic asset market.

We conjecture that this system, with appropriate nonlinearities added, will give rise to two coupled relaxation oscillations of the type we have considered in Chiarella, Flaschel and Zhu (1999a). It is therefore to be expected that the fluctuations in financial markets and their impact on the real part of the economy will become significantly more complicated in such situations of coupled (relaxation) oscillations and their effect on the real part of the economy without or with feedback on the financial sector via the interest rate policy rule of the central bank. In this regard we refer the reader to Asada, Chiarella, Flaschel and Franke (2003).

6. Numerical investigations of the full 18D dynamics

We have so far discussed in this paper various possibilities for a systematic approach towards an investigation of the numerical properties of the full 18D dynamics by mean of appropriate subdynamics. Before we now start the numerical investigation of the full 18D system we summarize the discussion so far by means of a flow diagram that shows the various feedback structures and feedback policy rules involved in dynamic interaction. The following thus provides a graphical representation of what we have discussed so far and it also gives a guide as to how we can go back and forth between appropriate subsystems and the full 18D dynamics in order to understand the outcome of the feedback chains this system contains. We refer the reader to section 3 and Chiarella, Flaschel and Zhu (1999a) for a detailed analysis of the partial feedback mechanisms these disequilibrium growth structures in fact integrates.

Note also with respect to the following graphical representation that there are some feedback mechanisms included (for reasons of completeness) that are not yet contained in the presently considered dynamics (namely the Fisher debt effect, based on investment behavior or also different consumption propensities of creditors and debtors) and the Pigou real balances or wealth effect (which would introduce wealth as an argument into the consumption functions of the model). Note also with respect to our basic 5D dynamics of

KMG type (discussed in section 3) that it brings together the Keynesian goods market view augmented by the Metzlerian inventory adjustment mechanism and the Goodwin real wage – capital stock growth dynamics augmented by Rose (1967) goods-market effects of the real wage on price inflation. The full downward causal nexus of Keynes (1936, ch.19) from asset via goods to labor markets extends these real dynamics in the way we have analyzed in the preceding section and it also allows for the influence of monetary policy rules besides fiscal policy rules as shown in the graph. The question of course again is (see Chiarella, Flaschel, Groh and Semmler (2000) for detailed discussions) whether the shown feedback mechanisms increase or decrease the stability features of the full dynamics close to the steady state (leading towards or away from NAIRU 'full' employment positions) and whether the downward causal nexus shown or the supply side real wage dynamics dominate the dynamics in the medium and longer run should the economy depart from their steady state due to centrifugal forces around it.

Let us begin our numerical investigations of the full 18D dynamics by showing a situation where all equations of the 18D system interact with each other, but where adjustment speeds in the asset markets, concerning asset revaluations (long-term bonds, exchange rate) and expectations on their rate of change, are still low so that there is not much movement present in this part of the model. Larger fluctuations, which are of a simple limit cycle type, therefore basically concern the interaction of prices and quantities on the real markets, as figure 12 shows.

The simulation of the full 18D dynamics in figure 12 (the parameters of this simulation run are shown in table 14) provides a first impression of a type of persistent economic fluctuations (here in fact a fairly simple limit cycle) as it may be generated by the intrinsic nonlinearities characterizing the dynamics. Of course, there can exist supply bottlenecks in the case of larger fluctuations, as discussed in Chiarella, Flaschel, Groh and Semmler (2000, ch.5), which must be taken into account in the formulation of the dynamics if certain thresholds are passed, but which are ignored in the present section. [14]

[14]See Chiarella, Flaschel, Groh and Semmler (2000, ch.6) for a treatment of such supply side restrictions.

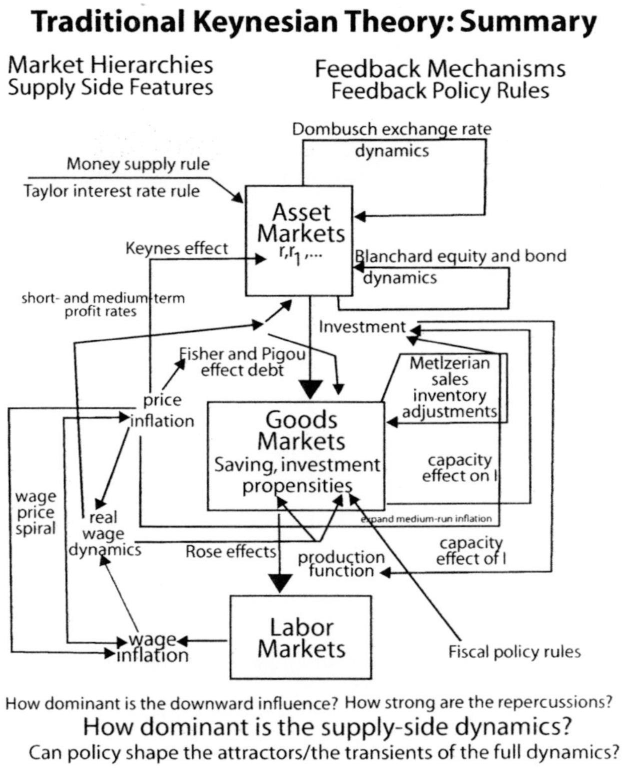

Figure 11. *An overview of the integrated dynamics.*

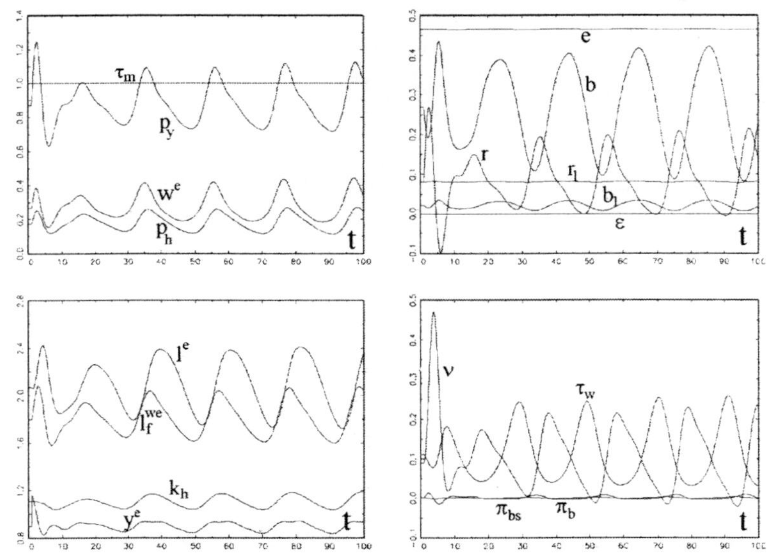

Figure 12. *Convergence to a limit cycle for the full 18D dynamics.*

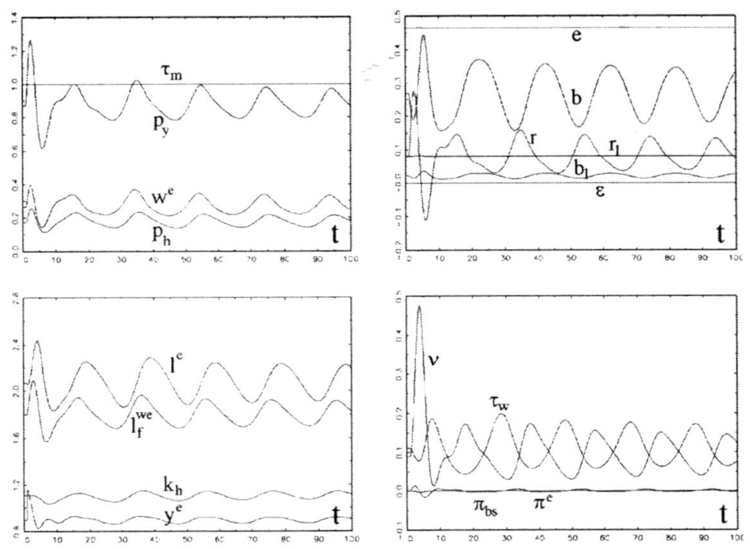

Figure 13. *Shrinking limit cycles when the parameter β_{w_2} is increased.*

Table 14: The parameters corresponding to figure 12.

$\beta_{w_1} = 0.4$	$\beta_{w_2} = 1$	$\beta_p = 0.7$	$\beta_{\pi^l} = 0.5$	$\beta_{p_b} = 0.1$	$\beta_{\pi_{bs}} = 0.1$	$\beta_e = 0.1$	$\beta_\epsilon = 0.1$
$\beta_n = 0.2$	$\beta_{n^d} = 0.1$	$\beta_{y^e} = 1$	$\beta_h = 0.8$	$\beta_l = 0.5$	$\beta_{r_1} = 0.1$	$\beta_{r_2} = 0.5$	$\beta_{r_3} = 0.1$
$\alpha_{\pi^l} = 0.1$	$\alpha_s = 0.5$	$\alpha_{h_1} = 0.1$	$\alpha_{h_2} = 0.5$	$\alpha_{h_3} = 0.1$	$\alpha_{k_1} = 0.1$	$\alpha_{k_2} = 0.5$	$\alpha_{k_3} = 0.1$
$\alpha_{\tau_w} = 0.5$	$\alpha_{\tau_m} = 0.5$	$\alpha_g = 0.2$	$\alpha_b^g = 0.5$	$\alpha_u = 0.5$	$\alpha_r = 0.5$	$L_1(0) = 20000$	$L_2(0) = 5000$
$\kappa_p = 0.5$	$\kappa_w = 0.5$	$\kappa_h = 0.5$	$\bar{U}_c = 0.9$	$\bar{U}_h = 0.9$	$\bar{V} = 0.9$	$\bar{d} = 0.6$	$g = 0.33$
$p_m^* = 1$	$p_x^* = 1$	$r_l^* = 0.08$	$\delta = 0.1$	$\delta_h = 0.1$	$\tau_c = 0.5$	$\tau_v = 0.15$	$\tau_p = 0.3$
$\gamma = 0.06$	$c_1 = 0.5$	$c_2 = 0.33$	$l_y = 2$	$x_y = 0.2$	$j_y = 0.1$	$y^p = 1$	$p_v = 1$

Table 14 shows that parameters that were critical with respect to the dynamic behavior of certain subdynamics, like the speed of adjustment for the wage taxation rate τ_w, need no longer be restricted to small values in order to obtain a meaningful dynamic evolution. However, the table also shows that asset prices still adjust very sluggishly with respect to the relevant interest rate differentials, which leaves for future research the task of investigating in more detail what thresholds must be applied to these dynamics in order to get bounded or viable dynamics also for larger adjustment speeds of asset prices and capital gains expectations around the steady state of the dynamics. Note also that rates of growth and of interest are now chosen in a more plausible range than was the case in some of the subdynamics considered in the preceding sections. The simulations of figure 12 and further ones (not shown) suggest that the full dynamics behaves more smoothly with respect to parameter changes than the various subdynamics we have investigated beforehand.

Increasing the parameter β_{w_2} to 1.14, the adjustment speed of nominal wages due to the employment rate of inside workers, stabilizes the dynamics further in the sense of making

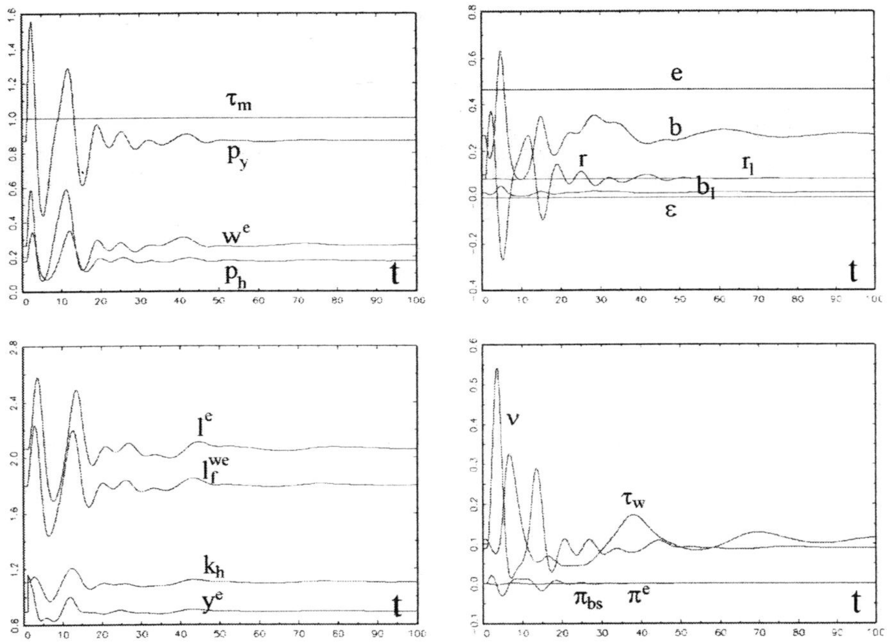

Figure 14. *Establishment of a point attractor as the parameter β_{w_2} is further increased (to the value 3).*

the limit cycle shown in figure 13 a smaller one. In fact, further increases of this parameter will remove the limit cycle totally and will create the situation of an asymptotically stable steady state or point attractor, as shown in figure 14. This indicates that a supercritical Hopf bifurcation is occurring from stable limit cycles back to convergence to the steady state as the parameter β_{w_2} goes beyond 1.14. This situation will be confirmed by a subsequent eigenvalue diagram calculation.

We note with respect to figure 13 that there is a long transient behavior shown in this figure with irregular fluctuations and varying cycle lengths of the time series of the 18 state variables that are shown. Note however that this is partly caused by the enormous shock that is here applied (a thirty percent increases in sales expectations).

In the situation shown in figure 14 we may increases the adjustment parameters on the asset markets, $\beta_{p_b}, \beta_{\pi_{bs}}, \beta_e, \beta_\epsilon$ up to 0.6 and will find that fluctuations will now occur in the corresponding state variables (still of a minor degree), but quite astonishingly accompanied by a further increase in stability, i.e., by a more rapid convergence to the steady state. Asset prices and capital gain expectations thus do not always destabilize the dynamics when their corresponding adjustment speeds are increased. This may be due to the Taylor rule, the steering of the short-term rate of interest by the central bank, which may move the term structure of returns on assets in a way that increases the stability of the steady state.

However, if the four parameters just considered are all in fact increased to 0.6 and if we change the portion α_{π^l} of people who form adaptive price inflation expectations from 0.1 to 0.5 the fluctuations of the economy, and also the transient behavior, are significantly changed as figure 15 shows. These fluctuations still converge to a limit cycle which however

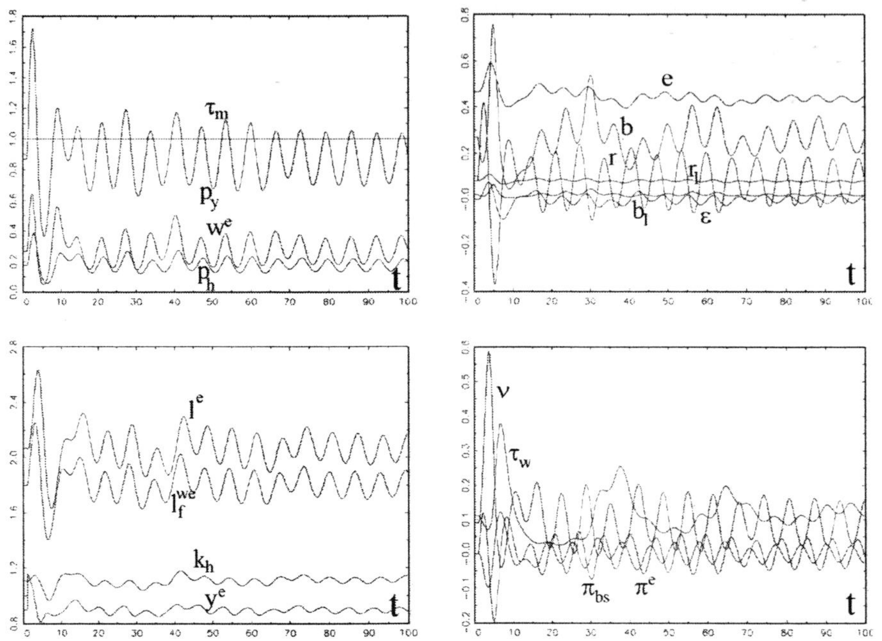

Figure 15. *A more dominant role for price inflation and adaptive expectations.*

is only revealed when the economy is simulated over a much longer time horizon than is here shown (100 years).

Next we come to the calculation of eigenvalue diagrams for speeds of adjustment and important other parameters characterizing fiscal or monetary policy and the behavior of the private sector of the economy. These eigenvalue diagrams show the maximum real part of the eighteen eigenvalues of the 18D core dynamics and they are based on the parameter values given in table 14, with $\beta_{w_2} = 1.14$ however. Note that due to the indeterminacy of the level of nominal magnitudes one eigenvalue must always be zero in these 18D dynamics, in distinction to the dynamics we have considered in Chiarella, Flaschel, Groh and Semmler (2000, ch.s 7/8). Therefore, local asymptotic stability of the remaining variables is given when we see a horizontal portion (at zero) in the eigenvalue diagrams shown below. The degree of asymptotic stability therefore cannot be seen from the depicted eigenvalue diagrams, but only the points where stability gets lost, presumably by way of a Hopf-bifurcation.

The eigenvalue diagrams shown in figure 16 are remarkable in that they confirm, in a very straightforward way, what intuition from the partial 1D or 2D perspectives would suggest, despite the fact that the partial stability analysis is often quite easy to understand since destabilizing feedback mechanism very often sit in the trace of the Jacobian of the dynamics at the steady state while they are distributed in the full 18D Jacobian in a very uninformative way at first glance. We thus see that the system very often behaves in a very simple way even though it integrates Rose type price adjustment, Metzler type quantity adjustment, Goodwin type growth cycles, a housing sector related to the Goodwin - Rose approach to the employment cycle, the dynamics of the government budget constraint, asset market dynamics of Dornbusch type, and monetary and fiscal policy rules.

Inspection of the parameter set underlying these eigenvalue diagrams, which is given by table 14, with β_{w_2} equal to 1.14, first of all shows that wage flexibility (on the outside labor market) should be destabilizing and price flexibility on the market for goods should be stabilizing, since broadly speaking aggregate demand y^d depends positively on the real wage, due to very low marginal propensities to invest as far as profitability component of investment behavior is concerned. These two diagrams therefore concern what has been called Rose effects in this paper. Indeed, this is what is shown in the first two diagrams in figure 16 over the range $(0, 1)$ in the case of the parameter β_{w_1} and the range $(0, 2)$ in the case of β_p. The Hopf-bifurcation value for these two parameter values, where stability gets lost, is slightly below (respectively above) the parameter values $\beta_{w_1} = 1.14$ and $\beta_p = 0.7$ since the parameter values of figure 13 already provide a stable limit cycle around an unstable steady state.

In the second row of figure 16 we see again what has already been demonstrated in relation to figures 12 and 13, namely that larger flexibility of the money wage with respect to the employment rate within firms is stabilizing. We also see in this row that increasing flexibility of adaptively formed inflationary expectations is stabilizing, which stands in striking contrast with what we know about the role of Mundell effects from the smaller KMG models considered in this paper. It is however easy to understand why this adverse situation arises here. The parameter characterizing the portion of adaptively behaving agents is, as table 14, shows in the present situation equal to $\alpha_{\pi^l} = 0.1$ which means that the other, regressive, component of inflationary expectations is the dominant one which is stabilizing. Increasing the parameter α_{π^l} to its extreme value of 1 indeed reverses this situation and gives for the β_{π^l} eigenvalue diagram the same form as for the β_{w_1} diagram and thus implies that the Mundell effect is working, as usual, in a destabilizing way when the adaptive expectations of price inflation become faster.

The third row in figure 16 shows very low bond price adjustment speeds turn the stable limit cycle situation given by the base parameter set into convergence to the steady state, while an increase has only moderate effect on instability for a while, until a point is reached (approximately $\beta_{p_b} = 1$) where instability increases significantly with the parameter β_{p_b}. Modifying the speed of adjustment $\beta_{\pi_{bs}}$ of the adaptive part of expectations formation in the market for long-term bonds, on the other hand, provides no way of obtaining stability in the present situation, i.e., the limit cycle will not shrink to zero in this case for either high or low values of this expectational parameter. Similar conclusions hold in the case of exchange rate dynamics, where however a small middle range of adjustment speeds for the exchange rate provides local asymptotic stability, while the system becomes unstable again for very low adjustment speeds of exchange rate dynamics. Asset markets thus behave by and large as expected for isolated changes towards higher adjustment speeds of prices and expectations. Note here however that we have found in connection with figure 14 that a simultaneous increase in the speeds of adjustment here involved could improve the rate of convergence of the dynamics.

Turning to the fourth row of figure 16 we see that there is a small range for inventory adjustment speeds β_n where local asymptotic stability holds, while there is instability below and above this range. Not only do faster inventory adjustments destroy stability, as expected from the 2D presentation of the Metzler dynamics in Chiarella, Flaschel, Groh and Semmler (2000, ch.2), but now also for very slow adjustments of inventories. The finding for sales

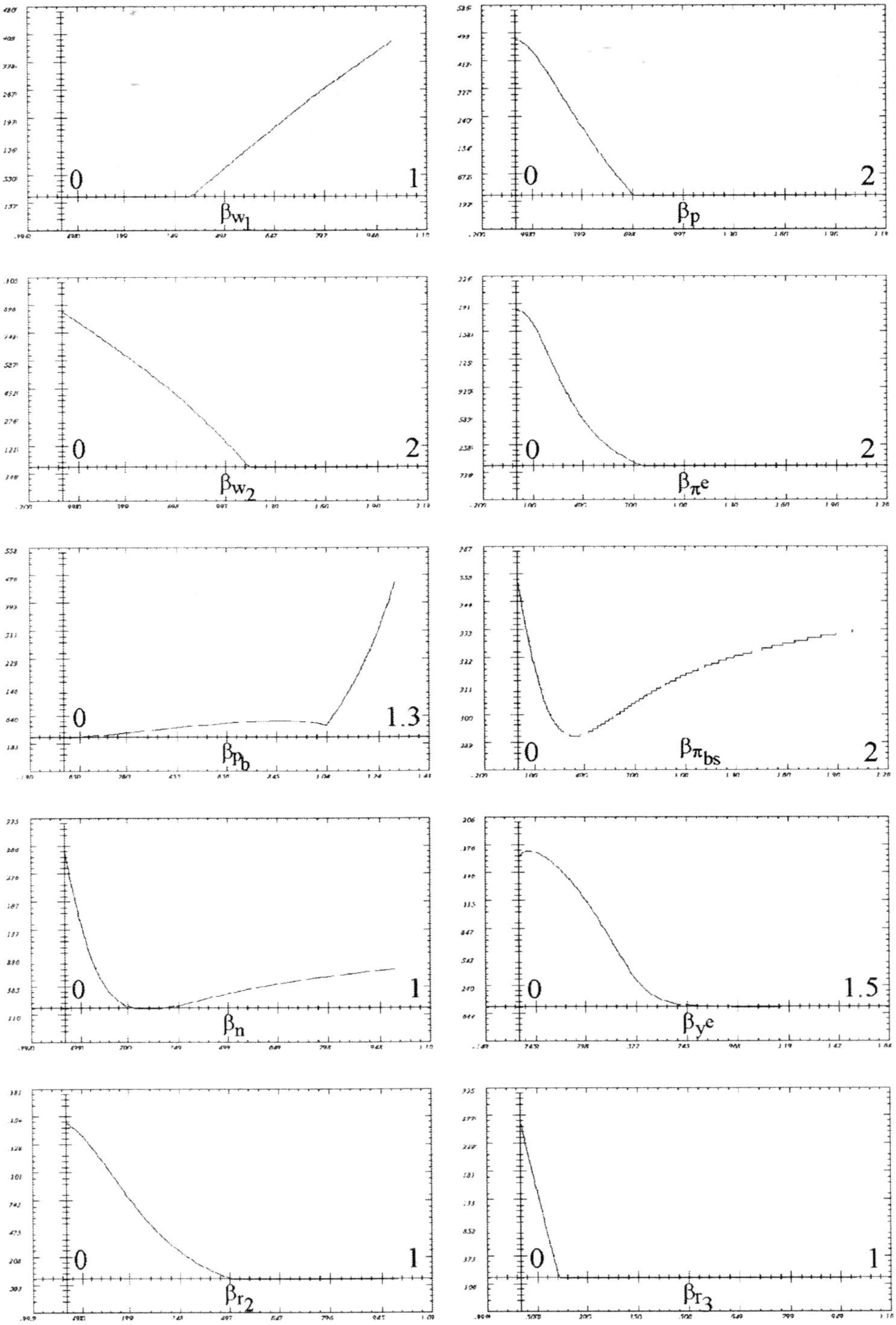

Figure 16. *Eigenvalue calculations for adjustment speed parameters.*

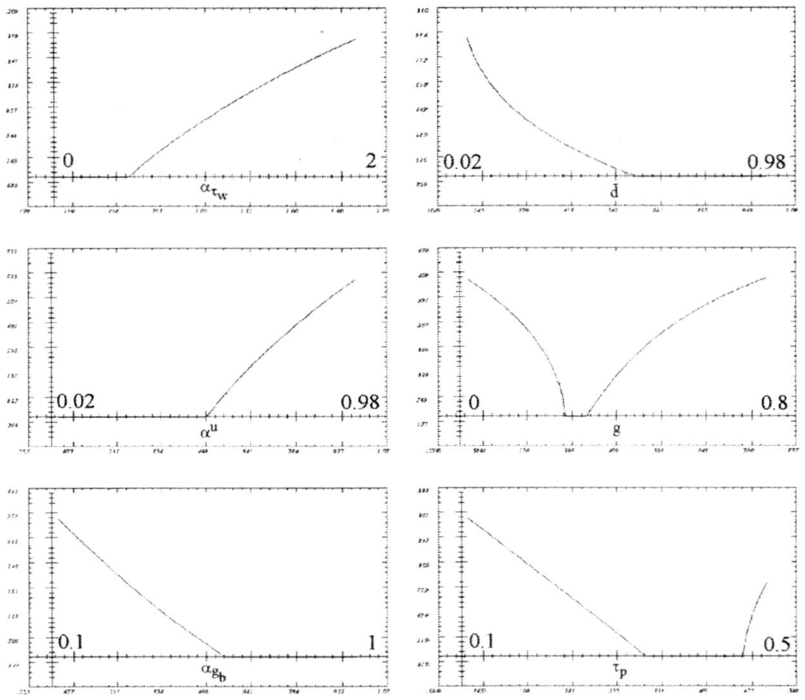

Figure 17. *Eigenvalue calculations for policy parameters.*

expectations, β_{y^e}, is as expected from the 2D situation, i.e., the stable limit cycle situation underlying the parameters of table 14 is turned into local asymptotic stability when the parameter β_{y^e} is increased, since the marginal propensity to spend is broadly speaking smaller than one in the considered situation and the dynamic multiplier process, here in expected sales, is therefore stabilizing.

Finally, the interest rate policy rule works as it is expected to work. Increasing inflation or activity levels here lead to increasing short-term nominal interest rates and this counteracts the increases in inflation and economic activity. Increasing the adjustment speeds with which the central bank reacts to inflation or economic activity changes thus leads to local asymptotic stability and makes the stable limit cycle around the then unstable steady state again disappear. We furthermore note, but do not demonstrate this here, that increasing adjustment speed β_h of the price level for housing services (from a certain point onwards) will destabilize the economy, as will increasing adjustment speeds in the employment policy of firms, β_l. However, in both cases, this will also occur if these adjustment speeds are decreased to a sufficient degree which again means that there is only a certain corridor for which it can be expected in the present situation that convergence to the steady state is assured.

Our next set of eigenvalue diagrams in figure 17 concerns important policy parameters of the 18D core model.

In the first row of figure 17 we see that an increase of the adjustment speed of the wage taxation rate (in order to approach a target level of 60 percent for the debt to (sold) output

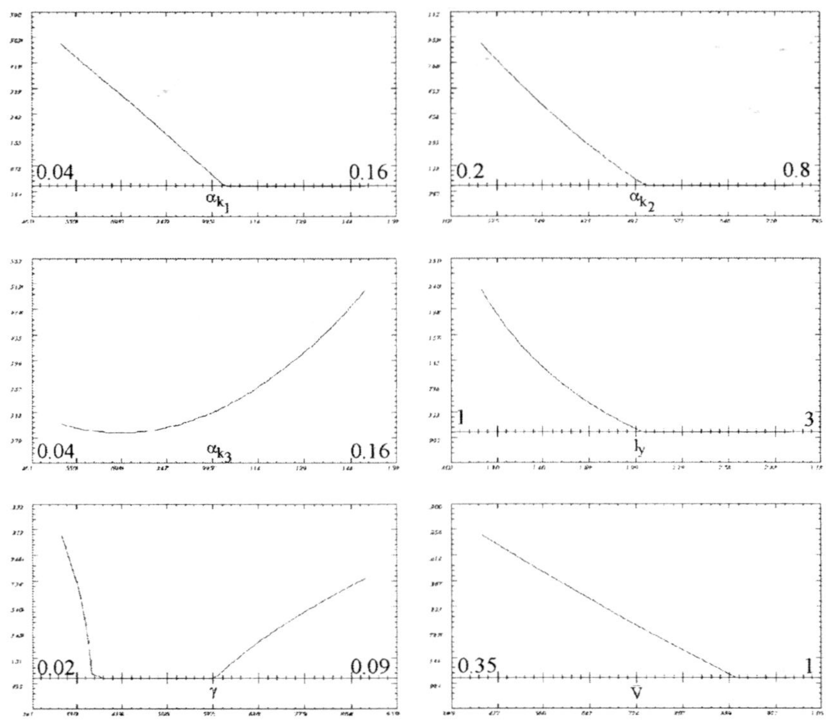

Figure 18. *Eigenvalue calculations for investment, growth, the NAIRU and labor productivity.*

ratio) is destabilizing further when started from the reference case of the limit cycle situation in figure 13, while a decrease of this speed will produce convergence to the steady state. By contrast, increasing the targeted debt to (sold) output ratio $\bar{d}$ removes the limit cycle and leads to asymptotic stability. The presently considered case therefore leads to the remarkable conclusion that the Maastricht criterion for the ratio $\bar{d}$ should be relaxed and / or the speed of adjustment towards this ratio be reduced if asymptotic stability of the steady state is a desired objective

The second row of diagrams in figure 17 shows to the left that (further) increases in the percentage of unemployment benefits, and also pension payments (not shown), as compared to the limit cycle reference situation tend to be destabilizing, while reductions in both of these ratios bring asymptotic stability and thus convergence to the steady state of the dynamics. To the right this row provides the eigenvalue diagram for the percentage of government expenditures per unit of (expected) sales, which shows that there is a small corridor for this ratio below the reference situation where local asymptotic stability of the steady state is given. Variations in this expenditure ratio therefore generally do not add much to the stability features of the reference situation.

Finally, in the last row of eigenvalue diagrams in figure 17, we consider to the left the shift in debt financing of government expenditures away from short-term bonds towards long-term bonds and find that this is stabilizing in the current situation. By contrast, in the diagram bottom right, we see again that there is a range of parameter values for the payroll-tax parameter τ_p, and similarly increase in capital income taxes τ_c and value added taxes τ_v, to the right of the reference situation where convergence to the steady state is obtained, i.e., increasing payroll taxes in the reference situation will produce asymptotic stability, while decreases from there will be destabilizing. Payroll tax increases are therefore only in a limited way comparable to increases in the adjustment speed of nominal wages with respect to the external labor market and thus must be considered as an independent event from the proposal that the (downward) adjustment speed of nominal wages should be increased somewhat.

Note that we here only consider stability issues, and not how steady state values themselves may be changed through those of the here considered parameters that do not concern adjustment speeds, which do not affect steady state positions. Such steady state comparisons have to use the set of steady state values presented at the beginning of this section. Note also that the stability assertions made are generally not confined to very limited basins around the steady state, but can in most cases be tested by means of considerable shocks out of the steady state.

We note that the parameter values α_{τ_m} and α_l, the speed of adjustment of import taxation and the participation rate of the labor forces, do not influence the eigenvalues of the Jacobian of the dynamics at the steady state, and that variations in the ratio of heterogeneity in capital gains expectations on the asset markets do not produce asymptotic stability in the presently considered situation. Not unexpectedly there is a band of intermediate ranges for the marginal propensities of workers to consume goods and housing services (below the reference ratio) where convergence is established, but low as well as high values of these ratios between zero and one do not produce such results. Note here that both ratios may exceed 1 in sum and thus give rise to unstable multiplier dynamics and also to the possibility of debt deflation since workers then become debtors of asset holders in and around the steady state. Finally, and also not demonstrated by an explicit presentation of such a numerical result, we have that a portion of adaptively formed expectations, α_{π^l}, that lies between 0.12 and 0.84 provides convergence instead of the limit cycle situation shown for the value $\alpha_{\pi^l} = 0.1$.

In the last set of eigenvalue diagrams (figure 18) we consider further important parameters of the 18D core dynamics, characterizing business fixed investment, labor productivity, external growth and the external labor market.

The first row in the diagrams in figure 18 shows that increased sensitivity with respect to both the profit / required interest differential and the sensitivity towards the term structure of interest rates increase the stability of the steady state as far as convergence towards it is concerned. The same however does not hold true for the impact of capacity utilization rates on the rate of investment which when varied does not create situations of local asymptotic stability (see second row to the left). On the right hand side of the second row we consider the ratio l_y, the labor coefficient which is the inverse of labor productivity. Increasing this ratio adds convergence to the dynamics, a thing one would have expected for the reciprocal ratio, the labor productivity of the economy. At the bottom left of figure 18 we consider the growth rate of the world economy which when lowered, starting from the reference situation of table 14, adds asymptotic stability to the dynamical system, unless it comes too close to zero. Finally, a higher NAIRU level for the employment rate, $\bar{V}$, equal to 0.9 in the reference situation, produces convergence, that is a smaller corridor for nominal wage

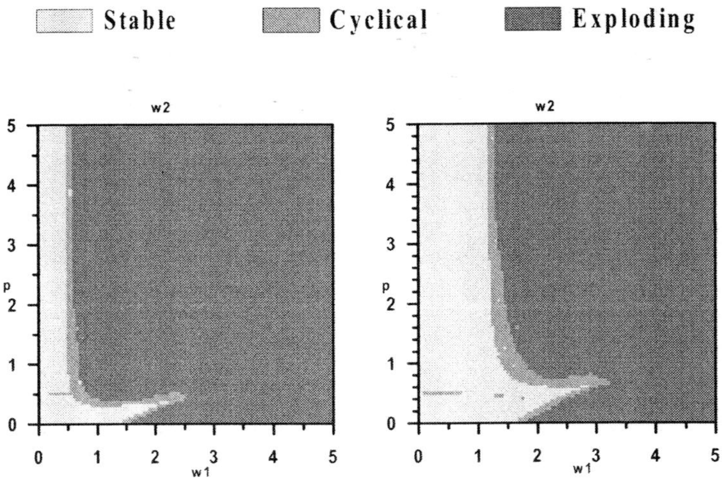

Figure 19. *The full 18D dynamics: Global considerations*

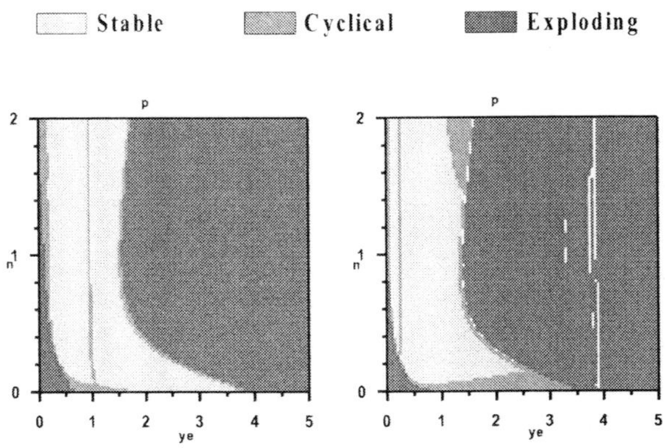

Figure 20. *The full 18D dynamics: Global considerations*

increases on the external labor market adds to the stability of the economy, see the diagram bottom right. The same holds true for the NAIRU rate for capacity utilization of firms as well as for housing services (not shown).
All of these stability investigations are of great importance since in particular in macroeconometric work convergence back to the steady state, if not enforced by the so-called jump variable technique, is a basic requirement in these types of approaches, not however in the present modeling framework. Nevertheless, adjustment speeds are difficult to estimate with respect to their most plausible range, and are therefore to be studied intensively in their role of creating or destroying convergence. As the figures of this section show the outcome for our 18D core dynamics, though basically only a single example in this direction, looks quite reasonable compared to the discussion of the basic feedback mechanism of such a model type that we have conducted on various levels of generality in parts I and II in Chiarella, Flaschel, Groh and Semmler (2000).
We conclude this section with an example of the global simulation studies we have used extensively in the preceding sections for studying the subsystems of the full 18D dynamics. The parameter set underlying the figures 19 and 20 is the one provided in table 9.
We see again, in figure 19, that price flexibility is stabilizing in the present situation, while wage flexibility, concerning the outside labor market, is not. However increasing the reaction speed of wages with respect to the inside employment rate improves the stability region for wage and (outside) wage flexibility. Figure 20, finally, shows that increased price flexibility does not significantly alter the domain where the quantity adjustment process exhibits convergence to the steady state. All these stability results heavily depend on the fact that the consumption propensity c_1 is situated in a certain economically meaningful range (of approximately 0.4 to 0.6).

7. Conclusions

We have considered in this paper the 18D core dynamics of the approach of Chiarella and Flaschel (1999a,b) from a variety of perspectives, in particular with respect to the various economically meaningful subdynamics it contains. Our general finding was that the implications of the 6D working KMG model, derived and investigated in Chiarella and Flaschel (2000) and Chiarella, Flaschel, Groh and Semmler (2000) from various perspectives, is confirmed if more structural details such as a housing sector, more complete asset market dynamics, exchange rate dynamics and fiscal and monetary policy rules are added to the picture. Though the descriptive relevance of the considered dynamics is considerably improved thereby, we still often simply find a set of three possible outcomes, namely convergence to the steady state, limit cycle behavior, or pure explosiveness as long as the dynamics are only intrinsically nonlinear and not augmented by extrinsic mechanisms that capture the fact that such economies will change their behavior far off the steady state. Furthermore, the range of persistent fluctuations found was often very small, so that increasing adjustment speed soon led us from convergence to explosive behavior around the steady state.
The paper has in addition discussed a variety of feedback chains that characterize the considered dynamics as well as others that are not yet present in it. It has provided a discussion of how the partial feedback mechanisms and their known (de-)stabilizing potential can be

investigated from a their partial as well as a more or less integrated perspective, giving rise to the general impression that the considered dynamics will more often be locally repelling than convergent. The study of extrinsic nonlinearities that bound the dynamics is therefore an important next step in the investigation of the disequilibrium growth model – with an applied orientation – introduced in Chiarella and Flaschel (1999a,b), Chiarella, Flaschel and Zhu (2000) and extended further in a variety of ways in Chiarella, Flaschel, Groh, Köper and Semmler (1999a,b) and Chiarella, Flaschel and Zhu (2003).
The general outcome of our investigation in the present paper is that such models of disequilibrium growth, due to the fact that most of their important feedback chains are more likely to be destabilizing, rather than stabilizing, their uniquely determined interior steady state solution that macroeconometric applications of the considered disequilibrium dynamics have to be prepared to find local instability of the steady state that is turned into globally bounded business fluctuations by important behavioral nonlinearities known to exist far off the steady state, the most prominent example maybe being an asymmetric (strictly convex) money-wage Phillips curve that is nearly horizontal for low rates of wage inflation as it was recently again confirmed to exist in the paper by Hoogenveen and Kuipers (2000). The new challenging task is, on the one hand, the macrodynamics has to have a high order orientation now in order to understand integrated feedback systems with respect to local as well as global stability, with the latter topic a still much neglected area, since knowledge about behavioral nonlinearities – to be associated with certain destabilizing feedback channels – is at best rudimentarily developed. Dynamic macroeconometrics, on the other hand, has to approach the situation, like in the work of Hoogenveen and Kuipers (2000), how such nonlinearities can be confirmed by the data, and if so that the business cycle is an endogenous phenomenon driven by local instabilities, global bounds and stochastic shocks, implying that the Frisch paradigm is not a good guiding line in this area of research, see here also Chen (1996, 1999, 2001). Structural macroeconomic model building must be aware of the important feedback channels that drive the macroeconomy (away from the steady state), [15] must handle their decomposition and re-integration (as demonstrated in this paper from the formal as well as numerical point of view) [16] and must finally be prepared that – when business cycles are endogenous components in working of modern market economies – that tools must be correspondingly and not that vice versa that tools determine what is to be investigated and what not.

References

Asada, T., C. Chiarella, P. Flaschel and R. Franke (2003): *Open Economy Macrodynamics. An Integrated Disequilibrium Approach*. Heidelberg: Springer, forthcoming.

Barnett, W., G. Gandolfo and C. Hillinger (1996): *Dynamic Disequilibrium Modeling: Theory and Applications.* Cambridge, UK: Cambridge University Press.

Barnett, W. and Y. He (1998): Bifurcations in Continuous-time Macroeconomic Systems.

[15]See Flaschel, Gong and Semmler (2001, 2002) for actual examples.

[16]see Chiarella, Flaschel and Semmler (2001), Asada et al. (2003), Chiarella, Flaschel and Franke (2003) with respect to the analytical possibilities that here meanwhile exist.

Washington University in St. Louis: Mimeo.

Barnett, W.A. and Y. He (1999a): Stability analysis of continuous-time macroeconometric systems. *Studies in Nonlinear Dynamics and Econometrics*, 3, 169 – 188.

Barnett, W. and Y. He (1999b): Center Manifold, Stability, and Bifurcations in Continuous Time Macroeconometric Systems. Washington University in St. Louis: Mimeo.

Bergstrom, A.R., K.B. Nowman and S. Wandasiewicz (1994): Monetary and fiscal policy in a second-order continuous time macroeconometric model of the United Kingdom. *Journal of Economic Dynamics and Control,* 18, 731 – 761.

Bodkin, R., Klein, L. and K. Marwah (1991): *A History of Macroeconometric Model-Building.* Aldershot: Edward Elgar.

Chen, P. (1996): Trends, shocks, persistent cycles in evolving economy: business cycle measurement in time-frequency representation. In: W.A. Barnett, A.P. Kirman and M. Salmon (eds.): *Nonlinear Dynamics and Economics*. Cambridge: Cambridge University Press, 307 – 331.

Chen, P. (1999): The Frisch model of business cycles – a spurious doctrine, but a mysterious success. China Center for Economy Research: Discussion paper.

Chen, P. (2001): Economic complexity: fundamental issues and policy implications. China Center for Economic Research: Working paper No. E2001002.

Chiarella, C. and P. Flaschel (2000): *The Dynamics of Keynesian Monetary Growth: Macrofoundations*. Cambridge, UK: Cambridge University Press.

Chiarella, C. and P. Flaschel (1999a): Towards Applied Disequilibrium Growth Theory: I. The starting model. UTS Sydney: Working Paper.

Chiarella, C. and P. Flaschel (1999b): Towards Applied Disequilibrium Growth Theory: II. Intensive form and steady state analysis of the model. UTS Sydney: Working Paper.

Chiarella, C., Flaschel, P. and R. Franke (2005): *Foundations for a Disequilibrium Theory of the Business Cycle. Qualitative Analysis and Quantitative Assessment*. Cambridge, UK: Cambridge University Press.

Chiarella, C., P. Flaschel, G. Groh, C. Köper and W. Semmler (1999a): Towards Applied Disequilibrium Growth Theory: VI. Substitution, money-holdings, wealth-effects and other extensions. UTS Sydney: Working Paper.

Chiarella, C., P. Flaschel, G. Groh, C. Köper and W. Semmler (1999b):: Towards Applied Disequilibrium Growth Theory: VII. Intensive form and steady state analysis in the case of substitution. UTS Sydney: Working Paper.

Chiarella, C., P. Flaschel, G. Groh and W. Semmler (2000): *Disequilibrium, Growth and Labor Market Dynamics. Macro Perspectives*. Heidelberg: Springer.

Chiarella, C., Flaschel, P. and W. Semmler (2001): Price flexibility and debt dynamics in a high order AS-AD model. *Central European Journal of Operations Research*, 9, 119 – 146.

Chiarella, C., P. Flaschel and P. Zhu (2000): Towards Applied Disequilibrium Growth Theory: III. Basic partial feedback structures and stability issues. UTS Sydney: Working Paper.

Chiarella, C., Flaschel, P. and P. Zhu (2003): Towards Applied Disequilibrium Growth Theory: VIII. The 22D core dynamics in the case of substitution. UTS Sydney: Working Paper.

Deleau, M., C. Le Van and P. Malgrange (1990): The long run of macroeconometric models. In: P. Champsaur et al.: *Essays in Honour of Edmond Malinvaud. Vol. 2: Macroeconomics.* Cambridge, MA: The MIT Press.

Fair, R. (1994): *Testing Macroeconometric Models.* Cambridge, MA: Harvard University Press.

Flaschel, P. and G. Groh (1998): Textbook Stagflation Theory and Beyond. University of Bielefeld: Discussion Paper.

Flaschel, P., Gong, G. and W. Semmler (2001): A Keynesian macroeconometric framework for the analysis of monetary policy rules. *Journal of Economic Behaviour and Organization*, 25, 101 – 136.

Flaschel, P., Gong, G. and W. Semmler (2002): A macroeconometric study on the labor market and monetary policy: Germany and the EMU. *Jahrbuch für Wirtschaftswissenschaften*, 53, 21 – 27.

Franke, R. and W. Semmler (2000): Bond rate, loan rate and Tobin's q in a temporary equilibrium model of the financial sector. *Metroeconomica*, 50, 351-385.

Goodwin, R.M. (1967): A growth cycle. In: C.H. Feinstein (ed.): *Socialism, Capitalism and Economic Growth.* Cambridge, UK: Cambridge University Press, 54 – 58.

Garratt, A., Lee, K., Peseran, M. and Y. Shin (1998): A long-run structural macroeconometric model of the UK. Cambridge, UK: Mimeo.

Hoogenveen, V. and S. Kuipers (2000): The long-run effects of low inflation rates. *Banca Nazionale del Lavoro Quarterly Review*, 214, 267–285.

Keynes, J.M. (1936): *The General Theory of Employment, Interest and Money.* New York: Macmillan.

McKibbin, W. and J. Sachs (1991): *Global Linkages. Macroeconomic Interdependence and Cooperation in the World Economy.* Washington, D.C.: The Brookings Institution.

Metzler, L. A. (1941): The nature and stability of inventory cycles. *Review of Economic Statistics*, 23, 113 – 129.

Powell, A. and C. Murphy (1997): *Inside a Modern Macroeconometric Model. A Guide to the Murphy Model*. Heidelberg: Springer.

Rose, H. (1967): On the non-linear theory of the employment cycle. *Review of Economic Studies*, 34, 153 – 173.

Whitley, J. (1994): *A Course in Macroeconomic Modelling and Forecasting.* New York: Harvester / Wheatsheaf.

Appendix: Notation

The following list of symbols contains only domestic variables and parameters. Foreign magnitudes are defined analogously and are indicated by an asterisk $(*)$. To ease verbal descriptions we shall consider in this paper the 'Australian Dollar' as the domestic currency (A$) and the 'US Dollar' ($) as a representation of the foreign currency (currencies).

A. Statically or dynamically endogenous variables:

y	Output (per K) of the domestic good
y^d	Aggregate demand (per K) for the domestic good
y^p	Potential output (per K) of the domestic good
y^{dp}	Normal sales (per K) of the domestic good
y^n	Normal output (per K) of the domestic good
y^e	Expected sales (per K) for the domestic good
y_w^D, y_c^D	Real disposable income (per K) of workers and asset-holders
l_1^e	Population aged $16 - 65$ in efficiency units (EU: $\times \exp(n_l t)$, per K)
l_2^e	Population aged $66 - \ldots$ in EU (per K)
l_0^e	Population aged $0 - 14$ in EU (per K)
l^{de}	Total employment of the employed in EU (per K)
l_f^{de}	Total employment of the work force of firms in EU (per K)
$l_g^{de} = l_g^{de}$	Total government employment in EU (per K)
l_f^{we}	Work force of firms in EU (per K)
l^{we}	Total active work force
V_f^w	Employment rate of those employed in the private sector
α_l	Participation rate of the potential work force
$V = l^{de}/l^e$	Rate of employment ($\bar{V}$ the employment–complement of the NAIRU)
$c_w\ (c_w^o)$	Real (equilibrium) goods consumption of workers (per K)
$c_c(c_c^o)$	Real (equilibrium) goods consumption of asset owners (per K)
$c = c_w + c_c$	Total goods consumption (per K)
c_h^s	Supply of dwelling services (per K)
c_h^d	Demand for dwelling services (per K)
g_k^d	Gross business fixed investment (per K)
g_h^d	Gross fixed housing investment (per K)
$I^a/K\ (I^{na}/K)$	Gross (net) actual total investment (per K)
$\mathcal{I}/K$	Planned inventory investment (per K)
N/K	Actual inventories (per K)
ν^d	Desired inventories (per K)
r	Nominal short-term rate of interest (price of bonds $p_b = 1$)
r^l	Nominal long-term rate of interest (price of bonds $p_b = 1/r^l$)
$\pi_b = \hat{p}_b^e$	expected appreciation in the price of long-term domestic bonds
ρ^r	Required rate of interest
p_e	Price of equities
$\pi_e = \hat{p}_e^e$	expected appreciation in the price of equities
$S^n/p_v K =$	$S_p^n/p_v K + S_f^n/p_v K + S_g^n/p_v K$ Total nominal savings (per $p_v K$)
$S_p^n/p_v K =$	$S_w^n/p_v K + S_c^n/p_v K$ Nominal savings of households (per $p_v K$)
$S_f^n/p_v K$	Nominal savings of firms ($= p_y Y_f/p_v K$, the income of firms) per $p_v K$
$S_g^n/p_v K$	Government nominal savings (per $p_v K$)
$T^n/p_v K\ (T/K)$	Nominal (real) taxes $p_v K, K$
g	Real government expenditure (per K)
ρ^e	Expected short-run rate of profit of firms
ρ^a	Actual short-run rate of profit of firms
ρ^n	Normal operation rate of profit of firms
ρ^l	Expected long-run rate of profit of firms
ρ_h	Actual rate of return for housing services

ρ_h^l	Expected long-run rate of return for housing services
K	Capital stock
k_h	Capital stock in the housing sector (per K)
w^{be}	Nominal wages including payroll tax (in EU)
w^e	Nominal wages before taxes (in EU)
w^{ue}	Unemployment benefit per unemployed (in EU)
w^{re}	Pension rate (in EU)
p_v	Price level of domestic goods including value added tax
p_y	Price level of domestic goods net of value added tax
p_x	Price level of export goods in domestic currency
p_m	Price level of import goods in domestic currency including taxation
p_h	Rent per unit of dwelling
$\pi^l = \hat{p}_v^e$	Expected rate of inflation (over the long run)
e	Exchange rate (units of domestic currency per unit of foreign currency: A\$/\$)
$\epsilon = \hat{e}^e$	Expected rate of change of the exchange rate
l^e	Labor supply (per K)
b	Stock of domestic short-term bonds (index d: stock demand) (per $p_v K$)
b_w	Short-term debt held by workers ($= B/p_v K$)
b_c	Short-term debt held by asset owners (per $= B_c/p_v K$)
b^l	Stock of domestic long-term bonds, of which b_1^l are held ($= B_1^l/p_v K$) by domestic asset-holders (index d: demand) and b_1^{l*} by foreigners (index d: demand)
b_2^l	Foreign bonds held by domestic asset-holders (index d: demand) ($= B_2^l/p_v K$)
ε	Equities (index d: demand) ($= E/p_v K$)
n	Natural growth rate of the labor force (adjustment towards $\tilde{n}$)
n_l	Rate of Harrod neutral technical change (adjustment towards $\tilde{n}_l$
τ_m	Tax rates on imported commodities
x	Exports (per K)
j^d	Imports (per K)
$nx = \frac{p_x x - e p_m^* j^d}{p_v}$	Net exports in terms of the domestic currency (per $p_v K$)
nfx	Net factor export payments (per $p_v K$)
ncx	Net capital exports (per $p_v K$)
τ_w	tax rate on wages, pensions and unemployment benefits
d	Actual public debt / output ratio

B. Parameters of the model

δ	Depreciation rate of the capital stock of firms
δ_h	Depreciation rate in the housing sector
α_i^j	All α-expressions (behavioral or other parameters)
β_x	All β-expressions (adjustment speeds)
γ	Steady growth rate in the rest of the world
$\bar{U}$	Normal rate of capacity utilization of firms
$\bar{U}_h$	Normal rate of capacity utilization in housing
κ_w, κ_p	Weights of short– and long–run inflation ($\kappa_w \kappa_p \neq 1$)
κ	$= (1 - \kappa_w \kappa_p)^{-1}$
y^p	Output–capital ratio
x_y	Export-output ratio
l_y	Labor-output ratio (labor in efficiency units)
j_y	Import-output ratio
$\bar{d}$	Desired public debt / output ratio
ξ	Risk and liquidity premium of long-term over short-term debt
ξ_e	Risk premium of long-term foreign debt over long-term domestic debt
τ_c	Tax rates on profit, rent and interest

τ_v	Value added tax rate
τ_p	Payroll tax
c_1	Propensity to consume goods (out of wages)
c_2	Propensity to consume housing services (out of wages)

In: Business Fluctuations and Cycles
Editor: T. Nagakawa, pp. 265-283
ISBN 978-1-60021-503-3

Chapter 10

INCREASED STABILIZATION AND THE G7 BUSINESS CYCLE

***Marcelle Chauvet*[1]* *and Fang Dong*[2†]**
[1]Department of Economics, University of California,
Riverside, CA 92521-0247
[2]Department of Economics, Providence College,
549 River Avenue, Providence, RI 02918-0001

Abstract

This paper models the G7 business cycle using a common factor model, which is used to investigate increased stabilization and its impact on business cycle phases. We find strong evidence of a decline in volatility in each of the G7 countries. We also find a break towards stability in their common business cycle. This reduction in volatility implies that recessions will be significantly less frequent in the future compared to the historical track.

Keywords: Recession, Common Factor, Business Cycle, Bayesian Methods.

1. Introduction

The US economy had the longest expansion phase in its history in the 1990s, which was followed by a shallow and short recession in 2001. Several authors have found a structural break in volatility of US GDP in 1984 such as McConnell and Perez-Quiros (2000), Kim and Nelson (1999), Koop and Potter (2000), among several others. Potter (2000) and Chauvet and Potter (2001) associate these recent business cycle changes with an increased stability of US GDP. In particular, they show how the decline in volatility since 1984 implies that subsequent recessions thereafter will be less frequent and, therefore, expansions will have a longer duration, given that there is no return to higher instability.

This chapter studies whether these business cycle changes have also occurred in the G7 countries and the implications for their business cycle. We examine potential breaks in the

*E-mail address: chauvet@ucr.edu
†E-mail address: fdong@providence.edu

variance of GDP in these countries and use statistical methods to investigate the potential impact in the frequency and duration of their business cycle phases.

We characterize the business cycle in the G7 countries by a common factor model that allows for structural breaks. Bayesian techniques are used to estimate the model, the potential endogenous breakpoint in volatility, and posterior means of a measure of the changes in the estimated business cycle. In particular, we investigate changes in the estimated coefficient of variation[1] and the frequency of negative growth in the common factor in order to asses the implications for future recessions in the G7 countries. We also use classical methods to test for breaks and to find their most probable dates for comparison. Thus, we examine both a potential decline in the volatility of the G7 countries and its business cycle, as well as the effects in the frequency of contractions.

We find strong evidence of a break in volatility towards increased stabilization for all countries in the early 1980s using both classical and Bayesian methods. We also find that the posterior mean of the common factor displays a break in volatility in the early 1980s. The estimated coefficient of variation indicates that the frequency and duration of future recessions since the break should be a lot lower. In particular, we find a decline of 50% in the number of quarters with negative growth in the G7 business cycle, since the breakpoint. The findings support the evidence that increased stabilization has been widespread, which implies that these changes might be permanent with a lower probability of reversal towards instability.

The structure of the chapter is as follows: Section 2 discusses the model and the estimation methods. Section 3 describes methods for measuring changes in the business cycle. Section 4 discusses the data used and report the empirical results, and Section 5 concludes.

2. Statistical Model and Methods

2.1. Common Factor Model

We propose a common factor model that represents the common dynamics in the GDP growth rates of the G7 countries. Chauvet (1998) and Chauvet and Yu (2006) estimate dynamic factor models with Markov switching as recurrent breaks in order to model recessions in the U.S. and in the G7 business cycle, respectively. We allow instead for a break in the common factor in order to capture structural changes in the G7 business cycle, rather than recessions.

Let $\mathbf{Y}_t$ be the $K \times 1$ vector of growth rates of real GDP for each of the G7 countries, which are the observable variables used to estimate the unobserved common business cycle in these countries, C_t:

$$\mathbf{Y}_t = \boldsymbol{\lambda} C_t + \mathbf{V}_t,$$

where $\boldsymbol{\lambda}$ is the $K \times 1$ vector of factor loadings, which measures the sensitivity of each one of the observable variables to business cycle fluctuations, and $\mathbf{V}_t$ is the vector of measurement errors. The common factor follows an autoregressive process and it is subject to a potential

[1]The coefficient of variation is the standard deviation divided by the mean.

structural break at τ :

$$C_t = \begin{cases} \alpha_1 + \phi_{1p}(L)C_{t-1} + \sigma_1\varepsilon_t & \text{if } t \le \tau \\ \alpha_2 + \phi_{2p}(L)C_{t-1} + \sigma_2\varepsilon_t & \text{if } t > \tau. \end{cases}$$

We also allow the measurement errors to follow an autoregressive progress:

$$\mathbf{V}_t = \Theta_1\mathbf{V}_{t-1} + \cdots + \Theta_q\mathbf{V}_{t-q} + \mathbf{U}_t,$$

where the innovations to the common factor, $\varepsilon_t \sim IIDN(0,1)$,and the idiosyncratic term, $\mathbf{U}_t \sim IIDN(\mathbf{0}, \mathbf{\Sigma}_K)$, $\mathbf{\Sigma}_K$ diagonal, are independent of each other at all leads and lags, and the autoregressive matrices are diagonal.

$$\Theta_i = \begin{bmatrix} \theta_{1i} & \cdots & 0 \\ \vdots & \ddots & \vdots \\ 0 & \cdots & \theta_{1K} \end{bmatrix}.$$

We cast the model in state space form assuming that $p = q + 1$. Let:

1. $\mathbf{Y}_t^* = (\mathbf{I}_k - \Theta(L))\mathbf{Y}_t$.
2. $\mathbf{C}_t^* = [C_t, \ldots, C_{t-p+1}]'$.
3. and the $K \times (q+1)$ matrix $\mathbf{H}$ be:

$$\begin{bmatrix} \lambda_1 & -\lambda_1\theta_{11} & \cdots & -\lambda_1\theta_{q1} \\ \lambda_2 & -\lambda_2\theta_{12} & \cdots & -\lambda_2\theta_{q2} \\ \vdots & \vdots & \ddots & \vdots \\ \lambda_K & -\lambda_K\theta_{1K} & \cdots & -\lambda_K\theta_{qK} \end{bmatrix}.$$

4. Define the $p \times p$ matrix $\mathbf{A}$ by:

$$\begin{bmatrix} \phi_1 & \phi_2 & \cdots & \phi_p \\ 1 & 0 & \cdots & 0 \\ 0 & 1 & \ddots & \vdots \\ 0 & \ddots & 1 & 0 \end{bmatrix}.$$

The measurement equation is:

$$\mathbf{Y}_t^* = \mathbf{H}\mathbf{C}_t^* + \mathbf{U}_t$$

and the transition equation:

$$\mathbf{C}_t^* = \begin{cases} \mathbf{a}_1 + \mathbf{A}_1\mathbf{C}_{t-1}^* + \mathbf{W}_1\varepsilon_t & \text{if } t \le \tau \\ \mathbf{a}_2 + \mathbf{A}_2\mathbf{C}_{t-1}^* + \mathbf{W}_2\varepsilon_t & \text{if } t > \tau, \end{cases}$$

where $\mathbf{W}_i = [\sigma_i, 0, \cdots, 0]'$ and $\mathbf{a}_i = [\alpha_i, 0, \ldots, 0]', i = 1, 2$, are $(p \times 1)$ vectors. The conditional mean coefficients in each regime is represented by the $p \times 1$ vector $\boldsymbol{\phi}_i = (\phi_{1i}, \ldots, \phi_{pi})$ or the $(p+1) \times 1$ vector $\boldsymbol{\beta}_i = (\alpha_i, \phi_{1i}, \ldots, \phi_{pi})$, where φ is the vector of all the parameters of the common factor model with a structural break and χ is the set of parameters of the common factor model without a break. The common factor is scaled by setting one of the factor loadings equal to unity.

In order to obtain evidence of changes in the G7 business cycle, we model the break in the transition equation for the common factor. This framework allows investigation of changes both in the factor volatility arising from the innovation variance and in the persistence of shocks from the autoregressive progress. The structural break in the common factor allows us to study these possible sources of decline in volatility separately.

2.2. Classical Methods

We test for structural stability in the variance of GDP growth rate assuming that breakpoint date is not known, using the asymptotically optimal tests by Andrews and Ploberger (1994). GDP growth, $\mathbf{Y}_t$, is modeled as following an autoregressive process:

$$\mathbf{Y}_t = \mu + \boldsymbol{v}\mathbf{Y}_{t-1} + \epsilon_t,$$

where $\epsilon_t|\Omega_{t-1} \sim N(0, \sigma^2)$, $\Omega_{t-1}$is the information set containing lagged values of $\mathbf{Y}_t$ and ϵ_t. We assume the following process for the estimated residuals:

$$\sqrt{\frac{\pi}{2}}|\widehat{\epsilon}_t| = \varsigma_1 D_{1t} + \varsigma_2 D_{2t} + \boldsymbol{\eta}_t,$$

for

$$\begin{cases} D_{1t} = 0 \quad \text{if } t \leq \tau \quad and\ D_{1t} = 1 \quad \text{if } t > \tau \\ D_{2t} = 0 \quad \text{if } t > \tau \quad and\ D_{2t} = 1 \quad \text{if } t \leq \tau \end{cases}$$

where ς is the estimator of the standard deviation and τ is the unknown break date. Given that ϵ_t follows a normal distribution, $\sqrt{\frac{\pi}{2}}|\widehat{\epsilon}_t|$is an unbiased estimator of ϵ_t.

We test the following hypothesis:

$$\begin{cases} H_1 : \varsigma_1 = \varsigma_2 \\ H_2 : \varsigma_1 \neq \varsigma_2 \end{cases}$$

The presence of the nuisance parameter τ under the alternative hypothesis implies that the Lagrange multiplier (LM), the Likelihood ratio (LR), and the Wald tests do not have standard asymptotic properties. Andrews and Ploberger's (1994) test and critical values overcome this problem.

We test for the possibility of a break in the variance of GDP growth assuming that the mean has remained constant. However, the results of this test could be compromised if there were a break in the mean parameters, as in this case the evidence of a break in volatility could be a result of neglected structural change in the conditional mean of GDP growth rate. We account for this by testing for breaks in the conditional mean, allowing for changing variance. This test is applied to each of the G7 country and for the estimated common factor for comparison with the Bayesian methods.

2.3. Bayesian Methods

This section follows closely Chauvet and Potter (2001). We will study the case in which the breakpoint τ is endogenous. If the breakpoint were known, we could use classical or Bayesian methods using the Kalman filter to evaluate the likelihood function. The Kalman filter iterations are given by:

1. Prediction Step: the conditional mean of the factor is

$$\mathbf{C}^*_{t+1|t} = \begin{cases} \mathbf{a}_1 + \mathbf{A}_1\mathbf{C}^*_{t|t} & \text{if } t \leq \tau \\ \mathbf{a}_2 + \mathbf{A}_2\mathbf{C}^*_{t|t} & \text{if } t > \tau \end{cases}.$$

The conditional variance of the factor is

$$\mathbf{P}_{t+1|t} = \begin{cases} \mathbf{A}_1\mathbf{P}_{t|t}\mathbf{A}_1' + \mathbf{W}_1\mathbf{W}_1' & \text{if } t \leq \tau \\ \mathbf{A}_2\mathbf{P}_{t|t}\mathbf{A}_2' + \mathbf{W}_2\mathbf{W}_2' & \text{if } t > \tau \end{cases}.$$

If we plug the conditional mean into the measurement equation we obtain the forecast error:

$$\mathbf{Y}^*_{t+1} - \widehat{\mathbf{Y}}^*_{t+1|t} = \mathbf{H}(\mathbf{C}^*_t - \mathbf{C}^*_{t+1|t}) + \mathbf{U}_t,$$

and variance:

$$E\left[(\mathbf{Y}^*_{t+1} - \widehat{\mathbf{Y}}^*_{t+1|t})(\mathbf{Y}^*_{t+1} - \widehat{\mathbf{Y}}^*_{t+1|t})'\right] = \mathbf{H}\mathbf{P}_{t+1|t}\mathbf{H}' + \Sigma_K.$$

2. Updating Step: first, the Kalman Gain matrix is constructed:

$$\mathbf{G}_{t+1} = \mathbf{P}_{t+1|t}\mathbf{H}'\left\{E\left[(\mathbf{Y}^*_{t+1} - \widehat{\mathbf{Y}}^*_{t+1|t})(\mathbf{Y}^*_{t+1} - \widehat{\mathbf{Y}}^*_{t+1|t})'\right]\right\}^{-1}.$$

Then, this is used to include the new information in the conditional mean of the factor

$$\mathbf{C}^*_{t+1|t+1} = \mathbf{C}^*_{t+1|t} + \mathbf{G}_{t+1}\left(\mathbf{Y}^*_{t+1} - \widehat{\mathbf{Y}}^*_{t+1|t}\right),$$

and to update the conditional variance:

$$\mathbf{P}_{t+1|t+1} = (\mathbf{I}_p - \mathbf{G}_{t+1}\mathbf{H})\,\mathbf{P}_{t+1|t}.$$

When the breakpoint is not known, one could estimate the model for each possible breakpoint and choose the ones that maximizes the likelihood function. Although this method is straightforward, it entails two main problems. First, the likelihood under the null is not known. Second, the method does not assess the uncertainty about the breakpoint, which makes inferences conditional on a breakpoint very fragile for classical estimation of recession frequencies, as shown in Potter (2000). In this chapter, we treat the breakpoint as unknown and use Bayesian methods to extract the sample evidence about its likelihood and date. We compare the results with the ones obtained from the Classical method used to find the endogenous breakpoint.

The Bayesian methods uses a Gibbs sampler to generate random draws from the posterior distribution by utilizing a sequence of conditioning distributions. In particular, the Gibbs sampler generates random draws of τ that allow analysis as if the breakpoint were known. In addition, a random draw of the common factor is generated as part of the iterations of the Gibbs sampler. The recursion used to generate the random draw of the common factor is as follows (see Carter and Kohn, 1994):

1. The last iteration of the Kalman filter yields:

$$\mathbf{C}_T^* \sim N(\mathbf{C}_{T|T}^*, \mathbf{P}_{T|T}).$$

Thus, using standard methods one can draw a realization $\widetilde{\mathbf{C}}_T^*$, from this multivariate normal. Then the draw of the most recent value of the common factor is given by:

$$\widetilde{C}_T = \mathbf{s}\widetilde{\mathbf{C}}_T^*,$$

where s $=[1, 0, \ldots, 0]$ is a $p \times 1$ selection vector. In practice, one only needs to draw from the univariate normal with mean given by the first element of $\mathbf{C}_{T|T}^*$ and variance by the first diagonal element of $\mathbf{P}_{T|T}$.

2. Given a draw at $t+1$ based on draws from $t+2$ to T, the information from the Kalman filter iterations is incorporated as if the filter were running backwards, combining prior information from the initial forward run of the filter with the 'sample' information generated by the random draw:

$$f_t = \widetilde{C}_{t+1} - \begin{cases} \alpha_1 + \phi_{1p}(L)C_{t|t} & \text{if } t \leq \tau \\ \alpha_2 + \phi_{2p}(L)C_{t|t} & \text{if } t > \tau \end{cases},$$

$$p_t = \begin{cases} \phi_1' \mathbf{P}_{t|t}\phi_1 + \sigma_1^2 & \text{if } t \leq \tau \\ \phi_2' \mathbf{P}_{t|t}\phi_2 + \sigma_2^2 & \text{if } t > \tau \end{cases},$$

$$\mathbf{g}_t = \begin{cases} \mathbf{P}_{t|t}\phi_1/p_t & \text{if } t \leq \tau \\ \mathbf{P}_{t|t}\phi_2/p_t & \text{if } t > \tau \end{cases},$$

$$\mathbf{C}_{t|T}^* = \mathbf{C}_{t|t}^* + \mathbf{g}_t f_t,$$

$$\mathbf{P}_{t|T} = \begin{cases} \left(\mathbf{I}_p - \mathbf{g}_t\phi_1'\right)\mathbf{P}_{t|t} & \text{if } t \leq \tau \\ \left(\mathbf{I}_p - \mathbf{g}_t\phi_2'\right)\mathbf{P}_{t|t} & \text{if } t > \tau \end{cases}.$$

Thus, after observing the whole sample $\mathbf{C}_t^* \sim N(\mathbf{C}_{t|T}^*, \mathbf{P}_{t|T})$, and standard methods can be used to obtain a random draw.

3. This iteration stops with $\mathbf{C}_p^* \sim N(\mathbf{C}_{p|T}^*, \mathbf{P}_{p|T})$, which is used to simultaneously draw the first p observations of the common factor.

Given this realization of the common factor, we apply the technique presented in Potter (2000) to study the breakpoint.

2.3.1. Estimation by Gibbs Sampler

Anticipating the empirical results, we find that the most probably date of a breakpoint, using both classical and Bayesian methods is 1983Q2. We initialize the Gibbs sampler by running the Kalman filter on the observed data assuming: a break date in 1983Q2, factor loadings equal to unity, measurement error equal to 1/4 of the observed variance, and point estimates obtained for GDP with a sample split in 1983Q2 as initial guesses for the parameters of the common factor. The results of the Kalman filter are then used to draw a sequence of realizations for the common factor.

The ordering of the Gibbs sampler is:

1. Conditional on $\{\widetilde{C}_t\}$, $\Theta(L)$, $\mathbf{\Sigma}_K$ we draw the $K \times 1$ vector of factor loadings $\boldsymbol{\lambda}$ from (independent) normal distributions. For the generic loading λ_k we have the sample information:

$$\left[\sum_{t=p+1}^{T} C_{kt}^{*2}\right]^{-1}, \sum_{t=p+1}^{T} C_{kt}^{*} Y_{kt}^{*},$$

where $C_{kt}^* = C_t - \theta_{1k} C_{t-1} - \cdots - \theta_{qk} C_{t-q}$. Let V_{λ_k} be the variance of the Gaussian prior on λ_k and M_{λ_k} be its prior mean. Then the posterior draw is from normal distribution with mean

$$\frac{V_{\lambda_k}^{-1} M_{\lambda_k} + \sum_{t=p+1}^{T} C_{kt}^{*} Y_{kt}^{*}}{V_{\lambda_k}^{-1} + \sum_{t=p+1}^{T} C_{kt}^{*2}}$$

and variance

$$\left[V_{\lambda_k}^{-1} + \sum_{t=p+1}^{T} C_{kt}^{*2}\right]^{-1}.$$

For the first element of $\boldsymbol{\lambda}$ we impose the prior belief that it is equal to 1.

2. Conditional on $\{\widetilde{C}_t\}$, $\Theta(L)$, $\boldsymbol{\lambda}$ we draw the measurement error variances from independent gamma distributions. For the generic measurement error Σ_{kk} we have the sample information

$$\sum_{t=p+1}^{T} (Y_{kt}^{*} - \lambda_k C_{kt}^{*})^2, T - p,$$

which is combined with the prior degrees of freedom of ξ and sum of squares ξs^2 to obtain the posterior degrees of freedom $\xi + T - p$ and sum of squares $\xi s^2 + \sum_{t=p+1}^{T} (Y_{kt}^{*} - \lambda_k C_{kt}^{*})^2$.

3. Conditional on $\{\widetilde{C}_t\}$,$\boldsymbol{\lambda}$, $\boldsymbol{\Sigma}_K$ we draw the measurement autoregressive coefficients from independent multivariate Gaussian distributions For the generic measurement error autoregression k the sample information is:

$$\left[\mathbf{Z}_k^{'}\mathbf{Z}_k\right]^{-1}, \mathbf{Z}_k^{'}\mathbf{W}_k,$$

where $\mathbf{W}_k = [Y_{kq+1}, \cdots, Y_{kT}]'$ and

$$\mathbf{Z}_k = \begin{bmatrix} Y_{kq} & \cdots & Y_{k1} \\ Y_{kq+1} & \cdots & Y_{k2} \\ \vdots & \vdots & \vdots \\ Y_{kT-1} & \cdots & Y_{kT-q} \end{bmatrix}.$$

This is combined with the prior Gaussian distribution, $N(0, V_{\theta_k})$ on the autoregressive coefficients in the standard way to obtain a posterior variance of:

$$\left[V_{\theta_k}^{-1} + \mathbf{Z}_k^{'}\mathbf{Z}_k\right]^{-1}$$

and posterior mean of

$$\left[V_{\theta_k}^{-1} + \mathbf{Z}_k^{'}\mathbf{Z}_k\right]^{-1}\left[\mathbf{Z}_k^{'}\mathbf{W}_k\right].$$

4. Conditional on $\{\widetilde{C}_t\}$ we calculate the posterior distribution of τ and the marginal likelihood of $\{\widetilde{C}_t\}$ under both the structural break model and the no break model. This requires that a normal-inverted gamma prior be used for both before and after the break values of the parameters (see Potter, 2000). We use the posterior distribution of τ to draw a particular breakpoint.

5. Conditional on $\{\widetilde{C}_t\}, \tau$ we draw the autoregressive model parameters for before and after the break from the inverted-gamma normal distribution. These draws of the autoregressive parameters are used to calculate various measures of changes in the common factor before and after the break.

6. Conditional on $\Theta(L), \boldsymbol{\lambda}, \boldsymbol{\Sigma}_K, \tau, \beta_1, \beta_2, \sigma_1, \sigma_2$ the Kalman filter is run on the observed data. The filter is initialized at the stationary distribution for $\{C_t\}$ implied by β_1, σ_1. Then, using the recursions described above, a draw of $\{\widetilde{C}_t\}$ is obtained and we return to step 1. The posterior mean for the smoothed factor is produced directly from a similar set of recursions, with the draw $\widetilde{C}_t$ replaced by $C_{t|T}$.

2.3.2. Evidence for a Structural Break

The sample evidence in favor of a structural break in the common factor model can be evaluated by comparing the average likelihood of the observed time series with and without a break. This calculation would require multiple integration but can be simplified using some shortcuts. The Bayes factor is the marginal likelihood of the no break model divided by the marginal likelihood of the break model:

$$B_{\text{no break vs.break}} = \frac{\int l(\mathbf{Y}|\chi)b(\chi)d\chi}{\int l(\mathbf{Y}|\varphi)b(\varphi)d\varphi}$$

Using the Basic likelihood identity (Chib 1995) we have:

$$\int l(\mathbf{Y}|\varphi)b(\varphi)d\varphi = \frac{l(\mathbf{Y}|\varphi)b(\varphi)}{p(\varphi|\mathbf{Y})}$$

for all points in the parameter space. In particular, consider the transformation of the parameter space for the common factor model from $(\beta_1, \sigma_1, \beta_2, \sigma_2, \tau)$ to $(\beta_1, \sigma_1, \beta_2 - \beta_1, \sigma_2/\sigma_1, \tau)$. If we evaluate the transformation at $\beta_2 - \beta_1 = 0, \sigma_2/\sigma_1 = 1$, then there is no information in the likelihood function about τ. As discussed in Koop and Potter (1999), one can use this lack of identification to simplify marginal likelihood calculations using the Savage-Dickey Density ratio. In this case we have:

$$\frac{\int l(\{\widetilde{C}_t\}|\beta_1, \sigma_1)b(\beta_1, \sigma_1)d\beta_1 d\sigma_1}{\int l(\{\widetilde{C}_t\}|\beta_1, \sigma_1, \beta_2, \sigma_2, \tau)b(\beta_1, \sigma_1, \beta_2, \sigma_2, \tau)d\beta_1 d\sigma_1 d\beta_2 d\sigma_2 d\tau}$$

$$= \frac{p(\beta_2 - \beta_1 = 0, \sigma_2/\sigma_1 = 1, \tau|\{\widetilde{C}_t\}, \mathbf{Y}, \varphi^-)}{b(\beta_2 - \beta_1 = 0, \sigma_2/\sigma_1 = 1, \tau|\varphi^-)},$$

where φ^- signifies the parameter space excluding the parameters of the common factor model. Using the methods of Koop and Potter (2000) one can directly calculate the LHS of this expression at each iteration of the Gibbs sampler. If this quantity is then averaged across draws of φ^- from the Gibbs sampler we will have

$$\frac{p(\beta_2 - \beta_1 = 0, \sigma_2/\sigma_1 = 1, \tau|\mathbf{Y})}{b(\beta_2 - \beta_1 = 0, \sigma_2/\sigma_1 = 1, \tau)},$$

which is the Savage Dickey ratio for the Bayes factor of a no break common factor model vs a structural break common factor model.

3. Business Cycle Frequency

One way to measure changes in the business cycle is to compare the inverse coefficient of variation of the estimated common factor before and after the break, and the frequency of negative growth in the common factor. In our framework, the inverse of the coefficient of variation is the ratio of the mean to the standard deviation of the estimated common factor. The coefficient of variation can account for longer expansion phases or, equivalently, for less frequent recessions, in three possible ways: first, the mean growth rate could be higher after the break given the same variance; second, the volatility of fluctuations could be lower after the break; and third, both the mean could be higher and the volatility be lower. In all cases, the inverse of the coefficient of variation would be higher, implying a lower frequency of negative growth rates.

Analysis of the observed data indicates that there is not a significant change in the mean growth rate of the G7 countries that would account for the changes in business cycle phases. In fact, we find changes in the mean growth rate of some countries, but they are generally towards lower growth, which would go against the evidence of longer expansions and less frequent recessions. On the other hand, we find strong evidence of lower volatility in these countries, which seems to be the source of the changes in business cycles, as discussed below.

The mean of the estimated common factor is scaled to match the mean of the observable variables in the model, that is, the mean growth rate of the G7 countries. Thus, we study the coefficient of variation relative to the mean. The volatility of the G7 real growth can be accounted for by the common factor and by the individual measurement errors, which allow assessment of whether its reduction is due to individual measurement errors. For the estimated model, the inverse coefficient of variation CV is:

$$1/CV = \frac{\alpha}{1-\phi_1-\phi_2} \times \frac{\sqrt{\frac{1+\phi_2}{1-\phi_1}\left\{(1-\phi_2)^2-\phi_1^2\right\}}}{\sigma},$$

As it can be seen, the coefficient of variation is a nonlinear function of the estimated parameters. Potter (2000) shows that estimates of these measures using classical methods can be substantially biased. In addition, this method does not yield straightforward sampling distributions that would allow for uncertainty over the break point. We use the realizations from the Gibbs sampler to calculate the coefficient of variation, and obtain its posterior mean by averaging across the realizations. That is, for each iteration of the Gibbs sampler we calculate the parameters before and after the break, and then average to form its posterior mean. In addition, since we do not know the true data generating process, we can not use the normal cumulative distribution function to calculate the probability of recession. We then calculate the estimated probability of a negative quarter at each iteration of the Gibbs sampler and obtain the average of this quantity, which allows assessment on how informative the posterior mean of the inverse coefficient of variation is with respect to the rest of its posterior distribution.

3.1. Priors

The hyperparameters are assumed to be Normal-inverted gamma priors. We start by assuming a noninformative prior, setting the means and covariances to zero for all conditional mean parameters in the model. The prior variance for the intercept is assumed to be 4. For the autoregressive coefficients, the variance of the first lag is 1, and the subsequent ones are reduced by 0.5^{p-1}. The degrees of freedom ($\underline{\nu}$) for the inverted gamma priors are set to be 3 before and after break. The other hyperparameter of the inverted gamma prior is $\underline{s}$, where $E(\sigma_i^2) = \frac{\underline{\nu}}{\underline{\nu}-2}\underline{s}^2$.We set $\underline{s}^2 = 8$, $c = 0.01$. These priors are noninformative but yet consistent with G7 fluctuations.

4. Empirical Results

4.1. Data

We obtain the time series of quarterly GDP growth from the International Financial Statistics-International Monetary Fund (IFS-IMF). We use data for the period from 1957Q1 to 2005Q1.[2] Real data are obtained using the GDP deflator. The data are transformed by taking 100 times the logarithmic differences.

4.2. Testing for Breaks

We apply Andrews and Ploberger's (1994) break test as described in section 3. We focus here on the results for breaks in variance, controlling for possible breaks in mean. As reported in Table 1, we find that all G7 countries display structural breaks towards stability in the 1980s, more specifically between 1980 and 1984. Canada, U.K., Germany, and Italy had also a second break in volatility in the early 1990s, which for some countries it is related to the impact of Germany unification in 1989.

Table 1. Structural Breaks in Variance

GDP	Sample	Break Date
US	1957.3-2005.1	1984.1
Canada	1957.3-2005.1	1983.2 1991.2
U.K.	1957.3-2005.1	1981.4 1992.2
Germany	1960.3-2005.1	1982.4 1993.2
France	1970.3-2005.1	1980.3
Italy	1980.3-2005.1	1981.3 1990.3
Japan	1957.3-2005.1	1982.2
Common Factor	1957.3-2005.1	**1983.2**

Figure 1 plots the smoothed growth rates of real GDP of the G7 countries together with the estimated breakpoints in volatility. The more dampened business cycle oscillations since the breaks can be visualized in the figure for most countries. For Germany, there was first a brusque oscillation in growth rates at the time of the unification in 1989, but a subsequent decrease in variance from that point on, particularly after 1993.2, which is found as the date of the second breakpoint in this country. Canada also had a milder decrease in volatility in the 1980s compared to the other countries, but a more substantial one in the early 1990s, right after the 1990-1991 U.S. recession.

[2]Data starts in 1960.Q1 for Germany and in 1970.Q1 for Italy and France. We estimate the model for the earlier sample using missing variable technique.

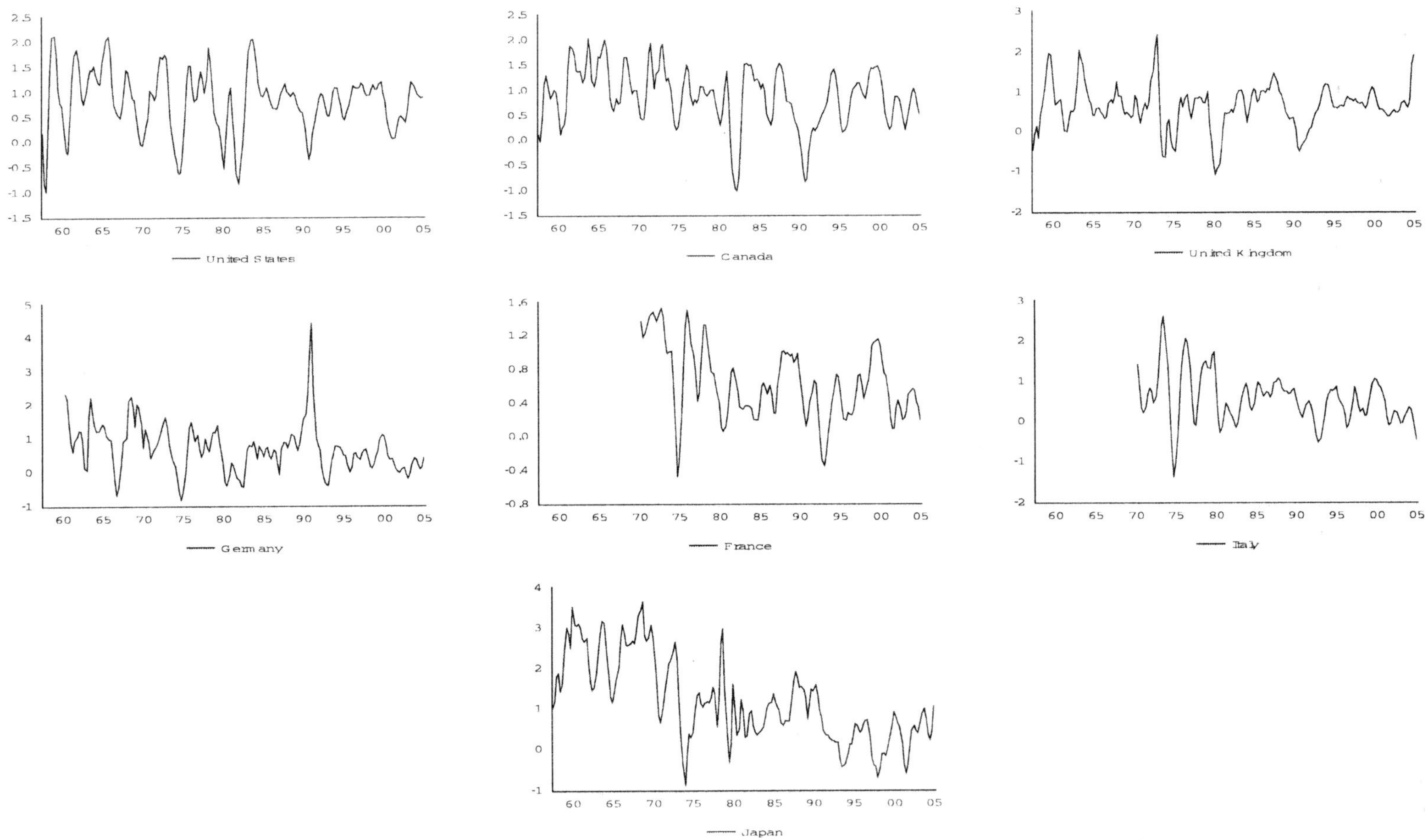

Figure 1. Smoothed Growth Rates of GDP for the G7 Countries and Breakpoints (dotted line).

Table 2 shows some statistics before and after the break found for each G7 country, which gives some insight on the changes in business cycle in these countries. The table shows the average growth, the standard deviation, the coefficient of variation, and the frequency of negative quarters. Most countries have displayed lower mean growth rate over time. With the exception of the United Kingdom, all other countries had a decline in average growth after the break. With respect to volatility, all countries experienced substantial stabilization after their individual breakpoint. The most accentuated decline in volatility was in Japan (112%), followed by Italy (60%), and United Kingdom (51%). Germany was the country that experienced the smallest decrease in volatility (11%), given the oscillations around the reunification. For almost all countries the coefficient of variation also declined after the break. The exceptions are Germany and France. However, if the quarters that followed the reunification of Germany are excluded, the coefficient of variation in these countries decreased as well.

Table 2. Statistics Before and After Individual Break for Each Country

Statistics	Before Break				After Break			
Series	Avg Growth	St. Dev.	CV	Neg. Quarter	Avg Growth	St. Dev.	CV	Neg. Quarter
U.S.	0.84	1.14	1.36	20	0.80	0.51	0.64	5
Canada	0.97	1.04	1.07	17	0.75	0.67	0.63	10
U.K.	0.59	1.33	2.25	28	0.69	0.65	0.94	9
Germany	0.80	1.56	1.95	27	0.61	1.38	2.26	25
France	0.92	0.74	0.80	4	0.49	0.45	0.92	15
Italy	0.84	1.13	1.35	1	0.50	0.46	0.92	22
Japan	1.79	1.89	1.06	13	0.54	0.89	1.65	22
Common Factor	**1**	**0.82**	**0.82**	**11**	**0.62**	**0.37**	**0.60**	**2**

4.3. Estimated Results

The model is estimated setting $q = 1, p = 2$, and the factor loading of the U.S. GDP equal to unity to normalize the common factor. The Gibbs sampler is run with a burn-in phase of $2,000$ iterations and additional $15,000$ iterations. We find that Bayes factor for no break and for a break show some initial uncertainty in the first $1,000$ iterations, but converges and stabilizes after $1,600$ iterations.

Figure 2 plots the averaged estimates across posterior draws of the smoothed common factor. The decrease in volatility of the common factor can be clearly visualized in the picture. As a first comparison with the breakdates found for each of the G7 countries, we apply Andrews and Ploberger's test to this estimate and find a structural break in its variance in 1983.2, which is shown in Table 1 and as the dotted line in the Figure 2. As discussed below, this is also the most probable date for the breakpoint indicated by the Bayes factors.

The G7 business cycle as represented by the common factor coincides with some U.S. recessions, as dated by the NBER. This is shown in Figure 3, which plots the estimated common factor and NBER recessions. The factor is negative around the same time as recessions occur in the U.S. We also compare the estimated common factor with the Center for Economic Policy Research (CEPR) business cycle dating of the Euro area. The CEPR

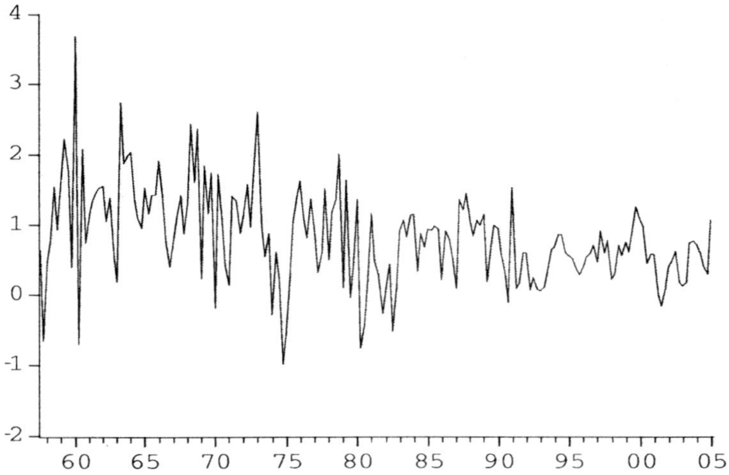

Figure 2. Posterior Mean of Common Factor and Breakpoint Date (dotted line).

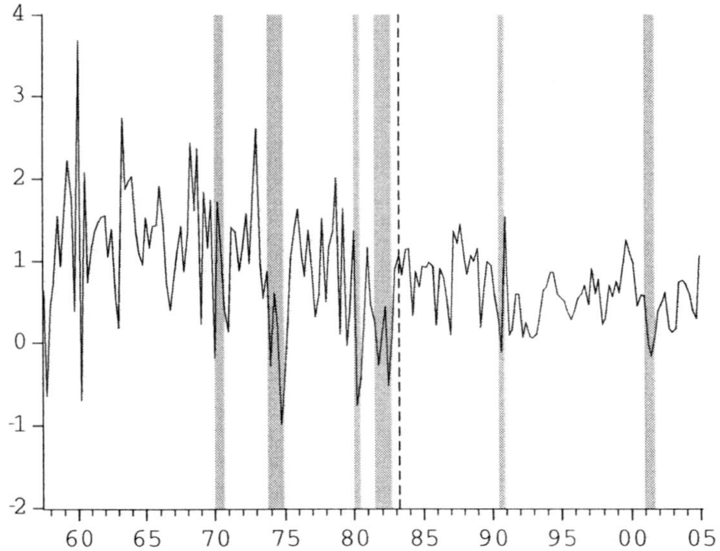

Figure 3. Posterior Mean of Common Factor, Breakpoint Date (dotted line), and NBER Recessions (Shaded Area)

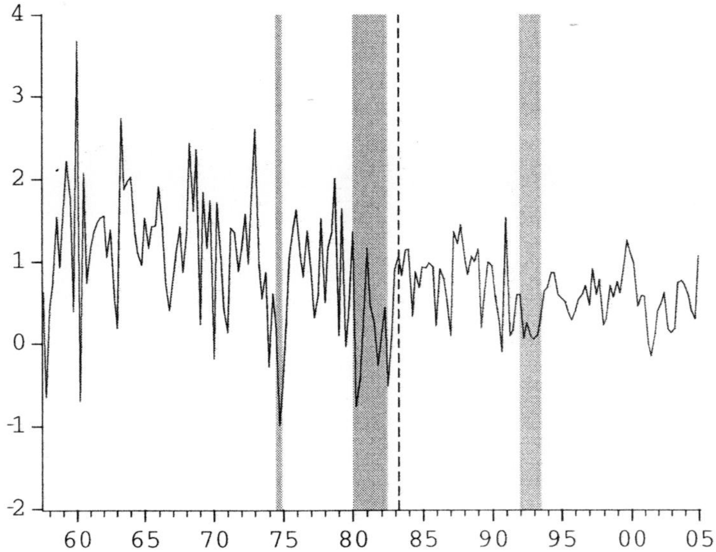

Figure 4. Posterior Mean of Common Factor, Breakpoint Date (dotted line), and Euro Recessions (Shaded Area).

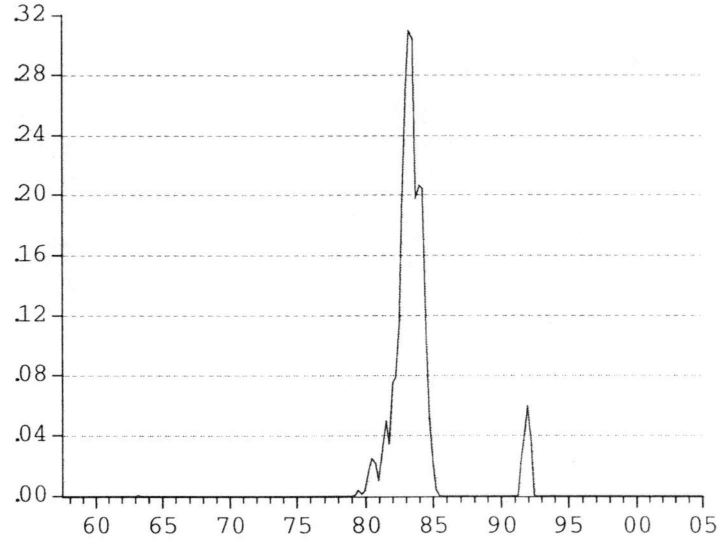

Figure 5. Posterior Probability for Breakpoint in the Common Factor.

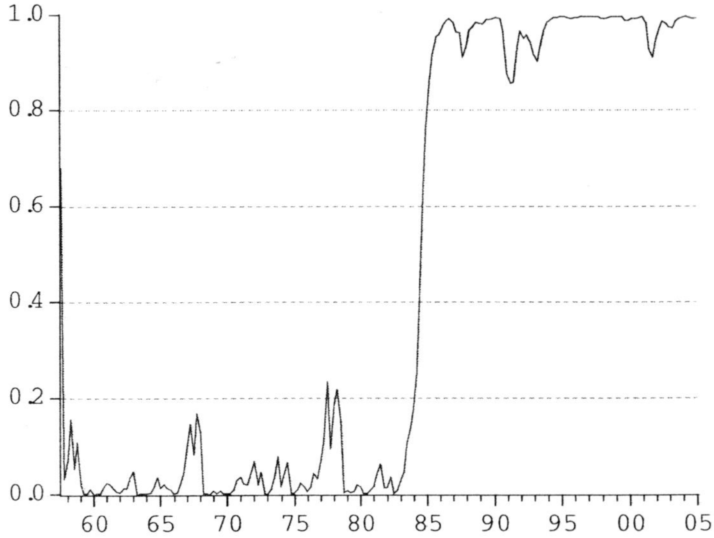

Figure 6. Cumulative Posterior Probability of Break.

business cycle committee is considered the European counterpart to the NBER dating committee for the U.S. The common factor for the G7 countries show a strong correlation with the Euro recessions as dated by the CEPR. In particular, the recession in the early 1980s was a deep and long one in the common factor and in the Euro area, whereas because of a recovery in 1981 in the U.S., this period was classified by the NBER as two short recessions instead. In addition, the recession in the 1990s started later in the common factor than as dated by the NBER for the U.S., more in accord with the Euro area business cycle. More recently, the common factor also became negative in 2001, indicating a contraction in the G7 countries at around the same time as the last U.S. recession. We can not compare this finding with the CEPR's dating, since the committee has not yet made a decision about a possible recession in 2001 (CEPR 2003).

The estimated Bayes factor in favor of no break is 0.0005, which implies that the posterior probability of a break is about $2,200$ to 1. This is a strong evidence in favor of a break, given that the model assumes that all countries had a break at the same time. As shown in Table 1, the break in volatility in these countries did not occur simultaneous, but were clustered between 1980 and 1984. This is consistent with the finding from Figure 6, which shows the posterior probability for breakpoint in the common factor. The model estimate the most likely date for the break as the second quarter of 1983, although the probability is high from 1980 to 1984. The odds of a break also show a slight increase in the early 1990s. This is related to the second break towards stability experienced in some countries, as reported in Table 1.

The last row of Table 2 shows the posterior statistic averages of the common factor for each iteration of the Gibbs sampler before and after the break. The volatility of the common factor declines 55% after the break in 1983.2. The inverse of the coefficient of variation give us the probability of a negative quarter using the cumulative distribution function of a normal. We calculate the implied probability of a negative quarter at each iteration of the

Gibbs sampler and average this quantity. The posterior mean of the inverse coefficient of variation before the break is 1.22, which from the normal CDF implies 11% of quarters having negative growth. The posterior mean after the break is 1.61, which implies only 5% of quarters having negative growth. This is close to the sample averages as reported in Table 2, although the model predicts slightly more percentage quarters of negative growth after the break than the sample average.

Table 3 reports the correlations between the estimated common factor and the growth rates of real GDP of the G7 countries used to estimate the factor. The full sample correlation is obtained from the posterior mean of the common factor. The subsamples correlation before and after break were calculated from average correlations across draws of the Gibbs Sampler. For the full sample, the factor has a balanced correlation with all countries, but is slightly more correlated with Germany and less so with the U.S. This is also the case for the sample before the break. After the break, the factor is more correlated with Germany, Italy and France and less correlated with Canada, U.K., and the U.S.

Table 3. Correlations – Observable Variables and the Common Factor

GDP	Full Sample	Before Break	After Break
U.S.	0.49	0.53	0.41
Canada	0.54	0.59	0.34
U.K.	0.50	0.56	0.43
Germany	0.68	0.72	0.55
France	0.61	0.62	0.61
Italy	0.51	0.45	0.62
Japan	0.62	0.61	0.53

5. Conclusion

This chapter investigates changes in the business cycle of the G7 countries. It finds strong evidence that the increased stabilization documented for the US business cycle is also experienced by the G7 countries, and by their common business cycle. In particular, we find structural breaks towards increased stability for each of the G7 countries. We also find a structural break for decreased volatility for the common G7 business cycle. This finding implies that recessions in these countries should be less frequent, and expansions longer than their historical record.

The evidence of widespread increased stabilization across countries indicates that these changes might be permanent. However, there is always the possibility that a break towards instability may occur in the future because of recessions, wars or natural disasters. However, since the breakpoints in volatility, these economies have experienced two long expansions and two short recessions. Yet, these economies have continued to show increased stabilization compared to the period before break. In fact, Chauvet and Popli (2003) show that stabilization is a secular trend shared by most industrialized countries.

References

[1] Andrews, D. W. K. and W. Ploberger (1994), "Optimal Tests when a Nuisance Parameter is Present Only Under the Alternative," *Econometrica*, **62-2**, 1383-1484.

[2] Carter, C and Kohn, P. (1994). "On Gibbs sampling for state space models," *Biometrika,* **81**, 541-553.

[3] Centre for Economic Policy Research. 2003. Euro Area Business Cycle Dating Committee. Press release, September 22. Available online at <www.cepr.org/press/dating.pdf>.

[4] Chauvet, M. (1998). "An Econometric Characterization of Business Cycle Dynamics with Factor Structure and Regime Switches," *International Economic Review*, Vol. 39, No. 4, November 1998, 969-96.

[5] Chauvet, M. and S. Potter (2001). "Recent Changes in the U.S. Business Cycle, with S. Potter, The Manchester School, 69, No. 5, 2001, 481-508.

[6] Chauvet, M. and G. Popli (2003). "Maturing Capitalism and Stabilization: International Evidence," *Journal of Business and Economics Research.*

[7] Chauvet, M. and C. Yu (2006). "International Business Cycles: G7 and OECD Countries," *Economic Review,* Federal Reserve Bank of Atlanta, First Quarter, 43-54.

[8] Chib, S. (1995). "Marginal likelihood from Gibbs Output," *Journal of American Statistical Association,* **90**, 1313-1321.

[9] Diebold, F. and Rudebusch, G. (1992) "Have Postwar Economic Fluctuations been stabilized?, *American Economic Review* **82**(4) pp 993-1005..

[10] Kim, C-J. and Nelson, C. (1999). "Has the US Economy become more stable? A Bayesian approach based on a Markov switching model of the Business Cycle," *Review of Economics and Statistics,* **81**(4) pp 1-10.

[11] Koop, G. and Potter, S.M.(1999) "Bayes factors and nonlinearity: Evidence from Economic Time series," *Journal of Econometrics,* **88**, 251-281.

[12] Koop, G. and Potter, S.M. (2000). "Nonlinearity, structural breaks or outliers in economic time series?" in *Nonlinear Econometric Modeling in Time Series Analysis*, William Barnett (ed.), Cambridge: Cambridge University Press pp 61-78.

[13] McConnell, M. and Perez-Quiros, G. (2000). "Output Fluctuations in the United States:What has changed since the early 1980s?" *American Economic Review.*

[14] Potter, S.M. (2000). "Forecasting the Frequency of Recessions" *mimeo* Federal Reserve Bank of New York

[15] Romer, C. (1994). "Remeasuring Business Cycles," *The Journal of Economic History,* **54**(3) pp 578-609.

[16] Stock, J and Watson, M. (1989) "New Indices of Coincident and Leading Indicators," In O. Blanchard and S. Fischer edited *NBER Macroeconomic Annual* Cambridge, MIT Press.

[17] Watson, M. (1994). "Business-Cycle Durations and Postwar stabilization in the US Economy," *American Economic Review* **84**(1) pp 24-46.

INDEX

A

B

C

D

E

F

G

H

I

J

K

L

M

N

R

S

T